MW00775143

Cost Accounting Standards Board Regulations

as of January 1, 2019

Compiled from CCH GOVERNMENT CONTRACTS REPORTER

(As of January 1, 2019)

© 2019 CCH Incorporated and its affiliates. All rights reserved.

2700 Lake Cook Road, Riverwoods, Illinois, 60015
866 529 6600
www.WoltersKluwerLR.com

All Rights Reserved
Printed in the United States of America
ISBN 978-1-5438-0650-2
Media Issue 10032338-0010

SUSTAINABLE FORESTRY INITIATIVE
Certified Sourcing
www.sfiprogram.org
SFI-01051

About the Cost Accounting Standards Board Regulations

This volume contains the cost accounting standards and related regulations issued by the Cost Accounting Standards Board as of January 1, 2019. The cost accounting standards provide rules for estimating, accumulating, and reporting costs under negotiated government contracts and subcontracts. Originally applicable only to defense contracts, the CAS now apply to civilian agency contracts as well. In addition, the set of standards and disclosure requirements for educational institutions is included.

This volume is intended for use as a convenient reference when it is not essential to have a text that reflects the latest amendments. Thus, no updating service will be provided. Future amendments will be reported as issued and incorporated at the appropriate places in the text of the regulations in the GOVERNMENT CONTRACTS REPORTER and the COST ACCOUNTING STANDARDS GUIDE.

January 1, 2019

WoltersKluwer

Editorial
Aaron M. Broaddus, Esq.
George M. Gullo, Esq.
Marilyn Helt, Esq.
David L. Stephanides, Esq.
William VanHuis, Esq.

Editorial Support
Theresa J. Jensen
Corann Kelly

COST ACCOUNTING STANDARDS BOARD REGULATIONS

Table of Contents

SOURCES

Cost Accounting Standards Board Acquisition Regulation Supplement Board Regulations, 57 FR 14148, April 17, 1992, effective 4/17/92; 56 FR 19304, 4/26/91.

Final rule, 83 FR 3146, 7/17/2018, effective 8/16/2018; see ¶ 70,055.28.

Final rule, 83 FR 8634, 2/28/2018, effective 3/30/2018; see ¶ 70,055.27.

Final rule, 77 FR 43542, 7/25/2012, effective 8/24/2012; see ¶ 70,055.26.

Final rule, 76 FR 81296, 12/27/2011, effective 2/27/2012; see ¶ 70,055.25.

Final rule, 76 FR 79545, 12/22/2011, effective 12/22/2011; see ¶ 70,055.24.

Final rule, 76 FR 49365, 8/10/2011, effective 10/11/2011; see ¶ 70,055.23.

Final rule, 76 FR 40817, 7/12/2011, effective 8/11/2011; see ¶ 70,055.22.

Final rule, 73 FR 15939, 3/26/2008, effective 4/25/2008; see ¶ 70,055.21.

Final rule, 73 FR 23961, 5/1/2008, effective 6/2/2008; see ¶ 70,055.20.

Final rule, 72 FR 36367, 7/3/2007, effective 7/3/2007; see ¶ 70,055.19.

Final rule, 72 FR 32809, 6/14/2007, effective 6/14/2007; see ¶ 70,055.18.

Final rule, 72 FR 32546, 6/13/2007, effective 6/13/2007; see ¶ 70,055.17.

Corrected final rule, 70 FR 37706, 6/30/2005, effective 6/30/2005; see ¶ 70,055.16.

Interim rule, 70 FR 29457, 5/23/2005, effective 5/23/2005; see ¶ 70,055.15.

Final rule, 65 FR 37470, 6/14/2000, effective 6/14/2000; see ¶ 70,055.14.

Final rule, 65 FR 36767, 6/9/2000, effective 6/9/2000; see ¶ 70,055.13.

Interim rule, 65 FR 5990, 2/7/2000, effective 4/2/2000; see ¶ 70,055.12.

Final rule, 62 FR 31294, 6/6/97, effective 6/6/97; see ¶ 70,055.11.

Final rule, 62 FR 31308, 6/6/97, effective 8/15/94; see ¶ 70,055.10.

Interim rule, 61 FR 39360, 7/29/96, effective 7/29/96; see ¶ 70,055.09.

Final rule, 61 FR 7616, 2/28/96, effective 2/28/96; see ¶ 70,055.08.

Final rule, 61 FR 5520, 2/13/96, effective 4/15/96; see ¶ 70,055.07.

Final rule, 60 FR 16534, 3/30/95, effective 3/30/95; see ¶ 70,055.06; Corrected, 61 FR 58011, 11/12/96.

Interim rule, 60 FR 12711, 3/8/95, effective 8/15/94; see ¶ 70,055.05.

Final rule, 59 FR 55746, 11/8/94, effective 1/9/95; see ¶ 70,055.04.

Final rule, 59 FR 48569, 9/22/94, effective 11/4/93; see ¶ 70,055.03.

Final rule, 58 FR 58798, 11/4/93, effective 11/4/93; Corrected 58 FR 61844, 11/23/93; corrected 58 FR 65556, 12 /15/93; corrected 59 FR 48568, 9/22/94; see ¶ 70,055.02.

Note: The ¶ 70,___ citations in the Sources list refer to the location of the source documents in **Government Contracts Reporter**, which is also available from **CCH** INCORPORATED.

PART 9900—SCOPE OF CHAPTER
Table of Contents

PART 9900—SCOPE OF CHAPTER

9900.000 Scope of chapter.

This chapter describes policies and procedures for applying the Cost Accounting Standards (CAS) to negotiated contracts and subcontracts. This chapter does not apply to sealed bid contracts or to any contract with a small business concern (see 9903.201-1(b) for these and other exemptions).

PART 9901—RULES AND PROCEDURES
Table of Contents

SUBCHAPTER A—ADMINISTRATION (Parts 9901-9902)

PART 9901—RULES AND PROCEDURES

9901.301 Purpose.

This part is published in compliance with Public Law 100-679, section 5(f)(3), 41 U.S.C. 422(f)(3), and constitutes the rules and procedures governing actions and the administration of the Cost Accounting Standards Board.

9901.302 Authority.

(a) The Cost Accounting Standards Board (hereinafter referred to as the "Board") is established by and operates in compliance with Public Law 100-679.

(b) The Board has the exclusive authority to make, promulgate, amend, and rescind cost accounting standards and regulations, including interpretations thereof, designed to achieve uniformity and consistency in the cost accounting practices governing measurement, assignment, and allocation of costs to contracts with the United States Government.

(c) All cost accounting standards, waivers, exemptions, interpretations, modifications, rules, and regulations promulgated under Section 719 of the Defense Production Act of 1950 (50 U.S.C. App. 2168) shall remain in effect unless and until amended, superseded, or rescinded by the Board pursuant to Public Law 100-679.

9901.303 Offices.

The Cost Accounting Standards Board's offices are located in the New Executive Office Building, 725 17th Street, NW., Washington, DC 20503. The hours of business for the Board are 9 a.m. to 5:30 p.m., local time, Monday through Friday, excluding holidays observed by the Federal Government in Washington, DC.

9901.304 Membership.

The Board consists of five members, including the Administrator of the Office of Federal Procurement Policy (hereinafter referred to as the "Administrator") who shall serve as Chairman, and four other members with experience in Government contract cost accounting who are to be appointed as follows:

(a) A representative of the Department of Defense appointed by the Secretary of Defense.

(b) An officer or employee of the General Services Administration appointed by the Administrator of the General Services Administration or his/her designee.

(c) A representative of industry appointed from the private sector by the Administrator.

(d) An individual who is particularly knowledgeable about cost accounting problems and systems appointed from the private sector by the Administrator.

(e) The term of office of each of the members of the Board, other than the Administrator, shall be four years, with the exception of the initial appointments of members. Of the initial appointments to the Board, two members shall hold appointment for a term of two years, one shall hold appointment for a term of three years, and one shall hold appointment for a term of four years.

(f) The members from the Department of Defense and the General Services Administration shall not be permitted to continue to serve on the Board after ceasing to be an officer or employee of their respective appointing agency. A vacancy on the Board shall be filled in the same manner in which the original appointment was made. A member may be reappointed for a subsequent term(s). Any member appointed to fill an interim vacancy on the Board shall serve for the remainder of the term for which his or her predecessor was appointed.

(g) In the event of the absence or incapacity of the Administrator or during a vacancy in the office, the official of the Office of Federal Procurement Policy, acting as Administrator, shall serve as the Chairman of the Board.

(h) In the event of the absence of any of the other Board members, a representative of that Board member may attend the Board meeting, but shall have no vote, and his or her attendance shall not be counted to establish a quorum.

9901.305 Requirements for standards and interpretive rulings.

Prior to the promulgation of cost accounting standards and interpretations thereof, the Board shall:

(a) Take into account, after consultation and discussion with the Comptroller General, professional accounting organizations, contractors, government agencies and other interested parties:

(1) The probable costs of implementation, including inflationary effects, if any, compared to the probable benefits;

(2) The advantages, disadvantages, and improvements anticipated in the pricing and administration of, and settlement of disputes concerning, contracts; and

(3) The scope of, and alternatives available to, the action proposed to be taken.

(b) Prepare and publish a report in the **Federal Register** on issues reviewed under subparagraph (a) above.

(c) Publish an advance notice of proposed rulemaking in the **Federal Register** in order to solicit comments on the report prepared pursuant to paragraph (b) of this section, and provide all parties affected a period of not less than 60 days after such publication to submit their views and comments. During this 60-day period, consult with the Comptroller General and consider any recommendation the Comptroller General may make.

(d) Publish a notice of such proposed rulemaking in the **Federal Register** and provide all parties affected a period of not less than 60 days after such publication to submit their views and comments.

(e) Rules, regulations, cost accounting standards, and modifications thereof promulgated or amended by the Board, shall have the full force and effect of law and shall become effective within 120 days after publication in the **Federal Register** in final form, unless the Board determines a longer period is necessary. Implementation dates for contractors and subcontractors shall be determined by the Board, but in no event shall

such dates be later than the beginning of the second fiscal year of affected contractors or subcontractors after the standard becomes effective. Rules, regulations, cost accounting standards, and modifications thereof promulgated or amended by the Board shall be accompanied by prefatory comments and by illustrations, if necessary.

(f) The above functions exercised by the Board are excluded from the operations of sections 551, 553 through 559, and 701 through 706 of Title 5, United States Code.

9901.306 Standards applicability.

Cost Accounting Standards promulgated by the Board shall be mandatory for use by all executive agencies and by contractors and subcontractors in estimating, accumulating, and reporting costs in connection with pricing and administration of, and settlement of disputes concerning, all negotiated prime contract and subcontract procurements with the United States Government in excess of the Truth in Negotiations Act (TINA) threshold, as adjusted for inflation (41 U.S.C. 1908 and 41 U.S.C. 1502(b)(1)(B)), other than contracts or subcontracts that have been exempted by the Board's regulations.

[Final rule, 72 FR 32809, 6/14/2007, effective 6/14/2007; Interim rule, 76 FR 40817, 7/12/2011, effective 8/11/2011; Final rule, 76 FR 79545, 12/22/2011, effective 12/22/2011]

9901.307 Exemptions and waivers.

The Board may exempt classes or categories of contractors and subcontractors from cost accounting standards requirements, and establish procedures for waiver of the requirements with respect to individual contracts and subcontracts. The official records of the Board shall be documented with supporting justification for class or category exemptions and individual waivers.

9901.308 Meetings.

The Board shall meet at the call of the Chairman. Agenda for Board meetings shall be proposed by the Chairman, but any Board member may request any item to be placed on the agenda.

9901.309 Quorum.

Three Board members, at least one of whom is appointed by the Administrator from the private sector, shall constitute a quorum of the Board.

9901.310 Board action.

Board action shall be by majority vote of the members present and voting, except that any vote to publish a proposed standard, rule or regulation in the **Federal Register** for comment or any vote to promulgate, amend or rescind a standard, rule or regulation, or any interpretation thereof, shall require at least three affirmative votes of the five Board members. The Chairman may vote on all matters presented for a vote, not merely to resolve tie votes. The results of final votes shall be reported in the minutes of the meeting, and the vote of a Board member may be recorded at his/her request.

9901.311 Executive sessions.

During the course of a Board meeting, any Board Member may request that for any portion of the meeting, the Board meet in executive session. The Chairman shall thereupon order such a session.

9901.312 Minutes.

The Executive Secretary of the Board shall be responsible for keeping accurate minutes of Board meetings and maintaining Board files.

9901.313 Public hearings.

Public hearings to assist the Board in the development and explanation of cost accounting standards and interpretive rulings may be held to the extent the Board in its sole discretion deems desirable. Notice of such hearings shall be given by publication in the **Federal Register.**

9901.314 Informal actions.

The Chairman may take actions on behalf of the Board on administrative issues, as determined by the Chairman, without holding an official meeting of the members. However, details of the actions so taken shall be provided to all of the members at the next Board meeting following such actions. Board members may be polled by telephone on other issues that must be processed on a timely basis when such matters cannot be deferred until the next formal meeting of the Board.

9901.315 Executive Secretary.

The Board's staff of professional, technical and supporting personnel is directed and supervised by the Executive Secretary.

9901.316 Files and records.

The files and records of the Board shall be maintained in accordance with the *Federal Records Creation, Maintenance, and Disposition Manual* of the Executive Office of The President, Office of Administration. As a minimum, the files and records shall include:

(a) A record of every Board meeting, including the minutes of Board proceedings and public hearings.

(b) Cost accounting standards promulgated, amended, or rescinded and interpretations thereof along with the supporting documentation and applicable research material.

(c) Applicable working papers, memoranda, research material, etc. related to issues under consideration by the Board and/or previously considered by the Board.

(d) Substantive regulations and statutes of general applicability and general policy and interpretations thereof.

(e) Any other file or record deemed important and relevant to the duties and responsibilities of the Board.

9901.317 Amendments.

This part 9901, Rules and Procedures, may be amended by the Chairman, after consultation with the Board.

PART 9902—[NO FAR SUPPLEMENT]

CASB 9901.317

PART 9903—CONTRACT COVERAGE
Table of Contents
Subpart 9903.1—General

Subpart 9903.2 CAS Program Requirements

Subpart 9903.3—CAS Rules and Regulations

SUBCHAPTER B—PROCUREMENT PRACTICES AND COST ACCOUNTING STANDARDS (Parts 9903-9905)

PART 9903—CONTRACT COVERAGE

SUBPART 9903.1—GENERAL

9903.101 Cost Accounting Standards.

Public Law 100-679 (41 U.S.C. 422) requires certain contractors and subcontractors to comply with Cost Accounting Standards (CAS) and to disclose in writing and follow consistently their cost accounting practices.

9903.102 OMB Approval Under the Paperwork Reduction Act.

The Paperwork Reduction Act of 1980 (Pub. L. 96-511) imposes a requirement on Federal agencies to obtain approval from the Office of Management and Budget (OMB) before collecting information from ten or more members of the public. The information collection and recordkeeping requirements contained in this regulation have been approved by OMB. OMB has assigned Control Numbers 0348-0051 and 0348-0055 to the paperwork, recordkeeping and forms associated with this regulation.

[Final rule, 59 FR 55746, 11/8/94, effective 1/9/95]

SUBPART 9903.2—CAS PROGRAM REQUIREMENTS

9903.201 Contract requirements. (No Text)

9903.201-1 CAS applicability.

(a) This subsection describes the rules for determining whether a proposed contract or subcontract is exempt from CAS. (See 9904 or 9905, as applicable.) Negotiated contracts not exempt in accordance with 9903.201-1(b) shall be subject to CAS. A CAS-covered contract may be subject to full, modified or other types of CAS coverage. The rules for determining the applicable type of CAS coverage are in 9903.201-2.

(b) The following categories of contracts and subcontracts are exempt from all CAS requirements:

(1) Sealed bid contracts.

(2) Negotiated contracts and subcontracts not in excess of the Truth in Negotiations Act (TINA) threshold, as adjusted for inflation (41 U.S.C. 1908 and 41 U.S.C. 1502(b)(1)(B)). For purposes of this paragraph (b)(2), an order issued by one segment to another segment shall be treated as a subcontract.

(3) Contracts and subcontracts with small businesses.

(4) Contracts and subcontracts with foreign governments or their agents or instrumentalities or, insofar as the requirements of CAS other than 9904.401 and 9904.402 are concerned, any contract or subcontract awarded to a foreign concern.

(5) Contracts and subcontracts in which the price is set by law or regulation.

(6) Contracts and subcontracts authorized in 48 CFR 12.207 for the acquisition of commercial items.

(7) Contracts or subcontracts of less than $7.5 million, provided that, at the time of award, the business unit of the contractor or subcontractor is not currently performing any CAS-covered contracts or subcontracts valued at $7.5 million or greater.

(8) [Reserved].

(9) [Reserved].

(10) [Reserved].

(11) [Reserved].

(12) [Reserved].

(13) Subcontractors under the NATO PHM Ship program to be performed outside the United States by a foreign concern.

(14) [Reserved].

(15) Firm-fixed-price contracts or subcontracts awarded on the basis of adequate price competition without submission of certified cost or pricing data.

[Corrected, 57 FR 34167, 8/3/92; Final rule, 58 FR 58798, 11/4/93, effective 11/4/93; Final rule, 59 FR 55746, 11/8/94, effective 1/9/95; Final rule, 60 FR 16534, 3/30/95, effective 3/30/95; Interim rule, 61

FR 39360, 7/29/96, effective 7/29/96; Final rule, 62 FR 31294, 6/6/97, effective 6/6/97; Interim rule, 65 FR 5990, 2/7/2000, effective 4/2/2000; Final rule, 65 FR 36767, 6/9/2000, effective 6/9/2000; Interim rule, 70 FR 29457, 5/23/2005, effective 5/23/2005; Final rule, 72 FR 32546, 6/13/2007, effective 6/13/2007; Final rule, 72 FR 32809, 6/14/2007, effective 6/14/2007; Final rule, 72 FR 36367, 7/3/2007, effective 7/3/2007; Interim rule, 76 FR 40817, 7/12/2011, effective 8/11/2011; Final rule, 76 FR 49365, 8/10/2011, effective 10/11/2011; Final rule, 76 FR 79545, 12/22/2011, effective 12/22/2011; Final rule, 83 FR 8634, 2/28/2018, effective 3/30/2018; Final rule, 83 FR 33146, 7/17/2018, effective 8/16/2018]

9903.201-2 Types of CAS coverage.

(a) Full coverage. Full coverage requires that the business unit comply with all of the CAS specified in Part 9904 that are in effect on the date of the contract award and with any CAS that become applicable because of later award of a CAS-covered contract. Full coverage applies to contractor business units that—

(1) Receive a single CAS-covered contract award of $50 million or more; or

(2) Received $50 million or more in net CAS-covered awards during its preceding cost accounting period.

(b) Modified coverage. (1) Modified CAS coverage requires only that the contractor comply with Standard 9904.401, Consistency in Estimating, Accumulating, and Reporting Costs, Standard 9904.402, Consistency in Allocating Costs Incurred for the Same Purpose, Standard 9904.405, Accounting for Unallowable Costs and Standard 9904.406, Cost Accounting Standard—Cost Accounting Period. Modified, rather, than full, CAS coverage may be applied to a covered contract of less than $50 million awarded to a business unit that received less than $50 million in net CAS-covered awards in the immediately preceding cost accounting period.

(2) If any one contract is awarded with modified CAS coverage, all CAS-covered contracts awarded to that business unit dur-

ing that cost accounting period must also have modified coverage with the following exception: if the business unit receives a single CAS-covered contract award of $50 million or more, that contract must be subject to full CAS coverage. Thereafter, any covered contract awarded in the same cost accounting period must also be subject to full CAS coverage.

(3) A contract awarded with modified CAS coverage shall remain subject to such coverage throughout its life regardless of changes in the business unit's CAS status during subsequent cost accounting periods.

(c) Coverage for educational institutions— (1) *Regulatory requirements.* Parts 9903 and 9905 apply to educational institutions except as otherwise provided in this paragraph (c) and at 9903.2021(f).

(2) *Definitions.* (i) The following term is prominent in Parts 9903 and 9905. Other terms defined elsewhere in this Chapter 99 shall have the meanings ascribed to them in those definitions unless paragraph (c)(2)(ii) of this subsection below requires otherwise.

Educational institution means a public or nonprofit institution of higher education, e.g., an accredited college or university, as defined in section 1201(a) of Public Law 89-329, November 8, 1965, Higher Education Act of 1965; (20 U.S.C. 1141(a)).

(ii) The following modifications of terms defined elsewhere in this Chapter 99 are applicable to educational institutions:

Business unit means any segment of an educational institution, or an entire educational institution which is not divided into segments.

Segment means one of two or more divisions, campus locations, or other subdivisions of an educational institution that operate as independent organizational entities under the auspices of the parent educational institution and report directly to an intermediary group office or the governing central system office of the parent educational institution. Two schools of instruction operating under one division, campus location or other subdivision would not be separate segments unless they follow different cost accounting practices, for example, the

School of Engineering should not be treated as a separate segment from the School of Humanities if they both are part of the same division's cost accounting system and are subject to the same cost accounting practices. The term includes Government-owned contractor-operated (GOCO) facilities, Federally Funded Research and Developments Centers (FFRDCs), and joint ventures and subsidiaries (domestic and foreign) in which the institution has a majority ownership. The term also includes those joint ventures and subsidiaries (domestic and foreign) in which the institution has less than a majority of ownership, but over which it exercises control.

(3) *Applicable standards.* Coverage for educational institutions requires that the business unit comply with all of the CAS specified in part 9905 that are in effect on the date of the contract award and with any CAS that become applicable because of later award of a CAS-covered contract. This coverage applies to business units that receive negotiated contracts in excess of the Truth in Negotiations Act (TINA) threshold, as adjusted for inflation (41 U.S.C. 1908 and 41 U.S.C. 1502(b)(1)(B)), except for CAS-covered contracts awarded to FFRDCs operated by an educational institution.

(4) *FFRDCs.* Negotiated contracts awarded to an FFRDC operated by an educational institution are subject to the full or modified CAS coverage prescribed in paragraphs (a) and (b) of this subsection. CAS-covered FFRDC contracts shall be excluded from the institution's universe of contracts when determining CAS applicability and disclosure requirements for contracts other than those to be performed by the FFRDC.

(5) *Contract clauses.* The contract clause at 9903.201-4(e) shall be incorporated in each negotiated contract and subcontract awarded to an educational institution when the negotiated contract or subcontract price exceeds the Truth in Negotiations Act (TINA) threshold, as adjusted for inflation (41 U.S.C. 1908 and 41 U.S.C. 1502(b)(1)(B)). For CAS-covered contracts awarded to an FFRDC operated by an educational institution, however, the full or modi-

fied CAS contract clause specified at 9903.201-4(a) or (c), as applicable, shall be incorporated.

(6) *Continuity in Fully CAS-Covered Contracts.* Where existing contracts awarded to an educational institution incorporate full CAS coverage, the contracting officer may continue to apply full CAS coverage, as prescribed at 9903.201-2(a), in future awards made to that educational institution.

(d) *Subcontracts.* Subcontract awards subject to CAS require the same type of CAS coverage as would prime contracts awarded to the same business unit. In measuring total net CAS-covered awards for a year, a transfer by one segment to another shall be deemed to be a subcontract award by the transferor.

(e) *Foreign concerns.* Contracts with foreign concerns subject to CAS shall only be subject to Standard 9904.401, Consistency in Estimating, Accumulating, and Reporting Costs, and Standard 9904.402, Consistency in Allocating Costs Incurred for the Same Purpose.

[Final rule, 58 FR 58798, 11/4/93, effective 11/4/93; Corrected, 58 FR 65556, 12/15/93; Final rule, 59 FR 48569, 9/22/94, effective 11/4/93; Final rule, 59 FR 55746, 11/8/94, effective 1/9/95; Interim rule, 65 FR 5990, 2/7/2000, effective 4/2/2000; Final rule, 65 FR 36767, 6/9/2000, effective 6/9/2000; Final rule, 72 FR 32809, 6/14/2007, effective 6/14/2007; Interim rule, 76 FR 40817, 7/12/2011, effective 8/11/2011; Final rule, 76 FR 79545, 12/22/2011, effective 12/22/2011]

9903.201-3 Solicitation provisions.

(a) Cost Accounting Standards Notices and Certification.

(1) The contracting officer shall insert the provision set forth below, Cost Accounting Standards Notices and Certification, in solicitations for proposed contracts subject to CAS as specified in 9903.201. The provision allows offerors to—

(i) Certify their Disclosure Statement status;

(ii) [Reserved];

(iii) Claim exemption from full CAS coverage and elect modified CAS coverage when appropriate; and

(iv) Certify whether award of the contemplated contract would require a change to existing cost accounting practices.

(2) If an award to an educational institution is contemplated prior to July 1, 1997, the contracting officer shall use the basic provision set forth below with its Alternate I, unless the contract is to be performed by an FFRDC (see 9903.201(c)(5)), or the provision at 9903.201(c)(6) applies.

COST ACCOUNTING STANDARDS NOTICES AND CERTIFICATION (JUL 2011)

Note: This notice does not apply to small businesses or foreign governments.

This notice is in three parts, identified by Roman numerals I through III.

Offerors shall examine each part and provide the requested information in order to determine Cost Accounting Standards (CAS) requirements applicable to any resultant contract.

If the offeror is an educational institution, Part II does not apply unless the contemplated contract will be subject to full or modified CAS-coverage pursuant to 9903.201-2(c)(5) or 9903.2012(c)(6).

I. Disclosure Statement—Cost Accounting Practices and Certification

(a) Any contract in excess of the Truth in Negotiations Act (TINA) threshold, as adjusted for inflation (41 U.S.C. 1908 and 41 U.S.C. 1502(b)(1)(B)), resulting from this solicitation, except for those contracts which are exempt as specified in 9903.201-1.

(b) Any offeror submitting a proposal which, if accepted, will result in a contract subject to the requirements of 48 CFR, Chapter 99 must, as a condition of contracting, submit a Disclosure Statement as required by 9903.202. When required, the Disclosure Statement must be submitted as a part of the offeror's proposal under this solicitation unless the offeror has already submitted a Disclosure Statement disclosing the practices used in connection with the pricing of this proposal. If an applicable Dis-

closure Statement has already been submitted, the offeror may satisfy the requirement for submission by providing the information requested in paragraph (c) of Part I of this provision.

Caution: In the absence of specific regulations or agreement, a practice disclosed in a Disclosure Statement shall not, by virtue of such disclosure, be deemed to be a proper, approved, or agreed-to-practice for pricing proposals or accumulating and reporting contract performance cost data.

(c) Check the appropriate box below:

[ ](1) Certificate of Concurrent Submission of Disclosure Statement.

The offeror hereby certifies that, as a part of the offer, copies of the Disclosure Statement have been submitted as follows: (i) Original and one copy to the cognizant Administrative Contracting Officer (ACO) or cognizant Federal agency official authorized to act in that capacity, as applicable, and (ii) one copy to the cognizant Federal auditor.

(Disclosure must be on Form No. CASB DS-1 or CASB DS-2, as applicable. Forms may be obtained from the cognizant ACO or cognizant Federal agency official acting in that capacity and/or from the looseleaf version of the Federal Acquisition Regulation.)

Date of Disclosure Statement:___

Name and Address of Cognizant ACO or Federal Official where filed:___

The offeror further certifies that the practices used in estimating costs in pricing this proposal are consistent with the cost accounting practices disclosed in the Disclosure Statement.

[ ] (2) Certificate of Previously Submitted Disclosure Statement. The offeror hereby certifies that the required Disclosure Statement was filed as follows:

Date of Disclosure Statement:___

Name and Address of Cognizant ACO or Federal Official where filed:___

The offeror further certifies that the practices used in estimating costs in pricing this proposal are consistent with the cost ac-

CASB 9903.201-3

counting practices disclosed in the applicable Disclosure Statement.

[ ] (3) Certificate of Monetary Exemption.

The offeror hereby certifies that the offeror, together with all divisions, subsidiaries, and affiliates under common control, did not receive net awards of negotiated prime contracts and subcontracts subject to CAS totaling $50 million or more in the cost accounting period immediately preceding the period in which this proposal was submitted.

The offeror further certifies that if such status changes before an award resulting from this proposal, the offeror will advise the Contracting Officer immediately.

[ ] (4) Certificate of Interim Exemption.

The offeror hereby certifies that (i) the offeror first exceeded the monetary exemption for disclosure, as defined in (3) above, in the cost accounting period immediately preceding the period in which this offer was submitted and (ii) in accordance with 9903.202-1, the offeror is not yet required to submit a Disclosure Statement. The offeror further certifies that if an award resulting from this proposal has not been made within 90 days after the end of that period, the offeror will immediately submit a revised certificate to the Contracting Officer, in the form specified under subparagraphs (c)(1) or (c)(2) of Part I of this provision, as appropriate, to verify submission of a completed Disclosure Statement.

Caution: Offerors currently required to disclose because they were awarded a CAS-covered prime contract or subcontract of $50 million or more in the current cost accounting period may not claim this exemption (4). Further, the exemption applies only in connection with proposals submitted before expiration of the 90-day period following the cost accounting period in which the monetary exemption was exceeded.

II. Cost Accounting Standards—Eligibility for Modified Contact Coverage

If the offeror is eligible to use the modified provisions of 9903.201-2(b) and elects to do so, the offeror shall indicate by checking the box below. Checking the box below shall mean that the resultant contract is subject to the Disclosure and Consistency of Cost Accounting Practices clause in lieu of the Cost Accounting Standards clause.

[ ] The offeror hereby claims an exemption from the Cost Accounting Standards clause under the provisions of 9903.201-2(b) and certifies that the offeror is eligible for use of the Disclosure and Consistency of Cost Accounting Practices clause because during the cost accounting period immediately preceding the period in which this proposal was submitted, the offeror received less than $50 million in awards of CAS-covered prime contracts and subcontracts. The offeror further certifies that if such status changes before an award resulting from this proposal, the offeror will advise the Contracting Officer immediately.

Caution: An offeror may not claim the above eligibility for modified contract coverage if this proposal is expected to result in the award of a CAS-covered contract of $50 million or more or if, during its current cost accounting period, the offeror has been awarded a single CAS-covered prime contract or subcontract of $50 million or more.

III. Additional Cost Accounting Standards Applicable to Existing Contracts

The offeror shall indicate below whether award of the contemplated contract would, in accordance with subparagraph (a)(3) of the Cost Accounting Standards clause, require a change in established cost accounting practices affecting existing contracts and subcontracts.

[ ] Yes [ ] No

(End of basic provision)

Alternate I(OCT 1994)

Insert the following subparagraph (5) at the end of Part I of the basic clause:

[ ] (5) Certificate of Disclosure Statement Due Date by Educational Institution. If the offeror is an educational institution that, under the transition provisions of 9903.202-1(f), is or will be required to submit a Disclosure Statement after receipt of this award, the offeror hereby certifies that (check one and complete):

CASB 9903.201-3

[ ] (a) A Disclosure Statement filing Due Date of ____ has been established with the cognizant Federal agency.

[ ] (b) The Disclosure Statement will be submitted within the six month period ending ____ months after receipt of this award.

Name and Address of Cognizant ACO or Federal Official where Disclosure Statement is to be filed:____

(End of Alternate I)

[Corrected, 57 FR 34079, 8/3/92; Final rule, 58 FR 58798, 11/4/93, effective 11/4/93; Corrected, 58 FR 61844, 11/23/93; Corrected, 58 FR 65556, 12/15/93; Final rule, 59 FR 55746, 11/8/94, effective 1/9/95; Interim rule, 61 FR 39360, 7/29/96, effective 7/29/96, finalized without change, 62 FR 31294, 6/6/97, effective 6/6/97; Interim rule, 65 FR 5990, 2/7/2000, effective 4/2/2000; Final rule, 65 FR 36767, 6/9/2000, effective 6/9/2000; Final rule, 72 FR 32809, 6/14/2007, effective 6/14/2007; Interim rule, 76 FR 40817, 7/12/2011, effective 8/11/2011; Final rule, 76 FR 79545, 12/22/2011, effective 12/22/2011]

9903.201-4 Contract clauses.

(a) *Cost Accounting Standards.* (1) The contracting officer shall insert the clause set forth below, Cost Accounting Standards, in negotiated contracts, unless the contract is exempted (see 9903.201-1), the contract is subject to modified coverage (see 9903.201-2), or the clause prescribed in paragraph (e) of this section is used.

(2) The clause below requires the contractor to comply with all CAS specified in part 9904, to disclose actual cost accounting practices (applicable to CAS-covered contracts only), and to follow disclosed and established cost accounting practices consistently.

COST ACCOUNTING STANDARDS (JUL 2011)

(a) Unless the contract is exempt under 9903.201-1 and 9903.201-2, the provisions of 9903 are incorporated herein by reference and the Contractor in connection with this contract, shall—

(1) (CAS-covered Contracts Only) By submission of a Disclosure Statement, disclosed in writing the Contractor's cost accounting practices as required by 9903.202-1 through 9903.202-5 including methods of distinguishing direct costs from indirect costs and the basis used for allocating indirect costs. The practices disclosed for this contract shall be the same as the practices currently disclosed and applied on all other contracts and subcontracts being performed by the Contractor and which contain a Cost Accounting Standards (CAS) clause. If the Contractor has notified the Contracting Officer that the Disclosure Statement contains trade secrets, and commercial or financial information which is privileged and confidential, the Disclosure Statement shall be protected and shall not be released outside of the Government.

(2) Follow consistently the Contractor's cost accounting practices in accumulating and reporting contract performance cost data concerning this contract. If any change in cost accounting practices is made for the purposes of any contract or subcontract subject to CAS requirements, the change must be applied prospectively to this contract and the Disclosure Statement must be amended accordingly. If the contract price or cost allowance of this contract is affected by such changes, adjustment shall be made in accordance with subparagraph (a)(4) or (a)(5) of this clause, as appropriate.

(3) Comply with all CAS, including any modifications and interpretations indicated thereto contained in part 9904, in effect on the date of award of this contract or, if the Contractor has submitted cost or pricing data, on the date of final agreement on price as shown on the Contractor's signed certificate of current cost or pricing data. The Contractor shall also comply with any CAS (or modifications to CAS) which hereafter become applicable to a contract or subcontract of the Contractor. Such compliance shall be required prospectively from the date of applicability of such contract or subcontract.

(4)(i) Agree to an equitable adjustment as provided in the Changes clause of this contract if the contract cost is affected by a change which, pursuant to subparagraph (a)(3) of this clause, the Contractor is required to make to the Contractor's established cost accounting practices.

(ii) Negotiate with the Contracting Officer to determine the terms and conditions under which a change may be made to a cost accounting practice, other than a change made under other provisions of subparagraph (a)(4) of this clause; provided that no agreement may be made under this provision that will increase costs paid by the United States.

(iii) When the parties agree to a change to a cost accounting practice, other than a change under subdivision (a)(4)(i) of this clause, negotiate an equitable adjustment as provided in the Changes clause of this contract.

(5) Agree to an adjustment of the contract price or cost allowance, as appropriate, if the Contractor or a subcontractor fails to comply with an applicable Cost Accounting Standard, or to follow any cost accounting practice consistently and such failure results in any increased costs paid by the United States. Such adjustment shall provide for recovery of the increased costs to the United States, together with interest thereon computed at the annual rate established under section 6621(a)(2) of the Internal Revenue Code of 1986 (26 U.S.C. 6621(a)(2)) for such period, from the time the payment by the United States was made to the time the adjustment is effected. In no case shall the Government recover costs greater than the increased cost to the Government, in the aggregate, on the relevant contracts subject to the price adjustment, unless the Contractor made a change in its cost accounting practices of which it was aware or should have been aware at the time of price negotiations and which it failed to disclose to the Government.

(b) If the parties fail to agree whether the Contractor or a subcontractor has complied with an applicable CAS in part 9904 or a CAS rule or regulation in part 9903 and as to any cost adjustment demanded by the United States, such failure to agree will constitute a dispute under the Contract Disputes Act (41 U.S.C. 601).

(c) The Contractor shall permit any authorized representatives of the Government to examine and make copies of any documents, papers, or records relating to compliance with the requirements of this clause.

(d) The contractor shall include in all negotiated subcontracts which the Contractor enters into, the substance of this clause, except paragraph (b), and shall require such inclusion in all other subcontracts, of any tier, including the obligation to comply with all CAS in effect on the subcontractor's award date or if the subcontractor has submitted cost or pricing data, on the date of final agreement on price as shown on the subcontractor's signed Certificate of Current Cost or Pricing Data. If the subcontract is awarded to a business unit which pursuant to 9903.201-2 is subject to other types of CAS coverage, the substance of the applicable clause set forth in 9903.201-4 shall be inserted. This requirement shall apply only to negotiated subcontracts in excess of the Truth in Negotiations Act (TINA) threshold, as adjusted for inflation (41 U.S.C. 1908 and 41 U.S.C. 1502(b)(1)(B)), except that the requirement shall not apply to negotiated subcontracts otherwise exempt from the requirement to include a CAS clause as specified in 9903.201-1.

(End of Clause)

(b) [Reserved]

(c) *Disclosure and Consistency of Cost Accounting Practices.* (1) The Contracting Officer shall insert the clause set forth below, Disclosure and Consistency of Cost Accounting Practices, in negotiated contracts when the contract amount is over $650,000 but less than $50 million, and the offeror certifies it is eligible for and elects to use modified CAS coverage (see 9903.201-2, unless the clause prescribed in paragraph (d) of this subsection is used).

(2) The clause below requires the Contractor to comply with CAS 9904.401, 9904.402, 9904.405, and 9904.406, to disclose (if it meets certain requirements) actual cost accounting practices, and to follow consistently disclosed and established cost accounting practices.

CASB 9903.201-4

DISCLOSURE AND CONSISTENCY OF COST ACCOUNTING PRACTICES (JUL 2011)

(a) The Contractor, in connection with this contract, shall—

(1) Comply with the requirements of 9904.401, Consistency in Estimating, Accumulating, and Reporting Costs; 9904.402, Consistency in Allocating Costs Incurred for the Same Purpose; 9904.405, Accounting for Unallowable Costs; and 9904.406, Cost Accounting Standard—Cost Accounting Period, in effect on the date of award of this contract, as indicated in part 9904.

(2) (CAS-covered Contracts Only) If it is a business unit of a company required to submit a Disclosure Statement, disclose in writing its cost accounting practices as required by 9903.202-1 through 9903.202-5. If the Contractor has notified the Contracting Officer that the Disclosure Statement contains trade secrets and commercial or financial information which is privileged and confidential, the Disclosure Statement shall be protected and shall not be released outside of the Government.

(3) (i) Follow consistently the Contractor's cost accounting practices. A change to such practices may be proposed, however, by either the Government or the Contractor, and the Contractor agrees to negotiate with the Contracting Officer the terms and conditions under which a change may be made. After the terms and conditions under which the change is to be made have been agreed to, the change must be applied prospectively to this contract, and the Disclosure Statement, if affected, must be amended accordingly.

(ii) The Contractor shall, when the parties agree to a change to a cost accounting practice and the Contracting Officer has made the finding required in 9903.201-6(c) that the change is desirable and not detrimental to the interests of the Government, negotiate an equitable adjustment as provided in the Changes clause of this contract. In the absence of the required finding, no agreement may be made under this contract clause that will increase costs paid by the United States.

(4) Agree to an adjustment of the contract price or cost allowance, as appropriate, if the Contractor or a subcontractor fails to comply

with the applicable CAS or to follow any cost accounting practice, and such failure results in any increased costs paid by the United States. Such adjustment shall provide for recovery of the increased costs to the United States, together with interest thereon computed at the annual rate established under section 6621(a)(2) of the Internal Revenue Code of 1986 (26 U.S.C. 6621(a)(2)) for such period, from the time the payment by the United States was made to the time the adjustment is effected.

(b) If the parties fail to agree whether the Contractor has complied with an applicable CAS rule, or regulation as specified in parts 9903 and 9904 and as to any cost adjustment demanded by the United States, such failure to agree will constitute a dispute under the Contract Disputes Act (41 U.S.C. 601).

(c) Disclosure and Consistency of Cost Accounting Practices. (1) The contracting officer shall insert the clause set forth below, Disclosure and Consistency of Cost Accounting Practices, in negotiated contracts when the contract amount is over the Truth in Negotiations Act (TINA) threshold, as adjusted for inflation (41 U.S.C. 1908 and 41 U.S.C. 1502(b)(1)(B)), but less than $50 million, and the offeror certifies it is eligible for and elects to use modified CAS coverage (see 9903.201-2, unless the clause prescribed in paragraph (d) of this subsection is used).

(d) The Contractor shall include in all negotiated subcontracts, which the Contractor enters into, the substance of this clause, except paragraph (b), and shall require such inclusion in all other subcontracts of any tier, except that—

(1) If the subcontract is awarded to a business unit which pursuant to 9903.201-2 is subject to other types of CAS coverage, the substance of the applicable clause set forth in 9903.201-4 shall be inserted.

(2) This requirement shall apply only to negotiated subcontracts in excess of the Truth in Negotiations Act (TINA) threshold, as adjusted for inflation (41 U.S.C. 1908 and 41 U.S.C. 1502(b)(1)(B)).

(3) The requirement shall not apply to negotiated subcontracts otherwise exempt

CASB 9903.201-4

from the requirement to include a CAS clause as specified in 9903.201-1.

(End of clause)

(d) [Reserved]

(e) *Cost Accounting Standards—Educational Institutions.* (1) The contracting officer shall insert the clause set forth below, Cost Accounting Standards—Educational Institutions, in negotiated contracts awarded to educational institutions, unless the contract is exempted (see 9903.201-1), the contract is to be performed by an FFRDC (see 9903.201-2(c)(5)), or the provision at 9903.201-2(c)(6) applies.

(2) The clause below requires the educational institution to comply with all CAS specified in part 9905, to disclose actual cost accounting practices as required by 9903.202-1(f), and to follow disclosed and established cost accounting practices consistently.

COST ACCOUNTING STANDARDS— EDUCATIONAL INSTITUTIONS (JUL 2011)

(a) Unless the contract is exempt under 9903.201-1 and 9903.201-2, the provisions of part 9903 are incorporated herein by reference and the Contractor in connection with this contract, shall—

(1) (CAS-covered Contracts Only) If a business unit of an educational institution required to submit a Disclosure Statement, disclose in writing the Contractor's cost accounting practices as required by 9903.202-1 through 9903.202-5 including methods of distinguishing direct costs from indirect costs and the basis used for accumulating and allocating indirect costs. The practices disclosed for this contract shall be the same as the practices currently disclosed and applied on all other contracts and subcontracts being performed by the Contractor and which contain a Cost Accounting Standards (CAS) clause. If the Contractor has notified the Contracting Officer that the Disclosure Statement contains trade secrets, and commercial or financial information which is privileged and confidential, the Disclosure Statement shall be protected and shall not be released outside of the Government.

(2) Follow consistently the Contractor's cost accounting practices in accumulating and reporting contract performance cost data concerning this contract. If any change in cost accounting practices is made for the purposes of any contract or subcontract subject to CAS requirements, the change must be applied prospectively to this contract and the Disclosure Statement, if required, must be amended accordingly. If an accounting principle change mandated under Office of Management and Budget (OMB) Circular A-21, Cost Principles for Educational Institutions, requires that a change in the Contractor's cost accounting practices be made after the date of this contract award, the change must be applied prospectively to this contract and the Disclosure Statement, if required, must be amended accordingly. If the contract price or cost allowance of this contract is affected by such changes, adjustment shall be made in accordance with subparagraph (a)(4) or (a)(5) of this clause, as appropriate.

(3) Comply with all CAS, including any modifications and interpretations indicated thereto contained in 48 CFR part 9905, in effect on the date of award of this contract or, if the Contractor has submitted cost or pricing data, on the date of final agreement on price as shown on the Contractor's signed certificate of current cost or pricing data. The Contractor shall also comply with any CAS (or modifications to CAS) which hereafter become applicable to a contract or subcontract of the Contractor. Such compliance shall be required prospectively from the date of applicability to such contract or subcontract.

(4) (i) Agree to an equitable adjustment as provided in the Changes clause of this contract if the contract cost is affected by a change which, pursuant to subparagraph (a)(3) of this clause, the Contractor is required to make to the Contractor's established cost accounting practices.

(ii) Negotiate with the Contracting Officer to determine the terms and conditions under which a change may be made to a cost accounting practice, other than a change made under other provisions of subparagraph (a)(4) of this clause; provided that no agree-

CASB 9903.201-4

ment may be made under this provision that will increase costs paid by the United States.

(iii) When the parties agree to a change to a cost accounting practice, other than a change under subdivision (a)(4)(i) or (a)(4)(iv) of this clause, negotiate an equitable adjustment as provided in the Changes clause of this contract.

(iv) Agree to an equitable adjustment as provided in the Changes clause of this contract, if the contract cost is materially affected by an OMB Circular A-21 accounting principle amendment which, on becoming effective after the date of contract award, requires the Contractor to make a change to the Contractor's established cost accounting practices.

(5) Agree to an adjustment of the contract price or cost allowance, as appropriate, if the Contractor or a subcontractor fails to comply with an applicable Cost Accounting Standard, or to follow any cost accounting practice consistently and such failure results in any increased costs paid by the United States. Such adjustment shall provide for recovery of the increased costs to the United States, together with interest thereon computed at the annual rate established under section 6621(a)(2) of the Internal Revenue Code of 1986 (26 U.S.C. 6621(a)(2)) for such period, from the time the payment by the United States was made to the time the adjustment is effected. In no case shall the Government recover costs greater than the increased cost to the Government, in the aggregate, on the relevant contracts subject to the price adjustment, unless the Contractor made a change in its cost accounting practices of which it was aware or should have been aware at the time of price negotiations and which it failed to disclose to the Government.

(b) If the parties fail to agree whether the Contractor or a subcontractor has complied with an applicable CAS or a CAS rule or regulation in 9903 and as to any cost adjustment demanded by the United States, such failure to agree will constitute a dispute under the Contract Disputes Act (41 U.S.C. 601).

(c) The Contractor shall permit any authorized representatives of the Government to examine and make copies of any documents, papers, or records relating to compliance with the requirements of this clause.

(d) The Contractor shall include in all negotiated subcontracts which the Contractor enters into, the substance of this clause, except paragraph (b), and shall require such inclusion in all other subcontracts, of any tier, including the obligation to comply with all applicable CAS in effect on the subcontractor's award date or if the subcontractor has submitted cost or pricing data, on the date of final agreement on price as shown on the subcontractor's signed Certificate of Current Cost or Pricing Data, except that—

(1) If the subcontract is awarded to a business unit which pursuant to 9903.201-2 is subject to other types of CAS coverage, the substance of the applicable clause set forth in 9903.201-4 shall be inserted; and

(2) This requirement shall apply only to negotiated subcontracts in excess of the Truth in Negotiations Act (TINA) threshold, as adjusted for inflation (41 U.S.C. 1908 and 41 U.S.C 1502(b)(1)B)).

(3) The requirement shall not apply to negotiated subcontracts otherwise exempt from the requirement to include a CAS clause as specified in 9903.201-1.

(End of clause)

(f) *Disclosure and Consistency of Cost Accounting Practices—Foreign Concerns.*

(1) The contracting officer shall insert the clause set forth below, Disclosure and Consistency of Cost Accounting Practices—Foreign Concerns, in negotiated contracts when the contract is with a foreign concern and the contract is not otherwise exempt under 9903.201-1 (see 9903.201-2(e)).

(2) The clause below requires the contractor to comply with 9904.401 and 9904.402, to disclose (if it meets certain requirements) actual cost accounting practices, and to follow consistently disclosed and established cost accounting practices.

DISCLOSURE AND CONSISTENCY OF COST ACCOUNTING PRACTICES—FOREIGN CONCERNS (JUL 2011)

(a) The Contractor, in connection with this contract, shall—

(1) Comply with the requirements of 9904.401, Consistency in Estimating, Accumulating, and Reporting Costs; and 9904.402, Consistency in Allocating Costs Incurred for the Same Purpose, in effect on the date of award of this contract, as indicated in Part 9904.

(2) (CAS-covered Contracts Only) If it is a business unit of a company required to submit a Disclosure Statement, disclose in writing its cost accounting practices as required by 9903.202-1 through 9903.202-5. If the Contractor has notified the Contracting Officer that the Disclosure Statement contains trade secrets and commercial or financial information which is privileged and confidential, the Disclosure Statement shall be protected and shall not be released outside of the Government.

(3) (i) Follow consistently the Contractor's cost accounting practices. A change to such practices may be proposed, however, by either the Government or the Contractor, and the Contractor agrees to negotiate with the Contracting Officer the terms and conditions under which a change may be made. After the terms and conditions under which the change is to be made have been agreed to, the change must be applied prospectively to this contract, and the Disclosure Statement, if affected, must be amended accordingly.

(ii) The Contractor shall, when the parties agree to a change to a cost accounting practice and the Contracting Officer has made the finding required in 9903.201-6(c) that the change is desirable and not detrimental to the interests of the Government, negotiate an equitable adjustment as provided in the Changes clause of this contract. In the absence of the required finding, no agreement may be made under this contract clause that will increase costs paid by the United States.

(4) Agree to an adjustment of the contract price or cost allowance, as appropriate, if the Contractor or a subcontractor fails to comply with the applicable CAS or to follow any cost accounting practice, and such failure results in any increased costs paid by the United States. Such adjustment shall provide for recovery of the increased costs to the United States, together with interest thereon computed at the annual rate established under section 6621(a)(2) of the Internal Revenue Code of 1986 (26 U.S.C. 6621(a)(2)) for such period, from the time the payment by the United States was made to the time the adjustment is effected.

(b) If the parties fail to agree whether the Contractor has complied with an applicable CAS rule, or regulation as specified in Parts 9903 and 9904 and as to any cost adjustment demanded by the United States, such failure to agree will constitute a dispute under the Contract Disputes Act (41 U.S.C. 601).

(c) The Contractor shall permit any authorized representatives of the Government to examine and make copies of any documents, papers, and records relating to compliance with the requirements of this clause.

(d) The Contractor shall include in all negotiated subcontracts, which the Contractor enters into, the substance of this clause, except paragraph (b), and shall require such inclusion in all other subcontracts of any tier, except that—

(1) If the subcontract is awarded to a business unit which pursuant to 9903.201-2 is subject to other types of CAS coverage, the substance of the applicable clause set forth in 9903.201-4 shall be inserted.

(2) This requirement shall apply only to negotiated subcontracts in excess of the Truth in Negotiations Act (TINA) threshold, as adjusted for inflation (41 U.S.C. 1908 and 41 U.S.C. 1502(b)(1)(B)).

(3) The requirement shall not apply to negotiated subcontracts otherwise exempt from the requirement to include a CAS clause as specified in 9903.201-1.

(End of Clause)

[Corrected, 57 FR 34079, 8/3/92; Corrected, 57 FR 43776, 9/22/92; Final rule, 58 FR 58798, 11/4/93, effective 11/4/93; Corrected, 58 FR 65556, 12/15/93; Corrected, 59 FR 48568, 9/22/94; Final rule, 59 FR 55746, 11/8/94, effective 1/9/95; Interim

CASB 9903.201-4

rule, 61 FR 39360, 7/29/96, effective 7/29/96; Final rule, 62 FR 31294, 6/6/97, effective 6/6/97; Interim rule, 65 FR 5990, 2/7/2000, effective 4/2/2000; Final rule, 65 FR 36767, 6/9/2000, effective 6/9/2000; Final rule, 65 FR 37470, 6/14/2000, effective 6/14/2000; Interim rule, 70 FR 29457, 5/23/2005, effective 5/23/2005; Final rule, 72 FR 32546, 6/13/2007, effective 6/13/2007; Final rule, 72 FR 32809, 6/14/2007, effective 6/14/2007; Final rule, 73 FR 15939, 3/26/2008, effective 4/25/2008; Interim rule, 76 FR 40817, 7/12/2011, effective 8/11/2011; Final rule, 76 FR 79545, 12/22/2011, effective 12/22/2011]

9903.201-5 Waiver.

(a) The head of an executive agency may waive the applicability of the Cost Accounting Standards for a contract or subcontract with a value of less than $15 million, if that official determines, in writing, that the business unit of the contractor or subcontractor that will perform the work—

(1) Is primarily engaged in the sale of commercial items; and

(2) Would not otherwise be subject to the Cost Accounting Standards under this Chapter.

(b) The head of an executive agency may waive the applicability of the Cost Accounting Standards for a contract or subcontract under exceptional circumstances when necessary to meet the needs of the agency. A determination to waive the applicability of the Cost Accounting Standards by the agency head shall be set forth in writing, and shall include a statement of the circumstances justifying the waiver.

(c) The head of an executive agency may not delegate the authority under paragraphs (a) and (b) of this section, to any official below the senior policymaking level in the agency.

(d) The head of each executive agency shall report the waivers granted under paragraphs (a) and (b) of this section, for that agency, to the Cost Accounting Standards Board, on an annual basis, not later than 90 days after the close of the Government's fiscal year.

(e) Upon request of an agency head or his designee, the Cost Accounting Standards Board may waive all or any part of the requirements of 9903.201-4(a), Cost Accounting Standards, or 9903.201-4(c), Disclosure and Consistency of Cost Accounting Practices, with respect to a contract subject to the Cost Accounting Standards. Any request for a waiver shall describe the proposed contract or subcontract for which the waiver is sought and shall contain—

(1) An unequivocal statement that the proposed contractor or subcontractor refuses to accept a contract containing all or a specified part of a CAS clause and the specific reason for that refusal;

(2) A statement as to whether the proposed contractor or subcontractor has accepted any prime contract or subcontract containing a CAS clause;

(3) The amount of the proposed award and the sum of all awards by the agency requesting the waiver to the proposed contractor or subcontractor in each of the preceding 3 years;

(4) A statement that no other source is available to satisfy the agency's needs on a timely basis;

(5) A statement of alternative methods considered for fulfilling the need and the agency's reasons for rejecting them;

(6) A statement of steps being taken by the agency to establish other sources of supply for future contracts for the products or services for which a waiver is being requested; and

(7) Any other information that may be useful in evaluating the request.

(f) Except as provided by the Cost Accounting Standards Board, the authority in paragraph (e) of this section shall not be delegated.

[Final rule, 65 FR 36767, 6/9/2000, effective 6/9/2000]

9903.201-6 Findings.

(a) Required change. (1) Finding. Prior to making any equitable adjustment under the provisions of paragraph (a)(4)(i) of the contract clause set forth in 9903.201-4(a) or 9903.201-4(e), or paragraph (a)(3)(i) of the contract clause set forth in 9903.201-4(c), the Contracting Officer shall make a finding that the practice change was required to comply with a CAS, modification or interpretation thereof, that subsequently became applicable to the contract; or, for planned changes being made in order to remain CAS compliant, that the former practice was in compliance with applicable CAS and the planned change is necessary for the contractor to remain in compliance.

(2) Required change means a change in cost accounting practice that a contractor is required to make in order to comply with applicable Standards, modifications, or interpretations thereto, that subsequently become applicable to an existing CAS-covered contract due to the receipt of another CAS-covered contract or subcontract. It also includes a prospective change to a disclosed or established cost accounting practice when the cognizant Federal agency official determines that the former practice was in compliance with applicable CAS and the change is necessary for the contractor to remain in compliance.

(b) Unilateral change. (1) Findings. Prior to making any contract price or cost adjustment(s) under the change provisions of paragraph (a)(4)(ii) of the contract clause set forth in 9903.201-4(a) or 9903.201-4(e), or paragraph (a)(3)(ii) of the contract clause set forth in 9903.201-4(c), the Contracting Officer shall make a finding that the contemplated contract price and cost adjustments will protect the United States from payment of increased costs, in the aggregate; and that the net effect of the adjustments being made does not result in the recovery of more than the estimated amount of such increased costs.

(2) Unilateral change by a contractor means a change in cost accounting practice from one compliant practice to another compliant practice that a contractor with a CAS-covered contract(s) elects to make that has not been deemed desirable by the cognizant Federal agency official and for which the Government will pay no aggregate increased costs.

(3) Action to preclude the payment of aggregate increased costs by the Government.

In the absence of a finding pursuant to paragraph (c) of this subsection that a compliant change is desirable, no agreement may be made with regard to a change to a cost accounting practice that will result in the payment of aggregate increased costs by the United States. For these changes, the cognizant Federal agency official shall limit upward contract price adjustments to affected contracts to the amount of downward contract price adjustments of other affected contracts, i.e., no net upward contract price adjustment shall be permitted.

(c) Desirable change. (1) Finding. Prior to making any equitable adjustment under the provisions of paragraph (a)(4)(iii) of the contract clause set forth in 9903.201-4(a) or 9903.201-4(e), or paragraph (a)(3)(ii) of the contract clause set forth in 9903.201-4(c), the cognizant Federal agency official shall make a finding that the change to a cost accounting practice is desirable and not detrimental to the interests of the Government.

(2) Desirable change means a compliant change to a contractor's established or disclosed cost accounting practices that the cognizant Federal agency official finds is desirable and not detrimental to the Government and is therefore not subject to the no increased cost prohibition provisions of CAS-covered contracts affected by the change. The cognizant Federal agency official's finding need not be based solely on the cost impact that a proposed practice change will have on a contractor's or subcontractor's current CAS-covered contracts. The change to a cost accounting practice may be determined to be desirable even though existing contract prices and/or cost allowances may increase. The determination that the change to a cost accounting practice is desirable, should be made on a case-by-case basis.

(3) Once a determination has been made that a compliant change to a cost accounting practice is a desirable change, associated management actions that also have an impact on contract costs should be considered when negotiating contract price or cost adjustments that may be needed to equitably resolve the overall cost impact of the aggregated actions.

CASB 9903.201-6

(4) Until the cognizant Federal agency official has determined that a change to a cost accounting practice is deemed to be a desirable change, the change shall be considered to be a change for which the Government will not pay increased costs, in the aggregate.

(d) Noncompliant cost accounting practices. (1) Findings. Prior to making any contract price or cost adjustment(s) under the provisions of paragraph (a)(5) of the contract clause set forth in 9903.201-4(a) or 9903.201-4(e), or paragraph (a)(4) of the contract clause set forth in 9903.201-4(c), the Contracting Officer shall make a finding that the contemplated contract price and cost adjustments will protect the United States from payment of increased costs, in the aggregate; and that the net effect of the adjustments being made does not result in the recovery of more than the estimated amount of such increased costs. While individual contract prices, including cost ceilings or target costs, as applicable, may be increased as well as decreased to resolve an estimating noncompliance, the aggregate value of all contracts affected by the estimating noncompliance shall not be increased.

[Final rule, 65 FR 37470, 6/14/2000, effective 6/14/2000]

9903.201-7 Cognizant Federal Agency Responsibilities.

(a) The requirements of Part 9903 shall, to the maximum extent practicable, be administered by the cognizant Federal agency responsible for a particular contractor organization or location, usually the Federal agency responsible for negotiating indirect cost rates on behalf of the Government. The cognizant Federal agency should take the lead role in administering the requirements of Part 9903 and coordinating CAS administrative actions with all affected Federal agencies. When multiple CAS-covered contracts or more than one Federal agency are involved, agencies should discourage Contracting Officers from individually administering CAS on a contract-by-contract basis. Coordinated administrative actions will provide greater assurances that individual contractors follow their cost accounting practices consistently under all their CAS-covered contracts and that changes in cost accounting practices or CAS noncompliance issues are resolved, equitably, in a uniform overall manner.

(b) Federal agencies shall prescribe regulations and establish internal policies and procedures governing how agencies will administer the requirements of CAS-covered contracts, with particular emphasis on interagency coordination activities. Procedures to be followed when an agency is and is not the cognizant Federal agency should be clearly delineated. Internal agency policies and procedures shall provide for the designation of the agency office(s) or officials responsible for administering CAS under the agency's CAS-covered contracts at each contractor business unit and the delegation of necessary contracting authority to agency individuals authorized to administer the terms and conditions of CAS-covered contracts, e.g., Administrative Contracting Officers (ACOs) or other agency officials authorized to perform in that capacity. Agencies are urged to coordinate on the development of such regulations.

[Final rule, 59 FR 55746, 11/8/94, effective 1/9/95]

9903.201-8 Compliant accounting changes due to external restructuring activities.

The contract price and cost adjustment requirements of this part 9903 are not applicable to compliant cost accounting practice changes directly associated with external restructuring activities that are subject to and meet the requirements of 10 U.S.C. 2325.

[Final rule, 65 FR 37470, 6/14/2000, effective 6/14/2000]

9903.202 Disclosure requirements. (No Text)

9903.202-1 General requirements.

(a) A Disclosure Statement is a written description of a contractor's cost accounting practices and procedures. The submission of a new or revised Disclosure Statement is not required for any non-CAS-covered contract or from any small business concern.

(b) Completed Disclosure Statements are required in the following circumstances:

(1) Any business unit that is selected to receive a CAS-covered contract or subcontract of $50 million or more shall submit a Disclosure Statement before award.

(2) Any company which, together with its segments, received net awards of negotiated prime contracts and subcontracts subject to CAS totaling $50 million or more in its most recent cost accounting period, must submit a Disclosure Statement before award of its first CAS-covered contract in the immediately following cost accounting period. However, if the first CAS-covered contract is received within 90 days of the start of the cost accounting period, the contractor is not required to file until the end of 90 days.

(c) When a Disclosure Statement is required, a separate Disclosure Statement must be submitted for each segment whose costs included in the total price of any CAS-covered contract or subcontract exceed the Truth in Negotiations Act (TINA) threshold, as adjusted for inflation (41 U.S.C. 1908 and 41 U.S.C. 1502(b)(1)(B)) unless (i) the contract or subcontract is of the type or value exempted by 9903.201-1 or (ii) in the most recently completed cost accounting period the segment's CAS-covered awards are less than 30 percent of total segment sales for the period *and* less than $10 million.

(d) Each corporate or other home office that allocates costs to one or more disclosing segments performing CAS-covered contracts must submit a Part VIII of the Disclosure Statement.

(e) Foreign contractors and subcontractors who are required to submit a Disclosure Statement may, in lieu of filing a Form No. CASB-DS-1, make disclosure by using a disclosure form prescribed by an agency of its Government, provided that the Cost Accounting Standards Board determines that the information disclosed by that means will satisfy the objectives of Public Law 100-679. The use of alternative forms has been approved for the contractors of the following countries:

(1) Canada.

(2) Federal Republic of Germany.

(3) United Kingdom.

(f) Educational institutions—disclosure requirements. (1) Educational institutions receiving contracts subject to the CAS specified in Part 9905 are subject to the requirements of 9903.202, except that completed Disclosure Statements are required in the following circumstances.

(2) Basic requirement. For CAS-covered contracts placed on or after January 1, 1996, completed Disclosure Statements are required as follows:

(i) Any business unit of an educational institution that is selected to receive a CAS-covered contract or subcontract in excess of the Truth in Negotiations Act (TINA) threshold, as adjusted for inflation (41 U.S.C. 1908 and 41 U.S.C. 1502(b)(1)(B)), and is part of a college or university location listed in Exhibit A of Office of Management and Budget (OMB) Circular A-21 shall submit a Disclosure Statement before award. A Disclosure Statement is not required; however, if the listed entity can demonstrate that the net amount of Federal contract and financial assistance awards received during its immediately preceding cost accounting period was less than $25 million.

(ii) Any business unit that is selected to receive a CAS-covered contract or subcontract of $25 million or more shall submit a Disclosure Statement before award.

(iii) Any educational institution which, together with its segments, received net awards of negotiated prime contracts and subcontracts subject to CAS totaling $25 million or more in its most recent cost accounting period, of which, at least one award exceeded $1 million, must submit a Disclosure Statement before award of its first CAS-covered contract in the immediately following cost accounting period. However, if the first CAS-covered contract is received within 90 days of the start of the cost accounting period, the institution is not required to file until the end of 90 days.

(3) Transition period requirement. For CAS-covered contracts placed on or before December 31, 1995, completed Disclosure Statements are required as follows:

CASB 9903.202-1

(i) For business units that are selected to receive a CAS-covered contract or subcontract in excess of the Truth in Negotiations Act (TINA) threshold, as adjusted for inflation (41 U.S.C. 1908 and 41 U.S.C. 1502(b)(1)(B)), and are part of the first 20 college or university locations (i.e., numbers 1 through 20) listed in Exhibit A of OMB Circular A-21, Disclosure Statements shall be submitted within six months after the date of contract award.

(ii) For business units that are selected to receive a CAS-covered contract or subcontract in excess of the Truth in Negotiations Act (TINA) threshold, as adjusted for inflation (41 U.S.C. 1908 and 41 U.S.C. 1502(b)(1)(B)), and are part of a college or university location that is listed as one of the institutions numbered 21 through 50, in Exhibit A of OMB Circular A-21, Disclosure Statements shall be submitted during the six month period ending twelve months after the date of contract award.

(iii) For business units that are selected to receive a CAS-covered contract or subcontract in excess of the Truth in Negotiations Act (TINA) threshold, as adjusted for inflation (41 U.S.C. 1908 and 41 U.S.C. 1502(b)(1)(B)), and are part of a college or university location that is listed as one of the institutions numbered 51 through 99, in Exhibit A of OMB Circular A-21, Disclosure Statements shall be submitted during the six month period ending eighteen months after the date of contract award.

(iv) For any other business unit that is selected to receive a CAS-covered contract or subcontract of $25 million or more, a Disclosure Statement shall be submitted within six months after the date of contract award.

(4) Transition period due dates. The educational institution and cognizant Federal agency should establish a specific due date within the periods prescribed in 9903.202-1(f)(3) when a Disclosure Statement is required under a CAS-covered contract placed on or before December 31, 1995.

(5) Transition period waiver authority. For a CAS-covered contract to be awarded during the period January 1, 1996 through June 30, 1997, the awarding agency may waive the preaward Disclosure Statement submission requirement specified in 9903.202-1(f)(2) when a due date for the submission of a Disclosure Statement has previously been established by the cognizant Federal agency and the educational institution under the provisions of 9903.202-1(f) (3) and (4). **CAUTION:** This waiver authority is not available unless the cognizant Federal agency and the educational institution have established a disclosure statement due date pursuant to a written agreement executed prior to January 1, 1996, and award is made prior to the established disclosure statement due date.

[Corrected, 57 FR 34167, 8/3/92; Final rule, 58 FR 58798, 11/4/93, effective 11/4/93; Final rule, 59 FR 55746, 11/8/94, effective 1/9/95; Interim rule, 65 FR 5990, 2/7/2000, effective 4/2/2000; Final rule, 65 FR 36767, 6/9/2000, effective 6/9/2000; Interim rule, 70 FR 29457, 5/23/2005, effective 5/23/2005; Final rule, 72 FR 32809, 6/14/2007, effective 6/14/2007; Interim rule, 76 FR 40817, 7/12/2011, effective 8/11/2011; Final rule, 76 FR 79545, 12/22/2011, effective 12/22/2011]

9903.202-2 Impracticality of submission.

The agency head may determine that it is impractical to secure the Disclosure Statement, although submission is required, and authorize contract award without obtaining the Statement. He shall, within 30 days of having done so, submit a report to the Cost Accounting Standards Board setting forth all material facts. This authority may not be delegated.

9903.202-3 Amendments and revisions.

Contractors and subcontractors are responsible for maintaining accurate Disclosure Statements and complying with disclosed practices. Amendments and revisions to Disclosure Statements may be submitted at any time and may be proposed by either the contractor or the Government. Resubmission of complete, updated, Disclosure Statements is discouraged except when extensive changes require it to assist the review process.

9903.202-4 Privileged and confidential information.

If the offeror or contractor notifies the contracting officer that the Disclosure Statement contains trade secrets and commercial or financial information, which is privileged and confidential, the Disclosure Statement shall be protected and shall not be released outside the Government.

9903.202-5 Filing Disclosure Statements.

(a) Disclosure must be on Form Number CASB DS-1 or CASB DS-2, as applicable. Forms may be obtained from the cognizant Federal agency (cognizant ACO or cognizant Federal agency official authorized to act in that capacity) or from the looseleaf version of the Federal Acquisition Regulation. When requested in advance by a contractor, the cognizant Federal agency may authorize contractor disclosure based on computer generated reproductions of the applicable Disclosure Statement Form.

(b) Offerors are required to file Disclosure Statements as follows:

(1) Original and one copy with the cognizant ACO or cognizant Federal agency official acting in that capacity, as applicable; and

(2) One copy with the cognizant Federal auditor.

(c) Amendments and revisions shall be submitted to the ACO or agency official acting in that capacity, as applicable, and the Federal auditor of the currently cognizant Federal agency.

[Final rule, 59 FR 55746, 11/8/94, effective 1/9/95]

9903.202-6 Adequacy of Disclosure Statement.

Federal agencies shall prescribe regulations and establish internal procedures by which each will promptly determine on behalf of the Government, when serving as the cognizant Federal agency for a particular contractor location, that a Disclosure Statement has adequately disclosed the practices required to be disclosed by the Cost Accounting Standards Board's rules, regulations and Standards. The determination of adequacy shall be distributed to all affected agencies. Agencies are urged to coordinate on the development of such regulations.

[Final rule, 59 FR 55746, 11/8/94, effective 1/9/95]

9903.202-7 [Reserved]

9903.202-8 Subcontractor Disclosure Statements.

(a) The contractor or higher tier subcontractor is responsible for administering the CAS requirements contained in subcontracts.

(b) If the subcontractor has previously furnished a Disclosure Statement to an ACO, the subcontractor may satisfy the submission requirement by identifying to the contractor or higher tier subcontractor the ACO to whom it was submitted.

(c) (1) If the subcontractor considers the Disclosure Statement (or other similar information) privileged or confidential, the subcontractor may submit it directly to the ACO and auditor cognizant of the subcontractor, notifying the contractor or higher tier subcontractor. A preaward determination of adequacy is not required in such cases. Instead, the ACO cognizant of the subcontractor shall

(i) Notify the auditor that the adequacy review will be performed during the postaward compliance review and, upon completion,

(ii) Notify the subcontractor, the contractor or higher tier subcontractor, and the cognizant ACOs of the findings.

(2) Even though a Disclosure Statement is not required, a subcontractor may

(i) Claim that CAS-related reviews by contractors or higher tier subcontractors would reveal proprietary data or jeopardize the subcontractor's competitive position and

(ii) Request that the Government perform the required reviews.

(d) When the Government requires determinations of adequacy or inadequacy, the ACO cognizant of the subcontractor shall make such recommendation to the ACO cognizant of the prime contractor or next higher tier subcontractor. ACOs cognizant of higher tier subcontractors or prime contractors shall not reverse the determination of the ACO cognizant of the subcontractor.

9903.202-9 Illustration of Disclosure Statement Form, CASB-DS-1.

The data which are required to be disclosed are set forth in detail in the Disclosure Statement Form, CASB-DS-1, which is illustrated below:

COST ACCOUNTING STANDARDS BOARD DISCLOSURE STATEMENT REQUIRED BY PUBLIC LAW 100-679	INDEX

COST ACCOUNTING STANDARDS BOARD DISCLOSURE STATEMENT REQUIRED BY PUBLIC LAW 100-679	GENERAL INSTRUCTIONS

1.   This Disclosure Statement has been designed to meet the requirements of Public Law 100-679, and persons completing it are to describe the contractor and its contract cost accounting practices. For complete regulations, instructions and timing requirements concerning submission of the Disclosure Statement, refer to Section 9903.202 of Chapter 99 Of Title 48 CFR (48 CFR 9903.202).

2.   Part I of the Statement provides general information concerning each reporting unit (e.g., segment, Corporate or other intermediate level home office, or a business unit). Parts II through VII pertain to the types of costs generally incurred by the segment or business unit directly performing Federal contracts or similar cost objectives. Part VIII pertains to the types of costs that are generally incurred by a Home office and are allocated to one or more segments performing Federal contracts. For a definition of the term "home office", see 48 CFR 9904.403.

3.   Each segment or business unit required to disclose its cost accounting practices should complete the Cover Sheet, the Certification, and Parts I through VII.

4.   Each home office required to disclose its cost accounting practices for measuring, assigning and allocating its costs to segments performing Federal contracts or similar cost objectives shall complete the Cover Sheet, the Certification, Part I and Part VIII of the Disclosure Statement. Where a home office either establishes practices or procedures for the types of costs covered by Parts V, VI and VII, or incurs and then allocates these types of cost to its segments, the home office may complete Parts V, VI and VII to be included in the Disclosure Statement submitted by its segments. While a home office may have more than one segment submitting Disclosure Statements, only one Statement needs to be submitted to cover the home office operations.

5.   The Statement must be signed by an authorized signatory of the reporting unit.

6.   The Disclosure Statement should be answered by marking the appropriate line or inserting the applicable letter code which describes the segment's (reporting unit's) cost accounting practices.

7.   A number of questions in this Statement may need narrative answers requiring more space than is provided. In such instances, the reporting unit should use the attached continuation sheet provided. The continuation sheet may be reproduced locally as needed. The number of the question involved should be indicated and the same coding required to answer the questions in the Statement should be used in presenting the answer on the continuation sheet. Continuation sheets should be inserted at the end of the pertinent Part of the Statement. On each continuation sheet, the reporting unit should enter the next sequential page number for that Part and, on the last continuation sheet used, the words "End of Part" should be inserted after the last entry.

8.   Where the cost accounting practice being disclosed is clearly set forth in the contractor's existing written accounting policies and procedures, such documents may be cited on a continuation sheet and incorporated by reference at the option of the contractor. In such cases, the contractor should provide the date of issuance and effective date for each accounting policy and/or procedures document cited. Alternatively, copies of the relevant parts of such documents may be attached as appendices to the pertinent Disclosure Statement Part. Such continuation sheets and appendices should be labeled and cross-referenced with the applicable Disclosure Statement number and follow the page number specified in paragraph 7. Any supplementary comments needed to adequately describe the cost accounting practice being disclosed should also be provided.

9.   Disclosure Statements must be amended when cost accounting practices are changed to comply with a new CAS or when practices are changed with or without knowledge of the Government (Also see 48 CFR 9903.202-3).

CASB 9903.202-9

COST ACCOUNTING STANDARDS BOARD DISCLOSURE STATEMENT REQUIRED BY PUBLIC LAW 100-679	GENERAL INSTRUCTIONS

10.   Amendments shall be submitted to the same offices to which submission would have been made were an original Disclosure Statement filed.

11.   *Each amendment, or set of amendments should be accompanied by an amended cover sheet (indicating revision number and effective date of the change) and a signed certification.* For all resubmissions, on each page, insert "Revision Number ☐" and "Effective Date ☐" in the Item Description block; and, insert a revision mark (e.g., "R") in the right hand margin of any line that is revised. Completely resubmitted Disclosure Statements must be accompanied by similar notations identifying the items which have been changed.

12.   Use of this Disclosure Statement, amended February 1996, shall be phased in as follows:

A. <u>New Contractors</u>. This form shall be used by new contractors when they are initially required to disclose their cost accounting practices pursuant to 9903.202-1.

B. <u>Existing Contractors</u>. If a contractor has disclosed its cost accounting practices on a prior edition of the Disclosure Statement (CASB DS-1), such disclosure shall remain in effect until the contractor amends or revises a significant portion of the Disclosure Statement in accordance with CAS 9903.202-3. Minor amendments to an existing DS-1 may continue to be made using the prior form. However, when a substantive change is made, a complete Disclosure Statement must be filed using this form. In any event, all contractors and subcontractors must submit a new Disclosure Statement (this version of the CASB DS-1) not later than the beginning of the contractor's next full fiscal year after December 31, 1998.

ATTACHMENT -   Blank Continuation Sheet

CASB 9903.202-9

COST ACCOUNTING STANDARDS BOARD DISCLOSURE STATEMENT REQUIRED BY PUBLIC LAW 100-679	CONTINUATION SHEET
	NAME OF REPORTING UNIT

Item No.	Item description

COST ACCOUNTING STANDARDS BOARD DISCLOSURE STATEMENT REQUIRED BY PUBLIC LAW 100-679	COVER SHEET AND CERTIFICATION

0.1 Company or Reporting Unit.

    Name

    Street Address

    City, State, & Zip Code

    Division or Subsidiary of (if applicable)

0.2 Reporting Unit: (Mark one.)

    A.   ☐ Business Unit comprising an entire business organization which is not divided into segments.

    B.1. ☐ Corporate Home Office

    2.   ☐ Intermediate Level Home Office

    3.   ☐ Segment or business unit reporting directly to a home office.

0.3 Official to Contact Concerning this Statement.

    Name and Title

    Phone number (including area code and extension)

0.4 Statement Type and Effective Date:

    A.   (Mark type of submission. If a revision, enter number)

       (a)☐ Original Statement

       (b)☐ Revised Statement; Revision No.☐

    B.   Effective Date of this Statement/Revision:☐

0.5 Statement Submitted To (Provide office name, location and telephone number, include area code and extension):

    (a) Cognizant Federal Agency:

    (b) Cognizant Federal Auditor:

CERTIFICATION

I certify that to the best of my knowledge and belief this Statement, as amended in the case of a revision, is the complete and accurate disclosure as of the above date by the above-named organization of its cost accounting practices, as required by the Disclosure Regulation (48 CFR 9903.202) of the Cost Accounting Standards Board under P.L. 100-679.

(Name)

(Title)

THE PENALTY FOR MAKING A FALSE STATEMENT IN THIS DISCLOSURE IS PRESCRIBED IN 18 U.S.C. § 1001

COST ACCOUNTING STANDARDS BOARD DISCLOSURE STATEMENT REQUIRED BY PUBLIC LAW 100-679	PART I - GENERAL INFORMATION
	NAME OF REPORTING UNIT

Item No.	Item description

Part I Instructions

Sales data for this part should cover the most recently completed fiscal year of the reporting unit. "Government CAS Covered Sales" includes sales under both prime contracts and subcontracts. "Annual CAS Covered Sales" includes intracorporate transactions.

1.1.0   Type of Business Entity of Which the Reporting Unit is a Part. (Mark one.)

     A.   [ ]   Corporation
     B.   [ ]   Partnership
     C.   [ ]   Proprietorship
     D.   [ ]   Not-for-profit organization
     E.   [ ]   Joint Venture
     F.   [ ]   Federally Funded Research and Development Center (FFRDC)
     Y.   [ ]   Other (Specify) [_____]

1.2.0   Predominant Type of Government Sales. (Mark one.) 1/

     A.   [ ]   Manufacturing
     B.   [ ]   Research and Development
     C.   [ ]   Construction
     D.   [ ]   Services
     Y.   [ ]   Other (Specify) [_____]

1.3.0   Annual CAS Covered Government Sales as Percentage of Total Sales (Government and Commercial). (Mark one. An estimate is permitted for this section.) 1/

     A.   [ ]   Less than 10%
     B.   [ ]   10%-50%
     C.   [ ]   51%-80%
     D.   [ ]   81% - 95%
     E.   [ ]   Over 95%

1.4.0   Description of Your Cost Accounting System for Government Contracts and Subcontracts. (Mark the appropriate line(s) and if more than one is marked, explain on a continuation sheet.) 1/

     A.   [ ]   Standard costs - Job order
     B.   [ ]   Standard costs - Process
     C.   [ ]   Actual costs - Job order
     D.   [ ]   Actual costs - Process
     Y.   [ ]   Other(s) 2/

1/ Do not complete when Part I is filed in conjunction with Part VIII.
2/ Describe on a Continuation Sheet.

CASB 9903.202-9

COST ACCOUNTING STANDARDS BOARD DISCLOSURE STATEMENT REQUIRED BY PUBLIC LAW 100-679	PART I - GENERAL INFORMATION
	NAME OF REPORTING UNIT

Item No.	Item description
1.5.0	**Identification of Differences Between Contract Cost Accounting and Financial Accounting Records.**
	List on a continuation sheet, the types of costs charged to Federal contracts that are supported by memorandum records and identify the method used to reconcile with the entity's financial accounting records.
1.6.0	**Unallowable Costs.** Costs that are not reimbursable as allowable costs under the terms and conditions of Federal awards are identified as follows: (Mark all that apply and if more than one is marked, describe on a continuation sheet the major cost groupings, organizations, or other criteria for using each marked technique.)
1.6.1	Incurred costs.
	A. [ ] Specifically identified and recorded separately in the formal financial accounting records.
	B. [ ] Identified in separately maintained accounting records or workpapers.
	C. [ ] Identifiable through use of less formal accounting techniques that permit audit verification.
	D. [ ] Determinable by other means. 1/
1.6.2	Estimated costs.
	A. [ ] By designation and description (in backup data, workpapers, etc) which have specifically been identified and recognized in making estimates.
	B. [ ] By description of any other estimating technique employed to provide appropriate recognition of any unallowable amounts pertinent to the estimates.
	C. [ ] Other. 1/
1.7.0	**Fiscal Year:** [ ] (Specify twelve month period used for financial accounting and reporting purposes, e.g., 1/1 to 12/31.)
1.7.1	**Cost Accounting Period:** [ ] (Specify period. If the cost accounting period used for the accumulation and reporting of costs under Federal contracts is other than the fiscal year identified in Item 1.7.0, explain circumstances on a continuation sheet.)
	1/ Describe on a Continuation Sheet.

CASB 9903.202-9

Item No.	Item description
	COST ACCOUNTING STANDARDS BOARD / **DISCLOSURE STATEMENT** / **REQUIRED BY PUBLIC LAW 100-679** — **PART II - DIRECT COSTS** / **NAME OF REPORTING UNIT**

Item No.	Item description
	<u>Part II Instructions</u>
	This part covers the three major categories of direct costs, i.e., Direct Material, Direct Labor, and Other Direct Costs.
	It is not the intent here to spell out or define the three elements of direct costs. Rather, each contractor should disclose practices based on its own definitions of what costs are, or will be, charged directly to Federal contracts or similar cost objectives as Direct Material, Direct Labor, or Other Direct Costs. For example, a contractor may charge or classify purchased labor of a direct nature as "Direct Material" for purposes of pricing proposals, requests for progress payments, claims for cost reimbursement, etc.; some other contractor may classify the same cost as "Direct Labor," and still another as "Other Direct Costs." In these circumstances, it is expected that each contractor will disclose practices consistent with its own classifications of Direct Material, Direct Labor, and Other Direct Costs.
2.1.0	<u>Description of Direct Material.</u> *Direct material as used here is <u>not</u> limited to those items of material actually incorporated into the end product; they also include material, consumable supplies, and other costs when charged to Federal contracts or similar cost objectives as Direct Material. (Describe on a continuation sheet the principal classes or types of material and services which are charged as direct material; group the material and service costs by those which are incorporated in an end product and those which are not.)*
2.2.0	<u>Method of Charging Direct Material.</u>
2.2.1	<u>Direct Charge Not Through an Inventory Account at</u>: (Mark the appropriate line(s) and if more than one is marked, explain on a continuation sheet.)
	A. ☐ Standard costs (Describe the type of standards used.) 1/
	B. ☐ Actual Costs
	Y. ☐ Other(s) 1/
	Z. ☐ Not applicable
2.2.2	<u>Charged Direct from a Contractor-owned Inventory Account at</u>: (Mark the appropriate line(s) and if more than one is marked, explain on a continuation sheet.)
	A. ☐ Standard costs 1/
	B. ☐ Average Costs 1/
	C. ☐ First in, first out
	D. ☐ Last in, first out
	Y. ☐ Other(s) 1/
	Z. ☐ Not applicable
	1/ Describe on a Continuation Sheet.

Item No.	Item description
	COST ACCOUNTING STANDARDS BOARD **DISCLOSURE STATEMENT** **REQUIRED BY PUBLIC LAW 100-679** / **PART II - DIRECT COSTS** **NAME OF REPORTING UNIT**
2.3.0	**Timing of Charging Direct Material.** (Mark the appropriate line(s) to indicate the point in time at which direct material are charged to Federal contracts or similar cost objectives, and if more than one line is marked, explain on a continuation sheet.) A. When orders are placed B. When both the material and invoice are received C. When material is issued or released to a process, batch, or similar intermediate cost objective D. When material is issued or released to a final cost objective E. When invoices are paid Y. Other(s) 1/ Z. Not applicable
2.4.0	**Variances from Standard Costs for Direct Material.** (Do not complete this item unless you use a standard cost method, i.e., you have marked Line A of Item 2.2.1, or 2.2.2. Mark the appropriate line(s) in Items 2.4.1, 2.4.2, and 2.4.4, and if more than one line is marked, explain on a continuation sheet.)
2.4.1	**Type of Variance.** A. Price B. Usage C. Combined (A and B) Y. Other(s) 1/
2.4.2	**Level of Production Unit used to Accumulate Variance.** Indicate which level of production unit is used as a basis for accumulating material variances. A. Plant-wide Basis B. By Department C. By Product or Product Line Y. Other(s) 1/
2.4.3	**Method of Disposing of Variance.** Describe on a continuation sheet the basis for, and the frequency of, the disposition of the variance.
2.4.4	**Revisions.** Standard costs for direct materials are revised: A. Semiannually B. Annually C. Revised as needed, but at least once annually Y. Other(s) 1/
	1/ Describe on a Continuation Sheet.

CASB 9903.202-9

COST ACCOUNTING STANDARDS BOARD DISCLOSURE STATEMENT REQUIRED BY PUBLIC LAW 100-679	PART II - DIRECT COSTS
	NAME OF REPORTING UNIT

Item No.	Item description
2.5.0	**Method of Charging Direct Labor**: (Mark the appropriate line(s) for each Direct Labor Category to show how such labor is charged to Federal contracts or similar cost objectives, and if more than one line is marked, explain on a continuation sheet. Also describe on a continuation sheet the principal classes of labor rates that are, or will be applied to Manufacturing Labor, Engineering Labor, and Other Direct Labor, in order to develop direct labor costs.

<table>
<tr><td></td><td colspan="3">Direct Labor Category</td></tr>
<tr><td></td><td>Manufacturing</td><td>Engineering</td><td>Other Direct</td></tr>
<tr><td>A. Individual/actual rates</td><td>☐</td><td>☐</td><td>☐</td></tr>
<tr><td>B. Average rates – uncompensated overtime hours included in computation 1/</td><td></td><td></td><td></td></tr>
<tr><td>C. Average rates – uncompensated overtime hours excluded from computation</td><td>☐</td><td>☐</td><td>☐</td></tr>
<tr><td>D. Standard costs/rates 1/</td><td>☐</td><td>☐</td><td>☐</td></tr>
<tr><td>Y. Other(s) 1/</td><td></td><td></td><td></td></tr>
<tr><td>Z. Labor category is not applicable</td><td></td><td></td><td></td></tr>
</table>

2.6.0	**Variances from Standard Costs for Direct Labor.** (Do not complete this item unless you use a standard costs/rate method, i.e., you have marked Line D of Item 2.5.0 for any direct labor category. Mark the appropriate line(s) in each column of Items 2.6.1, 2.6.2, and 2.6.4. If more than one is marked, explain on a continuation sheet.)
2.6.1	**Type of Variance.**

<table>
<tr><td></td><td colspan="3">Direct Labor Category</td></tr>
<tr><td></td><td>Manufacturing</td><td>Engineering</td><td>Other Direct</td></tr>
<tr><td>A. Rate</td><td>☐</td><td>☐</td><td>☐</td></tr>
<tr><td>B. Efficiency</td><td>☐</td><td>☐</td><td>☐</td></tr>
<tr><td>C. Combined (A and B)</td><td>☐</td><td>☐</td><td>☐</td></tr>
<tr><td>Y. Other(s) 1/</td><td>☐</td><td>☐</td><td>☐</td></tr>
<tr><td>Z. Labor category is not applicable</td><td>☐</td><td>☐</td><td>☐</td></tr>
</table>

1/ Describe on a Continuation Sheet.

CASB 9903.202-9

Item No.	Item description

COST ACCOUNTING STANDARDS BOARD DISCLOSURE STATEMENT REQUIRED BY PUBLIC LAW 100-679

PART II - DIRECT COSTS

NAME OF REPORTING UNIT

2.6.2 **Level of Production Unit used to Accumulate Variance.** Indicate which level of production unit is used as a basis for accumulating the labor variances.

Direct Labor Category: Manufacturing, Engineering, Other Direct

A. Plant-wide basis
B. By department
C. By product or product line
Y. Other(s) 1/
Z. Labor category is not applicable

2.6.3 **Method of Disposing of Variance.** Describe on a continuation sheet the basis for, and the frequency of, the disposition of the variance.

2.6.4 **Revisions.** Standard costs for direct labor are revised:

A. Semiannually
B. Annually
C. Revised as needed, but at least once annually
Y. Other(s) 1/

2.7.0 **Description of Other Direct Costs.** Other significant items of cost directly identified with Federal contracts or other final cost objectives. Describe on a continuation sheet the principal classes of other costs that are always charged directly, that is, identified specifically with final cost objectives, e.g., fringe benefits, travel costs, services, subcontracts, etc.

2.7.1 When Employee Travel Expenses for lodging and subsistence are charged direct to Federal contracts or similar cost objectives the charge is based on:

A. Actual Costs
B. Per Diem Rates
C. Lodging at actual costs and subsistence at per diem
Y. Other Method 1/
Z. Not Applicable

2.8.0 **Credits to Contract Costs.** When Federal contracts or similar cost objectives are credited for the following circumstances, are the rates of direct labor, direct materials, other direct costs and applicable indirect costs always the same as those for the original charges? (Mark one line for each circumstance, and for each "No" answer, explain on a continuation sheet how the credit differs from the original charge.)

Circumstance	A. Yes	B. No	Z. Not Applicable
(a) Transfers to other jobs/contracts			
(b) Unused or excess materials remaining upon completion of contract			

1/ Describe on a Continuation Sheet.

CASB 9903.202-9

COST ACCOUNTING STANDARDS BOARD DISCLOSURE STATEMENT REQUIRED BY PUBLIC LAW 100-679	PART III - DIRECT VS. INDIRECT COSTS
	NAME OF REPORTING UNIT

Item No.	Item description
3.1.0	**Criteria for Determining How Costs are Charged to Federal Contracts Or Similar Cost Objectives.** Describe on a continuation sheet your criteria for determining when costs incurred for the same purpose, in like circumstances, are treated either as direct costs only or as indirect costs only with respect to final cost objectives.
3.2.0	**Treatment of Costs of Specified Functions, Elements of Cost, or Transactions.** (For each of the functions, elements of cost or transactions listed in Items 3.2.1, 3.2.2, and 3.2.3, enter one of the Codes A through F, or Y, to indicate how the item is treated. Enter Code Z in those lines that are not applicable to you. Also, specify the name(s) of the indirect pool(s) (as listed in 4.1.0, 4.2.0 and 4.3.0) for each function, element of cost, or transaction coded E or F. If Code E, Sometimes direct/Sometimes indirect, is used, explain on a continuation sheet the circumstances under which both direct and indirect allocations are made.)

Treatment Code

A. Direct material	E. Sometimes direct/Sometimes indirect
B. Direct labor	F. Indirect only
C. Direct material and labor	Y. Other(s) 1/
D. Other direct costs	Z. Not applicable

Item No.				
3.2.1	**Functions, Elements of Cost, or Transactions Related to Direct Material**		Treatment Code	Name of Pool(s)
	(a)	Cash Discounts on Purchases	☐	☐
	(b)	Freight in	☐	☐
	(c)	Income from Sale of Scrap	☐	☐
	(d)	Income from Sale of Salvage	☐	☐
	(e)	Incoming Material Inspection (receiving)	☐	☐
	(f)	Inventory adjustment	☐	☐
	(g)	Purchasing	☐	☐
	(h)	Trade Discounts, Refunds, Rebates, and Allowances on Purchases	☐	☐

1/ Describe on a Continuation Sheet.

CASB 9903.202-9

COST ACCOUNTING STANDARDS BOARD *DISCLOSURE STATEMENT* **REQUIRED BY PUBLIC LAW 100-679**	PART III - DIRECT VS. INDIRECT COSTS
	NAME OF REPORTING UNIT

Item No.	Item description

3.2.2   <u>Functions, Elements of Cost,</u> <u>or Transactions Related to</u> <u>Direct Labor</u>

		Treatment Code	Name of Pool(s)
(a)	Incentive Compensation	☐	☐
(b)	Holiday Differential (Priemium Pay)	☐	☐
(c)	Vacation Pay	☐	☐
(d)	Overtime Premium Pay	☐	☐
(e)	Shift Premium Pay	☐	☐
(f)	Pension Costs	☐	☐
(g)	Post Retirement Benefits Other Than Pensions	☐	☐
(h)	Health Insurance	☐	☐
(i)	Life Insurance	☐	☐
(j)	Other Deferred Compensation 1/	☐	☐
(k)	Training	☐	☐
(l)	Sick Leave	☐	☐

1/ Describe on a Continuation Sheet.

CASB 9903.202-9

COST ACCOUNTING STANDARDS BOARD DISCLOSURE STATEMENT REQUIRED BY PUBLIC LAW 100-679	PART III - DIRECT VS. INDIRECT COSTS NAME OF REPORTING UNIT

Item No.	Item description		
3.2.3	**Functions, Elements of Cost, or Transactions - Miscellaneous**	**Treatment Code**	**Name of Pool(s)**
	(a) Design Engineering (in-house)	☐	☐
	(b) Drafting (in-house)	☐	☐
	(c) Computer Operations (in-house)	☐	☐
	(d) Contract Administration	☐	☐
	(e) Subcontract Administration Costs	☐	☐
	(f) Freight Out (finished product)	☐	☐
	(g) Line (or production) Inspection	☐	☐
	(h) Packaging and Preservation	☐	☐
	(i) Preproduction Costs and Start-up Costs	☐	☐
	(j) Departmental Supervision	☐	☐
	(k) Professional Services (consultant fees)	☐	☐
	(l) Purchased Labor of Direct Nature (on premises)	☐	☐
	(m) Purchased Labor of Direct Nature (off premises)	☐	☐
	(n) Rearrangement Costs	☐	☐
	(o) Rework Costs	☐	☐
	(p) Royalties	☐	☐
	(q) Scrap Work	☐	☐
	(r) Special Test Equipment	☐	☐
	(s) Special Tooling	☐	☐
	(t) Warranty Costs	☐	☐
	(u) Rental Costs	☐	☐
	(v) Travel and Subsistence	☐	☐
	(w) Employee Severance Pay	☐	☐
	(x) Security Guards	☐	☐

CASB 9903.202-9

COST ACCOUNTING STANDARDS BOARD DISCLOSURE STATEMENT REQUIRED BY PUBLIC LAW 100-679	PART IV - INDIRECT COSTS NAME OF REPORTING UNIT

Item No.	Item description

Part IV Instructions

For the purpose of this part, indirect costs have been divided into three categories: (i) manufacturing, engineering, and comparable indirect costs, (ii) general and administrative (G&A) expenses, and (iii) service center and expense pool costs, as defined in Item 4.3.0. The term "overhead," as used in this part, refers only to the first category of indirect costs.

The following Allocation Base Codes are provided for use in connection with Items 4.1.0, 4.2.0 and 4.3.0.

A.	Sales		H.	Direct labor dollars
B.	Cost of sales		I.	Direct labor hours
C.	Total Cost input (direct material, direct labor, other direct costs and applicable overhead)		J.	Machine hours
			K.	Usage
			L.	Unit of production
D.	Value-added cost input (total cost input less direct material and subcontract costs)		M.	Direct material cost
			N.	Total payroll dollars (direct and indirect employees)
E.	Total cost incurred (total cost input plus G&A expenses)		O.	Headcount or number of employees (direct and indirect employees)
F.	Prime cost (direct material, direct labor and other direct cost)		P.	Square feet
			Y.	Other(s), or more than one basis (Describe on a continuation sheet.)
G.	Processing or conversion cost (direct labor and applicable overhead)		Z.	Pool not applicable

4.1.0 Overhead Pools. List all the overhead pools, i.e., pools of indirect costs, other than general and administrative (G&A) expenses, that are allocated to final cost objectives without any intermediate allocations. A segment or business unit may have only a single pool encompassing all of its overhead costs or alternatively it may have several pools such as manufacturing overhead, engineering overhead, material handling overhead, etc. For each pool listed indicate the base used for allocating such pooled expenses to Federal contracts or similar cost objectives. Also, for each of the pools indicate (a) the major functions, activities, and elements of cost included, and (b) the make up of the allocation base. Use a continuation sheet if additional space is required.

Allocation
Base Code

1. [   ]   [   ]

(a) Major functions, activities, and elements of cost included:

[   ]
[   ]

(b) Description/Make up of the allocation base:

[   ]
[   ]

COST ACCOUNTING STANDARDS BOARD DISCLOSURE STATEMENT REQUIRED BY PUBLIC LAW 100-679	PART IV - INDIRECT COSTS
	NAME OF REPORTING UNIT

Item No.	Item description

4.1.0 Continued.

Allocation Base Code

2. ☐ ☐

    (a) Major functions, activities, and elements of cost included:

       ☐

       ☐

    (b) Description/Make up of the allocation base:

       ☐

       ☐

4.2.0 General and Administrative (G&A) Expense Pool(s). Select among the three categories of pools below that describe(s) the manner in which G&A expenses are allocated. For each category of pool(s) selected indicate the base(s) used for allocating such pooled expenses to Federal contracts or similar cost objectives. Also, for each category of pool(s) selected, indicate (a) the major functions, activities, and elements of cost included, and (b) the make up of the allocation base(s). For example, if direct labor dollars are used, are fringe benefits included? If a total cost input base is used, is the imputed cost of capital included? Use a continuation sheet if additional space is required.

Allocation Base Code

Single Pool Containing G&A Expenses Only

☐ ☐

    (a) Major functions, activities, and elements of cost included:

       ☐

       ☐

    (b) Description/Make up of the allocation base:

       ☐

       ☐

COST ACCOUNTING STANDARDS BOARD DISCLOSURE STATEMENT REQUIRED BY PUBLIC LAW 100-679	PART IV - INDIRECT COSTS
	NAME OF REPORTING UNIT

Item No.	Item description
4.2.0	Continued.

Single Pool Containing Both G&A and Non-G&A Expenses   Allocation Base Code

(a) Major functions, activities, and elements of cost included:

(b) Description/Make up of the allocation base:

Special Allocations   Allocation Base Code

1.

(a) Major functions, activities, and elements of cost included:

(b) Description/Make up of the allocation base:

2.

(a) Major functions, activities, and elements of cost included:

(b) Description/Make up of the allocation base:

COST ACCOUNTING STANDARDS BOARD DISCLOSURE STATEMENT REQUIRED BY PUBLIC LAW 100-679	PART IV - INDIRECT COSTS
	NAME OF REPORTING UNIT

Item No.	Item description
4.3.0	**Service Center and Expense Pool Allocation Bases.**

Service centers are departments or other functional units which perform specific technical and/or administrative services primarily for the benefit of other units within a reporting unit. Expense pools are pools of indirect costs that are allocated primarily to other units within a reporting unit. Examples of service centers are data processing centers, reproduction services and communications services. Examples of expense pools are use and occupancy pools and fringe benefit pools.

Category Code

Generally, costs incurred by such centers or pools are, or can be, charged or allocated (i) partially to specific final cost objectives as direct costs and partially to other indirect cost pools (such as a manufacturing overhead pool) for subsequent reallocation to several final cost objectives, referred to herein as Category "A", and (ii) only to several other indirect cost pools (such as a manufacturing overhead pool, engineering overhead pool and G&A expense pool) for subsequent reallocation to several final cost objectives, referred to herein as Category "B".

Rate Code

Some service centers or expense pools may use predetermined billing or costing rates to charge or allocate the costs (Rate Code A) while others may charge or allocate on an actual basis (Rate Code B).

List all the service centers and expense pools and enter in column (1) Code A or B to indicate the category of pool. Enter in Column (2) one of the Allocation Base Codes A through P, or Y, listed on Page [   ] to indicate the base used for charging or allocating service center or expense pool costs. Enter in Column (3) Rate Code A or B to describe the costing method used. Also, for each of the centers and pools indicate (a) the major functions, activities, and elements of cost included, and (b) the make up of the allocation base. Use a continuation sheet if additional space is required.

	Service Center or Expense Pool	Category Code (1)	Allocation Base Code (2)	Rate Code (3)
1.	[ ]	[ ]	[ ]	[ ]
(a)	Major functions, activities, and elements of cost included:			
(b)	Description/Make up of the allocation base:			
2.	[ ]	[ ]	[ ]	[ ]
(a)	Major functions, activities, and elements of cost included:			
(b)	Description/Make up of the allocation base:			

COST ACCOUNTING STANDARDS BOARD DISCLOSURE STATEMENT REQUIRED BY PUBLIC LAW 100-679	PART IV - INDIRECT COSTS NAME OF REPORTING UNIT

Item No.	Item description
4.4.0	**Treatment of Variances from Actual Cost (Underabsorption or Overabsorption).** Where predetermined billing or costing rates are used to charge costs of service centers and expense pools to Federal contracts or other indirect cost pools (Rate Code A in Column (3) of Item 4.3.0), variances from actual costs are: (Mark the appropriate line(s) and if more than one is marked, explain on a continuation sheet.) A. [ ] Prorated to users on the basis of charges made, at least once annually B. [ ] All charged or credited to indirect cost pool(s) at least once annually Y. [ ] Other(s) 1/ Z. [ ] Service center is not applicable to reporting unit

4.5.0	**Application of Overhead and G&A Rates to Specified Transactions or Costs.**
	
	    This item is directed to ascertaining your practice in special situations where, in lieu of establishing a separate indirect cost pool, allocation is made from an established overhead or G&A pool at a rate other than the normal full rate for that pool. In the case of such a special allocation, the terms "less than full rate" or "more than full rate" should be used to describe the practice. The terms do <u>not</u> apply to situations where, as in some cases of off-site activities, etc., a separate indirect cost pool and base are used and the rate for such activities is lower than the "in-house" rate.
	
	    For each of the transactions or costs listed below, enter one of the following codes to indicate your indirect cost allocation practice with respect to that transaction or cost. If Code A, full rate, is entered, identify on a continuation sheet the pool(s) reported under Items 4.1.0, 4.2.0, and 4.3.0, which are applicable. If Codes B or C, less than or more than the full rate, is entered, describe on a continuation sheet the major types of expenses that are covered by such a rate.
	
	 Rate Code
	A. Full rate C. Special allocation at more than full rate
	B. Special allocation at less than full rate D. No overhead or G&A is applied
	       Z. Transaction or cost is not applicable to reporting unit
	
	Transaction or Cost to Which **Rate**
	Indirect Costs May be Allocated **Code**
	
	(a) Subcontract costs [ ]
	(b) Purchased Labor [ ]
	(c) Government-furnished materials [ ]
	(d) Self-constructed depreciable assets [ ]
	(e) Labor on installation of assets [ ]
	(f) Off-site work [ ]
	(g) Interorganizational transfers out
	(h) Interorganizational transfers in (Also indicate on a continuation sheet the basis used by you as transferee to charge the cost or price of interorganizational transfers to Federal contracts or similar cost objectives. If the charge is based on cost, indicate whether the transferor's G&A expenses are included.) [ ]
	(i) Other transactions or costs (Enter Code B or C on this line if there are other transactions or costs to which either less than full rate or more than full rate is applied. List such transactions or costs on a continuation sheet, and for each describe the major types of expenses covered by such a rate. If there are no other such transactions or costs, enter code Z.) [ ]
	
	1/ Describe on a Continuation Sheet.

COST ACCOUNTING STANDARDS BOARD DISCLOSURE STATEMENT REQUIRED BY PUBLIC LAW 100-679	PART IV - INDIRECT COSTS
	NAME OF REPORTING UNIT

Item No.	Item description
4.6.0	**Independent Research and Development (IR&D) and Bid and Proposal (B&P) Costs.** Definitions of and requirements for the allocation of IR&D and B&P costs are contained in 48 CFR 9904.420. The full rate of all allocable manufacturing, engineering, and/or other overhead is applied to IR&D and B&P costs as if IR&D and B&P projects were under contract, and the "burdened" IR&D and B&P costs are: (Mark appropriate line(s).)

        A.   ☐   Allocated to Federal contracts or similar cost objectives by means of a composite pool with G&A expenses.

        B.   ☐   Allocated to Federal contracts or similar cost objectives by means of a separate pool.

        C.   ☐   Transferred to the corporate or home office level for reallocation to the benefiting segments.

        Y.   ☐   Other 1/

        Z.   ☐   Not applicable

| 4.7.0 | **Cost of Capital Committed to Facilities.** In accordance with instructions for Form CASB-CMF, undistributed facilities capital items are allocated to overhead and G&A expense pools: (Mark one.) |

        A.   ☐   On a basis identical to that used to absorb the actual depreciation or amortization from these facilities; land is assigned in the same manner as the facilities to which it relates.

        B.   ☐   On a basis not identical to that used to absorb the actual depreciation or amortization from these facilities. (Describe on a continuation sheet the difference for each step of the allocation process.)

        C.   ☐   By the "alternative allocation process" described in instructions for Form CASB-CMF.

        Z.   ☐   Not applicable.

1/ Describe on a Continuation Sheet.

CASB 9903.202-9

Item No.	Item description

COST ACCOUNTING STANDARDS BOARD DISCLOSURE STATEMENT REQUIRED BY PUBLIC LAW 100-679	PART V - DEPRECIATION AND CAPITALIZATION PRACTICES
	NAME OF REPORTING UNIT

Part V Instructions

Where a home office either establishes practices or procedures for the types of costs covered in this Part or incurs and then allocates these costs to its segments, the home office may complete this Part to be included in the submission by the segment as indicated on page (i) 4., **General Instructions.**

5.1.0   **Depreciating Tangible Assets for Government Contract Costing.** (For each of the asset categories listed on Page ___, enter a code from A through H in Column (1) describing the method of depreciation (Code F for assets that are expensed); a code from A through C in Column (2) describing the basis for determining useful life; a code from A through C in Column (3) describing how depreciation methods or use charges are applied to property units; and a Code A, B or C in Column (4) indicating whether or not residual value is deducted from the total cost of depreciable assets. Enter Code Y in each column of an asset category where another or more than one method applies. Enter Code Z in Column (1) only, if an asset category is not applicable.)

Column (1)–Depreciation Method Code

A. Straight Line
B. Declining balance
C. Sum-of-the years digits
D. Machine hours
E. Unit of production
F. Expensed at acquisition
G. Use charge
H. Method of depreciation used under the applicable Internal Revenue Procedures
Y. Other or more than one method 1/
Z. Asset category is not applicable

Column (2)–Useful Life Code

A. Replacement experience adjusted by expected changes in periods of usefulness
B. Term of Lease
C. Estimated on the basis of Asset Guidelines under Internal Revenue Procedures
Y. Other, or more than one method 1/

Column (3)–Property Units Code

A. Individual units are accounted for separately
B. Applied to groups of assets with similar service lives
C. Applied to groups of assets with varying service lives
Y. Other or more than one method 1/

Column (4)–Residual Value Code

A. Residual value is estimated and deducted
B. Residual value is covered by the depreciation method (e.g., declining balance)
C. Residual value is estimated but not deducted in accordance with the provisions of 48 CFR 9904.409 1/
Y. Other or more than one method 1/

1/ Describe on a Continuation Sheet.

CASB 9903.202-9

COST ACCOUNTING STANDARDS BOARD DISCLOSURE STATEMENT REQUIRED BY PUBLIC LAW 100-679	PART V - DEPRECIATION AND CAPITALIZATION PRACTICES NAME OF REPORTING UNIT

Item No.	Item description

5.1.0 Continued.

Asset Category	Depreciation Method Code (1)	Useful Life Code (2)	Property Units Code (3)	Residual Value Code (4)
(a) Land improvements	☐	☐	☐	☐
(b) Building	☐	☐	☐	☐
(c) Building improvements	☐	☐	☐	☐
(d) Leasehold improvements	☐	☐	☐	☐
(e) Machinery and equipment	☐	☐	☐	☐
(f) Furniture and fixtures	☐	☐	☐	☐
(g) Automobiles and trucks	☐	☐	☐	☐
(h) Data processing equipment	☐	☐	☐	☐
(i) Programming/reprogramming costs	☐	☐	☐	☐
(j) Patterns and dies	☐	☐	☐	☐
(k) Tools	☐	☐	☐	☐
(l) Other depreciable asset categories (Enter Code Y on this line if other asset categories are used and enumerate on a continuation sheet each such asset category and the applicable codes. Otherwise enter Code Z.)	☐			

5.2.0 Depreciation Practices for Costing, Financial Accounting, and Income Tax. Are depreciation practices the same for costing Federal contracts as for financial accounting and income tax? (Mark either (A) or (B) on each line under Financial Accounting and Income Tax. Not-for-profit organizations need not complete this item.)

Financial Accounting	A. Yes	B. No
(a) Methods	☐	☐
(b) Useful lives	☐	☐
(c) Property units	☐	☐
(d) Residual values	☐	☐

Income Tax	A. Yes	B. No
(e) Methods	☐	☐
(f) Useful lives	☐	☐
(g) Property units	☐	☐
(h) Residual values	☐	☐

CASB 9903.202-9

COST ACCOUNTING STANDARDS BOARD DISCLOSURE STATEMENT REQUIRED BY PUBLIC LAW 100-679	PART V - DEPRECIATION AND CAPITALIZATION PRACTICES
	NAME OF REPORTING UNIT

Item No.	Item description
5.3.0	**Fully Depreciated Assets.** Is a usage charge for fully depreciated assets charged to Federal contracts? (Mark one.) A. ☐ Yes 1/ B. ☐ No Z. ☐ Not applicable
5.4.0	**Treatment of Gains and Losses on Disposition of Depreciable Property.** Gains and losses are: (Mark the appropriate line(s) and if more than one is marked, explain on a continuation sheet.) A. ☐ Credited or charged currently to the same overhead or G&A pools to which the depreciation of the assets was charged B. ☐ Taken into consideration in the depreciation cost basis of the new items, where trade-in is involved C. ☐ Not accounted for separately, but reflected in the depreciation reserve account Y. ☐ Other(s) 1/ Z. ☐ Not applicable
5.5.0	**Capitalization or Expensing of Specified Costs.** (Mark one line on each item to indicate your practices regarding capitalization or expensing of specified costs incurred in connection with capital assets. If the same specified cost is sometimes expensed and sometimes capitalized, mark both lines and describe on a continuation sheet the circumstances when each method is used.) Cost A. Expensed B. Capitalized (a) Freight-in ☐ ☐ (b) Sales taxes ☐ ☐ (c) Excise taxes ☐ ☐ (d) Architect-engineer fees ☐ ☐ (e) Overhauls (extraordinary repairs) ☐ ☐ 1/ Describe on a Continuation Sheet.

Item No.	Item description

<table>
<tr><td colspan="2">
COST ACCOUNTING STANDARDS BOARD
DISCLOSURE STATEMENT
REQUIRED BY PUBLIC LAW 100-679
</td>
<td>
PART V - DEPRECIATION AND
CAPITALIZATION PRACTICES
NAME OF REPORTING UNIT
</td></tr>
</table>

5.6.0   Criteria for Capitalization. Enter (a) the minimum dollar amount of acquisition cost or expenditures for addition, alteration and improvement of depreciable assets capitalized, and (b) the minimum number of expected life years of capitalized assets.

> If more than one dollar amount or number applies, show the information for the majority of your depreciable assets, and enumerate on a continuation sheet the dollar amounts and/or number of years for each category or subcategory of assets involved which differ from those for the majority of assets.

(a)   Minimum dollar amount capitalized   [ ]

(b)   Minimum service life years   [ ]

5.7.0   Group or Mass Purchase. Are group or mass purchases (original complement) of low cost equipment, which individually are less than the capitalization amount indicated above, capitalized? (Mark one. If Yes is marked, provide the minimum aggregate dollar amount capitalized.)

A.   [ ]   Yes

[ ] Minimum aggregate dollar amount capitalized

B.   [ ]   No

COST ACCOUNTING STANDARDS BOARD **DISCLOSURE STATEMENT** **REQUIRED BY PUBLIC LAW 100-679**	**PART VI - OTHER COSTS AND CREDITS** **NAME OF REPORTING UNIT**

Item No.	Item description
	<center>**Part VI Instructions**</center>

Where a home office either establishes practices or procedures for the types of costs covered in this Part or incurs and then allocates these costs to its segments, the home office may complete this Part to be included in the submission by the segment as indicated on page (ii) 4., General Instructions.

6.1.0 Method of Charging and Crediting Vacation, Holiday, and Sick Pay. (Mark the appropriate line(s) in each column of Items 6.1.1, 6.1.2, 6.1.3 and 6.1.4 to indicate the method used to charge, or credit any unused or unpaid vacation, holiday, or sick pay. If more than one method is marked, explain on a continuation sheet.)

		Salaried	
	Hourly (1)	Non-exempt 1/ (2)	Exempt 1/ (3)

6.1.1 Charges for Vacation Pay

A.	When Accrued (earned)	☐	☐	☐
B.	When Taken			
Y.	Other(s) 2/	☐	☐	☐

6.1.2 Charges for Holiday Pay

A.	When Accrued (earned)	☐	☐	☐
B.	When Taken			
Y.	Other(s) 2/	☐	☐	☐

6.1.3 Charges for Sick Pay

A.	When Accrued (earned)	☐	☐	☐
B.	When Taken			
Y.	Other(s) 2/	☐	☐	☐

6.1.4 Credits for Unused or Unpaid Vacation, Holiday, or Sick Pay

A.	Credited to Accounts Originally charged at Least Once Annually	☐	☐	☐
B.	Credited to Indirect Cost Pools at Least Once Annually	☐	☐	☐
C.	Carried Over to Future Cost Accounting Periods 2/	☐	☐	☐
Y.	Other(s) 2/			
Z.	Not Applicable	☐	☐	☐

1/ For the definition of Non-exempt and Exempt salaries, see the Fair Labor Standards Act, 29 U.S.C. 206.

2/ Describe on a Continuation Sheet.

COST ACCOUNTING STANDARDS BOARD DISCLOSURE STATEMENT REQUIRED BY PUBLIC LAW 100-679	PART VI - OTHER COSTS AND CREDITS
	NAME OF REPORTING UNIT

Item No.	Item description

6.2.0   Supplemental Unemployment (Extended Layoff) Benefit Plans. Costs of such plans are charged to Federal contracts: (Mark the appropriate line(s) and if more than one is marked, explain on a continuation sheet.)

A. ☐   When actual payments are made directly to employees
B. ☐   When accrued (book accrual or funds set aside but no trust fund involved)
C. ☐   When contributions are made to a nonforfeitable trust fund
D. ☐   Not charged
Y. ☐   Other(s) 1/
Z. ☐   Not applicable

6.3.0   Severance Pay and Early Retirement. Costs of normal turnover severance pay and early retirement incentive plans, as defined in FAR 31.2 or other pertinent procurement regulations, which are charged directly or indirectly to Federal contracts, are based on: (Mark the appropriate line(s) and if more than one is marked, explain on a continuation sheet.)

A. ☐   Actual payments made
B. ☐   Accrued amounts on the basis of past experience
C. ☐   Not charged
Y. ☐   Other(s) 1/
Z. ☐   Not applicable

6.4.0   Incidental Receipts. (Mark the appropriate line(s) to indicate the method used to account for incidental or miscellaneous receipts, such as revenues from renting real and personal property or selling services, when related costs have been allocated to Federal contracts. If more than one is marked, explain on a continuation sheet.)

A. ☐   The entire amount of the receipt is credited to the same indirect cost pools to which related costs have been charged
B. ☐   Where the amount of the receipt includes an allowance for profit, the cost-related part of the receipt is credited to the same indirect cost pools to which related costs have been charged; the profits are credited to Other (Miscellaneous) Income
C. ☐   The entire amount of the receipt is credited directly to Other (Miscellaneous) Income
Y. ☐   Other(s) 1/
Z. ☐   Not applicable

1/ Describe on a Continuation Sheet.

COST ACCOUNTING STANDARDS BOARD DISCLOSURE STATEMENT REQUIRED BY PUBLIC LAW 100-679	PART VI - OTHER COSTS AND CREDITS
	NAME OF REPORTING UNIT

Item No.	Item description
6.5.0	*Proceeds from Employee Welfare Activities.* *Employee welfare activities include all of those activities set forth in FAR 31.2 . (Mark the appropriate line(s) to indicate the practice followed in accounting for the proceeds from such activities. If more than one is marked, explain on a continuation sheet.)*

A. ☐   Proceeds are turned over to an employee-welfare organization or fund; such proceeds are reduced by all applicable costs such as depreciation, heat, light and power

B. ☐   Same as above, except the proceeds are not reduced by all applicable costs

C. ☐   Proceeds are credited at least once annually to the appropriate cost pools to which costs have been charged

D. ☐   Proceeds are credited to Other (Miscellaneous) Income

Y. ☐   Other(s) 1/

Z. ☐   Not applicable

1/ Describe on a Continuation Sheet.

CASB 9903.202-9

COST ACCOUNTING STANDARDS BOARD DISCLOSURE STATEMENT REQUIRED BY PUBLIC LAW 100-679	PART VII - DEFERRED COMPENSATION AND INSURANCE COST NAME OF REPORTING UNIT

Item No.	Item description
	<u>Part VII Instructions</u> This part covers the measurement and assignment of costs for employee pensions, post retirement benefits other than pensions (including post retirement health benefits), certain other types of deferred compensation, and insurance. Some organizations may incur all of these costs at the corporate or home office level, while others may incur them at subordinate organizational levels. Still others may incur a portion of these costs at the corporate level and the balance at subordinate organizational levels. Where the segment (reporting unit) does not directly incur such costs, the segment should, on a continuation sheet, identify the organizational entity that incurs and records such costs, and should require that entity to complete the applicable portions of this Part VII. Each such entity is to fully disclose the methods and techniques used to measure, assign, and allocate such costs to the segment(s) performing Federal contracts or similar cost objectives. Necessary explanations required to achieve that objective should be provided by the entity on a continuation sheet. Where a home office either establishes practices or procedures for the types of costs covered in this Part VII or incurs and then allocates those costs to its segments, the home office may complete this Part to be included in the submission by the segment as indicated on page (i) 4., <u>General Instructions</u>.
7.1.0	<u>Pension Plans with Costs Charged to Federal Contracts.</u> Identify the types and number of pension plans whose costs are charged to Federal contracts or similar cost objectives: (Mark applicable line(s) and enter number of plans.)

<u>Type of Pension Plan</u>   Number of
Plans

A.   Defined-Contribution Plan (Other than ESOPs (see 7.5.0))

      1.   Non-Qualified   [ ]
      2.   Qualified   [ ]

B.   Defined-Benefit Plan

      1.   Non-Qualified
           a. Costs are measured and assigned on accrual basis   [ ]
           b. Costs are measured and assigned on cash
             (pay-as-you-go) basis   [ ]
      2.   Qualified
           a. Trusteed (Subject to ERISA's minimum funding requirements)   [ ]
           b. Fully-insured plan (Exempt from ERISA's minimum funding
             requirements) treated as a defined-contribution plan   [ ]
           c. Collectively bargained plan treated as a defined-
             contribution plan   [ ]

Y.   [ ]   Other 1/   [ ]

Z.   [ ]   Not Applicable (Proceed to Item 7.2.0)

1/ Describe on a Continuation Sheet.

COST ACCOUNTING STANDARDS BOARD DISCLOSURE STATEMENT REQUIRED BY PUBLIC LAW 100-679	PART VII - DEFERRED COMPENSATION AND INSURANCE COST NAME OF REPORTING UNIT

Item No.	Item description
7.1.1	General Plan Information. On a continuation sheet for each plan identified in Item 7.1.0, provide the following information: A. The plan name B. The Employer Identification Number (EIN) of the plan sponsor as reported on IRS Form 5500, if any C. The plan number as reported on IRS Form 5500, if any D. Is there a funding agency established for the plan? E. Indicate where costs are accumulated: (1) Home Office (2) Segment F. If the plan provides supplemental benefits to any other plan, identify the other plan(s).
7.1.2	Defined-Contribution Plan(s) and Certain Defined-Benefit Plans treated as Defined-Contribution Plans. Where numerous plans are listed under 7.1.0.A., 7.1.0.B.2.b., or 7.1.0.B.2.c., for those plans which represent the largest dollar amounts of costs charged to Federal contracts, or similar cost objectives, describe on a continuation sheet the basis for the contribution (including treatment of dividends, credits, and forfeitures) required for each fiscal year. (If there are not more than three plans, provide information for all the plans. If there are more than three plans, information should be provided for those plans that in the aggregate account for at least 80 percent of those defined-contribution plan costs allocable to this segment or business unit.) Z. ☐ Not applicable. (Proceed to Item 7.1.3)
7.1.3	Defined-Benefit Plan(s). Where numerous plans are listed under 7.1.0.B. (excluding certain defined-benefit plans treated as defined-contribution plans reported under 7.1.0.B.2.b. and 7.1.0.B.2.c.), for those plans which represent the largest dollar amounts of costs charged to Federal contracts, provide the information requested below on a continuation sheet. (If there are not more than three plans, provide information for all the plans. If there are more than three plans, information should be provided for those plans that in the aggregate account for at least 80 percent of those defined-benefit plan costs allocable to this segment or business unit.): A. Actuarial Cost Method. Identify the actuarial cost method used, including the cost method(s) used to value ancillary benefits, for each plan. Include the method used to determine the actuarial value of assets. Also, if applicable, include whether normal cost is developed as a level dollar amount or as a level percent of salary. For plans listed under 7.1.0.B.1.b., enter "pay-as-you-go". B. Actuarial Assumptions. Describe the events or conditions for which significant actuarial assumptions are made for each plan. Do not include the current numeric values of the assumptions, but provide a description of the basis used for determining these numeric values. Also, describe the criteria used to evaluate the validity of an actuarial assumption. For plans listed under 7.1.0.B.1.b., enter "not applicable". C. Market Value of Funding Agency Assets. Indicate if all assets of the funding agency are valued on the basis of a readily determinable market price. If yes, indicate the basis for the market value. If no, describe how the market values are determined for those assets that do not have a readily determinable market price. For plans listed under 7.1.0.B.1.b., enter "not applicable". D. Basis for Cost Computation. Indicate whether the cost for the segment is determined as: 1. An allocated portion of the total pension plan cost. 2. A separately computed pension cost for one or more segments. If so, identify those segments. Z. ☐ Not applicable, proceed to Item 7.2.0.

CASB 9903.202-9

COST ACCOUNTING STANDARDS BOARD DISCLOSURE STATEMENT REQUIRED BY PUBLIC LAW 100-679	PART VII - DEFERRED COMPENSATION AND INSURANCE COST NAME OF REPORTING UNIT

Item No.	Item description
7.2.0	**Post-retirement Benefits (PRBs) Other than Pensions (including post-retirement health care benefits) Charged to Federal Contracts.** Identify the accounting method used to determine the costs and the number of PRB plans whose costs are charged to Federal contracts or similar cost objectives. Where retiree benefits are provided as an integral part of an employee group insurance plan that covers active employees, report that plan under 7.3.0. (Mark applicable line(s) and enter number of plans.) Method Used to Determine Costs — Number of Plans A. Accrual Accounting B. Cash (pay-as-you-go) Accounting C. Purchased insurance from unrelated insurer D. Purchased insurance from Captive Insurer E. Self-insurance (including insurance obtained through Captive Insurer) F. Terminal Funding Y. Other 1/ Z. _____ Not Applicable (Proceed to Item 7.3.0)
7.2.1	General PRB Plan Information. On a continuation sheet for each plan identified in item 7.2.0, provide the following information grouped by method used to determine costs: A. The plan name B. The Employer Identification Number (EIN) of the plan sponsor as reported on IRS Form 5500, if any C. The plan number as reported on IRS Form 5500, if any D. Is there a funding agency or funded reserve established for the plan? E. Indicate where costs are accumulated: (1) Home Office (2) Segment F. Are benefits provided pursuant to a written plan or an established practice? If established practice, briefly describe. G. If this PRB plan is listed under 7.2.0.C., 7.2.0.D., or 7.2.0.E., indicate whether the plan is operated as an employee group insurance program. If this PRB plan is listed under 7.2.0.Y., indicate whether the plan is operated as a group insurance program. If the plan is operated as an employee group insurance program, report this plan under 7.3.0. and 7.3.1., as appropriate. If no, report the plan under 7.2.2. 1/ Describe on a Continuation Sheet.

CASB 9903.202-9

COST ACCOUNTING STANDARDS BOARD DISCLOSURE STATEMENT REQUIRED BY PUBLIC LAW 100-679	PART VII - DEFERRED COMPENSATION AND INSURANCE COST NAME OF REPORTING UNIT

Item No.	Item description
7.2.2	PRB Plan(s). Where numerous plans are listed under 7.2.0, for those plans which represent the largest dollar amounts of costs charged to Federal contracts, or other similar cost objectives, provide the information below on a continuation sheet. (If there are not more than three plans, provide information for all the plans. If there are more than three plans, information should be provided for those plans that in the aggregate account for at least 80 percent of those PRB costs allocable to this segment or business unit.)

    A.   Actuarial Cost Method. Identify the actuarial cost method used for each plan or each benefit, as appropriate. Include the method used to determine the actuarial value of assets. Identify the amortization methods and periods used, if any. For plans listed under 7.2.0.B., enter "cash accounting". For plans listed under 7.2.0.F., enter "terminal funding" and identify the amortization methods and periods used, if any.

    B.   Actuarial Assumptions. Describe the events or conditions for which significant actuarial assumptions are made for each plan. Do not include the current numeric values of the assumptions, but provide a description of the basis used for determining these numeric values. Also, describe the criteria used to evaluate the validity of an actuarial assumption. For plans under 7.2.0.B. or 7.2.0.F., enter "not applicable".

    C.   Funding. Provide the following information on the funding practice for the costs of the plan: (For plans under 7.2.0.B. or 7.2.0.F., enter "not applicable".)

        1.   Describe the criteria for or practice of funding the measured and assigned cost; e.g., full funding of the accrual, funding is made pursuant to VEBA or 401(h) rules.
        2.   Briefly describe the funding arrangement.
        3.   Are all assets valued on the basis of a readily determinable market price? If yes, indicate the basis used for the market value. If no, describe how the market value is determined for those assets that are not valued on the basis of a readily determinable market price.

    D.   Basis for Cost Computation. Indicate whether the cost for the segment is determined as:

        1.   An allocated portion of the total PRB plan cost
        2.   A separately computed PRB cost for one or more segments. If so, identify those segments.

    E.   Forfeitability. Does each participant have a non-forfeitable contractual right to their benefit or account balance? If no, explain.

    Z.   ☐ Not applicable, proceed to item 7.3.0.

COST ACCOUNTING STANDARDS BOARD DISCLOSURE STATEMENT REQUIRED BY PUBLIC LAW 100-679	**PART VII - DEFERRED COMPENSATION AND INSURANCE COST** **NAME OF REPORTING UNIT**

Item No.	Item description
7.3.0	**Employee Group Insurance Charged to Federal Contracts or Similar Cost Objectives.** Does your organization provide group insurance coverage to its employees? (Includes coverage for life, hospital, surgical, medical, disability, accident, and similar plans for both active and retired employees, even if the coverage was previously described in 7.2.0.) A. ☐ Yes (Complete Item 7.3.1) B. ☐ No (Proceed to Item 7.4.0)
7.3.1	Employee Group Insurance Programs. For each program that covers a category of insured risk (e.g., life, hospital, surgical, medical, disability, accident, and similar programs for both active and retired employees), provide the information below on a continuation sheet, using the codes described below: (If there are not more than three policies or self-insurance plans that comprise the program, provide information for all the policies and self-insurance plans. If there are more that three policies or self-insurance plans, information should be provided for those policies and self-insurance plans that in the aggregate account for at least 80 percent of the costs allocable to this segment or business unit for the program that covers each category of insured risk identified.) Description of Employee Group Insurance Program: [ ]

				Purchased	Self-insurance	
Policy or Self-Insurance Plan (1)	Cost Accumulation (2)	Cost Basis (3)	Includes Retirees (3)	Insurance Rating Basis (4)	Projected Average Loss (5)	Insurance Administrative Expenses (6)

Column (1) -- Cost Accumulation

Enter Code A, B, or Y, as appropriate.

A. Costs are accumulated at the Home Office.
B. Costs are accumulated at Segment
Y. Other 1/

Column (2) -- Cost Basis

Enter code A, B, C, or Y, as appropriate.

A. Purchased Insurance from unrelated third party
B. Self-insurance
C. Purchased Insurance from a captive insurer
Y. Other 1/

1/ Describe on a Continuation Sheet. |

COST ACCOUNTING STANDARDS BOARD DISCLOSURE STATEMENT REQUIRED BY PUBLIC LAW 100-679	PART VII - DEFERRED COMPENSATION AND INSURANCE COST
	NAME OF REPORTING UNIT

Item No.	Item description
7.3.1	**Continued.**

Column (3) – Includes Retirees

Enter code A, B, C, or Y, as appropriate.

A. No, does not include benefits for retirees.
B. Yes, PRB benefits for retirees that are a part of a policy or coverage for both active employees and retirees are reported here instead of 7.2.0.
C. Yes, PRB benefits for retirees are a part of a PRB plan previously reported under 7.2.0.
Y. Other 1/

Column (4) – Purchased Insurance Rating Basis

For each plan listed enter code A, B, C, Y, or Z, as appropriate.

A. Retrospective Rating (also called experience rating plan or retention plan).
B. Manually Rated
C. Community Rated
Y. Other, or more than one type 1/
Z. Not applicable

Column (5) – Projected Average Loss

For each self-insured group plan, or the self-insured portion of purchased insurance, enter code A, B, C, Y, or Z, as appropriate.

A. Self-insurance costs represent the projected average loss for the period estimated on the basis of the cost of comparable purchased insurance.
B. Self-insurance costs are based on the contractor's experience, relevant industry experience, and anticipated conditions in accordance with accepted actuarial principles.
C. Actual payments are considered to represent the projected average loss for the period.
Y. Other, or more than one method 1/
Z. Not applicable

Column (6) – Insurance Administration Expenses

For each self-insured group plan, or the self-insured portion of purchased insurance, enter code A, B, C, D, Y, or Z, as appropriate, to indicate how administrative costs are treated.

A. Separately identified and accumulated in indirect cost pool(s).
B. Separately identified, accumulated, and allocated to cost objectives either at the segment and/or home office level (Describe allocation method on a Continuation Sheet).
C. Not separately identified, but included in indirect cost pool(s). (Describe pool(s) on a Continuation Sheet)
D. Incurred by an insurance carrier or third party (Describe accumulation and allocation process on a Continuation Sheet).
Y. Other 1/
Z. Not applicable

1/ Describe on a Continuation Sheet.

CASB 9903.202-9

COST ACCOUNTING STANDARDS BOARD DISCLOSURE STATEMENT REQUIRED BY PUBLIC LAW 100-679	PART VII - DEFERRED COMPENSATION AND INSURANCE COST NAME OF REPORTING UNIT

Item No.	Item description
7.4.0	**Deferred Compensation, as defined in CAS 9904.415.** Does your organization award deferred compensation, other than ESOPs, which is charged to Federal contracts or similar cost objectives? (Mark one.) A. ☐ Yes (Complete Item 7.4.1.) B. ☐ No (Proceed to Item 7.5.0.)
7.4.1	General Plan Information. On a continuation sheet for all deferred compensation plans, as defined by CAS 9904.415, provide the following information: A. The plan name B. The Employer Identification Number (EIN) of the plan sponsor as reported on IRS Form 5500, if any C. The plan number as reported on IRS Form 5500, if any D. Indicate where costs are accumulated: (1) Home office (2) Segment E. Are benefits provided pursuant to a written plan or an established practice? If established practice, briefly describe .
7.4.2	Deferred Compensation Plans. Where numerous plans are listed under 7.4.1, for those plans which represent the largest dollar amounts of costs charged to Federal contracts, or other similar cost objectives, provide the information below on a continuation sheet. (If there are not more than three plans, provide information for all the plans. If there are more than three plans, information should be provided for those plans that in the aggregate account for at least 80% of these deferred compensation costs allocable to this segment or business unit): A. Description of Plan. 1. Stock Options 2. Stock Appreciation Rights 3. Cash Incentive 4. Other (explain) B. Method of Charging Costs to Federal Contracts or Similar Cost Objectives. 1. Costs charged when accrued and the accrual is fully funded 2. Costs charged when accrued and the accrual is partially funded or not funded 3. Costs charged when paid to employee (pay-as-you-go) 4. Other (explain)

CASB 9903.202-9

	PART VII - DEFERRED COMPENSATION AND INSURANCE COST
COST ACCOUNTING STANDARDS BOARD **DISCLOSURE STATEMENT** *REQUIRED BY PUBLIC LAW 100-679*	**NAME OF REPORTING UNIT**

Item No.	Item description
7.5.0	**Employee Stock Ownership Plans (ESOPs).** Does your organization make contributions to fund ESOPs that are charged directly or indirectly to Federal contracts or similar cost objectives? (Mark one) A. ☐ Yes (Proceed to Item 7.5.1) B. ☐ No (Proceed to Item 7.6.0)
7.5.1	General Plan Information. On a continuation sheet, for all ESOPs provide the following information: A. The plan name B. The Employer Identification Number (EIN) of the plan sponsor as reported on IRS Form 5500, if any C. The plan number as reported on IRS Form 5500, if any D. Indicate where costs are accumulated: (1) Home office (2) Segment E. Are benefits provided pursuant to a written plan or an established practice? If established practice, briefly describe. F. Indicate whether the ESOP plan is a defined-contribution plan subject to CAS 9904.412. (Answer Yes or No). G. Indicate whether the ESOP is leveraged or nonleveraged. H. Valuation of Stock or Non-Cash Assets. Are the plan assets valued on the basis of a readily determinable market price? If yes, indicate the basis for the market value. If no, indicate how the market value is determined for those assets that do not have a readily determinable market price. I. Forfeitures and Dividends. Describe the accounting treatment for forfeitures and dividends, on both allocated and unallocated shares, in the measurement of ESOP costs charged directly or indirectly to Federal contracts or similar cost objectives for each plan identified. J. Administrative Costs. Describe how the costs of administration of each plan listed are identified, grouped, and accumulated.

CASB 9903.202-9

COST ACCOUNTING STANDARDS BOARD DISCLOSURE STATEMENT REQUIRED BY PUBLIC LAW 100-679	PART VII - DEFERRED COMPENSATION AND INSURANCE COST
	NAME OF REPORTING UNIT

Item No.	Item description
7.6.0	**Worker's Compensation, Liability, and Property Insurance.** Does your organization have insurance coverage regarding worker's compensation, liability and property insurance?
	A. [ ] Yes (Complete Item 7.6.1.)
	B. [ ] No (Proceed to Part VIII)
7.6.1	Worker's Compensation, Liability and Property Insurance Coverage.

For each line of insurance that covers a category of insured risk (e.g., worker's compensation, fire and similar perils, automobile liability and property damage, general liability), provide the information below on a continuation sheet using the codes described below: (If there are not more than three policies or self-insurance plans that are applicable to the line of insurance, provide information for all the policies and self-insurance plans. If there are more than three policies or insurance plans, information should be provided for those policies and self-insurance plans that in the aggregate account for at least 80 percent of the costs allocable to this segment or business unit for each line of insurance identified.)

Description of Line of Insurance Coverage: [   ]

Policy or Self-Insurance Plan	Cost Accumulation (1)	Cost Basis (2)	Crediting of Dividends and Earned Refunds (3)	Self-insurance	
				Projected Average Loss (4)	Insurance Administrative Expenses (5)

Column (1) – Cost Accumulation

Enter code A, B, or Y, as appropriate.

A.   Costs are accumulated at the Home Office.
B.   Costs are accumulated at Segment
Y.   Other   1/

Column (2) – Cost Basis

Enter code A, B, C, or Y, as appropriate.

A.   Purchased Insurance from unrelated third party
B.   Self-insurance
C.   Purchased Insurance from a captive insurer
Y.   Other   1/

1/   Describe on a Continuation Sheet.

CASB 9903.202-9

COST ACCOUNTING STANDARDS BOARD DISCLOSURE STATEMENT REQUIRED BY PUBLIC LAW 100-679	PART VII - DEFERRED COMPENSATION AND INSURANCE COST
	NAME OF REPORTING UNIT

Item No.	Item description
7.6.1	Continued.

Column (3) – Crediting of Dividends and Earned Refunds

For each line of coverage listed, enter code A, B, C, D, E, Y, or Z, as appropriate.

A. Credited directly or indirectly to Federal contracts or similar cost objectives in the year earned
B. Credited directly or indirectly to Federal contracts or similar cost objectives in the year received, not necessarily in the year earned
C. Accrued each year, as applicable, to currently reflect the net annual cost of the insurance
D. Not credited or refunded to the contractor but retained by the carriers as reserves in accordance with 48 CFR 9904.416-50(a)(1)(iv)
E. Manually Rated - not applicable
Y. Other, or more than one 1/
Z. Not applicable

Column (4) – Projected Average Loss

For each self-insured group plan, or the self-insured portion of purchased insurance, enter code A, B, C, Y, or Z, as appropriate.

A. Costs that represent the projected average loss for the period estimated on the basis of the cost of comparable purchased insurance.
B. Costs that are based on the contractor's experience, relevant industry experience, and anticipated conditions in accordance with generally accepted actuarial principles and practices.
C. The actual amount of losses are considered to represent the projected average loss for the period.
Y. Other, or more than one method. 1/
Z. Not applicable

Column (5) – Insurance Administration Expenses

For each self-insured group plan, or the self-insured portion of purchased insurance, enter code A, B, C, D, Y, or Z, as appropriate, to indicate how administrative costs are treated.

A. Separately identified and accumulated in indirect cost pool(s).
B. Separately identified, accumulated, and allocated to cost objectives either at the segment and/or home office level (Describe allocation method on a Continuation Sheet).
C. Not separately identified, but included in indirect cost pool(s). (Describe pool(s) on a Continuation Sheet).
D. Incurred by an insurance carrier or third party. (Describe accumulation and allocation process on a Continuation Sheet).
Y. Other 1/
Z. Not applicable

1/   Describe on a Continuation Sheet.

CASB 9903.202-9

COST ACCOUNTING STANDARDS BOARD DISCLOSURE STATEMENT REQUIRED BY PUBLIC LAW 100-679	PART VIII - HOME OFFICE EXPENSES NAME OF REPORTING UNIT

Item No.	Item description
	Part VIII Instructions **FOR HOME OFFICE, AS APPLICABLE (Includes home office type operations of subsidiaries, joint ventures, partnerships, etc.). 1/** This part should be completed only by the office of a corporation or other business entity where such an office is responsible for administering two or more segments, where it allocates its costs to such segments and where at least one of the segments is required to file Parts I through VII of the Disclosure Statement. Data for this part should cover the reporting unit's (corporate or other intermediate level home office's) most recently completed fiscal year. For a corporate (home) office, such data should cover the entire corporation. For a intermediate level home office, they should cover the subordinate organizations administered by that group office.
8.1.0	**Organizational Structure.** On a continuation sheet, provide the following information: 1. In column (1) list segments and other intermediate level home offices reporting to this home office, 2. In column (2) insert "yes" or "no" to indicate if reporting units have recorded any CAS-covered Government Sales, and 3. In column (3) provide the percentage of annual CAS-covered Government Sales as a Percentage of Total Sales (Government and Commercial), if applicable, as follows: A. Less than 10% B. 10%-50% C. 51%-80% D. 81%-95% E. Over 95%

Segment or Other Intermediary Home Office (1)	CAS Covered Government Sales (2)	Government Sales as a Percentage of Total Sales (3)

Item No.	Item description
8.2.0	**Other Applicable Disclosure Statement Parts.** (Refer to page (i) 4., General Instructions, and Parts V, VI and VII of the Disclosure Statement. Indicate below the parts that the reporting unit has completed concurrently with Parts I and VIII.) A. ☐ Part V - Depreciation and Capitalization Practices B. ☐ Part VI - Other Costs and Credits C. ☐ Part VII - Deferred Compensation and Insurance Costs Z. ☐ Not Applicable
	1/ For definition of home office see 48 CFR 9904.403.

CASB 9903.202-9

COST ACCOUNTING STANDARDS BOARD DISCLOSURE STATEMENT REQUIRED BY PUBLIC LAW 100-679	PART VIII - HOME OFFICE EXPENSES
	NAME OF REPORTING UNIT

Item No.	Item description
8.3.0	**Expenses or Pools of Expenses and Methods of Allocation.** For classification purposes, three methods of allocation, defined as follows, are to be used: (i) Directly Allocated—those expenses that are charged to specific corporate segments or other intermediate level home offices based on a specific identification of costs incurred, as described in 9904.403; (ii) Homogeneous Expense Pools—those individual or groups of expenses which are allocated using a base which reflects beneficial or causal relationships, as described in 9904.403; and (iii) Residual Expense—the remaining expenses which are allocated to all segments by means of a base representative of the total activity of such segments. **Allocation Base Codes** A. Sales B. Cost of Sales C. Total Cost Input (Direct Material, Direct Labor, Other Direct Costs, and Applicable Overhead) D. Total Cost Incurred (Total Cost Input Plus G&A Expenses) E. Prime Cost (Direct Material, Direct Labor, and Other Direct Costs F. Three factor formula (CAS 9904.403-50(c)) G. Processing or Conversion Cost (Direct Labor and Applicable Overhead) H. Direct Labor Dollars I. Direct Labor Hours J. Machine Hours K. Usage L. Unit of Production M. Direct Material Cost N. Total Payroll Dollars (Direct and Indirect Employees) O. Headcount or Number of employees (Direct and Indirect Employees) P. Square Feet Q. Value Added Y. Other, or More than One Basis 1/ (On a continuation sheet, under each of the headings 8.3.1, 8.3.2, and 8.3.3 enter the type of expenses or the name of the expense pool(s). For each of the types of expense or expense pools listed, also indicate as item (a) the major functions, activities, and elements of cost included. In addition, for items listed under 8.3.2 and 8.3.3 enter one of the Allocation Base Codes A through Q, or Y, to indicate the basis of allocation and describe as item (b) the make up of the base(s). For example, if direct labor dollars are used, are overtime premiums, fringe benefits, etc. included? For items listed under 8.3.2 and 8.3.3, if a pool is not allocated to all reporting units listed under 8.1.0, then list those reporting units either receiving or not receiving an allocation. Also identify special allocations of residual expenses and/or fixed management charges (see 9904.403-40(c)(3)). 1/ Describe on a Continuation Sheet.

CASB 9903.202-9

COST ACCOUNTING STANDARDS BOARD DISCLOSURE STATEMENT REQUIRED BY PUBLIC LAW 100-679	PART VIII - HOME OFFICE EXPENSES
	NAME OF REPORTING UNIT

Item No.	Item description

Type of Expenses or Name of Pool of Expenses

8.3.1 Directly Allocated

  1.

  (a) Major functions, activities, and elements of cost include:

  2.

  (a) Major functions, activities, and elements of cost include:

8.3.2 Homogeneous Expense Pools   **Allocation Base Code**

  1.

  (a) Major functions, activities, and elements of cost include:

  (b) Description/Make up of the allocation base:

  2.

  (a) Major functions, activities, and elements of cost include:

  (b) Description/Make up of the allocation base:

CASB 9903.202-9

COST ACCOUNTING STANDARDS BOARD DISCLOSURE STATEMENT REQUIRED BY PUBLIC LAW 100-679	**PART VIII - HOME OFFICE EXPENSES** **NAME OF REPORTING UNIT**

Item No.	Item description

8.3.3 Residual Expenses   Allocation Base Code

(a)   Major functions, activities, and elements of cost include:

(b)   Description/Make up of the allocation base:

8.4.0 Transfer of Expenses. If there are normally transfers of expenses from reporting units to this home office, identify on a continuation sheet the classification of the expense and the name of the reporting unit incurring the expense.

FORM CASB DS-1 (REV 2/96)   VIII - 4

[Final rule, 61 FR 7616, 2/28/96, effective 2/28/96]

CASB 9903.202-9

**9903.202-10 Illustration of
Disclosure Statement Form, CASB
DS-2.**

The data which are required to be disclosed by educational institutions are set forth in detail in the Disclosure Statement Form, CASB DS-2, which is illustrated below:

FORM APPROVED OMB NUMBER
0348-0055

COST ACCOUNTING STANDARDS BOARD DISCLOSURE STATEMENT REQUIRED BY PUBLIC LAW 100-679 EDUCATIONAL INSTITUTIONS	INDEX

FORM CASB DS-2 (REV 10/94)

CASB 9903.202-10

COST ACCOUNTING STANDARDS BOARD DISCLOSURE STATEMENT REQUIRED BY PUBLIC LAW 100-679 EDUCATIONAL INSTITUTIONS	GENERAL INSTRUCTIONS

1.   This Disclosure Statement has been designed to meet the requirements of Public Law 100-679, and persons completing it are to describe the educational institution and its cost accounting practices. For complete regulations, instructions and timing requirements concerning submission of the Disclosure Statement, refer to Section 9903.202 of Chapter 99 of Title 48 CFR (49 CFR 9903).

2.   Part I of the Statement provides general information concerning each reporting unit (e.g., segments, business units, and central system or group (intermediate administration) offices). Parts II through VI pertain to the types of costs generally incurred by the segment or business unit directly performing under Federally sponsored agreements (e.g., contracts, grants and cooperative agreements). Part VII pertains to the types of costs that are generally incurred by a central or group office and are allocated to one or more segments performing under Federally sponsored agreements.

3.   Each segment or business unit required to disclose its cost accounting practices should complete the Cover Sheet, the Certification, and Parts I through VI.

4.   Each central or group office required to disclose its cost accounting practices for measuring, assigning and allocating its costs to segments performing under Federally sponsored agreements should complete the Cover Sheet, the Certification, Part I and Part VII of the Disclosure Statement. Where a central or group office incurs the types of cost covered by Parts IV, V and VI, and the cost amounts allocated to segments performing under Federally sponsored agrfeements are material, such office(s) should complete Parts IV, V, or VI for such material elements of cost. While a central or group office may have more than one reporting unit submitting Disclosure Statements, only one Statement needs to be submitted to cover the central or group office operations.

5.   The Statement must be signed by an authorized signatory of the reporting unit.

6.   The Disclosure Statement should be answered by marking the appropriate line or inserting the applicable letter code which describes the segment's (reporting unit's) cost accounting practices.

7.   A number of questions in this Statement may need narrative answers requiring more space than is provided. In such instances, the reporting unit should use the attached continuation sheet provided. The continuation sheet may be reproduced locally as needed. The number of the question involved should be indicated and the same coding required to answer the questions in the Statement should be used in presenting the answer on the continuation sheet. Continuation sheets should be inserted at the end of the pertinent Part of the Statement. On each continuation sheet, the reporting unit should enter the next sequential page number for that Part and, on the last continuation sheet used, the words "End of Part" should be inserted after the last entry.

FORM CASB DS-2 (REV 10/94)   (i)

COST ACCOUNTING STANDARDS BOARD DISCLOSURE STATEMENT REQUIRED BY PUBLIC LAW 100-679 EDUCATIONAL INSTITUTIONS	GENERAL INSTRUCTIONS

8. Where the cost accounting practice being disclosed is clearly set forth in the institution's existing written accounting policies and procedures, such documents may be cited on a continuation sheet and incorporated by reference. In such cases, the reporting unit should provide the date of issuance and effective date for each accounting policy and/or procedures document cited. Alternatively, copies of the relevant parts of such documents may be attached as appendices to the pertinent Disclosure Statement Part. Such continuation sheets and appendices should be labeled and cross-referenced with the applicable Disclosure Statement item number. Any supplementary comments needed to fully describe the cost accounting practice being disclosed should also be provided.

9. Disclosure Statements must be amended when disclosed practices are changed to comply with a new CAS or when practices are changed with or without agreement of the Government (Also see 48 CFR 9903.202-3).

10. Amendments shall be submitted to the same offices to which submission would have to be made were an original Disclosure Statement ebing filed.

11. Each amendment should be accompanied by an amended cover sheet (indicating revision number and effective date of the change) and a signed certification. For all resubmissions, on each page, insert "Revision Number ____" and "Effective Date ____" in the Item Description block; and, insert "Revised" under each Item Number amended. Resubmitted Disclosure Statements must be accompanied by similar notations identifying the items which have been changed.

ATTACHMENT — Blank Continuation Sheet

CASB 9903.202-10

COST ACCOUNTING STANDARDS BOARD DISCLOSURE STATEMENT REQUIRED BY PUBLIC LAW 100-679 EDUCATIONAL INSTITUTIONS	CONTINUATION SHEET
	NAME OF REPORTING UNIT

Item No.	Item Description

FORM CASB DS-2 (REV 10/94)   __ - __

CASB 9903.202-10

COST ACCOUNTING STANDARDS BOARD DISCLOSURE STATEMENT REQUIRED BY PUBLIC LAW 100-679 EDUCATIONAL INSTITUTIONS	COVER SHEET AND CERTIFICATION

0.1 Educational Institution

    (a)   Name

    (b)   Street Address

    (c)   City, State and ZIP Code

    (d)   Division or Campus of
           (if applicable)

0.2 Reporting Unit is: (Mark one.)

    A.   ____ Independently Administered Public Institution

    B.   ____ Independently Administered Nonprofit Institution

    C.   ____ Administered as Part of a Public System

    D.   ____ Administered as Part of a Nonprofit System

    E.   ____ Other (Specify) _____

0.3 Official to Contact Concerning this Statement:

    (a)   Name and Title

    (b)   Phone Number (include area code and extension)

0.4 Statement Type and Effective Date:

    A.   (Mark type of submission. If a revision, enter number)

         (a)   ____ Original Statement

         (b)   ____ Amended Statement; Revision No. _____

    B.   Effective Date of this Statement: (Specify) _____

0.5 Statement Submitted To (Provide office name, location and telephone number, include area code and extension):

    A.   Cognizant Federal Agency: _____

                            _____

    B.   Cognizant Federal Auditor: _____

                            _____

FORM CASB DS-2 (REV 10/94)   C-1

CASB 9903.202-10

COST ACCOUNTING STANDARDS BOARD DISCLOSURE STATEMENT REQUIRED BY PUBLIC LAW 100-679 EDUCATIONAL INSTITUTIONS	COVER SHEET AND CERTIFICATION

CERTIFICATION

I certify that to the best of my knowledge and belief this Statement, as amended in the case of a Revision, is the complete and accurate disclosure as of the date of certification shown below by the above-named organization of its cost accounting practices, as required by the Disclosure Regulations (49 CFR 9903.202) of the Cost Accounting Standards Board under 41 U.S.C. § 422.

Date of Certification: _____

_____
(Signature)

_____
(Print or Type Name)

_____
(Title)

THE PENALTY FOR MAKING A FALSE STATEMENT IN THIS DISCLOSURE
IS PRESCRIBED IN
18 U.S.C. § 1001

FORM CASB DS-2 (REV 10/94)   C-2

CASB 9903.202-10

COST ACCOUNTING STANDARDS BOARD DISCLOSURE STATEMENT	PART I—GENERAL INFORMATION
REQUIRED BY PUBLIC LAW 100-679 EDUCATIONAL INSTITUTIONS	NAME OF REPORTING UNIT

Item No.	Item Description

Part I

1.1.0 *Description of Your Cost Accounting System* for recording expenses charged to Federally sponsored agreements (e.g., contracts, grants and cooperative agreements). (Mark the appropriate line(s) and if more than one is marked, explain on a continuation sheet.)

A. _____ Accrual

B. _____ Modified Accrual Basis[1]

C. _____ Cash Basis

Y. _____ Other[1]

1.2.0 *Integration of Cost Accounting with Financial Accounting.* The cost accounting system is: (Mark one. If B or C is marked, describe on a continuation sheet the costs which are accumulated on memorandum records.)

A. _____ Integrated with financial accounting records (Subsidiary cost accounts are all controlled by general ledger control accounts.)

B. _____ Not integrated with financial accounting records (Cost data are accumulated on memorandum records.)

C. _____ Combination of A and B

1.3.0 *Unallowable Costs.* Costs that are not reimbursable as allowable costs under the terms and conditions of Federally sponsored agreements are: (Mark one)

A. _____ Specifically identified and recorded separately in the formal financial accounting records.[1]

B. _____ Identified in separately maintained accounting records or workpapers.[1]

C. _____ Identifiable through use of less formal accounting techniques that permit audit verification.[1]

D. _____ Combination of A, B or C [1]

E. _____ Determinable by other means.[1]

[1] Describe on a Continuation Sheet.

FORM CASB DS-2 (REV 10/94)   I-1

CASB 9903.202-10

COST ACCOUNTING STANDARDS BOARD DISCLOSURE STATEMENT	PART I—GENERAL INFORMATION
REQUIRED BY PUBLIC LAW 100-679 EDUCATIONAL INSTITUTIONS	NAME OF REPORTING UNIT

Item No.	Item Description
1.3.1	Treatment of Unallowable Costs. (Explain on a continuation sheet how unallowable costs and directly associated costs are treated in each allocation base and indirect expense pool, e.g., when allocating costs to a major function or activity; when determining indirect cost rates; or, when a central office or group office allocates costs to a segment.)
1.4.0	*Cost Accounting Period:* _____ (Specify the twelve month period used for the accumulation and reporting of costs under Federally sponsored agreements, e.g., 7/1 to 6/30. If the cost accounting period is other than the institution's fiscal year used for financial accounting and reporting purposes, explain circumstances on a continuation sheet.)
1.5.0	*State Laws or Regulations.* Identify on a continuation sheet any State laws or regulations which influence the institution's cost accounting practices, e.g., State administered pension plans, and any applicable statutory limitations or special agreements on allowance of costs.

[1] Describe on a Continuation Sheet.

FORM CASB DS-2 (REV 10/94)   I-2

CASB 9903.202-10

COST ACCOUNTING STANDARDS BOARD DISCLOSURE STATEMENT REQUIRED BY PUBLIC LAW 100-679 EDUCATIONAL INSTITUTIONS	PART II—DIRECT COSTS
	NAME OF REPORTING UNIT

Item No.	Item Description
	Instructions for Part II
	Institutions should disclose what costs are, or will be, charged directly to Federally sponsored agreements or similar cost objectives as Direct Costs. It is expected that the disclosed cost accounting practices (as defined at 48 CFR 9903.302-1) for classifying costs either as direct costs or indirect costs will be consistently applied to all costs incurred by the reporting unit.
2.1.0	*Criteria for Determining How Costs are Charged to Federally Sponsored Agreements or Similar Cost Objectives.* (For all major categories of cost under each major function or activity such, as instruction, organized research, other sponsored activities and other institutional activities, describe on a continuation sheet, your criteria for determining when costs incurred for the same purpose, in like circumstances, are treated either as direct costs only or as indirect costs only with respect to final cost ojbectives. Particular emphasis should be placed on items of cost that may be treated as either direct or indirect costs (e.g., Supplies, Materials, Salaries and Wages, Fringe Benefits, etc.) depending upon the purpose of the activity involved. Separate explanations on the criteria governing each direct cost category identified in this Part II are required. Also, list and explain if there are any deviations from the specified criteria.)
2.2.0	*Description of Direct Materials.* All materials and supplies directly identified with Federally sponsored agreements or similar cost objectives. (Describe on a continuation sheet the principal classes of materials which are charged as direct materials and supplies.)
2.3.0	*Method of Charging Direct Materials and Supplies.* (Mark the appropriate line(s) and if more than one is marked, explain on a continuation sheet.)
2.3.1	Direct Purchases for Projects are Charged to Projects at:
	A. _____ Actual Invoiced Costs
	B. _____ Actual Invoiced Costs Net of Discounts Taken
	Y. _____ Other(s) [1]
	Z. _____ Not Applicable
2.3.2	(Inventory Requisitions from Central or Common, Institution-owned Inventory. (Identify the inventory valuation method used to charge projects):
	A. _____ First In, First Out
	B. _____ Last In, First Out
	C. _____ Average Costs[1]
	D. _____ Predetermined Costs[1]
	Y. _____ Other(s) [1]
	Z. _____ Not Applicable
	[1] Describe on a Continuation Sheet.

CASB 9903.202-10

COST ACCOUNTING STANDARDS BOARD DISCLOSURE STATEMENT REQUIRED BY PUBLIC LAW 100-679 EDUCATIONAL INSTITUTIONS	PART II—DIRECT COSTS
	NAME OF REPORTING UNIT

Item No.	Item Description
2.4.0	*Description of Direct Personal Services.* All personal services directly identified with Federally sponsored agreements or similar cost objectives. (Describe on a continuation sheet the personal services compensation costs, including applicable fringe benefits costs, if any, within each major institutional function or activity that are charged as direct personal services.)
2.5.0	*Method of Charging Direct Salaries and Wages.* (Mark the appropriate line(s) for each Direct Personal Services Category to identify the method(s) used to charge direct salary and wage costs to Federally sponsored agreements or similar cost objectives. If more than one line is marked in a column, fully describe on a continuation sheet, the applicable methods used.)

Direct Personal Services Category

	Faculty (1)	Staff (2)	Students (3)	Other [1] (4)
A. Payroll Distribution Method (Individual time card/actual hours and rates)	——	——	——	——
B. Plan—Confirmation (Budgeted, planned or assigned work activity, updated to reflect significant changes)				
C. After-the-fact Activity Records (Percentage Distribution of employee activity)	——	——	——	——
D. Multiple Confirmation Records (Employee Reports prepared each academic term, to account for employee's activities, direct and indirect charges are certified separately.)	——	——	——	——
Y. Other(s) [1]	——	——	——	——

[1] Describe on a Continuation Sheet.

FORM CASB DS-2 (REV 10/94)   II-2

CASB 9903.202-10

COST ACCOUNTING STANDARDS BOARD DISCLOSURE STATEMENT REQUIRED BY PUBLIC LAW 100-679 EDUCATIONAL INSTITUTIONS	PART II—DIRECT COSTS
	NAME OF REPORTING UNIT

Item No.	Item Description
2.5.1	Salary and Wage Cost Distribution Systems. Within each major function or activity, are the methods marked in Item 2.5.0 used by all employees compensated by the reporting unit? (If "NO", describe on a continuation sheet, the types of employees not included and describe the methods used to identify and distribute their salary and wage costs to direct and indirect cost objectives.) ____ Yes ____ No
2.5.2	Salary and Wage Cost Accumulation System. (Within each major function or activity, describe, on a continuation sheet, the specific accounting records or memorandum records used to accumulate and record the share of the total salary and wage costs attributable to each employee's direct (Federally sponsored projects, non-sponsored projects or similar cost objectives) and indirect activities. Indicate how the salary and wage cost distributions are reconciled with the payroll data recorded in the institution's financial accounting records.)
2.6.0	*Description of Direct Fringe Benefits Costs.* All fringe benefits that are attributable to direct salaries and wages and are charged directly to Federally sponsored agreements or similar cost objectives. (Describe on a continuation sheet *all* of the different types of fringe benefits which are classified and charged as direct costs, e.g., actual or accrued costs of vacation, holidays, sick leave, sabbatical leave, premium pay, social security, pension plans, post-retirement benefits other than pensions, health insurance, training, tuition, tuition remission, etc.)
2.6.1	Method of Charging Direct Fringe Benefits. (Describe on a continuation sheet, how each type of fringe benefit cost identified in item 2.6.0. is measured, assigned and allocated (for definitions, See 9903.302-1); first, to the major functions (e.g., instruction, research); and, then to individual projects or direct cost objectives within each function.)
2.7.0	*Description of Other Direct Costs.* All other items of cost directly identified with Federally sponsored agreements or similar cost objectives. (List on a continuation sheet the principal classes of other costs which are charged directly, e.g., travel, consultants, services, subgrants, subcontracts, malpractice insurance, etc.)

CASB 9903.202-10

COST ACCOUNTING STANDARDS BOARD DISCLOSURE STATEMENT REQUIRED BY PUBLIC LAW 100-679 EDUCATIONAL INSTITUTIONS	PART II—DIRECT COSTS
	NAME OF REPORTING UNIT

Item No.	Item Description

2.8.0 *Cost Transfers.* When Federally sponsored agreements or similar cost objectives are credited for cost transfers to other projects, grants or contracts, is the credit amount for direct personal services, materials, other direct charges and applicable indirect costs always based on the same amount(s) or rate(s) (e.g., direct labor rate, indirect costs) originally used to charge or allocate costs to the project (Consider transactions where the original charge and the credit occur in different cost accounting periods). (Mark one, if "No", explain on a continuation sheet how the credit differs from original charge.)

_____ Yes

_____ No

2.9.0 *Interorganizational Transfers.* This item is directed only to those materials, supplies, and services which are, or will be transferred to you from other segments of the educational institution. (Mark the appropriate line(s) in each column to indicate the basis used by you as transferee to charge the cost or price of interorganizational transfers or materials, supplies, and services to Federally sponsored agreements or similar cost objectives. If more than one line is marked in a column, explain on a continuation sheet.)

		Materials (1)	Supplies (2)	Services (3)
A.	At full cost *excluding* indirect costs attributable to group or central office expenses.	____	____	____
B.	At full cost *including* indirect costs attributable to group or central office expenses.	____	____	____
C.	At established catalog or market price or prices based on adequate competition.	____	____	____
Y.	Other(s) [1]	____	____	____
Z.	Interorganizational transfers are not applicable.	____	____	____

[1] Describe on a Continuation Sheet.

FORM CASB DS-2 (REV 10/94)   II-4

CASB 9903.202-10

COST ACCOUNTING STANDARDS BOARD DISCLOSURE STATEMENT REQUIRED BY PUBLIC LAW 100-679 EDUCATIONAL INSTITUTIONS	PART III—INDIRECT COSTS
	NAME OF REPORTING UNIT

Item No.	Item Description

Instructions for Part III

Institutions should disclose how the segment's total indirect costs are identified and accumulated in specific indirect cost categories and allocated to applicable indirect cost pools and service centers within each major function or activity, how service center costs are accumulated and "billed" to users, and the specific indirect cost pools and allocation bases used to calculate the indirect cost reates that are used to allocate accumulated indirect costs to Federally sponsored agreements or similar final cost objectives. A continuation sheet should be used wherever additional space is required or when a response requires further explanation to ensure clarity and understanding.

The following Allocation Base Codes are provided for use in connection with Items 3.1.0 and 3.3.0.

A. Direct charge or Allocation
B. Total Expenditures
C. Modified Total Cost Basis
D. Modified Total Direct Cost Basis
E. Salaries and Wages
F. Salaries, Wages and Fringe Benefits
G. Number of Employees (head count)
H. Number of Employees (full-time equivalent basis)
I. Number of Students (head count)
J. Number of Students (full-time equivalent basis)
K. Student Hours—classroom and work performed
L. Square Footage
M. Usage
N. Unit of Product
O. Total Production
P. More than one base (Separate Cost Groupings) [1]
Y. Other(s) [1]
Z. Category or Pool not applicable

[1] List on a continuation sheet, the category and subgrouping(s) of expense involved and the allocation base(s) used.

FORM CASB DS-2 (REV 10/94)   III-1

CASB 9903.202-10

COST ACCOUNTING STANDARDS BOARD DISCLOSURE STATEMENT REQUIRED BY PUBLIC LAW 100-679 EDUCATIONAL INSTITUTIONS	PART III—INDIRECT COSTS
	NAME OF REPORTING UNIT

Item No.	Item Description
3.1.0	*Indirect Cost Categories—Accumulation and Allocation.* This item is directed at the identification, accumulation and allocation of all indirect costs of the institution. (Under the column heading, "Accumulation Method," insert "Yes" or "No" to indicate if the cost elements included in each indirect cost category are identified, recorded and accumulated in the institution's formal accounting system. If "No," describe on a continuation sheet, how the cost elements included in the indirect cost category are identified and accumulated. Under the column heading "Allocation Base," enter one of the allocation base codes A through P, Y, or Z, to indicate the basis used for allocating the accumulated costs of each indirect cost category to other applicable indirect cost categories, indirect cost pools, other institutional activities, specialized service facilities and other service centers. Under the column heading "Allocation Sequence," insert 1, 2, or 3 next to each of the first three indirect cost categories to indicate the sequence of the allocation process. If cross-allocation techniques are used, insert "CA." If an indirect cost category listed in this section is not used, insert "NA.")

Indirect Cost Category	Accumulation Method	Allocation Base Code	Allocation Sequence
(a) Depreciation/Use Allowances/Interest			____
Building	____	____	
Equipment	____	____	
Capital Improvements to Land [1]	____	____	
Interest [1]	____	____	
(b) Operation and Maintenance	____	____	____
(c) General Administration and General Expense	____	____	____
(d) Departmental Administration	____	____	
(e) Sponsored Projects Administration	____	____	
(f) Library	____	____	
(g) Student Administration and Services	____	____	
(h) Other [1]			

[1] Describe on a Continuation Sheet.

CASB 9903.202-10

COST ACCOUNTING STANDARDS BOARD DISCLOSURE STATEMENT REQUIRED BY PUBLIC LAW 100-679 EDUCATIONAL INSTITUTIONS	PART III—INDIRECT COSTS
	NAME OF REPORTING UNIT

Item No.	Item Description

3.2.0 *Service Centers.* Service centers are department or functional units which perform specific technical or administrative services primarily for the benefit of other units within a reporting unit. Service Centers include "recharge centers" and the "specialized service facilities" defined in Section J of Circular A-21. (The codes identified below should be inserted on the appropriate line for each service center listed. The column numbers correspond to the paragraphs listed below that provide the codes. Explain on a Continuation Sheet if any of the services are charged to users on a basis other than usage of the services. Enter "Z" in Column 1, if not applicable.)

	(1)	(2)	(3)	(4)	(5)	(6)
(a) Scientific Computer Operations	___	___	___	___	___	___
(b) Business Data Processing	___	___	___	___	___	___
(c) Animal Care Facilities	___	___	___	___	___	___
(d) Other Service Centers with Annual Operating Budgets exceeding $1,000,000 or that generate significant charges to Federally sponsored agreements either as a direct or indirect cost. (Specify below; use a Continuation Sheet, if necessary)						
_____	___	___	___	___	___	___
_____	___	___	___	___	___	___

(1) *Category Code:* Use code "A" if the service center costs are billed only as direct costs of final cost objectives; code "B" if billed only to indirect cost categories or indirect cost pools; code "C" if billed to both direct and indirect cost objectives.

(2) *Burden Code:* Code "A"—center receives an allocation of all applicable indirect costs; Code "B"—partial allocation of indirect costs; Code "C"—no allocation of indirect costs.

(3) *Billing Rate Code:* Code "A"—billing rates are based on historical costs; Code "B"—rates are based on projected costs; Code "C"—rates are based on a combination of historical and projected costs; Code "D"—billings are based on the actual costs of the billing period; Code "Y"—other (explain on a Continuation Sheet).

(4) *User Charges Code:* Code "A"—all users are charged at the same billing rates; Code "B"—some users are charged at different rates than other users (explain on a Continuation Sheet).

(5) *Actual Costs vs. Revenues Code:* Code "A"—billings (revenues) are compared to actual costs (expenditures) at least annually; Code "B"—billings are compared to actual costs less frequently than annually.

(6) *Variance Code:* Code "A"—Annual variances between billed and actual costs are prorated to users (as credits or charges); Code "B"—variances are carried forward as adjustments to billing rate of future periods; Code "C"—annual variances are charged or credited to indirect costs; Code "Y"—other (explain on a Continuation Sheet).

FORM CASB DS-2 (REV 10/94)   III-3

CASB **9903.202-10**

COST ACCOUNTING STANDARDS BOARD DISCLOSURE STATEMENT REQUIRED BY PUBLIC LAW 100-679 EDUCATIONAL INSTITUTIONS	PART III—INDIRECT COSTS
	NAME OF REPORTING UNIT

Item No.	Item Description

3.3.0	**Indirect Cost Pools and Allocation Bases**
	
	(Identify all of the indirect cost pools established for the accumulation of indirect costs, excluding service centers, and the allocation bases used to distributed accumulated indirect costs to Federally sponsored agreements or similar cost objectives within each major function or activity. For all applicable indirect cost pools, enter the applicable Allocation Base Code A through P, Y, or Z, to indicate the basis used for allocating accumulated pool costs to Federally sponsored agreements or similar cost objectives.)
	
	Indirect Cost Pools Allocation Base Code
	
	A. Instruction
	
	   _____ On-Campus _____
	   _____ Off-Campus _____
	   _____ Other[1] _____
	
	B. Organized Research
	
	   _____ On-Campus _____
	   _____ Off-Campus _____
	   _____ Other[1] _____
	
	C. Other Sponsored Activities
	
	   _____ On-Campus _____
	   _____ Off-Campus _____
	   _____ Other[1] _____
	
	D. Other Institutional Activities [1] _____

3.4.0	*Composition of Indirect Cost Pools.* (For each pool identified under Items 3.1.0 and 3.2.0, describe on a continuation sheet the major organizational components, subgroupings of expenses, and elements of cost included.) [1] Describe on a Continuation Sheet.

FORM CASB DS-2 (REV 10/94)   III-4

COST ACCOUNTING STANDARDS BOARD DISCLOSURE STATEMENT REQUIRED BY PUBLIC LAW 100-679 EDUCATIONAL INSTITUTIONS	PART III—INDIRECT COSTS
	NAME OF REPORTING UNIT

Item No.	Item Description
3.5.0	*Composition of Allocation Bases.* (For each allocation base code used in Items 3.1.0 and 3.3.0, describe on a continuation sheet the makeup of the base. For example, if a modified total direct cost base is used, specify which of the elements of direct cost identified in Part II, Direct Costs, that are included, e.g., materials, salaries and wages, fringe benefits, travel costs, and excluded, e.g., subcontract costs over first $25,000. Where applicable, explain if service centers are included or excluded. Specify the benefitting functions and activities included. If any cost objectives are excluded from the allocation base, such cost objectives and the alternate allocation method used should be identified. If an indirect cost allocation is based on Cost Analysis Studies, identify the study, and fully describe the study methods and techniques applied, the composition of the specific allocation base used, and the frequency of each recurring study.
3.6.0	*Allocation of Indirect Costs to Programs That Pay Less Than Full Indirect Costs.* Are appropriate direct costs of all programs and activites included in the indirect cost allocation bases, regardless of whether allocable indirect costs are fully reimbursed by the sponsoring organizations? A. _____ Yes B. _____ No [1] [1] Describe on a Continuation Sheet.

FORM CASB DS-2 (REV 10/94)   III-5

CASB 9903.202-10

COST ACCOUNTING STANDARDS BOARD DISCLOSURE STATEMENT REQUIRED BY PUBLIC LAW 100-679 EDUCATIONAL INSTITUTIONS	PART IV—DEPRECIATION AND USE ALLOWANCES
	NAME OF REPORTING UNIT

Item No.	Item Description
	Part IV
4.1.0	*Depreciation Charged to Federally Sponsored Agreements or Similar Cost Objectives.* (For each asset category listed below, enter a code from A through C in Column (1) describing the method of depreciation; a code from A through D in Column (2) describing the basis for determining userful life; a code from A through C in column (3) describing how depreciation methods or use allowance are applied to property units; and Code A or B in Column (4) indicating whether or not the estimated residual value is deducted from the total cost of depreciable assets. Enter Code Y is each column of an asset category where another or more than one method applies. Enter Code Z in Column (1) only, if an asset category is not applicable.)

Asset Category	Depreciation Method	Useful Life	Property Unit	Residual Value
	(1)	(2)	(3)	(4)
(a) Land Improvements	___	___	___	___
(b) Buildings	___	___	___	___
(c) Building Improvements	___	___	___	___
(d) Leasehold Improvements	___	___	___	___
(e) Equipment	___	___	___	___
(f) Furniture and Fixtures	___	___	___	___
(g) Automobiles and Trucks	___	___	___	___
(h) Tools	___	___	___	___
(i) Enter Code Y on this line if other asset categories are used and enumerate on a continuation sheet each such asset category and the applicable codes. (Otherwise enter Code Z.)	___	___	___	___

Column (1)—Depreciation Method Code

A. Straight Line
B. Expensed at Acquisition
C. Use Allowance
Y. Other or more than one method [1]

Column (2)—Useful Life Code

A. Replacement Experience
B. Term of Lease
C. Estimated service life
D. As prescribed for use allowance by Office of Management and Budget Circular No. A-21
Y. Other or more than one method [1]

Column (3)—Property Unit Code

A. Individual units are accounted for separately
B. Applied to groups of assets with similar service lives
C. Applied to groups of assets with varying service lives
Y. Other or more than one method [1]

Column (4)—Residual Value Code

A. Residual value is deducted
B. Residual value is not deducted
Y. Other or more than one method [1]

[1] Describe on a Continuation Sheet.

FORM CASB DS-2 (REV 10/94)   IV-1

CASB 9903.202-10

COST ACCOUNTING STANDARDS BOARD DISCLOSURE STATEMENT REQUIRED BY PUBLIC LAW 100-679 EDUCATIONAL INSTITUTIONS	PART IV—DEPRECIATION AND USE ALLOWANCES
	NAME OF REPORTING UNIT

Item No.	Item Description
4.1.1	Asset Valuations and Useful Lives. Are the asset valuations and useful lives used in your indirect cost proposal consistent with those used in the institution's financial statements? (Mark one.) A. _____ Yes B. _____ No [1]
4.2.0	*Fully Depreciated Assets.* Is a usage charge for fully depreciated assets charged to Federally sponsored agreements or similar cost objectives? (Mark one. If yes, describe the basis for the charge on a continuation sheet.) A. _____ Yes B. _____ No

4.3.0	*Treatment of Gains and Losses on Disposition of Depreciable Property.* Gains and losses are: (Mark the appropriate line(s) and if more than one is marked, explain on a continuation sheet.)
	
	A. _____ Excluded from determination of sponsored agreement costs
	B. _____ Credited or charged currently to the same pools to which the depreciation
	              of the assets was original charged
	C. _____ Taken into consideration in the depreciation cost basis of the new items,
	              where trade-in is involved
	D. _____ Not accounted for separately, but reflected in the depreciation reserve
	              account
	Y. _____ Other(s) [1]
	Z. _____ Not applicable

4.4.0	*Criteria for Capitalization.* (Enter (a) the minimum dollar amount of expenditures which are capitalized for acquisition, addition, alteration, donation and improvement of capital assets, and (b) the minimum number of expected life years of assets which are capitalized. If more than one dollar amount or number applies, show the information for the majority of your capitalized assets, and enumerate on a continuation sheet the dollar amounts and/or number of years for each category or subcategory of assets involved which differs from those for the majority of assets.) A. Minimum Dollar Amount _____ B. Minimum Life Years _____
4.5.0	*Group or Mass Purchase.* Are group or mass purchases (initial complement) of similar items, which individually are less than the capitalization amount indicated above, capitalized? (Mark one.) A. _____ Yes [1] B. _____ No [1] Describe on a Continuation Sheet.

CASB 9903.202-10

COST ACCOUNTING STANDARDS BOARD DISCLOSURE STATEMENT REQUIRED BY PUBLIC LAW 100-679 EDUCATIONAL INSTITUTIONS	PART V—OTHER COSTS AND CREDITS
	NAME OF REPORTING UNIT

Item No.	Item Description
	Part V
5.1.0	*Method of Charging Leave Costs.* Do you charge vacation, sick, holiday and sabbatical leave costs to sponsored agreements on the cash basis of accounting (i.e., when the leave is taken or paid), or on the accrual basis of accounting (when the leave is earned)? (Mark applicable line(s)) A. _____ Cash B. _____ Accrual [1]
5.2.0	*Applicable Credits.* This item is directed at the treatment of "applicable credits" as defined in Section C of OMB Circular A-21 and other incidental receipts (e.g., purchase discounts, insurance refunds, library fees and fines, parking fees, etc.). (Indicate how the principal types of credits and incidental receipts the institution receives are usually handled.) A. _____ The credits/receipts are offset against the specific direct or indirect costs to which they relate. B. _____ The credits/receipts are handled as a general adjustment to the indirect pool. C. _____ The credits/receipts are treated as income and are not offset against costs. D. _____ Combination of methods [1] Y. _____ Other [1] [1] Describe on a Continuation Sheet.

FORM CASB DS-2 (REV 10/94)   V-1

COST ACCOUNTING STANDARDS BOARD DISCLOSURE STATEMENT REQUIRED BY PUBLIC LAW 100-679 EDUCATIONAL INSTITUTIONS	PART VI—DEFERRED COMPENSATION AND INSURANCE COSTS
	NAME OF REPORTING UNIT

Item No.	Item Description
	Instructions for Part VI
	This part covers the measurement and assignment of costs for employee pensions, post retirement benefits other than pensions (including post retirement health benefits) and insurance. Some organizations may incur all of these costs at the main campus level or for public institutions at the governmental unit level, while others may incur them at subordinate organization levels. Still others may incur a portion of these costs at the main campus level and the balance at subordinate organization levels.
	Where the segment (reporting unit) does not directly incur such costs, the segment should, on a continuation sheet, identify the organizational entity that incurs and records such costs. When the costs allocated to Federally sponsored agreements are material, and the reporting unit does not have access to the information needed to complete an item, the reporting unit should require that entity to complete the applicable portions of this Part VI. (See item 4, page (i), General Instructions)
6.1.0	Pension Plans.
6.1.1	Defined-Contribution Pension Plans. Identify the types and number of pension plans whose costs are charged to Federally sponsored agreements. (Mark applicable line(s) and enter number of plans.)
	Type of Plan Number of Plans
	A. _____ Institution employees participate in _____ in State/Local Government Retirement Plan(s)
	B. _____ Institution uses TIAA/CREF plan or _____ other defined contribution plan that is managed by an organization not affiliated with the institution
	C. _____ Institution has its one Defined- _____ Contribution Plan(s) [1]
6.1.2	Defined-Benefit Pension Plan. (For each defined-benefit plan (other than plans that are part of a State or Local government pension plan) describe on a continuation sheet the actuarial cost method, the asset valuation method, the criteria for changing actuarial assumptions and computations, the amortization periods for prior service costs, the amortization periods for actuarial gains and losses, and the funding policy.)
	[1] Describe on a Continuation Sheet.

FORM CASB DS-2 (REV 10/94)   VI-1

CASB 9903.202-10

COST ACCOUNTING STANDARDS BOARD DISCLOSURE STATEMENT REQUIRED BY PUBLIC LAW 100-679 EDUCATIONAL INSTITUTIONS	PART VI—DEFERRED COMPENSATION AND INSURANCE COSTS
	NAME OF REPORTING UNIT

Item No.	Item Description
6.2.0	*Post Retirement Benefits Other Than Pensions (including post retirement health care benefits) (PRBs).* (Identify on a continuation sheet all PRB plans whose costs are charged to Federally sponsored agreements. For each plan listed, state the plan name and indicate the approximate number and type of employees covered by each plan.) Z. [ ] Not Applicable
6.2.1	Determination of Annual PRB Costs. (On a continuation sheet, indicate whether PRB costs charged to Federally sponsored agreements are determined on the cash or accrual basis of accounting. If costs are accrued, describe the accounting practices used, including actuarial cost method, the asset valuation method, the criteria for changing actuarial assumptions and computations, the amortization periods for prior service costs, the amortization periods for actuarial gains and losses, and the funding policy.)
6.3.0	*Self-Insurance Programs (Employee Group Insurance).* Costs of the self-insurance programs are charged to Federally sponsored agreements or similar cost objectives: (Mark one.) A. _____ When accrued (book accrual only) B. _____ When contributions are made to a nonforfeitable fund C. _____ When contributions are made to a forfeitable fund D. _____ When the benefits are paid to an employee E. _____ When amounts are paid to an employee welfare plan Y. _____ Other or more than one method [1] Z. _____ Not Applicable
6.4.0	*Self-Insurance Programs* (Worker's Compensation, Liability and Casualty Insurance.)
6.4.1	Worker's Compensation and Liability. Costs of such self-insurance programs are charged to Federally sponsored agreements or similar cost objectives: (Mark one.) A. _____ When claims are paid or losses are incurred (no provision for reserves) B. _____ When provision sfor reserves are recorded based on the present value of the liability C. _____ When provisions for reserves are recorded based on the full or undiscounted value, as contrasted with present value, of the liability D. _____ When funds are set aside or contributions are made to a fund Y. _____ Other or more than one method [1] Z. _____ Not Applicable [1] Describe on a Continuation Sheet.

FORM CASB DS-2 (REV 10/94)   VI-2

COST ACCOUNTING STANDARDS BOARD DISCLOSURE STATEMENT REQUIRED BY PUBLIC LAW 100-679 EDUCATIONAL INSTITUTIONS	PART VI—DEFERRED COMPENSATION AND INSURANCE COSTS
	NAME OF REPORTING UNIT

Item No.	Item Description
6.4.2	Casualty Insurance. Costs of such self-insurance programs are charged to Federally sponsored agreements or similar cost objectives: (Mark one.) A. _____ When losses are incurred (no provision for reserves) B. _____ When provisions for reserves are recorded based on replacement costs C. _____ When provisions for reserves are recorded based on reproduction costs new less observed depreciation (market value) excluding the value of land and other indestructibles. D. _____ Losses are charged to fund balance with no charge to contracts and grants (no provision for reserves) Y. _____ Other or more than one method [1] Z. _____ Not Applicable [1] Describe on a Continuation Sheet.

FORM CASB DS-2 (REV 10/94)   VI-3

CASB 9903.202-10

COST ACCOUNTING STANDARDS BOARD DISCLOSURE STATEMENT REQUIRED BY PUBLIC LAW 100-679 EDUCATIONAL INSTITUTIONS	PART VII—CENTRAL SYSTEM OR GROUP EXPENSES
	NAME OF REPORTING UNIT

Item No.	Item Description
	DISCLOSURE BY CENTRAL SYSTEM OFFICE, OR GROUP (INTERMEDIATE ADMINISTRATION) OFFICE, AS APPLICABLE. Instructions for Part VII This part should be completed *only* by the central system office or a group office of an educational system when that office is responsible for administering two or more segments, where it allocates its costs to such segments and where at least one of the segments is required to file Parts 1 through VI of the Disclosure Statement. The reporting unit (central system or group office) should disclose how costs of services provided by the reporting unit are, or will be, accumulated and allocated to applicable segments of the institution. For a central system office, disclosure should cover the entire institution. For a group office, disclosure should cover all of the subordinate organizations administered by that group office.
7.1.0	Organizational Structure. On a continuation sheet, list all segments of the university or university system, including hospitals, Federally Funded Research and Development Centers (FFRDC's), Government-owned Contractor-operated (GOCO) facilities, and lower-tier group offices serviced by the reporting unit.
7.2.0	Cost Accumulation and Allocation. On a continuation sheet, provide a description of: A. The services provided to segments of the university or university system (including hospitals, FFRDC's, GOCO facilities, etc.), in brief. B. How the costs of the services are identified and accumulated. C. The basis used to allocate the accumulated costs to the benefitting segments. D. Any costs that are transferred from a segment *to* the central system office or the intermediate administrative office, and which are reallocated to another segment(s). If none, so state. E. Any fixed management fees that are charged to a segment(s) in lieu of a prorata or allocation basis and the basis of such charges. If none, so state.

FORM CASB DS-2 (REV 10/94)   VII-1

[Final rule, 59 FR 55746, 11/8/94, effective 1/9/95]

SUBPART 9903.3—CAS RULES AND REGULATIONS

9903.301 Definitions.

(a) The definitions set forth below apply to this chapter 99.

Accrued benefit cost method. See 9904.412-30.

Accumulating costs. See 9904.401-30.

Actual cash value. See 9904.401-30.

Actual cost. See 9904.401-30 for the broader definition and 9904.407-30 for a more restricted definition applicable only to the standard on the use of standard costs for direct material and direct labor.

Actuarial assumption. See 9904.412-30 or 9904.413-30.

Actuarial cost method. See 9904.412-30 or 9904.413-30.

Actuarial gain and loss. See 9904.412-30 or 9904.413-30.

Actuarial liability. See 9904.412-30 or 9904.413-30.

Actuarial valuation. See 9904.412-30 or 9904.413-30.

Allocate. See 9904.402-30, 9904.403-30, 9904.406-30, 9904.410-30, 9904.411-30, 9904.418-30 or 9904.420-30.

Asset accountability unit. See 9904.404-30.

Assignment of cost to cost accounting periods. See 9903.302-1(b).

Bid and proposal (B&P) cost. See 9904.420-30.

Business unit. See 9904.410-30, 9904.411-30 or 9904.414-30.

CAS-covered contract, as used in this part, means any negotiated contract or subcontract in which a CAS clause is required to be included.

Category of material. See 9904.411-30.

Change to a cost accounting practice. See 9903.302-2.

Compensated personal absence. See 9904.408-30.

Cost accounting practice. See 9903.302-1.

Cost input. See 9904.410-30.

Cost objective. See 9904.402-30, 9904.406-30, 9904.410-30 or 9904.411-30.

Cost of capital committed to facilities. See 9904.414-30.

Currently performing, as used in this part, means that a contractor has been awarded a contract, but has not yet received notification of final acceptance of all supplies, services, and data deliverable under the contract (including options).

Deferred compensation. See 9904.415-30.

Defined-benefit pension plan. See 9904.412-30.

Defined-contribution pension plan. See 9904.412-30.

Direct cost. See 9904.402-30 or 9904.418-30.

Directly associated cost. See 9904.405-30.

Disclosure statement, as used in this part, means the Disclosure Statement required by 9903.202-1.

Entitlement. See 9904.408-30.

Estimating costs. See 9904.401-30.

Expressly unallowable cost. See 9904.405-30.

Facilities capital. See 9904.414-30.

Final cost objective. See 9904.402-30 or 9904.410-30.

Fiscal year. See 9904.406-30.

Funded pension cost. See 9904.412-30.

Funding agency. See 9904.412-30.

General and administrative (G&A) expense. See 9904.410-30 or 9904.420-30.

Home office. See 9904.403-30 or 9904.420-30.

Immediate-gain actuarial cost method See 9904.413-30.

Independent research and development (IR&D) cost. See 9904.420-30.

Indirect cost. See 9904.402-30, 9904.405-30, 9904.418-30 or 9904.420-30.

Indirect cost pool. See 9904.401-30, 9904.402-30, 9904.406-30 or 9904.418-30.

Insurance administration expenses. See 9904.416-30.

Intangible capital asset. See 9904.414-30 or 9904.417-30.

Labor cost at standard. See 9904.407-30.

Labor-rate standard. See 9904.407-30.

Labor-time standard. See 9904.407-30.

Material cost at standard. See 9904.407-30.

Material inventory record. See 9904.411-30.

Material-price standard. See 9904.407-30.

Material-quantity standard. See 9904.407-30.

Measurement of cost. See 9904.302-1(c).

Moving average cost. See 9904.411-30.

Multiemployer pension plan. See 9904.412-30.

Negotiated subcontract, as used in this part, means any subcontract except a firm fixed-price subcontract made by a contractor or subcontractor after receiving offers from at least two persons not associated with each other or with such contractor or subcontractor, providing

(1) The solicitation to all competitors is identical.

(2) Price is the only consideration in selecting the subcontractor from among the competitors solicited, and

(3) The lowest offer received in compliance with the solicitation from among those solicited is accepted.

Net awards, as used in this Chapter, means the total value of negotiated CAS-covered prime contract and subcontract awards, including the potential value of contract options, received during the reporting period minus cancellations, terminations, and other related credit transactions.

Normal cost. See 9904.412-30 or 9904.413-30.

Operating revenue. See 9904.403-30.

Original complement of low cost equipment. See 9904.404-30.

Pay-as-you-go cost method. See 9904.412-30.

Pension plan. See 9904.412-30 or 9904.413-30.

Pension plan participant. See 9904.413-30.

Pricing. See 9904.401-30.

Production unit. See 9904.407-30.

Projected average loss. See 9904.416-30.

Projected benefit cost method. See 9904.412-30 or 9904.413-30.

Proposal. See 9904.401-30.

Repairs and maintenance. See 9904.404-30.

Reporting costs. See 9904.401-30.

Residual value. See 9904.409-30.

Segment. See 9904.403-30, 9904.410-30, 9904.413-30 or 9904.420-30.

Self-insurance. See 9904.416-30.

Self-insurance charge. See 9904.416-30.

Service life. See 9904.409-30.

Small business, as used in this part, means any concern, firm, person, corporation, partnership, cooperative, or other business enterprise which, under 15 U.S.C. 637(b)(6) and the rules and regulations of the Small Business Administration in Part 121 of Title 13 of the Code of Federal Regulations, is determined to be a small business concern for the purpose of Government contracting.

Spread-gain actuarial cost method. See 9904.413-30.

Standard cost. See 9904.407-30.

Tangible capital asset. See 9904.403-30, 9904.404-30, 9904.409-30, 9904.414-30 or 9904.417-30.

Termination gain or loss. See 9904.413-30.

Unallowable cost. See 9904.405-30.

Variance. See 9904.407-30.

Weighted average cost. See 9904.411-30.

(b) The definitions set forth below are applicable exclusively to educational institutions and apply to this chapter 99.

Business unit. See 9903.201-2(c)(2)(ii).

Educational institution. See 9903.201-2(c)(2)(i).

Intermediate cost objective. See 9905.502-30(a)(7).

Segment. See 9903.201-2(c)(2)(ii).

[Final rule, 58 FR 58798, 11/4/93, effective 11/4/93; Final rule, 59 FR 55746, 11/8/94, effective 1/9/95; Interim rule, 61 FR 39360, 7/29/96, effective 7/29/96, finalized without change, 62 FR 31294, 6/6/97, effective 6/6/97]

9903.302 Definitions, explanations, and illustrations of the terms, "cost accounting practice" and "change to a cost accounting practice." (No Text)

9903.302-1 Cost accounting practice.

Cost accounting practice, as used in this part, means any disclosed or established accounting method or technique which is used for allocation of cost to cost objectives, assignment of cost to cost accounting periods, or measurement of cost.

(a) *Measurement of cost,* as used in this part, encompasses accounting methods and techniques used in defining the components of cost, determining the basis for cost measurement, and establishing criteria for use of alternative cost measurement techniques. The determination of the amount paid or a change in the amount paid for a unit of goods and services is not a cost accounting practice. Examples of cost accounting practices which involve measurement of costs are—

(1) The use of either historical cost, market value, or present value;

(2) The use of standard cost or actual cost; or

(3) The designation of those items of cost which must be included or excluded from tangible capital assets or pension cost.

(b) *Assignment of cost to cost accounting periods,* as used in this part, refers to a method or technique used in determining the amount of cost to be assigned to individual cost accounting periods. Examples of cost accounting practices which involve the assignment of cost to cost accounting periods are requirements for the use of specified accrual basis accounting or cash basis accounting for a cost element.

(c) *Allocation of cost to cost objectives,* as used in this part, includes both direct and indirect allocation of cost. Examples of cost accounting practices involving allocation of cost to cost objectives are the accounting methods or techniques used to accumulate cost, to determine whether a cost is to be directly or indirectly allocated to determine the composition of cost pools, and to determine the selection and composition of the appropriate allocation base.

9903.302-2 Change to a cost accounting practice.

Change to a cost accounting practice, as used in this part, means any alteration in a cost accounting practice, as defined in 9903.302-1, whether or not such practices are covered by a Disclosure Statement, except for the following:

(a) The initial adoption of a cost accounting practice for the first time a cost is incurred, or a function is created, is not a change in cost accounting practice. The partial or total elimination of a cost or the cost of a function is not a change in cost accounting practice. As used here, function is an activity or group of activities that is identifiable in scope and has a purpose or end to be accomplished.

(b) The revision of a cost accounting practice for a cost which previously had been immaterial is not a change in cost accounting practice.

9903.302-3 Illustrations of changes which meet the definition of "change to a cost accounting practice."

(a) The method or technique used for measuring costs has been changed.

Description	Accounting treatment
(1) Contractor changes its actuarial cost method for computing pension costs	(1)(i)Before change: The contractor computed pension costs using the aggregate cost method. (ii) After change: The contractor computes pension cost using the unit credit method.
(2) Contractor uses standard costs to account for its direct labor. Labor cost at standard was computed by multiplying labor-time	(2)(i) Before change: Contractor's direct labor cost was measured with only one component set at standard.

CASB 9903.302-3

Description	Accounting treatment
standard by actual labor rates. The contractor changes the computation by multiplying labor-time standard by labor-rate standard.	(ii) After change: Contractor's direct labor cost is measured with both the time and rate components set at standard.

(b) The method or technique used for assignment of cost to cost accounting periods has been changed.

Description	Accounting treatment
(1) Contractor changes his established criteria for capitalizing certain classes of tangible capital assets whose acquisition costs totaled $1 million per cost accounting period.	(1)(i) Before change: Items having acquisition costs of between $200 and $400 per unit were capitalized and depreciated over a number of cost accounting periods. (ii) After change: The contractor charges the value of assets costing between $200 and $400 per unit to an indirect expense pool which is allocated to the cost objectives of the cost accounting period in which the cost was incurred.
(2) Contractor changes his methods for computing depreciation for a class of assets.	(2)(i) Before change: The contractor assigned depreciation costs to cost accounting periods using an accelerated method. (ii) After change: The contractor assigns depreciation costs to cost accounting periods using the straight line method.
(3) Contractor changes his general method of determining asset lives for classes of assets acquired prior to the effective date of CAS 409.	(3)(i) Before change: The contractor identified the cost accounting periods to which the cost of tangible capital assets would be assigned using guideline class lives provided in IRS Rev. Pro. 72-10. (ii) After change: The contractor changes the method by which he identifies the cost accounting periods to which the costs of tangible capital assets will be assigned. He now uses the expected actual lives based on past usage.

(c) The method or technique used for allocating costs has been changed.

Description	Accounting treatment
(1) Contractor changes his method of allocating G&A expenses under the requirements of Cost Accounting Standard 410.	(1)(i) Before change: The contractor operating under Cost Accounting Standard 410 has been allocating his general and administrative expense pool to final cost objectives on a total cost input base in compliance with the Standard. The contractor's business changes substantially such that there are significant new projects which have only insignificant quantities of material.

Description	Accounting treatment
	(ii) After change: After the addition of the new work, an evaluation of the changed circumstances reveals that the continued use of a total cost input base would result in a significant distortion in the allocation of the G&A expense pool in relation to the benefits received. To remain in compliance with Standard 410, the contractor alters his G&A allocation base from a total cost input base to a value added base.
(2) The contractor changes the accounting for hardware common to all projects.	(2)(i) Before change: The contractor allocated the cost of purchased or requisitioned hardware directly to projects.
	(ii) After change: The contractor charges the cost of purchased or requisitioned hardware to an indirect expense pool which is allocated to projects using an appropriate allocation base.
(3) The contractor merges operating segments A and B which use different cost accounting practices in accounting for manufacturing overhead costs.	(3)(i) Before change: In segment A, the costs of the manufacturing overhead pool have been allocated to final cost objectives using a direct labor hours base; in segment B, the costs of the manufacturing overhead pool have been allocated to final cost objectives using a direct labor dollars base.
	(ii) After change: As a result of the merger of operations, the combined segment decides to allocate the cost of the manufacturing overhead pool to all final cost objectives, using a direct labor dollars base. Thus, for those final cost objectives referred to in segment A, the cost of the manufacturing overhead pool will be allocated to the final cost objectives of segment A using a direct labor dollars base instead of a direct labor hours base.

9903.302-4 Illustrations of changes which do not meet the definition of "Change to a cost accounting practice."

Description	Accounting treatment
(a) Changes in the interest rate levels in the national economy have invalidated the prior actuarial assumption with respect to anticipated investment earnings. The pension plan administrators adopted an increased (decreased) interest rate actuarial assumption. The company allocated the resulting pension costs to all final cost objectives.	(a) Adopting the increase (decrease) in the interest rate actuarial assumption is not a change in cost accounting practice.
(b) The basic benefit amount for a company's pension plan is increased from $8 to $10 per year of credited service. The change increases the dollar amount of pension cost allocated to all final cost objectives.	(b) The increase in the amount of the benefits is not a change in cost accounting practice.
(c) A contractor who has never paid pensions establishes for the first time a pension plan. Pension costs for the first year amounted to $3.5 million.	(c) The initial adoption of an accounting practice for the first time incurrence of a cost is not a change in cost accounting practice.

CASB 9903.302-4

Description	Accounting treatment
(d) A contractor maintained a Deferred Incentive Compensation Plan. After several years' experience, the plan was determined not to be attaining its objective, so it was terminated, and no future entitlements were paid.	(d) There was a termination of the Deferred Incentive Compensation Plan. Elimination of a cost is not a change in cost accounting practice.
(e) A contractor eliminates a segment that was operated for the purpose of doing research for development of products related to nuclear energy.	(e) The projects and expenses related to nuclear energy projects have been terminated. No transfer of these projects and no further work in this area is planned. This is an elimination of cost and not a change in cost accounting practice.
(f) For a particular class of assets for which technological changes have rarely affected asset lives, a contractor starts with a 5-year average of historical lives to estimate future lives. He then considers technological changes and likely use. For the past several years the process resulted in an estimated future life of 10 years for this class of assets. This year a technological change leads to a prediction of a useful life of 7 years for the assets acquired this year for the class of assets.	(f) The change in estimate (not in method) is not a change in cost accounting practice. The contractor has not changed the method or technique used to determine the estimate. The methodology applied has indicated a change in the estimated life, and this is not a change in cost accounting practice.
(g) The marketing department of a segment has reported directly to the general manager of the segment. The costs of the marketing department have been combined as part of the segment's G&A expense pool. The company reorganizes and requires the marketing department to report directly to a vice president at corporate headquarters.	(g) After the organization change in the company's reporting structure, the parties agree that the appropriate recognition of the beneficial or causal relationship between the costs of the marketing department and the segment is to continue to combine these costs as part of the segment's G&A expense pool. Thus, the organizational change has not resulted in a change in cost accounting practice.

9903.303 Effect of filing Disclosure Statement.

(a) A disclosure of a cost accounting practice by a contractor does not determine the allowability of particular items of cost. Irrespective of the practices disclosed by a contractor, the question of whether or not, or the extent to which, a specific element of cost is allowed under a contract remains for consideration in each specific instance. Contractors are cautioned that the determination of the allowability of cost items will remain a responsibility of the contracting officers pursuant to the provisions of the applicable procurement regulations.

(b) The individual Disclosure Statement may be used in audits of contracts or in negotiation of prices leading to contracts. The authority of the audit agencies and the contracting officers is in no way abrogated by the material presented by the contractor in his Disclosure Statement. Contractors are cautioned that their disclosures must be complete and accurate; the practices disclosed may have a significant impact on ways in which contractors will be required to comply with Cost Accounting Standards.

9903.304 Concurrent full and modified coverage.

Contracts subject to full coverage may be performed during a period in which a previously awarded contract subject to modified coverage is being performed. Compliance with full coverage may compel the use of cost accounting practices that are not required under modified coverage. Under these circumstances the cost accounting practices applicable to contracts subject to modified coverage need not be changed. Any resulting differences in practices between contracts subject to full coverage and those subject to modified coverage shall not constitute a violation of 9904.401 and 9904.402. This principle also applies to contracts subject to modified coverage being performed during a period in which a previously awarded contract subject to full coverage is being performed.

9903.305 Materiality.

In determining whether amounts of cost are material or immaterial, the following criteria shall be considered where appropriate; no one criterion is necessarily determinative:

(a) The absolute dollar amount involved. The larger the dollar amount, the more likely that it will be material.

(b) The amount of contract cost compared with the amount under consideration. The larger the proportion of the amount under consideration to contract cost, the more likely it is to be material.

(c) The relationship between a cost item and a cost objective. Direct cost items, especially if the amounts are themselves part of a base for allocation of indirect costs, will normally have more impact than the same amount of indirect costs.

(d) The impact on Government funding. Changes in accounting treatment will have more impact if they influence the distribution of costs between Government and non-Government cost objectives than if all cost objectives have Government financial support.

(e) The cumulative impact of individually immaterial items. It is appropriate to consider whether such impacts

(1) Tend to offset one another, or

(2) Tend to be in the same direction and hence to accumulate into a material amount.

(f) The cost of administrative processing of the price adjustment modification shall be considered. If the cost to process exceeds the amount to be recovered, it is less likely the amount will be material.

9903.306 Interpretations.

In determining amounts of increased costs in the clauses at 9903.201-4(a), Cost Accounting Standards, 9903.201-4(c), Disclosure and Consistency of Cost Accounting Practices, and 9903.201-4(d), Consistency in Cost Accounting, the following considerations apply:

(a) Increased costs shall be deemed to have resulted whenever the cost paid by the Government results from a change in a contractor's cost accounting practices or from failure to comply with applicable Cost Accounting Standards, and such cost is higher than it would have been had the practices not been changed or applicable Cost Accounting Standards complied with.

(b) If the contractor under any fixed-price contract, including a firm fixed-price contract, fails during contract performance to follow its cost accounting practices or to comply with applicable Cost Accounting Standards, increased costs are measured by the difference between the contract price agreed to and the contract price that would have been agreed to had the contractor proposed in accordance with the cost accounting practices used during contract performance. The determination of the contract price that would have been agreed to will be left to the contracting parties and will depend on the circumstances of each case.

(c) The statutory requirement underlying this interpretation is that the United States not pay increased costs, including a profit enlarged beyond that in the contemplation of the parties to the contract when the contract costs, price, or profit is negotiated, by reason of a contractor's failure to use applicable Cost Accounting Standards, or to follow consistently its cost accounting practices. In making price adjustments under the Cost Accounting Standards clause at 9903.201-4(a) in fixed price or cost reimbursement incentive contracts, or contracts providing for prospective or retroactive price redetermination, the Federal agency shall apply this requirement appropriately in the circumstances.

(d) The contractor and the contracting officer may enter into an agreement as contemplated by subdivision (a)(4)(ii) of the Cost Accounting Standards clause at 9903.201-4(a), covering a change in practice proposed by the Government or the contractor for all of the contractor's contracts for which the contracting officer is responsible, provided that the agreement does not permit any increase in the cost paid by the Government. Such agreement may be made final and binding, notwithstanding the fact that experience may subsequently establish that the actual impact of the change differed from that agreed to.

(e) An adjustment to the contract price or of cost allowances pursuant to the Cost Accounting Standards clause at 9903.201-4(a) may not be required when a change in cost accounting practices or a failure to follow Standards or cost accounting practices is estimated to result in increased costs being paid under a particular contract by the United States. This circumstance may arise when a contractor is performing two or more covered contracts, and the change or failure affects all such contracts. The change or failure may increase the cost paid under one or more of the contracts, while decreasing the cost paid under one or more of the contracts. In such case, the Government will not require price adjustment for any increased costs paid by the United States, so long as the cost decreases under one or more contracts are at least equal to the increased cost under the other affected contracts, provided that the contractor and the affected contracting officers agree on the method by which the price adjustments are to be made for all affected contracts. In this situation, the contracting agencies would, of course, require an adjustment of the contract price or cost allowances, as appropriate, to the extent that the increases under certain contracts were not offset by the decreases under the remaining contracts.

(f) Whether cost impact is recognized by modifying a single contract, several but not all contracts, or all contracts, or any other suitable technique, is a contract administration matter. The Cost Accounting Standards rules do not in any way restrict the capacity of the parties to select the method by which the cost impact attributable to a change in cost accounting practice is recognized.

9903.307 Cost Accounting Standards Preambles.

Preambles to the Cost Accounting Standards published by the original Cost Accounting Standards Board, as well as those preambles published by the signatories to the Federal Acquisition Regulation respecting changes made under their regulatory authorities, are available by writing to the: Publications Office, Office of Administration, Executive Office of the President, 725 17th Street NW., room 2200, Washington, DC 20500, or by calling (202) 395-7332.

PART 9904—COST ACCOUNTING STANDARDS
Table of Contents

PART 9904—COST ACCOUNTING STANDARDS

9904.400 [Reserved]

9904.401 Cost accounting standard—consistency in estimating, accumulating and reporting costs. (No Text)

9904.401-10 [Reserved]

9904.401-20 Purpose.

The purpose of this Cost Accounting Standard is to ensure that each contractor's practices used in estimating costs for a proposal are consistent with cost accounting practices used by him in accumulating and reporting costs. Consistency in the application of cost accounting practices is necessary to enhance the likelihood that comparable transactions are treated alike. With respect to individual contracts, the consistent application of cost accounting practices will facilitate the preparation of reliable cost estimates used in pricing a proposal and their comparison with the costs of performance of the resulting contract. Such comparisons provide one important basis for financial control over costs during contract performance and aid in establishing accountability for cost in the manner agreed to by both parties at the time of contracting. The comparisons also provide an improved basis for evaluating estimating capabilities.

9904.401-30 Definitions.

(a) The following are definitions of terms which are prominent in this Standard. Other terms defined elsewhere in this Part 99 shall have the meanings ascribed to them in those definitions unless paragraph (b) of this subsection, requires otherwise.

(1) *Accumulating costs* means the collecting of cost data in an organized manner, such as through a system of accounts.

(2) *Actual cost* means an amount determined on the basis of cost incurred (as distinguished from forecasted cost), including standard cost properly adjusted for applicable variance.

(3) *Estimating costs* means the process of forecasting a future result in terms of cost, based upon information available at the time.

(4) *Indirect cost pool* means a grouping of incurred costs identified with two or more objectives but not identified specifically with any final cost objective.

(5) *Pricing* means the process of establishing the amount or amounts to be paid in return for goods or services.

(6) *Proposal* means any offer or other submission used as a basis for pricing a contract, contract modification or termination settlement or for securing payments thereunder.

(7) *Reporting costs* means provision of cost information to others.

(b) The following modifications of terms defined elsewhere in this Chapter 99 are applicable to this Standard: None.

9904.401-40 Fundamental requirement.

(a) A contractor's practices used in estimating costs in pricing a proposal shall be consistent with his cost accounting practices used in accumulating and reporting costs.

(b) A contractor's cost accounting practices used in accumulating and reporting actual costs for a contract shall be consistent with his practices used in estimating costs in pricing the related proposal.

(c) The grouping of homogeneous costs in estimates prepared for proposal purposes shall not per se be deemed an inconsistent application of cost accounting practices under paragraphs (a) and (b) of this section when such costs are accumulated and reported in greater detail on an actual cost basis during contract performance.

9904.401-50 Techniques for application.

(a) The standard allows grouping of homogeneous costs in order to cover those cases where it is not practicable to estimate contract costs by individual cost element or function. However, costs estimated for proposal purposes shall be presented in such a manner and in such detail that any significant cost can be compared with the actual cost accumulated and reported therefor. In any event the cost accounting practices used

CASB 9904.401-50

in estimating costs in pricing a proposal and in accumulating and reporting costs on the resulting contract shall be consistent with respect to:

(1) The classification of elements or functions of cost as direct or indirect;

(2) The indirect cost pools to which each element or function of cost is charged or proposed to be charged; and

(3) The methods of allocating indirect costs to the contract.

(b) Adherence to the requirement of 9904.401-40(a) of this standard shall be determined as of the date of award of the contract, unless the contractor has submitted cost or pricing data pursuant to 10 U.S.C. 2306a or 41 U.S.C. 254(d) (Pub. L. 87-653), in which case adherence to the requirement of 9904.401-40(a) shall be determined as of the date of final agreement on price, as shown on the signed certificate of current cost or pricing data. Notwithstanding 9904.401-40(b), changes in established cost accounting practices during contract performance may be made in accordance with part 99.

9904.401-60 Illustrations.

(a) The following examples are illustrative of applications of cost accounting practices which are deemed to be consistent.

Practices used in estimating costs for proposals	Practices used in accumulating and reporting costs of contract performance
1. Contractor estimates an average direct labor rate for manufacturing direct labor by labor category or function.	1. Contractor records manufacturing direct labor based on actual cost for each individual and collects such costs by labor category or function.
2. Contractor estimates an average cost for minor standard hardware items, including nuts, bolts, washers, etc.	2. Contractor records actual cost for minor standard hardware items based upon invoices or material transfer slips.
3. Contractor uses an estimated rate for manufacturing overhead to be applied to an estimated direct labor base. He identifies the items included in his estimate of manufacturing overhead and provides supporting data for the estimated direct labor base.	3. Contractor accounts for manufacturing overhead by individual items of cost which are accumulated in a cost pool allocated to final cost objectives on a direct labor base.

(b) The following examples are illustrative of application of cost accounting practices which are deemed not to be consistent.

Practices used in estimating costs for proposals	Practices used in accumulating and reporting costs of contract performance
4. Contractor estimates a total dollar amount for engineering labor which includes disparate and significant elements or functions of engineering labor. Contractor does not provide supporting data reconciling this amount to the estimates for the same engineering labor cost functions for which he will separately account in contract performance.	4. Contractor accounts for engineering labor by cost function, i.e. drafting, designing, production, engineering, etc.
5. Contractor estimates engineering labor by cost function, i.e. drafting, production engineering, etc.	5. Contractor accumulates total engineering labor in one undifferentiated account.
6. Contractor estimates a single dollar amount for machining cost to cover labor, material and overhead.	6. Contractor records separately the actual costs of machining labor and material as direct costs, and factory overhead as indirect costs.

9904.401-61 Interpretation.

(a) 9904.401, Cost Accounting Standard—Consistency in Estimating, Accumulating and Reporting Costs, requires in 9904.401-40 that a contractor's "practices used in estimating costs in pricing a proposal shall be consistent with his cost accounting practices used in accumulating and reporting costs."

(b) In estimating the cost of direct material requirements for a contract, it is a common practice to first estimate the cost of the actual quantities to be incorporated in end items. Provisions are then made for additional direct material costs to cover expected material losses such as those which occur, for example, when items are scrapped, fail to meet specifications, are lost, consumed in the manufacturing process, or destroyed in testing and qualification processes. The cost of some or all of such additional direct material requirements is often estimated by the application of one or more percentage factors to the total cost of basic direct material requirements or to some other base.

(c) Questions have arisen as to whether the accumulation of direct material costs in an undifferentiated account where a contractor estimates a significant part of such costs by means of percentage factors is in compliance with 9904.401. The most serious questions pertain to such percentage factors which are not supported by the contractor with accounting, statistical, or other relevant data from past experience, nor by a program to accumulate actual costs for comparison with such percentage estimates. The accumulation of direct costs in an undifferentiated account in this circumstance is a cost accounting practice which is not consistent with the practice of estimating a significant part of costs by means of percentage factors. This situation is virtually identical with that described in Illustration 9904.401-60(b)(5), which deals with labor.

(d) 9904.401 does not, however, prescribe the amount of detail required in accumulating and reporting costs. The amount of detail required may vary considerably depending on the percentage factors used, the data presented in justification or lack thereof, and the significance of each situation. Accordingly, it is neither appropriate nor practical to prescribe a single set of accounting practices which would be consistent in all situations with the practices of estimating direct material costs by percentage factors. Therefore, the amount of accounting and statistical detail to be required and maintained in accounting for this portion of direct material costs has been and continues to be a matter to be decided by Government procurement authorities on the basis of the individual facts and circumstances.

9904.401-62 Exemption.

None for this Standard.

9904.401-63 Effective date.

This Standard is effective as of April 17, 1992.

[Corrected, 57 FR 34167, 8/3/92]

9904.402 Cost accounting standard—consistency in allocating costs incurred for the same purpose. (No Text)

9904.402-10 [Reserved]

9904.402-20 Purpose.

The purpose of this standard is to require that each type of cost is allocated only once and on only one basis to any contract or other cost objective. The criteria for determining the allocation of costs to a product, contract, or other cost objective should be the same for all similar objectives. Adherence to these cost accounting concepts is necessary to guard against the overcharging of some cost objectives and to prevent double counting. Double counting occurs most commonly when cost items are allocated directly to a cost objective without eliminating like cost items from indirect cost pools which are allocated to that cost objective.

9904.402-30 Definitions.

(a) The following are definitions of terms which are prominent in this standard. Other terms defined elsewhere in this Part 99 shall have the meanings ascribed to them in those definitions unless paragraph (b) of this section requires otherwise.

(1) *Allocate* means to assign an item of cost, or a group of items of cost, to one or more cost objectives. This term includes both direct assignment of cost and the reassignment of a share from an indirect cost pool.

(2) *Cost objective* means a function, organizational subdivision, contract, or other work unit for which cost data are desired and for which provision is made to accumulate and

CASB 9904.402-30

measure the cost to processes, products, jobs, capitalized projects, etc.

(3) *Direct cost* means any cost which is identified specifically with a particular final cost objective. Direct costs are not limited to items which are incorporated in the end product as material or labor. Costs identified specifically with a contract are direct costs of that contract. All costs identified specifically with other final cost objectives of the contractor are direct costs of those cost objectives.

(4) *Final cost objective* means a cost objective which has allocated to it both direct and indirect costs, and in the contractor's accumulation system, is one of the final accumulation points.

(5) *Indirect cost* means any cost not directly identified with a single final cost objective, but identified with two or more final cost objectives or with at least one intermediate cost objective.

(6) *Indirect cost pool* means a grouping of incurred costs identified with two or more cost objectives but not specifically identified with any final cost objective.

(b) The following modifications of terms defined elsewhere in this chapter 99 are applicable to this Standard: None.

9904.402-40 Fundamental requirement.

All costs incurred for the same purpose, in like circumstances, are either direct costs only or indirect costs only with respect to final cost objectives. No final cost objective shall have allocated to it as an indirect cost any cost, if other costs incurred for the same purpose, in like circumstances, have been included as a direct cost of that or any other final cost objective. Further, no final cost objective shall have allocated to it as a direct cost any cost, if other costs incurred for the same purpose, in like circumstances, have been included in any indirect cost pool to be allocated to that or any other final cost objective.

9904.402-50 Techniques for application.

(a) The Fundamental Requirement is stated in terms of cost incurred and is equally applicable to estimates of costs to be incurred as used in contract proposals.

(b) The Disclosure Statement to be submitted by the contractor will require that he set forth his cost accounting practices with regard to the distinction between direct and indirect costs. In addition, for those types of cost which are sometimes accounted for as direct and sometimes accounted for as indirect, the contractor will set forth in his Disclosure Statement the specific criteria and circumstances for making such distinctions. In essence, the Disclosure Statement submitted by the contractor, by distinguishing between direct and indirect costs, and by describing the criteria and circumstances for allocating those items which are sometimes direct and sometimes indirect, will be determinative as to whether or not costs are incurred for the same purpose. Disclosure Statement as used herein refers to the statement required to be submitted by contractors as a condition of contracting as set forth in subpart 9903.2.

(c) In the event that a contractor has not submitted a Disclosure Statement, the determination of whether specific costs are directly allocable to contracts shall be based upon the contractor's cost accounting practices used at the time of contract proposal.

(d) Whenever costs which serve the same purpose cannot equitably be indirectly allocated to one or more final cost objectives in accordance with the contractor's disclosed accounting practices, the contractor may either:

(1) Use a method for reassigning all such costs which would provide an equitable distribution to all final cost objectives, or

(2) Directly assign all such costs to final cost objectives with which they are specifically identified.

In the event the contractor decides to make a change for either purpose, the Disclosure Statement shall be amended to reflect the revised accounting practices involved.

(e) Any direct cost of minor dollar amount may be treated as an indirect cost for reasons of practicality where the accounting treatment for such cost is consistently applied to all final cost objectives, provided that such treatment produces results which are substantially the same as the results which would have been obtained if such cost had been treated as a direct cost.

9904.402-60 Illustrations.

(a) Illustrations of costs which are incurred for the same purpose:

(1) Contractor normally allocates all travel as an indirect cost and previously disclosed this accounting practice to the Government. For purposes of a new proposal, contractor intends to allocate the travel costs of personnel whose time is accounted for as direct labor directly to the contract. Since travel costs of personnel whose time is accounted for as direct labor working on other contracts are costs which are incurred for the same purpose, these costs may no longer be included within indirect cost pools for purposes of allocation to any covered Government contract. Contractor's Disclosure Statement must be amended for the proposed changes in accounting practices.

(2) Contractor normally allocates planning costs indirectly and allocates this cost to all contracts on the basis of direct labor. A proposal for a new contract requires a disproportionate amount of planning costs. The contractor prefers to continue to allocate planning costs indirectly. In order to equitably allocate the total planning costs, the contractor may use a method for allocating all such costs which would provide an equitable distribution to all final cost objectives. For example, he may use the number of planning documents processed rather than his former allocation base of direct labor. Contractor's Disclosure Statement must be amended for the proposed changes in accounting practices.

(b) Illustrations of costs which are not incurred for the same purpose:

(1) Contractor normally allocates special tooling costs directly to contracts. The costs of general purpose tooling are normally included in the indirect cost pool which is allocated to contracts. Both of these accounting practices were previously disclosed to the Government. Since both types of costs involved were not incurred for the same pur-

pose in accordance with the criteria set forth in the Contractor's Disclosure Statement, the allocation of general purpose tooling costs from the indirect cost pool to the contract, in addition to the directly allocated special tooling costs, is not considered a violation of the standard.

(2) Contractor proposes to perform a contract which will require three firemen on 24-hour duty at a fixed-post to provide protection against damage to highly inflammable materials used on the contract. Contractor presently has a firefighting force of 10 employees for general protection of the plant. Contractor's costs for these latter firemen are treated as indirect costs and allocated to all contracts; however, he wants to allocate the three fixed-post firemen directly to the particular contract requiring them and also allocate a portion of the cost of the general firefighting force to the same contract. He may do so but only on condition that his disclosed practices indicate that the costs of the separate classes of firemen serve different purposes and that it is his practice to allocate the general firefighting force indirectly and to allocate fixed-post firemen directly.

9904.402-61 Interpretation.

(a) 9904.402, Cost Accounting Standard—Consistency in Allocating Costs Incurred for the Same Purpose, provides, in 9904.402-40, that "no final cost objective shall have allocated to it as a direct cost any cost, if other costs incurred for the same purpose, in like circumstances, have been included in any indirect cost pool to be allocated to that or any other final cost objective."

(b) This interpretation deals with the way 9904.402 applies to the treatment of costs incurred in preparing, submitting, and supporting proposals. In essence, it is addressed to whether or not, under the Standard, all such costs are incurred for the same purpose, in like circumstances.

(c) Under 9904.402, costs incurred in preparing, submitting, and supporting proposals pursuant to a specific requirement of an existing contract are considered to have been incurred in different circumstances from the circumstances under which costs are incurred in preparing proposals which do not result from such specific requirement. The circumstances are different because the costs of preparing proposals specifically required by the provisions of an existing contract relate only to that contract while other proposal costs relate to all work of the contractor.

(d) This interpretation does not preclude the allocation, as indirect costs, of costs incurred in preparing all proposals. The cost accounting practices used by the contractor, however, must be followed consistently and the method used to reallocate such costs, of course, must provide an equitable distribution to all final cost objectives.

9904.402-62 Exemption.

None for this Standard.

9904.402-63 Effective date.

This Standard is effective as of April 17, 1992.

9904.403 Allocation of home office expenses to segments. (No Text)

9904.403-10 [Reserved]

9904.403-20 Purpose.

(a) The purpose of this Cost Accounting Standard is to establish criteria for allocation of the expenses of a home office to the segments of the organization based on the beneficial or causal relationship between such expenses and the receiving segments. It provides for:

(1) Identification of expenses for direct allocation to segments to the maximum extent practical;

(2) Accumulation of significant nondirectly allocated expenses into logical and relatively homogeneous pools to be allocated on bases reflecting the relationship of the expenses to the segments concerned; and

(3) Allocation of any remaining or residual home office expenses to all segments.

Appropriate implementation of this Standard will limit the amount of home office expenses classified as residual to the ex-

penses of managing the organization as a whole.

(b) This Standard does not cover the reallocation of a segment's share of home office expenses to contracts and other cost objectives.

9904.403-30 Definitions.

(a) The following are definitions of terms which are prominent in this Standard. Other terms defined elsewhere in this part 99 shall have the meanings ascribed to them in those definitions unless paragraph (b) of this subsection requires otherwise.

(1) *Allocate* means to assign an item of cost, or a group of items of cost, to one or more cost objectives. This term includes both direct assignments of cost and the reassignment of a share from an indirect cost pool.

(2) *Home office* means an office responsible for directing or managing two or more, but not necessarily all, segments of an organization. It typically establishes policy for, and provides guidance to the segments in their operations. It usually performs management, supervisory, or administrative functions, and may also perform service functions in support of the operations of the various segments. An organization which has intermediate levels, such as groups, may have several home offices which report to a common home office. An intermediate organization may be both a segment and a home office.

(3) *Operating revenue* means amounts accrued or charged to customers, clients, and tenants, for the sale of products manufactured or purchased for resale, for services, and for rentals of property held primarily for leasing to others. It includes both reimbursable costs and fees under cost-type contracts and percentage-of-completion sales accruals except that it includes only the fee for management contracts under which the contractor acts essentially as an agent of the Government in the erection or operation of Government-owned facilities. It excludes incidental interest dividends, royalty, and rental income, and proceeds from the sale of assets used in the business.

(4) *Segment* means one of two or more divisions, product departments, plants, or other subdivisions of an organization reporting directly to a home office, usually identified with responsibility for profit and/or producing a product or service. The term includes Government-owned contractor-operated (GOCO) facilities, and joint ventures and subsidiaries (domestic and foreign) in which the organization has a majority ownership. The term also includes those joint ventures and subsidiaries (domestic and foreign) in which the organization has less than a majority of ownership, but over which it exercises control.

(5) *Tangible capital asset* means an asset that has physical substance, more than minimal value, and is expected to be held by an enterprise for continued use or possession beyond the current accounting period for the services it yields.

(b) The following modifications of terms defined elsewhere in this Chapter 99 are applicable to this Standard: None.

9904.403-40 Fundamental requirement.

(a)(1) Home office expenses shall be allocated on the basis of the beneficial or causal relationship between supporting and receiving activities. Such expenses shall be allocated directly to segments to the maximum extent practical. Expenses not directly allocated, if significant in amount and in relation to total home office expenses, shall be grouped in logical and homogeneous expense pools and allocated pursuant to paragraph (b) of this subsection. Such allocations shall minimize to the extent practical the amount of expenses which may be categorized as residual (those of managing the organization as a whole). These residual expenses shall be allocated pursuant to paragraph (c) of this subsection.

(2) No segment shall have allocated to it as an indirect cost, either through a homogeneous expense pool, or the residual expense pool, any cost, if other costs incurred for the same purpose have been allocated directly to that or any other segment.

(b) The following subparagraphs provide criteria for allocation of groups of home office expenses.

(1) *Centralized service functions.* Expenses of centralized service functions performed by a home office for its segments shall be allocated to segments on the basis of the service furnished to or received by each segment. Centralized service functions performed by a home office for its segments are considered to consist of specific functions which, but for the existence of a home office, would be performed or acquired by some or all of the segments individually. Examples include centrally performed personnel administration and centralized data processing.

(2) *Staff management of certain specific activities of segments.* The expenses incurred by a home office for staff management or policy guidance functions which are significant in amount and in relation to total home office expenses shall be allocated to segments receiving more than a minimal benefit over a base, or bases, representative of the total specific activity being managed. Staff management or policy guidance to segments is commonly provided in the overall direction or support of the performance of discrete segment activities such as manufacturing, accounting, and engineering (but see paragraph (b)(6) of this subsection).

(3) *Line management of particular segments or groups of segments.* The expense of line management shall be allocated only to the particular segment or group of segments which are being managed or supervised. If more than one segment is managed or supervised, the expense shall be allocated using a base or bases representative of the total activity of such segments. Line management is considered to consist of management or supervision of a segment or group of segments as a whole.

(4) *Central payments or accruals.* Central payments or accruals which are made by a home office on behalf of its segments shall be allocated directly to segments to the extent that all such payments or accruals of a given type or class can be identified specifically with individual segments. Central payments or accruals are those which but for

CASB 9904.403-40

the existence of a number of segments would be accrued or paid by the individual segments. Common examples include centrally paid or accrued pension costs, group insurance costs, State and local income taxes and franchise taxes, and payrolls paid by a home office on behalf of its segments. Any such types of payments or accruals which cannot be identified specifically with individual segments shall be allocated to benefitted segments using an allocation base representative of the factors on which the total payment is based.

(5) *Independent research and development costs and bid and proposal costs.* Independent research and development costs and bid and proposal costs of a home office shall be allocated in accordance with 9904.420.

(6) *Staff management not identifiable with any certain specific activities of segments.* The expenses incurred by a home office for staff management, supervisory, or policy functions, which are not identifiable to specific activities of segments shall be allocated in accordance with paragraph (c) of this subsection as residual expenses.

(c) *Residual expenses.* (1) All home office expenses which are not allocable in accordance with paragraph (a) of this subsection and paragraphs (b)(1) through (b)(5) of this subsection shall be deemed residual expenses. Typical residual expenses are those for the chief executive, the chief financial officer, and any staff which are not identifiable with specific activities of segments. Residual expenses shall be allocated to all segments under a home office by means of a base representative of the total activity of such segments, except where paragraph (c)(2) or (3) of this subsection applies.

(2) Residual expenses shall be allocated pursuant to 9904.403-50(c)(1) if the total amount of such expenses for the contractor's previous fiscal year (excluding any unallowable costs and before eliminating any amounts to be allocated in accordance with paragraph (c)(3) of this subsection) exceeds the amount obtained by applying the following percentage(s) to the aggregate operating revenue of all segments for such previous year: 3.35 percent of the first $100 million: 0.95 percent of the next $200 million: 0.30

percent of the next $2.7 billion; 0.20 percent of all amounts over $3 billion. The determination required by this paragraph for the 1st year the contractor is subject to this Standard shall be based on the pro forma application of this Standard to the home office expenses and aggregate operating revenue for the contractor's previous fiscal year.

(3) Where a particular segment receives significantly more or less benefit from residual expenses than would be reflected by the allocation of such expenses pursuant to paragraph (c)(1) or (2) of this subsection (see 9904.403-50(d)), the Government and the contractor may agree to a special allocation of residual expenses to such segment commensurate with the benefits received. The amount of a special allocation to any segment made pursuant to such an agreement shall be excluded from the pool of residual expenses to be allocated pursuant to paragraph (c)(1) or (2) of this subsection, and such segment's data shall be excluded from the base used to allocate this pool.

9904.403-50 Techniques for application.

(a) (1) Separate expense groupings will ordinarily be required to implement 9904.403-40. The number of groupings will depend primarily on the variety and significance of service and management functions performed by a particular home office. Ordinarily, each service or management function will have to be separately identified for allocation by means of an appropriate allocation technique. However, it is not necessary to identify and allocate different functions separately, if allocation in accordance with the relevant requirements of 9904.403-40(b) can be made using a common allocation base. For example, if the personnel department of a home office provides personnel services for some or all of the segments (a centralized service function) and also established personnel policies for the same segments (a staff management function), the expenses of both functions could be allocated over the same base, such as the number of personnel, and the separate functions do not have to be identified.

(2) Where the expense of a given function is to be allocated by means of a particular

allocation base, all segments shall be included in the base unless;

(i) Any excluded segment did not receive significant benefits from, or contribute significantly to the cause of the expense to be allocated and,

(ii) Any included segment did receive significant benefits from or contribute significantly to the cause of the expense in question.

(b) (1) Section 9904.403-60 illustrates various expense pools which may be used together with appropriate allocation bases. The allocation of centralized service functions shall be governed by a hierarchy of preferable allocation techniques which represent beneficial or causal relationships. The preferred representation of such relationships is a measure of the activity of the organization performing the function. Supporting functions are usually labor-oriented, machine-oriented, or space-oriented. Measures of the activities of such functions ordinarily can be expressed in terms of labor hours, machine hours, or square footage. Accordingly, costs of these functions shall be allocated by use of a rate, such as a rate per labor hour, rate per machine hour or cost per square foot, unless such measures are unavailable or impractical to ascertain. In these latter cases the basis for allocation shall be a measurement of the output of the supporting function. Output is measured in terms of units of end product produced by the supporting function, as for example, number of printed pages for a print shop, number of purchase orders processed by a purchasing department, number of hires by an employment office.

(2) Where neither activity nor output of the supporting function can be practically measured, a surrogate for the beneficial, or causal relationship must be selected. Surrogates used to represent the relationship are generally measures of the activity of the segments receiving the service: for example, for personnel services reasonable surrogates would be number of personnel, labor hours, or labor dollars of the segments receiving the service. Any surrogate used should be a reasonable measure of the services received

and, logically, should vary in proportion to the services received.

(c) (1) Where residual expenses are required to be allocated pursuant to 9904.403-40(c)(2), the three factor formula described below must be used. This formula is considered to result in appropriate allocations of the residual expenses of home offices. It takes into account three broad areas of management concern: The employees of the organization, the business volume, and the capital invested in the organization. The percentage of the residual expenses to be allocated to any segment pursuant to the three factor formula is the arithmetical average of the following three percentages for the same period.

(i) The percentage of the segment's payroll dollars to the total payroll dollars of all segments.

(ii) The percentage of the segment's operating revenue to the total operating revenue of all segments. For this purpose, the operating revenue of any segment shall include amounts charged to other segments and shall be reduced by amounts charged by other segments for purchases.

(iii) The percentage of the average net book value of the sum of the segment's tangible capital assets plus inventories to the total average net book value of such assets of all segments. Property held primarily for leasing to others shall be excluded from the computation. The average net book value shall be the average of the net book value at the beginning of the organization's fiscal year and the net book value at the end of the year.

(d) The following paragraphs provide guidance for implementing the requirements of 9904.403-40(c)(3).

(1) An indication that a segment received significantly less benefit in relation to other segments can arise if a segment, unlike all or most other segments, performs on its own many of the functions included in the residual expense. Another indication may be that, in relation to its size, comparatively little or no costs are allocable to a segment pursuant to 9904.403-40(b)(1) through (5). Evidence of comparatively little communica-

CASB 9904.403-50

tion or interpersonal relations between a home office and a segment, in relation to its size, may also indicate that the segment receives significantly less benefit from residual expenses. Conversely, if the opposite conditions prevail at any segment, a greater allocation than would result from the application of 9904.403-40(c)(1) or (2) may be indicated. This may be the case, for example, if a segment relies heavily on the home office for certain residual functions normally performed by other segments on their own.

(2) Segments which may require special allocations of residual expenses pursuant to 9904.403-40(c)(3) include, but are not limited to foreign subsidiaries, GOCO's, domestic subsidiaries with less than a majority ownership, and joint ventures.

(3) The portion of residual expenses to be allocated to a segment pursuant to 9904.403-40(c)(3) shall be the cost of estimated or recorded efforts devoted to the segments.

(e) Home office functions may be performed by an organization which for some purposes may not be a part of the legal entity with which the Government has contracted. This situation may arise, for example, in instances where the Government contracts directly with a corporation which is wholly or partly owned by another corporation. In this case, the latter corporation serves as a "home office," and the corporation with which the contract is made is a "segment" as those terms are defined and used in this Standard. For purposes of contracts subject to this Standard, the contracting corporation may only accept allocations from the other corporation to the extent that such allocations meet the requirements set forth in this Standard for allocation of home office expenses to segments.

9904.403-60 Illustrations.

(a) The following table lists some typical pools, together with illustrative allocation bases, which could be used in appropriate circumstances:

Home office expense or function	Illustrative allocation bases
Centralized service functions:	
1. Personnel administration	1. Number of personnel, labor hours, payroll, number of hires.
2. Data processing services	2. Machine time, number of reports.
3. Centralized purchasing and subcontracting	3. Number of purchase orders, value of purchases, number of items.
4. Centralized warehousing	4. Square footage, value of material, volume.
5. Company aircraft service.	5. Actual or standard rate per hour, mile, passenger mile, or similar unit.
6. Central telephone service.	6. Usage costs, number of instruments.

(b) The selection of a base for allocating centralized service functions shall be governed by the criteria established in 9904.403-50(b).

(c) The listed allocation bases in this section are illustrative. Other bases for allocation of home office expenses to segments may be used if they are substantially in accordance with the beneficial or casual relationships outlined in 9904.403-40.

Home office expenses or function	Illustrative allocation bases
Staff management or specific activities:	
1. Personnel management	1. Number of personnel, labor hours, payroll, number of hires.
2. Manufacturing policies, (quality control, industrial engineering, production, scheduling, tooling, inspection and testing, etc.	2. Manufacturing cost input, manufacturing direct labor.
3. Engineering policies	3. Total engineering costs, engineering direct labor, number of drawings.
4. Material/purchasing policies...............	4. Number of purchase orders, value of purchases.
5. Marketing policies	5. Sales, segment marketing costs.
Central Payments or accruals:	
1. Pension expenses	1. Payroll or other factor on which total payment is based.
2. Group insurance expenses	2. Payroll or other factor on which total payment is based.
3. State and local income taxes and franchise taxes	3. Any base or method which results in an allocation that equals or approximates a segment's proportionate share of the tax imposed by the jurisdiction in which the segment does business, as measured by the same factors used to determine taxable income for that jurisdiction.

9904.403-61 Interpretation.

(a) Questions have arisen as to the requirements of 9904.403, Cost Accounting Standard, Allocation of Home Office Expenses to Segments, for the purpose of allocating State and local income taxes and franchise taxes based on income (hereinafter collectively referred to as income taxes) from a home office of an organization to its segments.

(b) By means of an illustrative allocation base in 9904.403-60, the Standard provides that income taxes are to be allocated by "any base or method which results in an allocation that equals or approximates a segment's proportionate share of the tax imposed by the jurisdiction in which the segment does business, as measured by the same factors used to determine taxable income for that jurisdiction." This provision contains two essential criteria for the allocation of income taxes from a home office to segments. First, the taxes of any particular jurisdiction are to be allocated only to those segments that do business in the taxing jurisdiction. Second, where there is more than one segment in a taxing jurisdiction, the taxes are to be allocated among those segments on the basis of "the same factors used to determine the taxable income for that jurisdiction." The questions that have arisen relate primarily to whether segment book income or loss is a "factor" for this purpose.

(c) Most States tax a fraction of total organization income, rather than the book income of segments that do business within the State. The fraction is calculated pursuant to a formula prescribed by State statute. In these situations the book income or loss of individual segments is not a factor used to determine taxable income for that jurisdiction. Accordingly, in States that tax a fraction of total organization income, rather than the book income of segments within the State, such book income is irrelevant for tax allocation purposes. Therefore, segment book income is to be used as a factor in allocating income tax expense from a home office to segments only where this amount is expressly used by the taxing jurisdiction in computing the income tax.

9904.403-62 [Reserved]

[Reserved, 57 FR 34079, 8/3/92]

9904.403-63 Effective date.

This Standard is effective as of April 17, 1992. Contractors with prior CAS-covered contracts with full coverage shall continue this Standard's applicability upon receipt of a contract to which this Standard is applicable. For contractors with no previous contracts subject to this Standard, this Standard shall be applied beginning with the contractor's next full fiscal year beginning after the receipt of a contract to which this Standard is applicable.

CASB 9904.403-63

9904.404 Capitalization of tangible assets. (No Text)

9904.404-10 [Reserved]

9904.404-20 Purpose.

This Standard requires that, for purposes of cost measurement, contractors establish and adhere to policies with respect to capitalization of tangible assets which satisfy criteria set forth herein. Normally, cost measurements are based on the concept of enterprise continuity; this concept implies that major asset acquisitions will be capitalized, so that the cost applicable to current and future accounting periods can be allocated to cost objectives of those periods. A capitalization policy in accordance with this Standard will facilitate measurement of costs consistently over time.

9904.404-30 Definitions.

(a) The following are definitions of terms which are prominent in this Standard. Other terms defined elsewhere in this Part 99 shall have the meanings ascribed to them in those definitions unless paragraph (b) of this subsection requires otherwise.

(1) *Asset accountability unit* means a tangible capital asset which is a component of plant and equipment that is capitalized when acquired or whose replacement is capitalized when the unit is removed, transferred, sold, abandoned, demolished, or otherwise disposed of.

(2) *Original complement of low cost equipment* means a group of items acquired for the initial outfitting of a tangible capital asset or an operational unit, or a new addition to either. The items in the group individually cost less than the minimum amount established by the contractor for capitalization for the classes of assets acquired but in the aggregate they represent a material investment. The group, as a complement, is expected to be held for continued service beyond the current period. Initial outfitting of the unit is completed when the unit is ready and available for normal operations.

(3) *Repairs and maintenance* generally means the total endeavor to obtain the expected service during the life of tangible capital assets. Maintenance is the regularly recurring activity of keeping assets in normal or expected operating condition while repair is the activity of putting them back into such condition.

(4) *Tangible capital assets* means an asset that has physical substance, more than minimal value, and is expected to be held by an enterprise for continued use or possession beyond the current accounting period for the service it yields.

(b) The following modifications of terms defined elsewhere in this Chapter 99 are applicable to this Standard: None.

9904.404-40 Fundamental requirement.

(a) The acquisition cost of tangible capital assets shall be capitalized. Capitalization shall be based upon a written policy that is reasonable and consistently applied.

(b) The contractor's policy shall designate economic and physical characteristics for capitalization of tangible assets.

(1) The contractor's policy shall designate a minimum service life criterion, which shall not exceed 2 years, but which may be a shorter period. The policy shall also designate a minimum acquisition cost criterion which shall not exceed $5,000, but which may be a smaller amount.

(2) The contractor's policy may designate other specific characteristics which are pertinent to his capitalization policy decisions (e.g., class of asset, physical size, identifiability and controllability, the extent of integration or independence of constituent units).

(3) The contractor's policy shall provide for identification of asset accountability units to the maximum extent practical.

(4) The contractor's policy may designate higher minimum dollar limitations for original complement of low cost equipment and for betterments and improvements than the limitation established in accordance with paragraph (b)(1) of this subsection, provided such higher limitations are reasonable in the contractor's circumstances.

(c) Tangible assets shall be capitalized when both of the criteria in the contractor's policy as required in paragraph (b)(1) of this subsection are met, except that assets described in subparagraph (b)(4) of this subsection shall be capitalized in accordance with the criteria established in accordance with that paragraph.

(d) Costs incurred subsequent to the acquisition of a tangible capital asset which result in extending the life or increasing the productivity of that asset (e.g., betterments and improvements) and which meet the contractor's established criteria for capitalization shall be capitalized with appropriate accounting for replaced asset accountability units. However, costs incurred for repairs and maintenance to a tangible capital asset which either restore the asset to, or maintain it at, its normal or expected service life or production capacity shall be treated as costs of the current period.

[Final rule, 61 FR 5520, 2/13/96, effective 4/15/96]

9904.404-50 Techniques for application.

(a) The cost to acquire a tangible capital asset includes the purchase price of the asset and costs necessary to prepare the asset for use.

(1) The purchase price of an asset shall be adjusted to the extent practical by premiums and extra charges paid or discounts and credits received which properly reflect an adjustment in the purchase price.

(i) Purchase price is the consideration given in exchange for an asset and is determined by cash paid, or to the extent payment is not made in cash, in an amount equivalent to what would be the cash price basis. Where this amount is not available, the purchase price is determined by the current value of the consideration given in exchange for the asset. For example, current value for a credit instrument is the amount immediately required to settle the obligation or the amount of money which might have been raised directly through the use of the same instrument employed in making the credit purchase. The current value of an equity security is its market value. Market value is the current or prevailing price of the security as indicated by recent market quota-

tions. If such values are unavailable or not appropriate (thin market, volatile price movement, etc.), an acceptable alternative is the fair value of the asset acquired.

(ii) Donated assets which, at the time of receipt, meet the contractor's criteria for capitalization shall be capitalized at their fair value at that time.

(2) Costs necessary to prepare the asset for use include the cost of placing the asset in location and bringing the asset to a condition necessary for normal or expected use. Where material in amount, such costs, including initial inspection and testing, installation and similar expenses, shall be capitalized.

(b) Tangible capital assets constructed or fabricated by a contractor for its own use shall be capitalized at amounts which include all indirect costs properly allocable to such assets. This requires the capitalization of general and administrative expenses when such expenses are identifiable with the constructed asset and are material in amount (e.g., when the in-house construction effort requires planning, supervisory, or other significant effort by officers or other personnel whose salaries are regularly charged to general and administrative expenses). When the constructed assets are identical with or similar to the contractor's regular product, such assets shall be capitalized at amounts which include a full share of indirect costs.

(c) In circumstances where the acquisition by purchase or donation of previously used tangible capital assets is not an arm's-length transaction, acquisition cost shall be limited to the capitalized cost of the asset to the owner who last acquired the asset through an arm's-length transaction, reduced by depreciation charges from date of that acquisition to date of gift or sale.

(d) The capitalized values of tangible capital assets acquired in a business combination, accounted for under the "purchase method" of accounting, shall be assigned to these assets as follows:

(1) All the tangible capital assets of the acquired company that during the most recent cost accounting period prior to a business combination generated either

CASB 9904.404-50

depreciation expense or cost of money charges that were allocated to Federal government contracts or subcontracts negotiated on the basis of cost, shall be capitalized by the buyer at the net book value(s) of the asset(s) as reported by the seller at the time of the transaction.

(2) All the tangible capital asset(s) of the acquired company that during the most recent cost accounting period prior to a business combination did not generate either depreciation expense or cost of money charges that were allocated to Federal government contracts or subcontracts negotiated on the basis of cost, shall be assigned a portion of the cost of the acquired company not to exceed their fair value(s) at the date of acquisition. When the fair value of identifiable acquired assets less liabilities assumed exceeds the purchase price of the acquired company in an acquisition under the "purchase method," the value otherwise assignable to tangible capital assets shall be reduced by a proportionate part of the excess.

(e) Under the "pooling of interest method" of accounting for business combinations, the values established for tangible capital assets for financial accounting shall be the values used for determining the cost of such assets.

(f) Asset accountability units shall be identified and separately capitalized at the time the assets are acquired. However, whether or not the contractor identifies and separately capitalizes a unit initially, the contractor shall remove the unit from the asset accounts when it is disposed of and, if replaced, its replacement shall be capitalized.

[Final rule, 61 FR 5520, 2/13/96, effective 4/15/96]

9904.404-60 Illustrations.

(a) Illustrations of costs which must be capitalized. (1) Contractor has an established policy of capitalizing tangible assets which have a service life of more than 1 year and a cost of $6,000. The contractor's policy must be modified to conform to the $5,000 policy limitation on minimum acquisition cost established by the Standard.

(i) Contractor acquires a tangible capital asset with a life of 18 months at a cost of $6,500. The Standard requires that the asset be capitalized in compliance with contractor's policy as to service life.

(ii) Contractor acquires a tangible asset with a life of 18 months at a cost of $900. The asset need not be capitalized unless the contractor's revised policy establishes a minimum cost criterion below $900.

(2) Contractor has an established policy of capitalizing tangible assets which have a service life of more than 1 year and a cost of $250. Contractor acquires a tangible asset with a life of 18 months and a cost of $300. The Standard requires that, based upon contractor's policy, the asset be capitalized.

(3) Contractor establishes a major new production facility. In the process, a number of large and small items of equipment were acquired to outfit it. The contractor has an established policy of capitalizing individual items of tangible assets which have a service life of over 1 year and a cost of $500, and all items meeting these requirements were capitalized. In addition, the contractor's policy requires capitalization of an original complement which has a service life of over 1 year and a cost of $5,000. Items of durable equipment acquired for the production facility costing less than $500 each aggregated $50,000. Based upon the contractor's policy, the durable equipment items must be capitalized as the original complement of low cost equipment. (The concept of original complement applies to such items as books in a new library, impact wrenches in a new factory, work benches and racks in a new production facility, or furniture and fixtures in a new office building.)

(4) Contractor has an established policy for treating its heavy presses and their power supplies as separate asset accountability units. A power supply is replaced during the service life of the related press. The Standard requires that, based upon the contractor's policy, the new power supply be capitalized with appropriate accounting for the replaced unit.

(b) Illustrations of costs which need not be capitalized. (1) The contractor has an established policy of capitalizing tangible assets which have a service life of 2 years and a cost of $500. The contractor acquires an asset with a useful life of 18 months and a cost of $5,000. The tangible asset should be expensed because it does not meet the 2-year criterion.

(2) The contractor establishes a new assembly line. In outfitting the line, the contractor acquires $5,000 of small tools. On similar assembly lines under similar conditions, the original complement of small tools was expensed because the complement was replaced annually as a result of loss, pilferage, breakage, and physical wear and tear. Because the unit of original complement does not meet the contractor's service life criterion for capitalization (1 year), the small tools may be expensed.

[Correction, 70 FR 37706, 6/30/2005, effective 6/30/2005]

9904.404-61 [Reserved]

9904.404-62 Exemption.

None for this Standard.

9904.404-63 Effective date.

(a) This Standard is effective April 15, 1996.

(b) This Standard shall be applied beginning with the contractor's next full cost accounting period beginning after the receipt of a contract or subcontract to which this Standard is applicable.

(c) Contractors with prior CAS-covered contracts with full coverage shall continue to follow Standard 9904.404 in effect prior to April 15, 1996, until this Standard, effective April 15, 1996, becomes applicable after the receipt of a contract or subcontract to which this revised Standard applies.

[Final rule, 61 FR 5520, 2/13/96, effective 4/15/96]

9904.405 Accounting for unallowable costs. (No Text)

9904.405-10 [Reserved]

9904.405-20 Purpose.

(a) The purpose of this Cost Accounting Standard is to facilitate the negotiation, audit, administration and settlement of contracts by establishing guidelines covering:

(1) Identification of costs specifically described as unallowable, at the time such costs first become defined or authoritatively designated as unallowable, and

(2) The cost accounting treatment to be accorded such identified unallowable costs in order to promote the consistent application of sound cost accounting principles covering all incurred costs. The Standard is predicated on the proposition that costs incurred in carrying on the activities of an enterprise—regardless of the allowability of such costs under Government contracts—are allocable to the cost objectives with which they are identified on the basis of their beneficial or causal relationships.

(b) This Standard does not govern the allowability of costs. This is a function of the appropriate procurement or reviewing authority.

9904.405-30 Definitions.

(a) The following are definitions of terms which are prominent in this Standard. Other terms defined elsewhere in this part 99 shall have the meanings ascribed to them in those definitions unless paragraph (b) of this subsection, requires otherwise.

(1) *Directly associated cost* means any cost which is generated solely as a result of the incurrence of another cost, and which would not have been incurred had the other cost not been incurred.

(2) *Expressly unallowable cost* means a particular item or type of cost which, under the express provisions of an applicable law, regulation, or contract, is specifically named and stated to be unallowable.

(3) *Indirect cost* means any cost not directly identified with a single final cost objective, but identified with two or more final cost objectives or with at least one intermediate cost objective.

(4) *Unallowable cost* means any cost which, under the provisions of any pertinent law, regulation, or contract, cannot be included in prices, cost reimbursements, or settlements under a Government contract to which it is allocable.

(b) The following modifications of terms defined elsewhere in this chapter 99 are applicable to this Standard: None.

9904.405-40 Fundamental requirement.

(a) Costs expressly unallowable or mutually agreed to be unallowable, including costs mutually agreed to be unallowable directly associated costs, shall be identified and excluded from any billing, claim, or proposal applicable to a Government contract.

(b) Costs which specifically become designated as unallowable as a result of a written decision furnished by a contracting officer pursuant to contract disputes procedures shall be identified if included in or used in the computation of any billing, claim, or proposal applicable to a Government contract. This identification requirement applies also to any costs incurred for the same purpose under like circumstances as the costs specifically identified as unallowable under either this paragraph or paragraph (a) of this subsection.

(c) Costs which, in a contracting officer's written decision furnished pursuant to contract disputes procedures, are designated as unallowable directly associated costs or unallowable costs covered by either paragraph (a) or (b) of this subsection shall be accorded the identification required by paragraph (b) of this subsection.

(d) The costs of any work project not contractually authorized, whether or not related to performance of a proposed or existing contract, shall be accounted for, to the extent appropriate, in a manner which permits ready separation from the costs of authorized work projects.

(e) All unallowable costs covered by paragraphs (a) through (d) of this subsection shall be subject to the same cost accounting principles governing cost allocability as allowable costs. In circumstances where these unallowable costs normally would be part of a regular indirect-cost allocation base or bases, they shall remain in such base or bases. Where a directly associated cost is part of a category of costs normally included in an indirect-cost pool that will be allocated over a base containing the

unallowable cost with which it is associated, such a directly associated cost shall be retained in the indirect-cost pool and be allocated through the regular allocation process.

(f) Where the total of the allocable and otherwise allowable costs exceeds a limitation-of-cost or ceiling-price provision in a contract, full direct and indirect cost allocation shall be made to the contract cost objective, in accordance with established cost accounting practices and Standards which regularly govern a given entity's allocations to Government contract cost objectives. In any determination of unallowable cost overrun, the amount thereof shall be identified in terms of the excess of allowable costs over the ceiling amount, rather than through specific identification of particular cost items or cost elements.

9904.405-50 Techniques for application.

(a) The detail and depth of records required as backup support for proposals, billings, or claims shall be that which is adequate to establish and maintain visibility of identified unallowable costs (including directly associated costs), their accounting status in terms of their allocability to contract cost objectives, and the cost accounting treatment which has been accorded such costs. Adherence to this cost accounting principle does not require that allocation of unallowable costs to final cost objectives be made in the detailed cost accounting records. It does require that unallowable costs be given appropriate consideration in any cost accounting determinations governing the content of allocation bases used for distributing indirect costs to cost objectives. Unallowable costs involved in the determination of rates used for standard costs, or for the indirect-cost bidding or billing, need be identified only at the time rates are proposed, established, revised or adjusted.

(b)(1) The visibility requirement of paragraph (a) of this subsection, may be satisfied by any form of cost identification which is adequate for purposes of contract cost determination and verification. The Standard does not require such cost identification for purposes which are not relevant to the determination of Government contract cost. Thus, to

CASB 9904.405-40

provide visibility for incurred costs, acceptable alternative practices would include:

(i) The segregation of unallowable costs in separate accounts maintained for this purpose in the regular books of account,

(ii) The development and maintenance of separate accounting records or workpapers, or

(iii) The use of any less formal cost accounting techniques which establishes and maintains adequate cost identification to permit audit verification of the accounting recognition given unallowable costs.

(2) Contractors may satisfy the visibility requirements for estimated costs either:

(i) By designation and description (in backup data, workpapers, etc.) of the amounts and types of any unallowable costs which have specifically been identified and recognized in making the estimates, or

(ii) By description of any other estimating technique employed to provide appropriate recognition of any unallowable costs pertinent to the estimates.

(c) Specific identification of unallowable cost is not required in circumstances where, based upon considerations of materiality, the Government and the contractor reach agreement on an alternate method that satisfies the purpose of the Standard.

9904.405-60 Illustrations.

(a) An auditor recommends disallowance of certain direct labor and direct materials costs, for which a billing has been submitted under a contract, on the basis that these particular costs were not required for performance and were not authorized by the contract. The contracting officer issues a written decision which supports the auditor's position that the questioned costs are unallowable. Following receipt of the contracting officer's decision, the contractor must clearly identify the disallowed direct labor and direct material costs in his accounting records and reports covering any subsequent submission which includes such costs. Also, if the contractor's base for allocation of any indirect cost pool relevant to the subject contract consists of direct labor, direct material, total prime cost, total cost input, etc., he must include the disallowed direct labor and material costs in his allocation base for such pool. Had the contracting officer's decision been against the auditor, the contractor would not, of course, have been required to account separately for the costs questioned by the auditor.

(b) A contractor incurs, and separately identifies, as a part of his manufacturing overhead, certain costs which are expressly unallowable under the existing and currently effective regulations. If manufacturing overhead is regularly a part of the contractor's base for allocation of general and administrative (G&A) or other indirect expenses, the contractor must allocate the G&A or other indirect expenses to contracts and other final cost objectives by means of a base which includes the identified unallowable manufacturing overhead costs.

(c) An auditor recommends disallowance of the total direct indirect costs attributable to an organizational planning activity. The contractor claims that the total of these activity costs are allowable under the Federal Acquisition Regulation (FAR) as "Economic planning costs" (48 CFR 31.205-12); the auditor contends that they constitute "Organization costs" (48 CFR 31.205-27) and therefore are unallowable. The issue is referred to the contracting officer for resolution pursuant to the contract disputes clause. The contracting officer issues a written decision supporting the auditor's position that the total costs questioned are unallowable under the FAR. Following receipt of the contracting officer's decision, the contractor must identify the disallowed costs and specific other costs incurred for the same purpose in like circumstances in any subsequent estimating, cost accumulation or reporting for Government contracts, in which such costs are included. If the contracting officer's decision had supported the contractor's contention, the costs questioned by the auditor would have been allowable "Economic planning costs," and the contractor would not have been required to provide special identification.

(d) A defense contractor was engaged in a program of expansion and diversification of corporate activities. This involved internal corporate reorganization, as well as mergers and acquisitions. All costs of this activity were charged by the contractor as corporate or segment general and administrative (G&A) expense. In the contractor's proposals for final Segment G&A rates (including corporate home office allocations) to be applied in determining allowable costs of its defense contracts subject to 48 CFR part 31, the contractor identified and excluded the expressly unallowable costs (as listed in 48 CFR 31.205-12) incurred for incorporation fees and for charges for special services of outside attorneys, accountants, promoters, and consultants. In addition, during the course of negotiation of interim bidding and billing G&A rates, the contractor agreed to classify as unallowable various in-house costs incurred for the expansion program, and various directly associated costs of the identifiable unallowable costs. On the basis of negotiations and agreements between the contractor and the contracting officers' authorized representatives, interim G&A rates were established, based on the net balance of allowable G&A costs. Application of the rates negotiated to proposals, and on an interim basis to billings, for covered contracts constitutes compliance with the Standard.

(e) An official of a company, whose salary, travel, and subsistence expenses are charged regularly as general and administrative (G&A) expenses, takes several business associates on what is clearly a business entertainment trip. The entertainment cost of such trips is expressly unallowable because it constitutes entertainment expense, and is separately identified by the contractor. The contractor does not regularly include his expenses in any indirect-expense allocation base. In these circumstances, the official's travel and subsistence expenses would be directly associated costs for identification with the unallowable entertainment expense. However, unless this type of activity constituted a significant part of the official's regular duties and responsibilities on which his salary was based, no part of the official's salary would be required to be identified as a directly associated cost of the unallowable entertainment expense.

[Corrected, 57 FR 34167, 8/3/92; Corrected, 57 FR 43776, 9/22/92]

CASB 9904.405-61

9904.405-61 [Reserved]

9904.405-62 Exemption.

None for this Standard.

9904.405-63 Effective date.

This Standard is effective as of April 17, 1992.

9904.406 Cost accounting standard—cost accounting period. (No Text)

9904.406-10 [Reserved]

9904.406-20 Purpose.

The purpose of this Cost Accounting Standard is to provide criteria for the selection of the time periods to be used as cost accounting periods for contract cost estimating, accumulating, and reporting. This Standard will reduce the effects of variations in the flow of costs within each cost accounting period. It will also enhance objectivity, consistency, and verifiability, and promote uniformity and comparability in contract cost measurements.

9904.406-30 Definitions.

(a) The following are definitions of terms which are prominent in this Standard. Other terms defined elsewhere in this part 99 shall have the meanings ascribed to them in those definitions unless paragraph (b) of this subsection, requires otherwise.

(1) *Allocate* means to assign an item of cost, or a group of items of cost, to one or more cost objectives. This term includes both direct assignment of cost and the reassignment of a share from an indirect cost pool.

(2) *Cost objective* means a function, organizational subdivision, contract, or other work unit for which cost data are desired and for which provision is made to accumulate and measure the cost of processes, products, jobs, capitalized projects, etc.

(3) *Fiscal year* means the accounting period for which annual financial statements are regularly prepared, generally a period of 12 months, 52 weeks, or 53 weeks.

(4) *Indirect cost pool* means a grouping of incurred costs identified with two or more cost objectives but not identified specifically with any final cost objective.

(b) The following modification of terms defined elsewhere in this chapter 99 are applicable to this Standard: None.

9904.406-40 Fundamental requirement.

(a) A contractor shall use this fiscal year as his cost accounting period, except that:

(1) Costs of an indirect function which exists for only a part of a cost accounting period may be allocated to cost objectives of that same part of the period as provided in 9904.406-50(a).

(2) An annual period other than the fiscal year may, as provided in 9904.406-50(d), be used as the cost accounting period, if its use is an established practice of the contractor.

(3) A transitional cost accounting period other than a year shall be used whenever a change of fiscal year occurs.

(4) Where a contractor's cost accounting period is different from the reporting period used for Federal income tax reporting purposes, the latter may be used for such reporting.

(b) A contractor shall follow consistent practices in his selection of the cost accounting period or periods in which any types of expense and any types of adjustment to expense (including prior-period adjustments) are accumulated and allocated.

(c) The same cost accounting period shall be used for accumulating costs in an indirect cost pool as for establishing its allocation base, except that the contracting parties may agree to use a different period for establishing an allocation base as provided in 9904.406-50(e).

[Corrected, 57 FR 34167, 8/3/92]

9904.406-50 Techniques for application.

(a) The cost of an indirect function which exists for only a part of a cost accounting period may be allocated on the basis of data for that part of the cost accounting period if the cost is:

(1) Material in amount,

(2) Accumulated in a separate indirect cost pool, and

(3) Allocated on the basis of an appropriate direct measure of the activity or output of the function during that part of the period.

(b) The practices required by 9904.406-40(b) of this Standard shall include appropriate practices for deferrals, accruals, and other adjustments to be used in identifying the cost accounting periods among which any types of expense and any types of adjustment to expense are distributed. If an expense, such as taxes, insurance or employee leave, is identified with a fixed, recurring, annual period which is different from the contractor's cost accounting period, the Standard permits continued use of that different period. Such expenses shall be distributed to cost accounting periods in accordance with the contractor's established practices for accruals, deferrals, and other adjustments.

(c) Indirect cost allocation rates, based on estimates, which are used for the purpose of expediting the closing of contracts which are terminated or completed prior to the end of a cost accounting period need not be those finally determined or negotiated for that cost accounting period. They shall, however, be developed to represent a full cost accounting period, except as provided in paragraph (a) of this subsection.

(d) A contractor may, upon mutual agreement with the Government, use as his cost accounting period a fixed annual period other than his fiscal year, if the use of such a period is an established practice of the contractor and is consistently used for managing and controlling the business, and appropriate accruals, deferrals or other adjustments are made with respect to such annual periods.

(e) The contracting parties may agree to use an annual period which does not coincide precisely with the cost accounting period for developing the data used in establishing an allocation base: Provided,

(1) The practice is necessary to obtain significant administrative convenience,

(2) The practice is consistently followed by the contractor,

(3) The annual period used is representative of the activity of the cost accounting period for which the indirect costs to be allocated are accumulated, and

(4) The practice can reasonably be estimated to provide a distribution to cost objectives of the cost accounting period not materially different from that which otherwise would be obtained.

(f) When a transitional cost accounting period is required under the provisions of 9904.406-40(a)(3), the contractor may select any one of the following:

(1) The period, less than a year in length, extending from the end of his previous cost accounting period to the beginning of his next regular cost accounting period,

(2) A period in excess of a year, but not longer than 15 months, obtained by combining the period described in paragraph (f)(1) of this subsection with the previous cost accounting period, or

(3) A period in excess of a year, but not longer than 15 months, obtained by combining the period described in paragraph (f)(1) of this subsection with the next regular cost accounting period. A change in the contractor's cost accounting period is a change in accounting practices for which an adjustment in the contract price may be required in accordance with paragraph (a)(4) (ii) or (iii) of the contract clause set out at 9903.201-4(a).

9904.406-60 Illustrations.

(a) A contractor allocates general management expenses on the basis of total cost input. In a proposal for a covered negotiated fixed-price contract, he estimates the allocable expenses based solely on the estimated amount of the general management expense pool and the amount of the total cost input base estimated to be incurred during the 8 months in which performance is scheduled to be commenced and completed. Such a proposal would be in violation of the requirements of this Standard that the calculation of the amounts of both the indirect cost pools

and the allocation bases be based on the contractor's cost accounting period.

(b) A contractor whose cost accounting period is the calendar year, installs a computer service center to begin operations on May 1. The operating expense related to the new service center is expected to be material in amount, will be accumulated in a separate indirect cost pool, and will be allocated to the benefiting cost objectives on the basis of measured usage. The total operating expenses of the computer service center for the 8-month part of the cost accounting period may be allocated to the benefiting cost objectives of that same 8-month period.

(c) A contractor changes his fiscal year from a calendar year to the 12-month period ending May 31. For financial reporting purposes, he has a 5-month transitional "fiscal year." The same 5-month period must be used as the transitional cost accounting period; it may not be combined as provided in 9904.406-50(f), because the transitional period would be longer than 15 months. The new fiscal year must be adopted thereafter as his regular cost accounting period. The change in his cost accounting period is a change in accounting practices; adjustments of the contract prices may thereafter be required in accordance with paragraph (a)(4) (ii) or (iii) of the contract clause at 9903.201-4(a).

(d) Financial reports to stockholders are made on a calendar year basis for the entire contractor corporation. However, the contracting segment does all internal financial planning, budgeting, and internal reporting on the basis of a "model year." The contracting parties agree to use a "model year" and they agree to overhead rates on the "model year" basis. They also agree on a technique for prorating fiscal year assignment of corporate home office expenses between model years. This practice is permitted by the Standard.

(e) Most financial accounts and contract cost records are maintained on the basis of a fiscal year which ends November 30 each year. However, employee vacation allowances are regularly managed on the basis of a vacation year which ends September 30 each year. Vacation expenses are estimated uniformly during each "vacation year." Adjustments are made each October to adjust the accrued liability to actual, and the estimating rates are modified to the extent deemed appropriate. This use of a separate annual period for determining the amounts of vacation expense is permitted under 9904.406-50(b).

9904.406-61 Interpretation.

(a) Questions have arisen as to the allocation and period cost assignment of certain contract costs (primarily under defense contracts and subcontracts). This section deals primarily with the assignment of restructuring costs to cost accounting periods. In essence, it clarifies whether restructuring costs are to be treated as an expense of the current period or as a deferred charge that is subsequently amortized over future periods.

(b) "Restructuring costs" as used in this Interpretation means costs that are incurred after an entity decides to make a significant nonrecurring change in its business operations or structure in order to reduce overall cost levels in future periods through work force reductions, the elimination of selected operations, functions or activities, and/or the combination of ongoing operations, including plant relocations. Restructuring activities do not include ongoing routine changes an entity makes in its business operations or organizational structure. Restructuring costs are comprised both of direct and indirect costs associated with contractor restructuring activities taken after a business combination is effected or after a decision is made to execute a significant restructuring event not related to a business combination. Typical categories of costs that have been included in the past and may be considered in the future as restructuring charges include severance pay, early retirement incentives, retraining, employee relocation, lease cancellation, asset disposition and write-offs, and relocation and rearrangement of plant and equipment. Restructuring costs do not include the cost of such activities when they do not relate either to business combinations or to other significant nonrecurring restructuring decisions.

(c) The costs of betterments or improvements of capital assets that result from restructuring activities shall be capitalized and depreciated in accordance with the provisions of 9904.404 and 9904.409.

(d) When a procuring agency imposes a net savings requirement for the payment of restructuring costs, the contractor shall submit data specifying

(1) the estimated restructuring costs by period,

(2) the estimated restructuring savings by period (if applicable), and

(3) the cost accounting practices by which such costs shall be allocated to cost objectives.

(e) Contractor restructuring costs defined pursuant to this section may be accumulated as deferred cost, and subsequently amortized, over a period during which the benefits of restructuring are expected to accrue. However, a contractor proposal to expense restructuring costs for a specific event in a current period is also acceptable when the Contracting Officer agrees that such treatment will result in a more equitable assignment of costs in the circumstances.

(f) If a contractor incurs restructuring costs but does not have an established or disclosed cost accounting practice covering such costs, the deferral of such restructuring costs may be treated as the initial adoption of a cost accounting practice (see 9903.302-2(a)). If a contractor incurs restructuring costs but does have an existing established or disclosed cost accounting practice that does not provide for deferring such costs, any resulting change in cost accounting practice to defer such costs may be presumed to be desirable and not detrimental to the interests of the Government (see 9903.201-6). Changes in cost accounting practices for restructuring costs shall be subject to disclosure statement revision requirements (see 9903.202-3), if applicable.

(g) Business changes giving rise to restructuring costs may result in changes in cost accounting practice (see 9903.302). If a contract price or cost allowance is affected by such changes in cost accounting practice, adjustments shall be made in accordance with subparagraph (a)(4) of the CAS clause (see 9903.201-4(a)(2), 9903.201-4(c)(2) and 9903.201-4(e)(2)).

(h) The amortization period for deferred restructuring costs shall not exceed five years. The straight-line method of amortization should normally be used, unless another method results in a more appropriate matching of cost to expected benefits.

(i) Restructuring costs that are deferred shall not be included in the computation to determine facilities capital cost of money (see 9904.414). Specifically, deferred charges are not tangible or intangible capital assets and therefore are excluded from the facilities capital values for the computation of facilities capital cost of money.

(j) Restructuring costs incurred at a home office level shall be treated in accordance with the provisions of 9904.403. Restructuring costs incurred at the segment level that benefit more than one segment should be allocated to the home office and treated as home office expense pursuant to 9904.403. Restructuring costs incurred at the segment level that benefit only that segment shall be treated in accordance with the provisions of 9904.418. If one or more indirect cost pools do not comply with the homogeneity requirements of 9904.418 due to the inclusion of the costs of restructuring activities, then the restructuring costs shall be accumulated in indirect cost pools that are distinct from the contractor's ongoing indirect cost pools.

(k) This section is applicable to contractor "restructuring costs" paid or approved on or after August 15, 1994.

[Final rule, 62 FR 31308, 6/6/97, effective 8/15/94]

9904.406-62 Exemption.

None for this Standard.

9904.406-63 Effective date.

This Standard is effective as of April 17, 1992. Contractors with prior CAS-covered contracts with full coverage shall continue this Standard's applicability upon receipt of a contract to which this Standard is applicable. For contractors with no previous contracts subject to this Standard, this Standard shall be applied beginning with the contractor's next full fiscal year beginning after the receipt of a contract to which this Standard is applicable.

9904.407 Use of standard costs for direct material and direct labor. (No Text)

9904.407-10 [Reserved]

9904.407-20 Purpose.

(a) The purpose of this Cost Accounting Standard is to provide criteria under which standard costs may be used for estimating, accumulating, and reporting costs of direct material and direct labor; and to provide criteria relating to the establishment of standards, accumulation of standard costs, and accumulation and disposition of variances from standard costs. Consistent application of these criteria where standard costs are in use will improve cost measurement and cost assignment.

(b) This Cost Accounting Standard is not intended to cover the use of pre-established measures solely for estimating.

9904.407-30 Definitions.

(a) The following are definitions of terms which are prominent in this Standard. Other terms defined elsewhere in this Chapter 99 shall have the meanings ascribed to them in those definitions unless paragraph (b) of this subsection requires otherwise.

(1) *Labor cost at standard* means a pre-established measure of the labor element of cost, computed by multiplying labor-rate standard by labor-time standard.

(2) *Labor-rate standard* means a pre-established measure, expressed in monetary terms, of the price of labor.

(3) *Labor time standard* means a pre-established measure, expressed in temporal terms, of the quantity of labor.

(4) *Material cost at standard* means a pre-established measure of the material element of cost, computed by multiplying material-price standard by material-quantity standard.

(5) *Material-price standard* means a pre-established measure, expressed in monetary terms, of the price of material.

(8) *Material quantity standard* means a pre-established measure, expressed in physical terms, of the quantity of material.

(7) *Production unit* means a grouping of activities which either uses homogeneous inputs of direct material and direct labor or yields homogeneous outputs such that the costs or statistics related to these homogeneous inputs or outputs are appropriate as bases for allocating variances.

(8) *Standard cost* means any cost computed with the use of pre-established measures.

(9) *Variance* means the difference between a pre-established measure and an actual measure.

(b) The following modifications of terms defined elsewhere in this Chapter 99 are applicable to this Standard:

(1) *Actual cost.* An amount determined on the basis of cost incurred.

(2) [Reserved].

9904.407-40 Fundamental requirement.

Standard costs may be used for estimating, accumulating, and reporting costs of direct material and direct labor only when all of the following criteria are met:

(a) Standard costs are entered into the books of account.

(b) Standard costs and related variances are appropriately accounted for at the level of the production unit.

(c) Practices with respect to the setting and revising of standards, use of standard costs, and disposition of variances are stated in writing and are consistently followed.

9904.407-50 Techniques for application.

(a) (1) A contractor's written statement of practices with respect to standards shall include the bases and criteria (such as engineering studies, experience, or other supporting data) used in setting and revising standards; the period during which standards are to remain effective; the level (such as ideal or realistic) at which material-quantity standards and labor-time standards are

set; and conditions (such as those expected to prevail at the beginning of a period) which material-price standards and labor-rate standards are designed to reflect.

(2) Where only either the material price or material quantity is set at standard, with the other component stated at actual, the result of the multiplication shall be treated as material cost at standard. Similarly, where only either the labor rate or labor time is set at standard, with the other component stated at actual, the result of the multiplication shall be treated as labor cost at standard.

(3) A labor-rate standard may be set to cover a category of direct labor only if the functions performed within that category are not materially disparate and the employees involved are interchangeable with respect to the functions performed.

(4) A labor-rate standard may be set to cover a group of direct labor workers who perform disparate functions only under either one of the following conditions:

(i) Where that group of workers all work in a single production unit yielding homogeneous outputs (in this case, the same labor-rate standard shall be applied to each worker in that group).

(ii) Where that group of workers, in the performance of their respective functions, forms an integral team (in this case, a labor-rate standard shall be set for each integral team).

(b) (1) Material-price standards may be used and their related variances may be recognized either at the time purchases of material are entered into the books of account, or at the time material cost is allocated to production units.

(2) Where material-price standards are used and related variances are recognized at the time purchases of material are entered into the books of account, they shall be accumulated separately by homogeneous groupings of material. Examples of homogeneous groupings of material are:

(i) Where prices of all items in that grouping of material are expected to fluctuate in the same direction and at substantially the same rate, or

CASB **9904.407-50**

(ii) Where items in that grouping of material are held for use in a single production unit yielding homogeneous outputs.

(3) Where material-price variances are recognized at the time purchases of material are entered into the books of account, variances of each homogeneous grouping of material shall be allocated (except as provided in paragraph (b)(4) of this subsection), at least annually, to items in purchased-items inventory and to production units receiving items from that homogeneous grouping of material, in accordance with either one of the following practices, which shall be consistently followed:

(i) Items in purchased-items inventory of a homogeneous grouping of material are adjusted from standard cost to actual cost; the balance of the material-price variance, after reflecting these adjustments, shall be allocated to production units on the basis of the total of standard cost of material received from that homogeneous grouping of material by each of the production units; or

(ii) Items, at standard cost, in purchased-items inventory of a homogeneous grouping of material, are treated, collectively, as a production unit; the material-price variance shall be allocated to production units on the basis of standard cost of material received from that homogeneous grouping of material by each of the production units.

(4) Where material-price variances are recognized at the time purchases of material are entered into the books of account, variances of each homogeneous grouping of material which are insignificant may be included in appropriate indirect cost pools for allocation to applicable cost objectives.

(5) Where a material-price variance is allocated to a production unit in accordance with paragraph (b)(3) of this subsection, it may be combined with material-quantity variance into one material-cost variance for that production unit. A separate material-cost variance shall be accumulated for each production unit.

(6) Where material-price variances are recognized at the time material cost is allocated to production units, these variances and material-quantity variances may be com-

bined into one material-cost variance account.

(c) Labor-cost variances shall be recognized at the time labor cost is introduced into production units. Labor-rate variances and labor-time variances may be combined into one labor-cost variance account. A separate labor-cost variance shall be accumulated for each production unit.

(d) A contractor's established practice with respect to the disposition of variances accumulated by production unit shall be in accordance with one of the following subparagraphs:

(1) Variances are allocated to cost objectives (including ending in-process inventory) at least annually. Where a variance related to material is allocated, the allocation shall be on the basis of the material cost at standard, or, where outputs are homogeneous, on the basis of units of output. Similarly, where a variance related to labor is allocated, the allocation shall be on the basis of the labor cost at standard or labor hours at standard or, where outputs are homogeneous, on the basis of units of output; or

(2) Variances which are immaterial may be included in appropriate indirect cost pools for allocation to applicable cost objectives.

(e) Where variances applicable to covered contracts are allocated by memorandum worksheet adjustments rather than in the books of account, the bases used for adjustment shall be in accordance with those stated in paragraph (b)(3) and paragraph (d) of this subsection.

9904.407-60 Illustrations.

(a) Contractor A's written practice is to set his material-price standard for an item on the basis of average purchase prices expected to prevail during the calendar year. For that item whose usage from month to month is stable, a purchase contract is generally signed on May 1 of each year for a 1-year commitment. The current purchase contract calls for a purchase price of $3 per pound; an increase of 5 percent, or 15 per pound, has been announced by the vendor when the new purchase contract comes into effect next May. Contractor A sets his material-price standard for this item at $3.10 per pound for the year ([$3.00 4 + $3.15 8] 12). Since Contractor A sets his material-price standard in accordance with his written practice, he complies with provisions of 9904.407-40(c) of this Cost Accounting Standard.

(b) Contractor B accumulates, in one account, labor cost at standard for a department in which several categories of direct labor of disparate functions, in different combinations, are used in the manufacture of various dissimilar outputs of the department. Contractor B's department is not a production unit as defined in 9904.407-30(a)(7) of this Cost Accounting Standard. Modifying his practice so as to comply with the definition of production unit in 9904.407-30(a)(7), he could accumulate the standard costs and variances separately,

(1) For each of the several categories of direct labor, or

(2) For each of several subdepartments, with homogeneous output for each of the subdepartments.

(c) Contractor C allocates variances at the end of each month. During the month of March, a production unit has accumulated the following data with respect to labor:

	Labor hours at standard	Labor dollars at standard	Labor cost variance
Balance, March 1....	5,000	$25,000	$2,000
Additions in March ..	15,000	75,000	5,000
Total.........	20,000	100,000	7,000
Transfers-out in March	8,000	40,000	....
Balance, March 31...	12,000	60,000	....

Using labor hours at standard as the base, Contractor C establishes a labor-cost variance rate of $.35 per standard labor hour ($7,000 20,000), and deducts $2,000 ($.35 × 8,000) from the labor-cost variance account, leaving a balance of $4,200 ($7,000 ÷ $2,800). Contractor C's practice complies with provisions of 9904.407-50(d)(1) of this Cost Accounting Standard.

(d) Contractor D, who uses materials the prices of which are expected to fluctuate at different rates, recognizes material-price variances at the time purchases of material are entered into the books of account. He maintains one purchase-price variance account for the whole plant. Purchased items are requisitioned by various production units in the plant. Since prices of material are expected to fluctuate at different rates, this plant-wide grouping does not constitute a homogeneous grouping of material. Contractor D's practice does not comply with provisions of 9904.407-50(b)(2) of this Cost Accounting Standard. However, if he would maintain several purchased-items inventory accounts, each representing a homogeneous grouping of material, and maintain a material-price variance account for each of these homogeneous groupings of material, Contractor D's practice would comply with 9904.407-50(b)(2) of this Cost Accounting Standard.

(e)(1) Contractor E recognizes material-price variances at the time purchases of material are entered into the books of account and allocates variances at the end of each month. During the month of May, a homogeneous grouping of material has accumulated the following data:

	Material cost at standard	Material price variance
Inventory, May 1	$150,000	$20,000
Additions in May	1,850,000	120,000
Total	2,000,000	140,000
Requisitions:		
Production Unit 1	900,000	....
Production Unit 2	450,000	....
Production Unit 3	300,000	....
Production Unit 4	150,000	....
Inventory, May 31	200,000	....

(2) Contractor E establishes a material-price variance rate of 7 ($140,000 $2,000,000) and allocates as follows:

	Material cost at standard	Material-price variance rate (percent)	Material-price variance allocation
Production unit 1	$900,000	7	$63,000
Production unit 2	450,000	7	31,500
Production unit 3	300,000	7	21,000
Production unit 4	150,000	7	10,500
Ending inventory of homogeneous grouping of material	200,000	7	14,000
Total	2,000,000	....	140,000

Contractor E's practice complies with provisions of 9904.407-50(b)(3)(ii) of this Cost Accounting Standard.

(f)(1) Contractor F makes year-end adjustments for variances attributable to covered contracts. During the year just ended, a covered contract was processed in four production units, each with homogeneous outputs. Data with respect to output and to labor of each of the four production units are as follows:

Production unit	Total units of output	Total units used by the covered contract	Total labor cost at standard	Total labor cost variance
1	100,000	10,000	$400,000	$20,000
2	30,000	6,000	900,000	30,000
3	20,000	5,000	600,000	10,000
4	10,000	4,000	500,000	20,000

(2) Since the outputs of each production unit are homogeneous, Contractor F uses the units of output as the basis of making memorandum worksheet adjustments concerning applicable variances, and establishes the following figures:

	Labor-cost variance per unit of output	Units used by the covered contract	Labor-cost variance attributable to the covered contract
Production unit 1	$0.20	10,000	$2,000
Production unit 2	1.00	6,000	6,000
Production unit 3	.50	5,000	2,500
Production unit 4	2.00	4,000	8,000
Total labor-cost variance attributable to the covered contract	. . . .	. . . .	18,500

(3) Contractor F makes a year-end adjustment of $18,500 as the labor-cost variances attributable to the covered contract. Contractor F's practice complies with provisions of 9904.407-50(e) of this Cost Accounting Standard.

[Corrected, 57 FR 34167, 8/3/92]

9904.407-61 [Reserved]

9904.407-62 Exemption.

None for this Standard.

9904.407-63 Effective date.

This Standard is effective as of April 17, 1992. Contractors with prior CAS-covered contracts with full coverage shall continue this Standard's applicability upon receipt of a contract to which this Standard is applicable. For contractors with no previous contracts subject to this Standard, this Standard shall be applied beginning with the contractor's next full fiscal year beginning after the receipt of a contract to which this Standard is applicable.

9904.408 Accounting for costs of compensated personal absence. (No Text)

9904.408-10 [Reserved]

9904.408-20 Purpose.

The purpose of this Standard is to improve, and provide uniformity in, the measurement of costs of vacation, sick leave, holiday, and other compensated personal absence for a cost accounting period, and thereby increase the probability that the measured costs are allocated to the proper cost objectives.

9904.408-30 Definitions.

(a) The following are definitions of terms which are prominent in this Standard. Other terms defined elsewhere in this part 99 shall have the meanings ascribed to them in those definitions unless paragraph (b) of this subsection, requires otherwise.

(1) *Compensated personal absence* means any absence from work for reasons such as illness, vacation, holidays, jury duty or military training, or personal activities, for which an employer pays compensation directly to an employee in accordance with a plan or custom of the employer.

(2) *Entitlement* means an employee's right, whether conditional or unconditional, to receive a determinable amount of compensated personal absence, or pay in lieu thereof

(b) The following modifications of terms defined elsewhere in this Chapter 99 are applicable to this Standard: None.

9904.408-40 Fundamental requirement.

(a) The costs of compensated personal absence shall be assigned to the cost accounting period or periods in which the entitlement was earned.

(b) The costs of compensated personal absence for an entire cost accounting period shall be allocated pro-rata on an annual basis among the final cost objectives of that period.

CASB 9904.408-40

9904.408-50 Techniques for application.

(a) *Determinations.* Each plan or custom for compensated personal absence shall be considered separately in determining when entitlement is earned. If a plan or custom is changed or a new plan or custom is adopted, then a new determination shall be made beginning with the first cost accounting period to which such new or changed plan or custom applies.

(b) *Measurement of entitlement.* (1) For purposes of compliance with 9904.408-40(a), compensated personal absence is earned at the same time and in the same amount as the employer becomes liable to compensate the employee for such absence if the employer terminates the employee's employment for lack of work or other reasons not involving disciplinary action, in accordance with a plan or custom of the employer. Where a new employee must complete a probationary period before the employer becomes liable, the employer may nonetheless treat such service as creating entitlement in any computations required by this Standard, provided that he does so consistently.

(2) Where a plan or custom provides for entitlement to be determined as of the first calendar day or the first business day of a cost accounting period based on service in the preceding cost accounting period, the entitlement shall be considered to have been earned, and the employer's liability to have arisen, as of the close of the preceding cost accounting period.

(3) In the absence of a determinable liability, in accordance with paragraph (b)(1) of this subsection, compensated personal absence will be considered to be earned only in the cost accounting period in which it is paid.

(c) *Determination of employer's liability.* In computing the cost of compensated personal absence, the computation shall give effect to the employer's liability in accordance with the following paragraphs:

(1) The estimated liability shall include all earned entitlement to compensated personal absence which exists at the time the liability is determined, in accordance with paragraph (b) of this subsection.

(2) The estimated liability shall be reduced to allow for anticipated nonutilization, if material.

(3) The liability shall be estimated consistently either in terms of current or of anticipated wage rates. Estimates may be made with respect to individual employees, but such individual estimates shall not be required if the total cost with respect to all employees in the plan can be estimated with reasonable accuracy by the use of sample data, experience or other appropriate means.

(d) *Adjustments.* (1) The estimate of the employer's liability for compensated personal absence at the beginning of the first cost accounting period for which a contractor must comply with this standard shall be based on the contractor's plan or custom applicable to that period, notwithstanding that some part of that liability has not previously been recognized for contract costing purposes. Any excess of the amount of the liability as determined in accordance with paragraph (c) of this subsection over the corresponding amount of the liability as determined in accordance with the contractor's previous practice shall be held in suspense and accounted for as described in subparagraph (d)(3) of this subsection.

(2) If a plan or custom is changed or a new plan or custom is adopted, and the new determination made in accordance with paragraph (a) of this subsection results in an increase in the estimate of the employer's liability for compensated personal absence at the beginning of the first cost accounting period for which the new plan is effective over the estimate made in accordance with the contractor's prior practice, then the amount of such increase shall be held in suspense and accounted for as described in paragraph (d)(3) of this subsection.

(3) At the close of each cost accounting period, the amount held in suspense shall be reduced by the excess of the amount held in suspense at the beginning of the cost accounting period over the employer's liability (as estimated in accordance with paragraph (c) of this subsection) at the end of that cost accounting period. The cost of compensated

personal absence assigned to that cost accounting period shall be increased by the amount of the excess.

(e) *Allocations.* Except where the use of a longer or shorter period is permitted by the provisions of the Cost Accounting Standard on Cost Accounting Period (9904.406), the cost of compensated personal absence shall be allocated to cost objectives on a pro-rata basis which reflects the total of such costs and the total of the allocation base for the entire cost accounting period. However, this provision shall not preclude revisions to an allocation rate during a cost accounting period based on revised estimates of period totals.

9904.408-60 Illustrations.

(a) Company A's vacation plan provides that on the anniversary of each employee's hiring date, that employee shall become eligible to receive a 2-week vacation with pay. Vacation entitlement must be used within 2 years or forfeited. An employee who leaves the company voluntarily will be paid for any remaining unused vacation entitlement which was earned through the employee's last anniversary date. An employee who is laid off for lack of work will also be paid a pro-rata vacation allowance for service since the employee's last anniversary date. Company A accrues vacation costs each month based on an estimate of the anniversary years which will be completed in that month. At the end of its cost accounting period, Company A adjusts its estimated liability to agree with its actual liability for completed years of service on an individual employee basis.

(1) In order to comply with 9904.408-50(c), Company A must increase its estimated liability for vacation pay at all times to include the estimated additional amount which would be payable to employees in the event of layoff. The additional liability may be calculated on an individual employee basis or it may be estimated for the employees as a group by the use of sample or historical data.

(2) The following illustrates one method of estimating Company A's liability at the end of its cost accounting period, December

31, with respect to individual employees, in accordance with 9904.408-50(c).

John Doe, Anniversary date July 10:

Unused entitlement resulting from completed service years, 24 hrs. at $5	$120
Full months of service since anniversary, 5:	
Pro-rata entitlement on lay-off = 80 hrs. 5/12 = 33.3 hrs. at 15	167
Total	287
Less estimated allowance for forfeitures, 3½ percent ...	10
Net liability	277

(b) Company B has a vacation plan similar to Company A's, but Company B does not pay pro-rata vacation pay on lay-off for service since the last anniversary date. Company B must include in its estimate of its liability at the end of its cost accounting period only that unused vacation entitlement which results from completed years of service, with allowance for forfeitures if material.

(c) Company C's sick leave plan provides that an employee will accumulate one-half day of sick leave entitlement for each full month of service. Sick leave entitlement may be accumulated without limit, but an employee is paid for sick leave only during actual illness; the Company does not pay for unused sick leave on lay-off. Despite the fact that Company C might be able to estimate the amount which will be paid for sick leave in a future cost accounting period with a high degree of accuracy, it has no liability for payment for unused sick leave entitlement in the event of lay-off. Therefore, in accordance with 9904.408-50(b)(3), it must assign to each cost accounting period only the costs of sick leave which it pays in that period.

(d) Company D's vacation plan provides that on July 1, each employee who has been employed by the Company for at least 1 year shall be entitled to 2 weeks of vacation. All vacation must be taken between July 1 and September 30. An employee who terminates after September 30 and before July 1 receives no vacation pay. Company D has a cost accounting period which ends on December 31; however, Company D customarily accrues its anticipated liability for vacation pay at July 1 in 12 equal installments over the "vacation year" starting on July 1 of the previous year and ending on June 30 of the current year. Company D has no liability for vacation pay at January 1 or at December 31. In accordance with 9904.408-50(b)(3), the amount of vacation cost which Company D must assign to each cost accounting period is the amount of such costs paid in that period. Therefore, Company D may not use the "vacation year" ending June 30 to apportion these costs between cost accounting periods.

(e) Company E's cost accounting period ends on December 31. Its vacation plan provides that on January 1, each employee who has been employed for at least 1 year shall become entitled to 2 weeks of vacation. The Company does not recognize a liability for vacation pay at December 31 because an employee must be employed on January 1 to be eligible.

(1) Despite the requirement that the employee also be employed on January 1, the necessary service was completed in the preceding cost accounting period. If the other terms of the plan are such that in accordance with this Standard, Company E must recognize its vacation costs on the accrual basis, then in accordance with 9904.408-50(b)(2). Company E must estimate its vacation costs as if the liability arose on December 31 rather than on the following January 1.

(2) Assume that Company E must comply with this Standard beginning on January 1, 1976. Assume that the employees of Company E earned $90,000 in vacation pay in 1975, all of which will be taken in 1976. Assume, further, that because of reduced employment levels, the employees of Company E will earn only $80,000 in vacation pay in 1976, $5,000 of which will be paid in 1978 because of layoffs. The following example illustrates the computation of vacation pay costs for Company E in 1976:

1976 beginning liability:
    With Standard (30.408-50(d)(1)) $90,000

Without Standard	0
Amount to be held in suspense (9904.408-50(d)(1))	90,000
1976 ending liability	75,000
Plus: Paid in 1976	95,000
Subtotal	170,000
Less: 1976 beginning liability	90,000
1976 vacation cost, basic amount . .	80,000
Amount in suspense at beginning of 1976	90,000
Less: 1976 ending liability	75,000
Suspense to be written off in 1976; additional 1976 vacation cost (9904.408-50(d)(3))	15,000
1976 basic vacation cost	80,000
Plus: 1976 reduction of suspense	15,000
1976 total vacation cost	95,000

(3) Assume, further, that all of the vacation entitlement which remained at December 31, 1976 ($75,000), is taken in 1977. Also, Company E hires a substantial number of additional employees in 1977, so that the amount of vacation entitlement earned in 1977 is $85,000. The following example illustrates the computation of vacation pay costs for Company E in 1977:

1977 ending liability	$85,000
Plus: Paid in 1977	75,000
Subtotal	160,000
Less: 1977 beginning liability	75,000
1977 vacation cost, basic amount	85,000
Amount in suspense at beginning of 1977 (Note 1) . .	75,000
1977 ending liability (Note 1)	85,000
1977 basic vacation cost	85,000
Plus: reduction of suspense (Note 1)	0
1977 total vacation cost	85,000

Note 1—Because the 1977 ending liability exceeds the amount in suspense at the beginning of 1977, there is no reduction of suspense in 1977.

(4) Assume further, that Company E goes out of business in 1978. All employees are terminated and paid both for the $85,000 vacation liability at the end of 1977 and an additional $40,000 earned in 1978. The following example illustrates the computation of vacation pay costs for Company E in 1978:

1978 ending liability	0
Plus: Paid in 1978	$125,000
Subtotal	125,000
Less: 1978 beginning liability	85,000
1978 vacation cost, basic amount	40,000
Amount in suspense at beginning of 1978	75,000
Less: 1978 ending liability	0

Suspense to be written off in 1978: additional 1978 vacation cost (9904.408-50(d)(3))	75,000
1978 basic vacation cost	40,000
Plus: 1978 reduction in suspense	75,000
1978 total vacation cost	115,000

(f) All of the salary costs of Company F's salaried employees are charged to service, administrative, or overhead functions. No accounting entries are made to segregate costs of compensated personal absence of these employees from their other salary costs, although other records are maintained to control the total amount of such absences.

(1) This policy does not violate the requirement of 9904.408-40(b) if such salaries are charged to overhead or indirect cost pools for subsequent allocation to final cost objectives over annually determined allocation bases which are appropriate for those pools.

(2) If the same policy were followed in the case of engineers whose salaries were directly allocated to two or more final cost objectives, or to both intermediate and final cost objectives, so that costs of compensated personal absence were charged directly to the jobs on which the individuals were working when paid, then this would violate the requirement of 9904.408-40(b) that these costs be allocated among cost objectives on the basis of the costs of the entire cost accounting period. Only if all salaries were directly allocated to a single final cost objective, as might be the case with personnel assigned to an overseas base for the performance of a single contract, would this practice be in accord with that requirement.

(g) Company G determines a "charging rate" for each employee. The charging rate includes an allowance for compensated personal absence based on average experience. As the employee performs services, the related cost objectives are charged for the services at the charging rate, the employee is paid at his base rate, and the excess is credited to the accrued liability for each benefit. As benefits are paid, the costs are charged against the accrued liabilities. The amount of each accrued liability is adjusted at the end of the cost accounting period, and any difference is adjusted through appropri-ate overhead accounts in accordance with company policy.

(1) This method is not a violation of 9904.408-40(b) if it results in allocating the estimated annual costs of compensated personal absence at a rate which reflects the anticipated costs of the entire cost accounting period.

(2) The computation itself must comply with the criteria of 9904.408-40(a). For example, if the terms of the Company's sick leave plan are such that in accordance with this Standard, the costs should be recognized in the cost accounting period when they are paid, then the computation should be intended to amortize the expected costs of sick leave over the activity of that cost accounting period, leaving no accrued liability for sick leave at the end of the cost accounting period.

[Corrected, 57 FR 34167, 8/3/92]

9904.408-61 [Reserved]

9904.408-62 Exemption.

This Standard shall not apply to contracts and grants with state, local, and Federally recognized Indian Tribal Governments.

9904.408-63 Effective date.

This Standard is effective as of April 17, 1992. Contractors with prior CAS-covered contracts with full coverage shall continue this Standard's applicability upon receipt of a contract to which this Standard is applicable. For contractors with no previous contracts subject to this Standard, this Standard shall be applied beginning with the contractor's next full fiscal year beginning after the receipt of a contract to which this Standard is applicable.

9904.409 Cost accounting standard depreciation of tangible capital assets. (No Text)

9904.409-10 [Reserved]

9904.409-20 Purpose.

The purpose of this Standard is to provide criteria and guidance for assigning costs of tangible capital assets to cost accounting periods and for allocating such costs in cost objectives within such periods in an objective and consistent manner. The Standard is based on the concept that depreciation costs identified with cost accounting periods and benefiting cost objectives within periods should be a reasonable measure of the expiration of service potential of the tangible assets subject to depreciation. Adherence to this Standard should provide a systematic and rational flow of the costs of tangible capital assets to benefitted cost objectives over the expected service lives of the assets. This Standard does not cover nonwasting assets or natural resources which are subject to depletion.

9904.409-30 Definitions.

(a) The following are definitions of terms which are prominent in this Standard. Other terms defined elsewhere in this Chapter 99 shall have the meanings ascribed to them in those definitions unless paragraph (b) of this subsection, requires otherwise.

(1) *Residual value* means the proceeds (less removal and disposal costs, if any) realized upon disposition of a tangible capital asset. It usually is measured by the net proceeds from the sale or other disposition of the asset, or its fair value if the asset is traded in on another asset. The estimated residual value is a current forecast of the residual value.

(2) *Service life* means the period of usefulness of a tangible asset (or group of assets) to its current owner. The period may be expressed in units of time or output. The estimated service life of a tangible capital asset (or group of assets) is a current forecast of its service life and is the period over which depreciation cost is to be assigned.

(3) *Tangible capital asset* means an asset that has physical substance, more than minimal value, and is expected to be held by an enterprise for continued use or possession beyond the current accounting period for the services it yields.

(b) The following modifications of terms defined elsewhere in this Chapter 99 are applicable to this Standard: None.

9904.409-40 Fundamental requirement.

(a) The depreciable cost of a tangible capital asset (or group of assets) shall be assigned to cost accounting periods in accordance with the following criteria:

(1) The depreciable cost of a tangible capital asset shall be its capitalized cost less its estimated residual value.

(2) The estimated service life of a tangible capital asset (or group of assets) shall be used to determine the cost accounting periods to which the depreciable cost will be assigned.

(3) The method of depreciation selected for assigning the depreciable cost of a tangible capital asset (or group of assets) to the cost accounting periods representing its estimated service life shall reflect the pattern of consumption of services over the life of the asset.

(4) The gain or loss which is recognized upon disposition of a tangible capital asset shall be assigned to the cost accounting period in which the disposition occurs.

(b) The annual depreciation cost of a tangible capital asset (or group of assets) shall be allocated to cost objectives for which it provides service in accordance with the following criteria:

(1) Depreciation cost may be charged directly to cost objectives only if such charges are made on the basis of usage and only if depreciation costs of all like assets used for similar purposes are charged in the same manner.

(2) Where tangible capital assets are part of, or function as, an organizational unit whose costs are charged to other cost objectives based on measurement of the services provided by the organizational unit, the depreciation cost of such assets shall be included as part of the cost of the organizational unit.

(3) Depreciation costs which are not allocated in accordance with paragraph (b)(1) or (2) of this subsection, shall be included in appropriate indirect cost pools.

(4) The gain or loss which is recognized upon disposition of a tangible capital asset,

CASB 9904.409-30

where material in amount, shall be allocated in the same manner as the depreciation cost of the asset has been or would have been allocated for the cost accounting period in which the disposition occurs. Where such gain or loss is not material, the amount may be included in an appropriate indirect cost pool.

9904.409-50 Techniques for application.

(a) Determination of the appropriate depreciation charges involves estimates both of service life and of the likely pattern of consumption of services in the cost accounting periods included in such life. In selecting service life estimates and in selecting depreciation methods, many of the same physical and economic factors should be considered. The following are among the factors which may be taken into account: Quantity and quality of expected output and the timing thereof; costs of repair and maintenance, and the timing thereof; standby or incidental use and the timing thereof; and technical or economic obsolescence of the asset (or group of assets), or of the product or service it is involved in producing.

(b) Depreciation of a tangible capital asset shall begin when the asset and any others on which its effective use depends are ready for use in a normal or acceptable fashion. However, where partial utilization of a tangible capital asset is identified with a specific operation, depreciation shall commence on any portion of the asset which is substantially completed and used for that operation. Depreciable spare parts which are required for the operation of such tangible capital assets shall be accounted for over the service life of the assets.

(c) A consistent policy shall be followed in determining the depreciable cost to be assigned to the beginning and ending cost accounting periods of asset use. The policy may provide for any reasonable starting and ending dates in computing the first and last year depreciable cost.

(d) Tangible capital assets may be accounted for by treating each individual asset as an accounting unit, or by combining two or more assets as a single accounting unit,

provided such treatment is consistently applied over the service life of the asset or group of assets.

(e) Estimated service lives initially established for tangible capital assets (or groups of assets) shall be reasonable approximations of their expected actual periods of usefulness, considering the factors mentioned in paragraph (a) of this subsection. The estimate of the expected actual periods of usefulness need not include the additional period tangible capital assets are retained for standby or incidental use where adequate records are maintained which reflect the withdrawal from active use.

(1) The expected actual periods of usefulness shall be those periods which are supported by records of either past retirement or, where available, withdrawal from active use (and retention for standby or incidental use) for like assets (or groups of assets) used in similar circumstances appropriately modified for specifically identified factors expected to influence future lives. The factors which can be used to modify past experience include:

(i) Changes in expected physical usefulness from that which has been experienced such as changes in the quantity and quality of expected output.

(ii) Changes in expected economic usefulness, such as changes in expected technical or economic obsolescence of the asset (or group of assets), or of the product or service produced.

(2) Supporting records shall be maintained which are adequate to show the age at retirement or, if the contractor so chooses, at withdrawal from active use (and retention for standby or incidental use) for a sample of assets for each significant category. Whether assets are accounted for individually or by groups, the basis for estimating service life shall be predicated on supporting records of experienced lives for either individual assets or any reasonable grouping of assets as long as that basis is consistently used. The burden shall be on the contractor to justify estimated service lives which are shorter than such experienced lives.

CASB 9904.409-50

(3) The records required in subparagraphs (e)(1) and (2) of this subsection, if not available on the date when the requirements of this Standard must first be followed by a contractor, shall be developed from current and historical fixed asset records and be available following the second fiscal year after that date. They shall be used as a basis for estimates of service lives of tangible capital assets acquired thereafter. Estimated service lives used for financial accounting purposes (or other accounting purposes where depreciation is not recorded for financial accounting purposes for some non-commercial organizations), if not unreasonable under the criteria specified in paragraph (e) of this subsection, shall be used until adequate supporting records are available.

(4) Estimated service lives for tangible capital assets for which the contractor has no available data or no prior experience for similar assets shall be established based on a projection of the expected actual period of usefulness, but shall not be less than asset guideline periods (mid-range) established for asset guideline classes under Internal Revenue Procedures which are in effect as of the first day of the cost accounting period in which the assets are acquired. Use of this alternative procedure shall cease as soon as the contractor is able to develop estimates which are appropriately supported by his own experience.

(5) The contracting parties may agree on the estimated service life of individual tangible capital assets where the unique purpose for which the equipment was acquired or other special circumstances warrant a shorter estimated service life than the life determined in accordance with the other provisions of this 9904.409-50(e) and where the shorter life can be reasonably predicted.

(f)(1) The method of depreciation used for financial accounting purposes (or other accounting purposes where depreciation is not recorded for financial accounting purposes) shall be used for contract costing unless:

(i) Such method does not reasonably reflect the expected consumption of services for the tangible capital asset (or group of assets) to which applied, or

(ii) The method is unacceptable for Federal income tax purposes.

If the contractors' method of depreciation used for financial accounting purposes (or other accounting purposes as provided above) does not reasonably reflect the expected consumption of services or is unacceptable for Federal income tax purposes, he shall establish a method of depreciation for contract costing which meets these criteria, in accordance with subparagraph (f)(3) of this subsection.

(2) After the date of initial applicability of this Standard, selection of methods of depreciation for newly acquired tangible capital assets, which are different from the methods currently being used for like assets in similar circumstances, shall be supported by projections of the expected consumption of services of those assets (or groups of assets) to which the different methods of depreciation shall apply. Support in accordance with paragraph (f)(3) of this subsection shall be based on the expected consumption of services of either individual assets or any reasonable grouping of assets as long as the basis selected for grouping assets is consistently used.

(3) The expected consumption of asset services over the estimated service life of a tangible capital asset (or group of assets) is influenced by the factors mentioned in paragraph (a) of this subsection which affect either potential activity or potential output of the asset (or group of assets). These factors may be measured by the expected activity or the expected physical output of the assets, as for example: Hours of operation, number of operations performed, number of units produced, or number of miles traveled. An acceptable surrogate for expected activity or output might be a monetary measure of that activity or output generated by use of tangible capital assets, such as estimated labor dollars, total cost incurred or total revenues, to the extent that such monetary measures can reasonably be related to the usage of specific tangible capital assets (or groups of assets). In the absence of reliable data for the measurement or estimation of the consumption of asset services by the techniques mentioned, the expected consumption of

CASB 9904.409-50

services may be represented by the passage of time. The appropriate method of depreciation should be selected as follows:

(i) An accelerated method of depreciation is appropriate where the expected consumption of asset services is significantly greater in early years of asset life.

(ii) The straight-line method of depreciation is appropriate where the expected consumption of asset services is reasonably level over the service life of the asset (or group of assets).

(g) The estimated service life and method of depreciation to be used for an original complement of low-cost equipment shall be based on the expected consumption of services over the expected useful life of the complement as a whole and shall not be based on the individual items which form the complement.

(h) Estimated residual values shall be determined for all tangible capital assets (or groups of assets). For tangible personal property, only estimated residual values which exceed ten percent of the capitalized cost of the asset (or group of assets) need be used in establishing depreciable costs. Where either the declining balance method of depreciation or the class life asset depreciation range system is used consistent with the provisions of this Standard, the residual value need not be deducted from capitalized cost to determine depreciable costs. No depreciation cost shall be charged which would significantly reduce book value of a tangible capital asset (or group of assets) below its residual value.

(i) Estimates of service life, consumption of services, and residual value shall be reexamined for tangible capital assets (or groups of assets) whenever circumstances change significantly. Where changes are made to the estimated service life, residual value, or method of depreciation during the life of a tangible capital asset, the remaining depreciable costs for cost accounting purposes shall be limited to the undepreciated cost of the assets and shall be assigned only to the cost accounting period in which the change is made and to subsequent periods.

(j) (1) Gains and losses on disposition of tangible capital assets shall be considered as adjustments of depreciation costs previously recognized and shall be assigned to the cost accounting period in which disposition occurs except as provided in subparagraphs (j) (2) and (3) of this subsection. The gain or loss for each asset disposed of is the difference between the net amount realized, including insurance proceeds in the event of involuntary conversion, and its undepreciated balance. However, the gain to be recognized for contract costing purposes shall be limited to the difference between the original acquisition cost of the asset and its undepreciated balance.

(2) Gains and losses on the disposition of tangible capital assets shall not be recognized where:

(i) Assets are grouped and such gains and losses are processed through the accumulated depreciation account, or

(ii) The asset is given in exchange as part of the purchase price of a similar asset and the gain or loss is included in computing the depreciable cost of the new asset.

Where the disposition results from an involuntary conversion and the asset is replaced by a similar asset, gains and losses may either be recognized in the period of disposition or used to adjust the depreciable cost base of the new asset.

(3) The contracting parties may account for gains and losses arising from mass or extraordinary dispositions in a manner which will result in treatment equitable to all parties.

(4) Gains and losses on disposition of tangible capital assets transferred in other than an arms-length transaction and subsequently disposed of within 12 months from the date of transfer shall be assigned to the transferor.

(5) The provisions of this subsection 9904.409-50(j) do not apply to business combinations. The carrying values of tangible capital assets acquired subsequent to a business combination shall be established in accordance with the provisions of subsection 9904.40450(d).

CASB 9904.409-50

(k) Where, in accordance with 9904.409-40(b)(1), the depreciation costs of like tangible capital assets used for similar purposes are directly charged to cost objectives on the basis of usage, average charging rates based on cost shall be established for the use of such assets. Any variances between total depreciation cost charged to cost objectives and total depreciation cost for the cost accounting period shall be accounted for in accordance with the contractor's established practice for handling such variances.

(l) Practices for determining depreciation methods, estimated service lives and estimated residual values need not be changed for assets acquired prior to compliance with this Standard if otherwise acceptable under applicable procurement regulations. However, if changes are effected such changes must conform to the criteria established in this Standard and may be effected on a prospective basis to cover the undepreciated balance of cost by agreement between the contracting parties pursuant to negotiation under subdivision (a)(4)(ii) or (iii) of the contract clause set out at 9903.201-4(a).

[Corrected, 57 FR 34167, 8/3/92; Final rule, 61 FR 5520, 2/13/96, effective 4/15/96]

9904.409-60 Illustrations.

The following examples are illustrative of the provisions of this Standard.

(a) Companies X, Y, and Z purchase identical milling machines to be used for similar purposes.

(1) Company X estimates service life for tangible capital assets on an individual asset basis. Its experience with similar machines is that the average replacement period is 14 years. Under the provisions of the Standard, Company X shall use the estimated service life of 14 years for the milling machine unless it can demonstrate changed circumstances or new circumstances to support a different estimate.

(2) Company Y estimates service life for tangible capital assets by grouping assets of the same general kind and with similar service lives. Accordingly, all machine tools are accounted for as a single group. The average replacement life for machine tools for Company Y is 12 years. In accordance with the

provisions of the Standard, Company Y shall use a life of 12 years for the acquisition unless it can support a different estimate for the entire group.

(3) Company Z estimates service life for tangible capital assets by grouping assets according to use without regard to service lives. Accordingly, all machinery and equipment is accounted for as a single group. The average replacement life for machinery and equipment in Company Z is 10 years. In accordance with the provisions of the Standard, Company Z shall use an estimated service life of ten years for the acquisition unless it can support a different estimate for the entire group.

(b) Company X desires to charge depreciation of the milling machine described in paragraph (a) of this subsection, directly to final cost objectives. Usage of the milling machine can be measured readily based on hours of operation. Company X may charge depreciation cost directly on a unit of time basis provided he uses one depreciation charging rate for all like milling machines in the machine shop and charges depreciation for all such milling machines directly to benefiting cost objectives.

(c) A contractor acquires, and capitalizes as an asset accountability unit, a new lathe. The estimated service life is 10 years for the lathe. He acquires, and capitalizes as an original complement of low-cost equipment related to the lathe, a collection of tool holders, chucks, indexing heads, wrenches, and the like. Although individual items comprising the complement have an average life of 6 years, replacements of these items will be made as needed and, therefore, the expected useful life of the complement is equal to the life of the lathe. An estimated service life of 10 years should be used for the original complement.

(d) A contractor acquires a test facility with an estimated physical life of 10 years, to be used on contracts for a new program. The test facility was acquired for $5 million. It is expected that the program will be completed in 6 years and the test facility acquired is not expected to be required for other products of the contractor. Although the facility will last 10 years, the contracting parties may agree in advance to depreciate the facility over 6 years.

(e) Contractor acquires a building by donation from its local Government. The building had been purchased new by another company and subsequently acquired by the local Government. Contractor capitalizes the building at its fair value. Under the Standard the depreciable cost of the asset based on that value may be accounted for over its estimated service life and allocated to cost objectives in accordance with contractor's cost allocation practices.

(f) A major item of equipment which was acquired prior to the applicability of this Standard was estimated, at acquisition, to have a service life of 12 years and a residual value of no more than 10 percent of acquisition cost. After 4 years of service, during which time this Standard has become applicable, a change in the production situation results in a well-supported determination to shorten the estimated service life to a total of 7 years. The revised estimated residual value is 15 percent of acquisition cost. The annual depreciation charges based on this particular asset will be appropriately increased to amortize the remaining cost, less the current estimate of residual value, over the remaining 3 years of expected usefulness. This change is not a change of cost accounting practice, but a correction of numeric estimates. The requirement of 9904.409.50(1) for an adjustment pursuant to subdivision (a)(4)(ii) or (iii) of the CAS clause does not apply.

(g) The support required by 9904.409-50(e) can, in all likelihood, be derived by sampling from almost any reasonable fixed asset records. Of course, the more complete the data in the records which are available, the more confidence there can be in determinations of asset service lives. The following descriptions of sampling methods are illustrations of techniques which may be useful even with limited fixed asset records.

(1) A company maintains an inventory of assets in use. The company should select a sampling time period which, preferably, is significantly longer than the anticipated life of the assets for which lives are to be established. Of course, the inventory must be available for each year in the sampling time period. The company would then select a random sample of items in each year except the most recent year of the time period. Each item in the sample would be compared to the subsequent year's inventory to determine if the asset is still in service; if not, then the asset had been retired in the year from which the sample was drawn. The item is then traced to prior year inventories to determine the year in which acquired.

Note: Sufficient items must be drawn in each year to ensure an adequate sample.

(2) A company maintains an inventory of assets in use and also has a record of retirements. In this case the company does not have to compare the sample to subsequent years to determine if disposition has occurred. As in Example (g)(1) of this subsection, the sample items are traced to prior years to determine the year in which acquired.

(3) A company maintains retirement records which show acquisition dates. The company should select a sampling time period which, preferably, is significantly longer than the anticipated life of the assets for which lives are to be estimated. The company would then select a random sample of items retired in each year of the sampling time period and tabulate age at requirement.

(4) A company maintains only a record of acquisitions for each year. The company should select a random sample of items acquired in the most recent complete year and determine from current records or observations whether each item is currently in service. The acquisitions of each prior year should be samples in turn to determine if sample items are currently in service. This sampling should be performed for a time period significantly longer than the anticipated life of assets for which the lives are to be established, but can be discontinued at the point at which sample items no longer appear in current use. From the data obtained, mortality tables can be constructed to determine average asset life.

(5) A company does not maintain accounting records on fully depreciated assets. However, property records are maintained, and such records are retained for 3 years after

disposition of an asset in groups by year of disposition. An analysis of these retirements may be made by selecting the larger dollar items for each category of assets for which lives are to be determined (for example, at least 75 percent of the acquisition values retired each year). The cases cited above are only examples and many other examples could have been used. Also, in any example, a company's individual circumstances must be considered in order to take into account possible biased results because of changes in organizations, products, acquisition policies, economic factors, etc. The results from example (g)(5) of this subsection, for instance, might be substantially distorted if the 3-year period was unusual with respect to dispositions. Therefore, the examples are illustrative only and any sampling performed in compliance with this Standard should take into account all relevant information to ensure that reasonable results are obtained.

9904.409-61 [Reserved]

9904.409-62 Exemption.

This Standard shall not apply where compensation for the use of tangible capital assets is based on use rates or allowances provided by other appropriate Federal acquisition regulations such as those governing:

(a) Educational institutions,

(b) State, local, and Federally recognized Indian tribal government, or

(c) Construction equipment rates (See 48 CFR 31.105(d)).

9904.409-63 Effective date.

(a) This Standard is effective April 15, 1996.

(b) This Standard shall be applied beginning with the contractor's next full cost accounting period beginning after the receipt of a contract or subcontract to which this Standard is applicable.

(c) Contractors with prior CAS-covered contracts with full coverage shall continue to follow Standard 9904.409 in effect prior to April 15, 1996, until this Standard, effective April 15, 1996, becomes applicable after the receipt of a contract or subcontract to which this revised Standard applies.

CASB 9904.409-61

[Final rule, 61 FR 5520, 2/13/96, effective 4/15/96]

9904.410 Allocation of business unit general and administrative expenses to final cost objectives. (No Text)

9904.410-10 [Reserved]

9904.410-20 Purpose.

The purpose of this Cost Accounting Standard is to provide criteria for the allocation of business unit general and administrative (G&A) expenses to business unit final cost objectives based on their beneficial or causal relationship. These expenses represent the cost of the management and administration of the business unit as a whole. The Standard also provides criteria for the allocation of home office expenses received by a segment to the cost objectives of that segment. This Standard will increase the likelihood of achieving objectivity in the allocation of expenses to final cost objectives and comparability of cost data among contractors in similar circumstances.

9904.410-30 Definitions.

(a) The following are definitions of terms which are prominent in this standard. Other terms defined elsewhere in this part 99 shall have the meanings ascribed to them in those definitions unless paragraph (b) of this section, requires otherwise.

(1) *Allocate* means to assign an item of cost or a group of items of cost, to one or more cost objectives. This term includes both direct assignment of cost and the reassignment of a share from an indirect cost pool.

(2) *Business unit* means any segment of an organization, or an entire business organization which is not divided into segments.

(3) *Cost input* means the cost, except G&A expenses, which for contract costing purposes is allocable to the production of goods and services during a cost accounting period.

(4) *Cost objective* means a function, organizational subdivision, contract or other work unit for which cost data are desired and for which provision is made to accumulate and

measure the cost of processes, products, jobs, capitalized projects, etc.

(5) *Final cost objective* means a cost objective which has allocated to it both direct and indirect costs, and, in the contractor's accumulation systems, is one of the final accumulation points.

(6) *General and administrative (G&A) expense* means any management, financial, and other expense which is incurred by or allocated to a business unit and which is for the general management and administration of the business unit as a whole. G&A expense does not include those management expenses whose beneficial or causal relationship to cost objectives can be more directly measured by a base other than a cost input base representing the total activity of a business unit during a cost accounting period.

(7) *Segment* means one of two or more divisions, product departments, plants, or other subdivisions of an organization reporting directly to a home office, usually identified with responsibility for profit and/or producing a product or service. The terms include Government-owned contractor-operated (GOCO) facilities, and joint ventures and subsidiaries (domestic and foreign) in which the organization has a majority ownership. The term also includes those joint ventures and subsidiaries (domestic and foreign) in which the organization has less than a majority of ownership, but over which it exercises control.

(b) The following modifications of terms defined elsewhere in this chapter 99 are applicable to this Standard: None.

9904.410-40 Fundamental requirements.

(a) Business unit G&A expenses shall be grouped in a separate indirect cost pool which shall be allocated only to final cost objectives.

(b)(1) The G&A expense pool of a business unit for a cost accounting period shall be allocated to final cost objectives of that cost accounting period by means of a cost input base representing the total activity of the business unit except as provided in subparagraph (b)(2) of this subsection. The cost input base selected shall be the one which

best represents the total activity of a typical cost accounting period.

(2) The allocation of the G&A expense pool to any particular final cost objectives which receive benefits significantly different from the benefits accruing to other final cost objectives shall be determined by special allocation (9994.410-50(j)).

(c) Home office expenses received by a segment shall be allocated to segment cost objectives as required by 9904.410-50(g).

(d) Any costs which do not satisfy the definition of G&A expense but which have been classified by a business unit as G&A expenses, can remain in the G&A expense pool unless they can be allocated to business unit cost objectives on a beneficial or causal relationship which is best measured by a base other than a cost input base.

9904.410-50 Techniques for application.

(a) G&A expenses of a segment incurred by another segment shall be removed from the incurring segment's G&A expense pool. They shall be allocated to the segment for which the expenses were incurred on the basis of the beneficial or causal relationship between the expenses incurred and all benefiting or causing segments. If the expenses are incurred for two or more segments, they shall be allocated using an allocation base common to all such segments.

(b) The G&A expense pool may be combined with other expenses for allocation to final cost objectives provided that—

(1) The allocation base used for the combined pool is appropriate both for the allocation of the G&A expense pool under this Standard and for the allocation of the other expenses; and

(2) Provision is made to identify the components and total of the G&A expense pool separately from the other expenses in the combined pool.

(c) Expenses which are not G&A expenses and are insignificant in amount may be included in the G&A expense pool for allocation to final cost objectives.

(d) The cost input base used to allocate the G&A expense pool shall include all significant elements of that cost input which represent the total activity of the business unit. The cost input base selected to represent the total activity of a business unit during a cost accounting period may be: Total cost input; value-added cost input; or single element cost input. The determination of which cost input base best represents the total activity of a business unit must be judged on the basis of the circumstances of each business unit.

(1) A total cost input base is generally acceptable as an appropriate measure of the total activity of a business unit.

(2) Value-added cost input shall be used as an allocation base where inclusion of material and subcontract costs would significantly distort the allocation of the G&A expense pool in relation to the benefits received, and where costs other than direct labor are significant measures of total activity. A value-added cost input base is total cost input less material and subcontract costs.

(3) A single element cost input base; e.g., direct labor hours or direct labor dollars, which represents the total activity of a business unit may be used to allocate the G&A expense pool where it produces equitable results. A single element base may not produce equitable results where other measures of activity are also significant in relation to total activity. A single element base is inappropriate where it is an insignificant part of the total cost of some of the final cost objectives.

(e) Where, prior to the effective date of this Standard, a business unit's disclosed or established cost accounting practice was to use a cost of sales or sales base, that business unit may use the transition method set out in appendix A hereof.

(f) Cost input shall include those expenses which by operation of this Standard are excluded from the G&A expense pool and are not part of a combined pool of G&A expenses and other expenses allocated using the same allocation base.

(g)(1) Allocations of the home office expenses of: (i) Line management of particular segments or groups of segments, (ii)

residual expenses, and (iii) directly allocated expenses related to the management and administration of the receiving segment as a whole, shall be included in the receiving segment's G&A expense pool.

(2) Any separate allocation of the expenses of home office centralized service functions, staff management of specific activities of segments, and central payments or accruals, which is received by a segment, shall be allocated to the segment cost objectives in proportion to the beneficial or causal relationship between the cost objectives and the expense if such allocation is significant in amount. Where a beneficial or causal relationship for the expense is not identifiable with segment cost objectives, the expense may be included in the G&A expense pool.

(h) Where a segment performs home office functions and also performs as an operating segment having a responsibility for final cost objectives, the expense of the home office functions shall be segregated. These expenses shall be allocated to all benefiting or causing segments, including the segment performing the home office functions, pursuant to disclosed or established accounting practices for the allocation of home office expenses to segments.

(i) For purposes of allocating the G&A expense pool, items produced or worked on for stock or product inventory shall be accounted for as final cost objectives in accordance with the following paragraphs:

(1) Where items are produced or worked on for stock or product inventory in a given cost accounting period, the cost input to such items in that period shall be included only once in the computation of the G&A expense allocation base and in the computation of the G&A expense allocation rate for that period and shall not be included in the computation of the base or rate for any other cost accounting period.

(2) A portion of the G&A expense pool shall be allocated to items produced or worked on for stock or product inventory in the cost accounting period or periods in which such items are produced at the rates determined for such periods except as provided in subparagraph (i)(3) of this subsection.

CASB 9904.410-50

(3) Where the contractor does not include G&A expense in inventory as part of the cost of stock or product inventory items, the G&A rate of the cost accounting period in which such items are issued to final cost objectives may be used to determine the G&A expenses applicable to issues of stock or product inventory items.

(j) Where a particular final cost objective in relation to other final cost objectives receives significantly more or less benefit from G&A expense than would be reflected by the allocation of such expenses using a base determined pursuant to paragraph (d) of this subsection, the business unit shall account for this particular final cost objective by a special allocation from the G&A expense pool to the particular final cost objective commensurate with the benefits received. The amount of a special allocation to any such final cost objective shall be excluded from the G&A expense pool required by 9904.410-40(a), and the particular final cost objective's cost input data shall be excluded from the base used to allocate this pool.

9904.410-60 Illustrations.

(a) Business Unit A has been including the cost of scientific computer operations in its G&A expense pool. The scientific computer is used predominantly for research and development, rather than for the management and administration of the business unit as a whole. The costs of the scientific computer operation do not satisfy the Standard's definition of G&A expense; however, they may remain in the G&A expense pool unless they can be allocated to business unit cost objectives on a beneficial or causal relationship which is best measured by a base other than a cost input base representing the total activity of a business unit during a cost accounting period.

(b) Segment B performs a budgeting function, the cost of which is included in its G&A expense pool. This function includes the preparation of budgets for another segment. The cost of preparing the budgets for the other segment should be removed from B's G&A expense pool and transferred to the other segment.

(c)(1) Business Unit C has a personnel function which is divided into two parts: A vice president of personnel who establishes personnel policy and overall guidance, and a personnel department which handles hirings, testing, evaluations, etc. The expense of the vice president is included in the G&A expense pool. The expense of the personnel department is allocated to the other indirect cost pools based on the beneficial or causal relationship between that expense and the indirect cost pools. This procedure is in compliance with the requirements of this Standard.

(2) Business Unit C has included selling costs as part of its G&A expense pool. Unit C wishes to continue to include selling costs in its G&A pool. Under the provisions of this Standard, Unit C may continue to include selling costs in its G&A pool, and these costs will be allocated over a cost input base selected in accordance with the provisions of 9904.410-50(d).

(3) Business Unit C has included IR&D and B&P costs in its G&A expense pool. Unit C has used a cost of sales base to allocate its G&A expense pool. As of January 1, 1978 (assumed for purposes of this illustration), the date on which Unit C must first allocate its G&A expense pool in accordance with the requirements of this Standard, Unit C has among its final cost objectives several cost reimbursement contracts and fixed price contracts subject to the G&S clause (referred to as the preexisting contracts). If Unit C chooses to use the transition method in 9904.410-50(e):

(i) Unit C shall allocate IR&D and B&P costs during the transition period (from January 1, 1978, to and including the cost accounting period during which the preexisting contracts are completed), to the preexisting contracts as part of its G&A expense pool using a cost of sales base pursuant to 9904.410-50(e) and appendix A to 9904.410.

(ii) During the transition period such costs, as part of the G&A expense pool, shall be allocated to new cost reimbursement contracts and new fixed price contracts subject to the G&S clause using a cost input base as required by 9904.410-50(d) and (e) and appendix A to 9904.410.

(iii) Beginning with the cost accounting period after the transition period the IR&D and B&P costs, as part of the G&A expense pool, shall be allocated to all final cost objectives using a cost input base as required by 9904.410-50(d). If Unit C chooses not to use the transition method in 9904.410-50(e), the contractual provision requiring appropriate equitable adjustment of the prices of affected prime contracts and subcontracts will be implemented.

(4) Business Unit C has accounted for and allocated IR&D and B&P costs in a cost pool separate and apart from the G&A expense pool. Unit C may continue to account for these costs in a separate cost pool under the provision of this Standard. If Unit C is to use a total cost input base, these costs when accounted for and allocated in a cost pool separate and apart from the G&A expense pool will become part of the total cost input base used by Unit C to allocate the G&A expense pool.

(5) Business Unit C has included selling costs as part of its G&A expense pool. Unit C has used a cost of sales base to allocate the G&A expense pool. Unit C desires to continue to allocate selling costs using the costs of sales base. Under the provisions of this Standard, Unit C would account for selling costs as a cost pool separate and apart from the G&A expense pool, and continue to allocate these costs over a cost of sales base. If Unit C uses a total cost input base to allocate the G&A expense pool, the selling costs will become part of the total cost input base.

(d) (1) Business Unit D has accounted for selling costs in a cost pool separate and apart from its G&A expense pool and has allocated these costs using a cost of sales base. Under the provisions of this Standard, Unit D may continue to account for those costs in a separate pool and allocate them using a cost of sales base. Unit D has a total cost input base to allocate its G&A expense pool. The selling costs will become part of the cost input base used by Unit D to allocate the G&A expense pool.

(2) During a cost accounting period, Business Unit D buys $2,000,000 of raw materials. At the end of that cost accounting period, $500,000 of raw materials inventory have not been charged out to contracts or other cost objectives. The $500,000 of raw materials are not part of the total cost input base for the cost accounting period, because they have not been charged to the production of goods and services during that period. If all of the $2,000,000 worth of raw material had been charged to cost objectives during the cost accounting period, the cost input base for the allocation of the G&A expense pool would include the entire $2,000,000.

(3) Business Unit D manufactures a variety of testing devices. During a cost accounting period, Unit D acquires and uses a small building, constructs a small production facility using its own resources, and keeps for its own use one unit of a testing device that it manufactures and sells to its customers. The acquisition cost of the building is not part of the total cost input base; however, the depreciation taken on the building would be part of the total cost input base. The costs of construction of the small production facility are not part of the total cost input base. The requirements of 9904.404 provide that those G&A expenses which are identifiable with the constructed asset and are material in amount shall be capitalized as part of the cost of the production facility. If there are G&A expenses material in amount and identified with the constructed asset, these G&A expenses would be removed from the G&A expense pool prior to the allocation of this pool to final cost objectives. The cost of the testing device shall be part of the total cost input base per the requirements of 9904.404 which provides that the costs of constructed assets identical with the contractor's regular product shall include a full share of indirect cost.

(e) (1) Business Unit E produces Item Z for stock or product inventory. The business unit does not include G&A expense as part of the inventory cost of these items for costing or financial reporting purposes. A production run of these items occurred during Cost Accounting Period 1. A number of the units produced were not issued during Period 1 and are issued in Period 2. However,

CASB 9904.410-60

those units produced in Period 1 shall be included in the cost input of that period for calculating the G&A expense allocation base and shall not be included in the cost input of Period 2.

(2) Business Unit E should apply the G&A expense rate of Period 1 to those units of Item Z issued during Period 1 and may apply the rate of Period 2 to the units issued in Period 2.

(3) If the practice of Business Unit E is to include G&A expense as part of the cost of stock or product inventory, the inventory cost of all units of Item Z produced in Period 1 and remaining in inventory at the end of Period 1, should include G&A expense using the G&A rate of Period 1.

(f)(1) Business Unit F produced Item X for stock or product inventory. The business unit does not include G&A expense as part of the inventory cost of these items. A production run of these items was started, finished, and placed into inventory in a single cost accounting period. These items are issued during the next cost accounting period.

(2) The cost of items produced for stock or product inventory should be included in the G&A base in the same year they are produced. The cost of such items is not to be included in the G&A base on the basis of when they are issued to final cost objectives. Therefore, the time of issuance of these items from inventory to a final cost objective is irrelevant in computing the G&A base.

(g) The normal productive activity of Business Unit G includes the construction of base operating facilities for others. Unit G uses a total cost input base to allocate G&A expense to final cost objectives. As part of a contract to construct an operating facility, Unit G agrees to acquire a large group of trucks and other mobile equipment to equip the base operating facility. Unit G does not usually supply such equipment. The cost of the equipment constitutes a significant part of the contract cost. A special G&A allocation to this contract shall be agreed to by the parties if they agree that in the circumstances the contract as a whole receives substantially less benefit from the G&A expense pool than that which would be represented by a cost allocation based on inclusion of the contract cost in the total cost input base.

(h)(1) The home office of Segment H separately allocates to benefiting or causing segments significant home office expenses of staff management functions relative to manufacturing, staff management functions relative to engineering, central payment of health insurance costs, and residual expenses. Segment H receives these expenses as separate allocations and maintains three indirect cost pools; i.e., G&A expense, manufacturing overhead, and engineering overhead; all home office expenses allocated to Segment H are included in Segment H's G&A expense pool.

(2) This accounting practice of Segment H does not comply with 9904.410-50(g)(2). Home office residual expenses should be in the G&A expense pool, and the expenses of the staff management functions relative to manufacturing and engineering should be included in the manufacturing overhead and engineering overhead pools, respectively. The health insurance costs should be allocated in proportion to the beneficial and causal relationship between these costs and Segment H's cost objectives.

9904.410-61 [Reserved]

9904.410-62 Exemption.

This Standard shall not apply to contracts and grants with state, local, and Federally recognized Indian tribal governments.

9904.410-63 Effective date.

This Standard is effective as of April 17, 1992. Contractors with prior CAS-covered contracts with full coverage shall continue this Standard's applicability upon receipt of a contract to which this Standard is applicable. For contractors with no previous contracts subject to this Standard, this Standard shall be applied beginning with the contractor's next full fiscal year beginning after the receipt of a contract to which this Standard is applicable.

[Corrected, 57 FR 34167, 8/3/92]

APPENDIX A TO 9904.410—
TRANSITION FROM A COST OF SALES

CASB 9904.410-App. A

OR SALES BASE TO A COST INPUT BASE

A business unit may use the method described below for transition from the use of a cost of sales or sales base to a cost input base.

(1) Calculate the cost of sales or sales base in accordance with the cost accounting practice disclosed or established prior to the date established by 9904.410-80(b) of the original Cost Accounting Standard.

(2) Calculate the G&A expense allocation rate using the base determined in subparagraph (1) of this appendix and use that rate to allocate from the G&A expense pool to the final cost objectives which were in existence prior to the date on which the business unit must first allocate costs in accordance with the requirements of this Cost Accounting Standard.

(3) Calculate a cost input base in compliance with 9904.410-50(d).

(4) Calculate the G&A expense rate using the base determined in subparagraph (3) of this appendix and use that rate to allocate from the G&A expense pool to those final cost objectives which arise under contracts entered into on or after the date on which the business unit must first allocate costs in accordance with the requirements of this Cost Accounting Standard.

(5) The calculations set forth in subparagraphs (1)-(4) of this appendix shall be performed for each cost accounting period during which final cost objectives described in (2) are being performed.

(6) The business unit shall establish an inventory suspense account. The amount of the inventory suspense account shall be equal to the beginning inventory of contracts subject to the CAS clause of the cost accounting period in which the business unit must first allocate costs in accordance with the requirements of this Cost Accounting Standard.

(7) In any cost accounting period, after the cost accounting periods described in subparagraph (5) of this Appendix, if the ending inventory of contracts subject to the CAS clause is less than the balance of the inventory suspense account, the business unit shall calculate two G&A expense allocation rates, one to allocate G&A expenses to contracts subject to the CAS clause and one applicable to other work.

(a) The G&A expense pool shall be divided in the proportion which the cost input of the G&A expense allocation base of the contracts subject to the CAS clause bears to the total of the cost input allocation base, selected in accordance with 9904.410-50(d), for the cost accounting period.

(b) The G&A expenses applicable to contracts subject to the CAS clause shall be reduced by an amount determined by multiplying the difference between the balance of the inventory suspense account and the ending inventory of contracts subject to the CAS clause by the cost of sales rate, as determined under subparagraph (1) of this Appendix, of the cost accounting period in which a business unit must first allocate costs in accordance with the requirements of this Cost Accounting Standard.

(8) In any cost accounting period in which such a reduction is made, the balance of the inventory suspense account shall be reduced to be equal to the ending inventory of contracts subject to the CAS clause of that cost accounting period.

The following illustrates how a business unit would use this transition method.

1. Business Unit R has been using a cost of sales base to allocate its G&A expense pool to final cost objectives. Unit R uses a calendar year as its cost accounting period. On October 1, 1976 (assumed for purposes of this illustration) Cost Accounting Standard 410 becomes effective. On October 2, 1976, Unit R receives a 3-year contract containing the Cost Accounting Standards clause. As a result, Unit R must comply with the requirements of the Standard in the cost accounting period beginning in January 1978. As of January 3, 1978, Business Unit R has the following contracts:

(1) Contract I—A 4-year contract awarded in January 1975.

(2) Contract II—A 3-year contract which was negotiated in March 1976, and was awarded on October 2, 1976.

CASB 9904.410-App. A

(3) Contract III—A 4-year contract awarded on January 2, 1978.

If Business Unit R chooses to use the transition method provided in 9904.410-50(e), it will allocate the G&A expense pool to these contracts as follows:

(a) Contract I—Since Contract I was in existence prior to January 1, 1978, the G&A expense pool shall be allocated to it using a cost of sales base as provided in 9904.410-50(e).

(b) Contract II—Since this contract was in existence prior to January 1, 1978, the G&A expense pool shall be allocated to it using a cost of sales base as provided in 9904.410-50(e).

(c) Contract III—Since this contract was awarded after January 1, 1978, the G&A expense pool shall be allocated to this contract using a cost input base.

Having chosen to use 9904.410-50(e), Business Unit R will use the transition method of allocating the G&A expense pool to final cost objectives until all contracts awarded prior to January 1, 1978, are completed (1979 if the contracts are completed on schedule). Beginning with the cost accounting period subsequent to that time, 1980, Unit R will use a cost input base to allocate the G&A expense pool to all cost objectives. Unit R will also carry forward an inventory suspense account in accordance with the requirements of this Standard.

2.A. Business Unit N is first required to allocate its costs in accordance with the requirements of 9904.410 during the fiscal year beginning January 1, 1978. Unit N has used a cost of sales base to allocate its G&A expense pool.

During the years 1978, 1979, 1980, Business Unit N reported the following data:

		Contracts prior to Jan. 1, 1978			Contracts after Jan. 1, 1978		
	Total	Non-CAS work	CAS-fixed price work	CAS-cost contracts	Non-CAS work	CAS-fixed price work	CAS-cost contracts
Year 1978:							
Beginning inventory	$500	300	200	0	0	0	0
Cost input	+3000	400	600	700	500	500	300
Total	3500	700	800	700	500	500	300
Cost of sales	−3000	600	550	700	450	400	300
Ending inventory	500	100	250	0	50	100	0
Year 1979:							
Beginning inventory	500	100	250	0	50	100	0
Cost input	+3000	400	600	700	500	500	300
Total	3500	500	850	700	550	600	300
Cost of sales	−2500	450	650	700	150	250	300
Ending inventory	1000	50	200	0	400	350	0
Year 1980:							
Beginning inventory	1000	50	200	0	400	350	0
Cost input	+3000	400	600	700	500	500	300
Total	4000	450	800	700	900	850	300
Cost of sales	−3250	450	800	700	450	550	300
Ending inventory	750	0	0	0	450	300	0

NOTES:
Operating data is in thousands of dollars.
G. & A. expense $375,000 in accordance with the requirements of this standard.

CASB 9904.410-App. A

Work existing prior to January 1, 1978, may include—

(1) Government contracts which contain the CAS clause;

(2) Government contracts which do not contain the CAS clause;

(3) Contracts other than Government contracts or customer orders; and

(4) Production not specifically identified with contracts or customer orders under production or work orders existing prior to the date on which a business unit must first allocate its costs in compliance with this Standard and which are limited in time or quantity.

Production under standing or unlimited work orders, continuous flow processes and the like, not identified with contracts or customer orders are to be treated as final cost objectives awarded after the date on which a business unit must first allocate its costs in compliance with the requirements of this Standard.

Business Unit N may allocate the G&A expense pool as follows:

[In dollars]

		Year 1978		Year 1979		Year 1980	
1.	G. & A. expense pool		375		375		375
	Cost of sales rate .	375⁄3,000=	.125	375⁄2,500=	.150	375⁄3,250=	.115
	Cost input	375⁄3,000=	.125	375⁄3,000=	.125	375⁄3,000=	.125
2.	G.& A. allocations:						
	Prior contracts:						
	Non-CAS work . . .	600⁄0.125=	75.00	450⁄0.15=	67.50	450⁄0.115=	51.75
	CAS-fixed price work	550⁄0.125=	68.75	650⁄0.15=	97.50	800⁄0.115=	92.00
	CAS-cost contracts	700⁄0.125=	87.50	700⁄0.15=	105.00	700⁄0.115=	80.50
	After contracts:						
	Non-CAS work . . .	500⁄0.125=	62.50	500⁄0.125=	62.50	500⁄0.125=	62.50
	CAS-fixed price work	500⁄0.125=	62.50	500⁄0.125=	62.50	500⁄0.125=	62.50
	CAS-cost contracts	300⁄0.125=	37.50	300⁄0.125=	37.50	300⁄0.125=	37.50
			393.75	432.50		386.80	
3.	Inventory suspense account[1]		200				
	G. & A. rate applicable		.125				

[1] Beginning inventory of contracts subject to the CAS clause, January 1978.

2.B. In cost accounting period 1982, Business Unit N has an ending inventory of contracts subject to the CAS clause of $100,000. This is the first cost accounting period after the transition in which the amount of the ending inventory is less than the amount of the inventory suspense account. During this cost accounting period, Business Unit N had G&A expenses of $410,000 and cost input of $3,500,000; $1,500,000 applicable to contracts subject to the CAS clause and $2,000,000 applicable to other work.

Business Unit N would compute its G&A expense allocation rate applicable to contracts subject to the CAS clause as follows:

CASB 9904.410-App. A

(1) Amount of inventory suspense
account $200,000

Amount of ending inventory . .   100,000

Difference   100,000

G. & A. rate applicable (see 2.A.
above) 0.125

Adjustment to G. & A. expense
applicable to contracts subject
to the CAS clause   12,500

(2) G. & A. expense pool   410,000

G. & A. expenses applicable to
contracts subject to the CAS
clause ($1,500,000/$3,500,000 ×
$410,000)   175,890

G. & A. expenses applicable to
other work   234,110

(3) G. & A. expenses applicable to
contracts subject to the CAS
clause   175,890

Adjustment to G. & A. expenses
applicable to contracts subject
to the CAS clause   12,500

G. & A. expenses allocable to
contracts subject to the CAS
clause   163,390

(4) G. & A. expense allocation rate
applicable to contracts subject
to the CAS clause for cost
accounting period 1982—
$163,390/$1,500,000 = 0.109.

The amount of the inventory suspense account would be reduced to $100,000.

[Corrected, 57 FR 34081, 8/3/92]

9904.411 Cost accounting standard—accounting for acquisition costs of material. (No Text)

9904.411-10 [Reserved]

9904.411-20 Purpose.

(a) The purpose of this Cost Accounting Standard is to provide criteria for the accounting for acquisition costs of material. The Standard includes provisions on the use of inventory costing methods. Consistent application of this Standard will improve the measurement and assignment of costs to cost objectives.

(b) This Cost Accounting Standard does not cover accounting for the acquisition costs of tangible capital assets nor accountability for Government-furnished materials.

[Corrected, 57 FR 34167, 8/3/92]

9904.411-30 Definitions.

(a) The following are definitions of terms which are prominent in this Standard. Other terms elsewhere in this chapter 99 shall have the meanings ascribed to them in those definitions unless paragraph (b) of this subsection, requires otherwise.

(1) *Allocate* means to assign an item of cost, or a group of items of cost, to one or more cost objectives. This term includes both direct assignment of cost and the reassignment of a share from an indirect cost pool.

(2) *Business unit* means any segment of an organization, or an entire business organization which is not divided into segments.

(3) *Category of material* means a particular kind of goods, comprised of identical or interchangeable units, acquired or produced by a contractor, which are intended to be sold, or consumed or used in the performance of either direct or indirect functions.

(4) *Cost objective* means a function, organizational subdivision, contract or other work unit for which cost data are desired and for which provision is made to accumulate and measure the cost of processes, products, jobs, capitalized projects, etc.

(5) *Material inventory record* means any record used for the accumulation of actual or standard costs of a category of material recorded as an asset for subsequent cost allocation to one or more cost objectives.

(6) *Moving average cost* means an inventory costing method under which an average unit cost is computed after each acquisition by adding the cost of the newly acquired units to the cost of the units of inventory on hand and dividing this figure by the new total number of units.

(7) *Weighted average cost* means an inventory costing method under which an average

CASB 9904.411-30

unit cost is computed periodically by dividing the sum of the cost of beginning inventory plus the cost of acquisitions by the total number of units included in these two categories.

(b) The following modifications of terms defined elsewhere in this chapter 99 are applicable to this Standard: None.

9904.411-40 Fundamental requirement.

(a) The contractor shall have, and consistently apply, written statements of accounting policies and practices for accumulating the costs of material and for allocating costs of material to cost objectives.

(b) The cost of units of a category of material may be allocated directly to a cost objective provided the cost objective was specifically identified at the time of purchase or production of the units.

(c) The cost of material which is used solely in performing indirect functions, or is not a significant element of production cost, whether or not incorporated in an end product, may be allocated to an indirect cost pool. When significant, the cost of such indirect material not consumed in a cost accounting period shall be established as an asset at the end of the period.

(d) Except as provided in paragraphs (b) and (c) of this subsection, the cost of a category of materials shall be accounted for in material inventory records.

(e) In allocating to cost objectives the costs of a category of material issued from company-owned material inventory, the costing method used shall be selected in accordance with the provisions of 9904.411-50, and shall be used in a manner which results in systematic and rational costing of issues of material to cost objectives. The same costing method shall, within the same business unit, be used for similar categories of materials.

9904.411-50 Techniques for application.

(a) Material cost shall be the acquisition cost of a category of material, whether or not a material inventory record is used. The purchase price of material shall be adjusted by extra charges incurred or discounts and credits earned. Such adjustments shall be charged or credited to the same cost objective as the purchase price of the material, except that where it is not practical to do so, the contractor's policy may provide for the consistent inclusion of such charges or credits in an appropriate indirect cost pool.

(b) One of the following inventory costing methods shall be used when issuing material from a company-owned inventory:

(1) The first-in, first-out (FIFO) method.

(2) The moving average cost method.

(3) The weighted average cost method.

(4) The standard cost method.

(5) The last-in, first-out (LIFO) method.

(c) The method of computation used for any inventory costing method selected pursuant to the provisions of this Standard shall be consistently followed.

(d) Where the excess of the ending inventory over the beginning inventory of material of the type described in 9904.411-40(c) is estimated to be significant in relation to the total cost included in the indirect cost pool, the cost of such unconsumed material shall be established as an asset at the end of the period by reducing the indirect cost pool by a corresponding amount.

9904.411-60 Illustrations.

(a) Contractor "A" has one contract which requires two custom-ordered, high-value, airborne cameras. The contractor's established policy is to order such special items specifically identified to a contract as the need arises and to charge them directly to the contract. Another contract is received which requires three more of these cameras, which the contractor purchases at a unit cost which differs from the unit cost of the first two cameras ordered. When the purchase orders were placed, the contractor identified the specific contracts on which the cameras being purchased were to be used. Although these cameras are identical, the actual cost of each camera is charged to the contract for which it was acquired without establishing a material inventory record. This practice would not be a violation of this Standard.

(b) (1) A Government contract requires use of electronic tubes identified as "W." The contractor expects to receive other contracts requiring the use of tubes of the same type. In accordance with its written policy, the contractor establishes a material inventory record for electronic tube "W," and allocates the cost of units issued to the existing Government contract by the FIFO method. Such a practice would conform to the requirements of this Standard.

(2) The contractor is awarded several additional contracts which require an electronic tube which the contractor concludes is similar to the one described in paragraph (b) (1) of this subsection and which is identified as "Y." At the time a purchase order for these tubes is written, the contractor cannot identify the specific number of tubes to be used on each contract. Consequently, the contractor establishes an inventory record for these tubes and allocates their cost to the contracts on an average cost method. Because a FIFO method is used for a similar category of material within the same business unit, the use of an average cost method for "Y" would be a violation of this Standard.

(c) A contractor complies with the Cost Accounting Standard on standard costs (9904.407), and he uses a standard cost method for allocating the costs of essentially all categories of material. Also, it is the contractor's established practice to charge the cost of purchased parts which are incorporated in his end products, and which are not a significant element of production cost to an indirect cost pool. Such practices conform to this Standard.

(d) A contractor has one established inventory for type "R" transformers. The contractor allocates by the LIFO method the current costs of the individual units issued to Government contracts. Such a practice would conform to the requirements of this Standard.

(e) A contractor has established inventories for various categories of material which are used on Government contracts. During the year the contractor allocates the costs of the units of the various categories of material issued to contracts by the moving average cost method. The contractor uses the LIFO method for tax and financial reporting purposes and, at year end, applies a pooled LIFO inventory adjustment for all categories of material to Government contracts. This application of pooled costs to Government contracts would be a violation of this Standard because the lump sum adjustment to all of the various categories of material is, in effect, a noncurrent repricing of the material issues.

9904.411-61 [Reserved]

9904.411-62 Exemption.

None for this Standard.

9904.411-63 Effective date.

This Standard is effective as of April 17, 1992. Contracts with prior CAS-Covered contract with full coverage shall continue this Standard's applicability upon receipt of a contract to which this Standard is applicable. For contractors with no previous contracts subject to this Standard, this Standard shall be applied beginning with the contractor's next full fiscal year beginning after the receipt of a contract to which this Standard is applicable.

9904.412 Cost accounting standard for composition and measurement of pension cost. (No Text)

9904.412-10 [Reserved]

9904.412-20 Purpose.

(a) The purpose of this Standard 9904.412 is to provide guidance for determining and measuring the components of pension cost. The Standard establishes the basis on which pension costs shall be assigned to cost accounting periods. The provisions of this Cost Accounting Standard should enhance uniformity and consistency in accounting for pension costs and thereby increase the probability that those costs are properly allocated to cost objectives.

(b) This Standard does not cover the cost of Employee Stock Ownership Plans (ESOPs) that meet the definition of a pension plan. Such plans are considered a form of deferred compensation and are covered under 9904.415.

[Final rule, 73 FR 23961, 5/1/2008, effective 6/2/2008]

9904.412-30 Definitions.

(a) The following are definitions of terms which are prominent in this Standard. Other terms defined elsewhere in this chapter 99 shall have the meanings ascribed to them in those definitions unless paragraph (b) of this subsection requires otherwise.

(1) *Accrued benefit cost method* means an actuarial cost method under which units of benefits are assigned to each cost accounting period and are valued as they accrue, that is, based on the services performed by each employee in the period involved. The measure of normal cost under this method for each cost accounting period is the present value of the units of benefit deemed to be credited to employees for service in that period. The measure of the actuarial accrued liability at a plan's measurement date is the present value of the units of benefit credited to employees for service prior to that date. (This method is also known as the Unit Credit cost method without salary projection.)

(2) *Actuarial accrued liability* means pension cost attributable, under the actuarial cost method in use, to years prior to the current period considered by a particular actuarial valuation. As of such date, the actuarial accrued liability represents the excess of the present value of future benefits and administrative expenses over the present value of future normal costs for all plan participants and beneficiaries. The excess of the actuarial accrued liability over the actuarial value of the assets of a pension plan is the Unfunded Actuarial Liability. The excess of the actuarial value of the assets of a pension plan over the actuarial accrued liability is an actuarial surplus and is treated as a negative unfunded actuarial liability.

(3) *Actuarial assumption* means an estimate of future conditions affecting pension cost; for example, mortality rate, employee turnover, compensation levels, earnings on pension plan assets, changes in values of pension plan assets.

(4) *Actuarial cost method* means a technique which uses actuarial assumptions to measure the present value of future pension benefits and pension plan administrative expenses, and which assigns the cost of such benefits and expenses to cost accounting periods. The actuarial cost method includes the asset valuation method used to determine the actuarial value of the assets of a pension plan.

(5) *Actuarial gain and loss* means the effect on pension cost resulting from differences between actuarial assumptions and actual experience.

(6) *Actuarial valuation* means the determination, as of a specified date, of the normal cost, actuarial accrued liability, actuarial value of the assets of a pension plan, and other relevant values for the pension plan.

(7) *Assignable cost credit* means the decrease in unfunded actuarial liability that results when the pension cost computed for a cost accounting period is less than zero.

(8) *Assignable cost deficit* means the increase in unfunded actuarial liability that results when the pension cost computed for a qualified defined-benefit pension plan exceeds the maximum tax-deductible amount for the cost accounting period determined in accordance with the Internal Revenue Code at Title 26 of the U.S.C.

(9) *Assignable cost limitation* means the excess, if any, of the actuarial accrued liability and the normal cost for the current period over the actuarial value of the assets of the pension plan.

(10) *Defined-benefit pension plan* means a pension plan in which the benefits to be paid or the basis for determining such benefits are established in advance and the contributions are intended to provide the stated benefits.

(11) *Defined-contribution pension plan* means a pension plan in which the contributions are established in advance and the benefits are determined thereby.

(12) *Funded pension cost* means the portion of pension cost for a current or prior cost accounting period that has been paid to a funding agency.

(13) *Funding agency* means an organization or individual which provides facilities to

receive and accumulate assets to be used either for the payment of benefits under a pension plan, or for the purchase of such benefits, provided such accumulated assets form a part of a pension plan established for the exclusive benefit of the plan participants and their beneficiaries. The fair market value of the assets held by the funding agency as of a specified date is the Funding Agency Balance as of that date.

(14) *Immediate-gain actuarial cost method* means any of the several cost methods under which actuarial gains and losses are included as part of the unfunded actuarial liability of the pension plan, rather than as part of the normal cost of the plan.

(15) *Market value of the assets* means the sum of the funding agency balance plus the accumulated value of any permitted unfunded accruals belonging to a pension plan. The Actuarial Value of the Assets means the value of cash, investments, permitted unfunded accruals, and other property belonging to a pension plan, as used by the actuary for the purpose of an actuarial valuation.

(16) *Multiemployer pension plan* means a plan to which more than one employer contributes and which is maintained pursuant to one or more collective bargaining agreements between an employee organization and more than one employer.

(17) *Nonforfeitable* means a right to a pension benefit, either immediate or deferred, which arises from an employee's service, which is unconditional, and which is legally enforceable against the pension plan or the contractor. Rights to benefits that do not satisfy this definition are considered forfeitable. A right to a pension benefit is not forfeitable solely because it may be affected by the employee's or beneficiary's death, disability, or failure to achieve vesting requirements. Nor is a right considered forfeitable because it can be affected by the unilateral actions of the employee.

(18) *Normal cost* means the annual cost attributable, under the actuarial cost method in use, to current and future years as of a particular valuation date, excluding any payment in respect of an unfunded actuarial liability.

(19) *Pay-as-you-go cost method* means a method of recognizing pension cost only when benefits are paid to retired employees or their beneficiaries.

(20) *Pension plan* means a deferred compensation plan established and maintained by one or more employers to provide systematically for the payment of benefits to plan participants after their retirement, provided that the benefits are paid for life or are payable for life at the option of the employees. Additional benefits such as permanent and total disability and death payments, and survivorship payments to beneficiaries of deceased employees may be an integral part of a pension plan.

(21) *Pension plan participant* means any employee or former employee of an employer, or any member or former member of an employee organization, who is or may become eligible to receive a benefit from a pension plan which covers employees of such employer or members of such organization who have satisfied the plan's participation requirements, or whose beneficiaries are receiving or may be eligible to receive any such benefit. A participant whose employment status with the employer has not been terminated is an active participant of the employer's pension plan.

(22) *Permitted unfunded accrual* means the amount of pension cost for nonqualified defined-benefit pension plans that is not required to be funded under 9904.412-50(d)(2). The Accumulated Value of Permitted Unfunded Accruals means the value, as of the measurement date, of the permitted unfunded accruals adjusted for imputed earnings and for benefits paid by the contractor.

(23) *Prepayment credit* means the amount funded in excess of the pension cost assigned to a cost accounting period that is carried forward for future recognition. The Accumulated Value of Prepayment Credits means the value, as of the measurement date, of the prepayment credits adjusted for income and expenses in accordance with 9904.413-50(c)(7) and decreased for amounts used to fund pension costs or liabilities, whether assignable or not.

CASB 9904.412-30

(24) *Projected benefit cost method* means either (i) any of the several actuarial cost methods which distribute the estimated total cost of all of the employees' prospective benefits over a period of years, usually their working careers, or (ii) a modification of the accrued benefit cost method that considers projected compensation levels.

(25) *Qualified pension plan* means a pension plan comprising a definite written program communicated to and for the exclusive benefit of employees which meets the criteria deemed essential by the Internal Revenue Service as set forth in the Internal Revenue Code for preferential tax treatment regarding contributions, investments, and distributions. Any other plan is a Nonqualified Pension Plan.

(b) The following modifications of terms defined elsewhere in this chapter 99 are applicable to this Standard: None.

[Final rule, 60 FR 16534, 3/30/95, effective 3/30/95; Final rule, 76 FR 81296, 12/27/2011, effective 2/27/2012]

9904.412-40 Fundamental requirement.

(a) Components of pension cost. (1) For defined-benefit pension plans, except for plans accounted for under the pay-as-you-go cost method, the components of pension cost for a cost accounting period are (i) the normal cost of the period, (ii) a part of any unfunded actuarial liability, (iii) an interest equivalent on the unamortized portion of any unfunded actuarial liability, and (iv) an adjustment for any actuarial gains and losses.

(2) For defined-contribution pension plans, the pension cost for a cost accounting period is the net contribution required to be made for that period, after taking into account dividends and other credits, where applicable.

(3) For defined-benefit pension plans accounted for under the pay-as-you-go cost method, the components of pension cost for a cost accounting period are:

(i) The net amount of periodic benefits paid for that period, and

(ii) An amortization installment, including an interest equivalent on the unamortized

settlement amount, attributable to amounts paid to irrevocably settle an obligation for periodic benefits due in current and future cost accounting periods.

(b) Measurement of pension cost. (1) For defined-benefit pension plans other than those accounted for under the pay-as-you-go cost method, the amount of pension cost of a cost accounting period shall be determined by use of an immediate-gain actuarial cost method.

(2) Each actuarial assumption used to measure pension cost shall be separately identified and shall represent the contractor's best estimates of anticipated experience under the plan, taking into account past experience and reasonable expectations. The validity of each assumption used shall be evaluated solely with respect to that assumption. Actuarial assumptions used in calculating the amount of an unfunded actuarial liability shall be the same as those used for other components of pension cost.

(3) For qualified defined benefit pension plans, the measurement of pension costs shall recognize the requirements of 9904.412-50(b)(7) for periods beginning with the "Applicability Date of the CAS Pension Harmonization Rule." However, paragraphs 9904.413-50(c)(8), (9) and (12) are exempt from the requirements of 9904.412-50(b)(7).

(c) Assignment of pension cost. Except costs assigned to future periods by 9904.412-50(c)(2) and (5), the amount of pension cost computed for a cost accounting period is assignable only to that period. For defined-benefit pension plans other than those accounted for under the pay-as-you-go cost method, the pension cost is assignable only if the sum of (1) the unamortized portions of assignable unfunded actuarial liability developed and amortized pursuant to 9904.412-50(a)(1), and (2) the unassignable portions of unfunded actuarial liability separately identified and maintained pursuant to 9904.412-50(a)(2) equals the total unfunded actuarial liability.

(d) Allocation of pension cost. Pension costs assigned to a cost accounting period are allocable to intermediate and final cost objectives only if they meet the requirements for allocation in 9904.412-50(d). Pension costs not meeting these requirements may not be reassigned to any future cost accounting period.

[Final rule, 60 FR 16534, 3/30/95, effective 3/30/95; Final rule, 76 FR 81296, 12/27/2011, effective 2/27/2012]

9904.412-50 Techniques for application.

(a) Components of pension cost. (1) The following portions of unfunded actuarial liability shall be included as a separately identified part of the pension cost of a cost accounting period and shall be included in equal annual installments. Each installment shall consist of an amortized portion of the unfunded actuarial liability plus an interest equivalent on the unamortized portion of such liability. The period of amortization shall be established as follows:

(i) If amortization of an unfunded actuarial liability has begun prior to the date this Standard first becomes applicable to a contractor, no change in the amortization period is required by this Standard.

(ii) If amortization of an unfunded actuarial liability has not begun prior to the date this Standard first becomes applicable to a contractor, the amortization period shall begin with the period in which the Standard becomes applicable and shall be no more than 30 years nor less than 10 years. However, if the plan was in existence as of January 1, 1974, the amortization period shall be no more than 40 years nor less than 10 years.

(iii) Each increase or decrease in unfunded actuarial liability resulting from the institution of new pension plans, from the adoption of improvements, or other changes to pension plans subsequent to the date this Standard first becomes applicable to a contractor shall be amortized over no more than 30 years nor less than 10 years.

(iv) If any assumptions are changed during an amortization period, the resulting increase or decrease in unfunded actuarial liability shall be separately amortized over no more than 30 years nor less than 10 years.

(v) Actuarial gains and losses shall be identified separately from unfunded actuarial liabilities that are being amortized pursuant to the provisions of this Standard. The accounting treatment to be afforded to such gains and losses shall be in accordance with Cost Accounting Standard 9904.413.

(vi) Each increase or decrease in unfunded actuarial liability resulting from an assignable cost deficit or credit, respectively, shall be amortized over a period of 10 years.

(vii) Each increase or decrease in unfunded actuarial liability resulting from a change in actuarial cost method, including the asset valuation method, shall be amortized over a period of 10 to 30 years. This provision shall not affect the requirements of 9903.302 to adjust previously priced contracts.

(2) (i) Except as provided in 9904.412-50(d)(2), any portion of unfunded actuarial liability attributable to either pension costs applicable to prior years that were specifically unallowable in accordance with then existing Government contractual provisions or pension costs assigned to a cost accounting period that were not funded in that period, shall be separately identified and eliminated from any unfunded actuarial liability being amortized pursuant to paragraph (a)(1) of this subsection.

(ii) Such portions of unfunded actuarial liability shall be adjusted for interest based on the interest assumption established in accordance with 9904.412-50(b)(4) without regard to 9904.412-50(b)(7). The contractor may elect to fund, and thereby reduce, such portions of unfunded actuarial liability and future interest adjustments thereon. Such funding shall not be recognized for purposes of 9904.412-50(d).

(3) A contractor shall establish and consistently follow a policy for selecting specific amortization periods for unfunded actuarial liabilities, if any, that are developed under the actuarial cost method in use. Such policy may give consideration to factors such as the size and nature of the unfunded actuarial liabilities. Except as provided in 9904.412-50(c)(2) or 9904.413-50(c)(12), once the amortization period for a portion of unfunded actuarial liability is selected, the

CASB 9904.412-50

amortization process shall continue to completion.

(4) Any amount funded in excess of the pension cost assigned to a cost accounting period shall be accounted for as a prepayment credit. The accumulated value of such prepayment credits shall be adjusted for income and expenses in accordance with 9904.413-50(c)(7) until applied towards pension cost in a future accounting period. The accumulated value of prepayment credits shall be reduced for portions of the accumulated value of prepayment credits used to fund pension costs or to fund portions of unfunded actuarial liability separately identified and maintained in accordance with 9904.412-50(a)(2). The accumulated value of any prepayment credits shall be excluded from the actuarial value of the assets used to compute pension costs for purposes of this Standard and Cost Accounting Standard 9904.413.

(5) An excise tax assessed pursuant to a law or regulation because of excess, inadequate, or delayed funding of a pension plan is not a component of pension cost. Income taxes paid from the funding agency of a nonqualified defined-benefit pension plan on earnings or other asset appreciation of such funding agency shall be treated as an administrative expense of the fund and not as a reduction to the earnings assumption.

(6) For purposes of this Standard, defined-benefit pension plans funded exclusively by the purchase of individual or group permanent insurance or annuity contracts, and thereby exempted from the minimum funding requirements implemented by the Employee Retirement Income Security Act of 1974 (ERISA), 29 U.S.C. 1001 *et seq.*, as amended, shall be treated as defined-contribution pension plans. However, all other defined-benefit pension plans administered wholly or in part through insurance company contracts shall be subject to the provisions of this Standard relative to defined-benefit pension plans

(7) If a pension plan is supplemented by a separately-funded plan which provides retirement benefits to all of the participants in the basic plan, the two plans shall be considered as a single plan for purposes of this Standard. If the effect of the combined plans is to provide defined-benefits for the plan participants, the combined plans shall be treated as a defined-benefit plan for purposes of this Standard.

(8) A multiemployer pension plan established pursuant to the terms of a collective bargaining agreement shall be considered to be a defined-contribution pension plan for purposes of this Standard.

(9) A pension plan applicable to a Federally-funded Research and Development Center (FFRDC) that is part of a State pension plan shall be considered to be a defined-contribution pension plan for purposes of this Standard.

(b) Measurement of pension cost. (1) For defined-benefit pension plans other than those accounted for under the pay-as-you-go cost method, the amount of pension cost assignable to cost accounting periods shall be measured by an immediate-gain actuarial cost method.

(2) Where the pension benefit is a function of salaries and wages, the normal cost shall be computed using a projected benefit cost method. The normal cost for the projected benefit shall be expressed either as a percentage of payroll or as an annual accrual based on the service attribution of the benefit formula. Where the pension benefit is not a function of salaries and wages, the normal cost shall be based on employee service.

(3) For defined-benefit plans accounted for under the pay-as-you-go cost method, the amount of pension cost assignable to a cost accounting period shall be measured as the sum of:

(i) The net amount for any periodic benefits paid for that period, and

(ii) The level annual installment required to amortize over 15 years any amounts paid to irrevocably settle an obligation for periodic benefits due in current or future cost accounting periods.

(4) Actuarial assumptions shall reflect long-term trends so as to avoid distortions caused by short-term fluctuations.

(5) Pension cost shall be based on provisions of existing pension plans. This shall

not preclude contractors from making salary projections for plans whose benefits are based on salaries and wages, or from considering improved benefits for plans which provide that such improved benefits must be made. For qualified defined benefit plans whose benefits are subject to a collectively bargained agreement(s) and whose benefits are not based on salaries and wages, the contractor may recognize benefit improvements expected to occur in succeeding plan years determined on the basis of the average annual increase in benefits over the 6 immediately preceding plan years.

(6) If the evaluation of the validity of actuarial assumptions shows that any assumptions were not reasonable, the contractor shall:

(i) Identify the major causes for the resultant actuarial gains or losses, and

(ii) Provide information as to the basis and rationale used for retaining or revising such assumptions for use in the ensuing cost accounting period(s).

(7) *CAS Pension Harmonization Rule:* For qualified defined benefit pension plans, the pension cost shall be determined in accordance with the provisions of paragraph (b)(7)(i) of this section.

(i) In any period that the sum of the minimum actuarial liability and the minimum normal cost exceeds the sum of the actuarial accrued liability and the normal cost, the contractor shall measure and assign the pension cost for the period in accordance with 9904.412 and 9904.413 by using the minimum actuarial liability and minimum normal cost as the actuarial accrued liability and normal cost, respectively, for all purposes unless otherwise excepted.

(ii) Special definitions to be used for this paragraph:

(A) The *minimum actuarial liability* shall be the actuarial accrued liability measured under the accrued benefit cost method and using an interest rate assumption as described in 9904.412-50(b)(7)(iii).

(B) The *minimum normal cost* shall be the normal cost measured under the accrued benefit cost method and using an interest rate assumption as described in

9904.412-50(b)(7)(iii). Anticipated administrative expense for the period shall be recognized as a separate incremental component of normal cost.

(iii) *Actuarial Assumptions:* The actuarial assumptions used to measure the minimum actuarial liability and minimum normal cost shall meet the following criteria:

(A) The interest assumption used to measure the pension cost for the current period shall reflect the contractor's best estimate of rates at which the pension benefits could effectively be settled based on the current period rates of return on investment grade fixed-income investments of similar duration to the pension benefits and that are in the top 3 quality levels available, *e.g.,* Moody's' single "A" rated or higher;

(B) The contractor may elect to use the same rate or set of rates, for investment grade corporate bonds of similar duration to the pension benefits, as may be published by the Secretary of the Treasury and used for determination of the minimum contribution required by ERISA. The contractor's cost accounting practice includes the election of the specific published rate or set of rates and must be consistently followed;

(C) For purposes of 9904.412-50(b)(7)(ii)(A) and (B), use of current period rates of return on investment grade corporate bonds of similar duration to the pension benefits shall not violate the provisions of 9904.412-40(b)(2) and 9904.412-50(b)(4) regarding the interest rate used to measure the minimum actuarial liability and minimum normal cost; and

(D) All actuarial assumptions, other than interest assumptions, used to measure the minimum actuarial liability and minimum normal cost shall be the same as the assumptions used elsewhere in this Standard.

(c) Assignment of pension cost. (1) Amounts funded in excess of the pension cost assigned to a cost accounting period pursuant to the provisions of this Standard shall be accounted for as a prepayment credit and carried forward to future accounting periods.

(2) For qualified defined-benefit pension plans, the pension cost measured for a cost

accounting period is assigned to that period subject to the following adjustments, in order of application:

(i) Any amount of pension cost measured for the period that is less than zero shall be assigned to future accounting periods as an assignable cost credit. The amount of pension cost assigned to the period shall be zero.

(ii) When the pension cost equals or exceeds the assignable cost limitation:

(A) The amount of pension cost, adjusted pursuant to paragraph (c)(2)(i) of this subsection, shall not exceed the assignable cost limitation,

(B) All amounts described in 9904.412-50(a)(1) and 9904.413-50(a), which are required to be amortized, shall be considered fully amortized, and

(C) Except for portions of unfunded actuarial liability separately identified and maintained in accordance with 9904.412-50(a)(2), any portion of unfunded actuarial liability, which occurs in the first cost accounting period after the pension cost has been limited by the assignable cost limitation, shall be considered an actuarial gain or loss for purposes of this Standard. Such actuarial gain or loss shall exclude any increase or decrease in unfunded actuarial liability resulting from a plan amendment, change in actuarial assumptions, or change in actuarial cost method effected after the pension cost has been limited by the assignable cost limitation.

(iii) An amount of pension cost of a qualified pension plan, adjusted pursuant to paragraphs (c)(2)(i) and (ii) of this subsection that exceeds the sum of (A) the maximum tax-deductible amount, determined in accordance with the Internal Revenue Code at Title 26 of the U.S.C., and (B) the accumulated value of prepayment credits, shall be assigned to future accounting periods as an assignable cost deficit. The amount of pension cost assigned to the current period shall not exceed the sum of the maximum tax-deductible amount and the accumulated value of prepayment credits.

(3) The cost of nonqualified defined-benefit pension plans shall be assigned to cost accounting periods in the same manner as qualified plans (with the exception of paragraph (c)(2)(iii) of this subsection) under the following conditions:

(i) The contractor, in disclosing or establishing his cost accounting practices, elects to have a plan so accounted for;

(ii) The plan is funded through the use of a funding agency; and,

(iii) The right to a pension benefit is nonforfeitable and is communicated to the participants.

(4) The costs of nonqualified defined-benefit pension plans that do not meet all of the requirements in 9904.412-50(c)(3) shall be assigned to cost accounting periods using the pay-as-you-go cost method.

(5) Any portion of pension cost measured for a cost accounting period and adjusted in accordance with 9904.412-50(c)(2) that exceeds the amount required to be funded pursuant to a waiver granted under the provisions of ERISA shall not be assigned to the current period. Rather, such excess shall be treated as an assignable cost deficit, except that it shall be assigned to future cost accounting periods using the same amortization period as used for ERISA purposes.

(d) Allocation of pension costs. The amount of pension cost assigned to a cost accounting period allocated to intermediate and final cost objectives shall be limited according to the following criteria:

(1) Except for nonqualified defined-benefit plans, the costs of a pension plan assigned to a cost accounting period are allocable to the extent that they are funded.

(2) For nonqualified defined-benefit pension plans that meet the criteria set forth at 9904.412-50(c)(3), pension costs assigned to a cost accounting period are fully allocable if they are funded at a level at least equal to the percentage of the complement (i.e., 100 minus tax rate percentage of assigned cost to be funded) of the highest published Federal corporate income tax rate in effect on the first day of the cost accounting period. If the contractor is not subject to Federal income tax, the assigned costs are allocable to the extent such costs are funded. Funding at

CASB 9904.412-50

other levels and benefit payments of such plans are subject to the following:

(i) Funding at less than the foregoing levels shall result in proportional reductions of the amount of assigned cost that can be allocated within the cost accounting period.

(ii) (A) Payments to retirees or beneficiaries shall contain an amount drawn from sources other than the funding agency of the pension plan that is, at least, proportionately equal to the accumulated value of permitted unfunded accruals divided by an amount that is the market value of the assets of the pension plan excluding any accumulated value of prepayment credits.

(B) The amount of assigned cost of a cost accounting period that can be allocated shall be reduced to the extent that such payments are drawn in a higher ratio from the funding agency.

(iii) The permitted unfunded accruals shall be identified and accounted for year to year, adjusted for benefit payments directly paid by the contractor and for interest at the actual annual earnings rate on the funding agency balance.

(3) For nonqualified defined-benefit pension plans accounted for under the pay-as-you-go method, pension costs assigned to a cost accounting period are allocable in that period.

(4) Funding of pension cost shall be considered to have taken place within the cost accounting period if it is accomplished by the corporate tax filing date for such period including any permissible extensions thereto.

[Final rule, 60 FR 16534, 3/30/95, effective 3/30/95, corrected 61 FR 58011, 11/12/96; Final rule, 76 FR 81296, 12/27/2011, effective 2/27/2012]

9904.412-60 Illustrations.

(a) Components of pension cost. (1) Contractor A has insured pension plans for each of two small groups of employees. One plan is exclusively funded through a group permanent life insurance contract and is exempt from the minimum funding requirements of ERISA. The other plan is funded through a deposit administration contract, which is a form of group deferred annuity contract that is not exempt from ERISA's minimum funding requirements. Both plans provide for defined benefits. Pursuant to 9904.412-50(a)(6), for purposes of this Standard the plan financed through a group permanent insurance contract shall be considered to be a defined-contribution pension plan; the net premium required to be paid for a cost accounting period (after deducting dividends and any credits) shall be the pension cost for that period. However, the deposit administration contract plan is subject to the provisions of this Standard that are applicable to defined-benefit plans.

(2) Contractor B provides pension benefits for certain hourly employees through a multiemployer defined-benefit plan. Under the collective bargaining agreement, the contractor pays six cents into the fund for each hour worked by the covered employees. Pursuant to 9904.412-50(a)(8), the plan shall be considered to be a defined contribution pension plan. The payments required to be made for a cost accounting period shall constitute the assignable pension cost for that period.

(3) Contractor C provides pension benefits for certain employees through a defined-contribution pension plan. However, the contractor has a separate fund that is used to supplement pension benefits for all of the participants in the basic plan in order to provide a minimum monthly retirement income to each participant. Pursuant to 9904.412-50(a)(7), the two plans shall be considered as a single plan for purposes of this Standard. Because the effect of the supplemental plan is to provide defined-benefits for the plan's participants, the provisions of this Standard relative to defined-benefit pension plans shall be applicable to the combined plan.

(4) Contractor D provides supplemental benefits to key management employees through a nonqualified defined-benefit pension plan funded by a so-called "Rabbi Trust." The trust agreement provides that Federal income taxes levied on the earnings of the Rabbi trust may be paid from the trust. The contractor's actuarial cost method recognizes the administrative expenses of the

plan and trust, such as broker and attorney fees, by adding the prior year's expenses to the current year's normal cost. The income taxes paid by the trust on trust earnings shall be accorded the same treatment as any other administrative expense in accordance with 9904.412-50(a)(5).

(5) (i) Contractor E has been using the entry age normal actuarial cost method to compute pension costs. The contractor has three years remaining under a firm fixed price contract subject to this Standard. The contract was priced using the unfunded actuarial liability, normal cost, and net amortization installments developed using the entry age normal method. The contract was priced as follows:

ENTRY AGE NORMAL VALUES

Cost component	Year 1	Year 2	Year 3
Normal cost	$100,000	$105,000	$110,000
Amortization	50,000	50,000	50,000
Pension cost	150,000	155,000	160,000

(ii) The contractor, after notifying the cognizant Federal official, switches to the projected unit credit actuarial cost method. The unfunded actuarial liability and normal cost decreased when redetermined under the projected unit credit method. Pursuant to 9904.412-50(a)(1)(vii), the contractor determines that an annual installment credit of $20,000 will amortize the decrease in unfunded actuarial liability (UAL) over ten years. The following pension costs are determined under the projected unit credit method:

PROJECTED UNIT CREDIT VALUES

Cost component	Year 1	Year 2	Year 3
Normal cost	$ 80,000	$ 85,000	$ 90,000
Amortization:			
Prior method	50,000	50,000	50,000
UAL decrease	(20,000)	(20,000)	(20,000)
Pension cost	110,000	115,000	120,000

(iii) The change in cost method is a change in accounting method that decreased previously priced pension costs by $40,000 per year. In accordance with 9903.302, Contractor E shall adjust the cost of the firm fixed-price contract for the remaining three years by $120,000 ($40,000 3 years).

(6) Contractor F has a defined-benefit pension plan for its employees. Prior to being subject to this Standard the contractor's policy was to compute and fund as annual pension cost normal cost plus only interest on the unfunded actuarial liability. Pursuant to 9904.412-40(a)(1), the components of pension cost for a cost accounting period must now include not only the normal cost for the period and interest on the unfunded actuarial liability, but also an amortized portion of the unfunded actuarial liability. The amortization of the liability and the interest equivalent on the unamortized portion of the liability must be computed in equal annual installments.

(b) Measurement of pension cost. (1) Contractor G has a pension plan whose costs are assigned to cost accounting periods by use of an actuarial cost method that does not separately identify actuarial gains and losses or the effect on pension cost resulting from changed actuarial assumptions. Contractor G's method is not an immediate-gain cost method and does not comply with the provisions of 9904.412-50(b)(1).

(2) For several years Contractor H has had an unfunded nonqualified pension plan which provides for payments of $200 a month to employees after retirement. The

contractor is currently making such payments to several retired employees and recognizes those payments as its pension cost. The contractor paid monthly annuity benefits totaling $24,000 during the current year. During the prior year, Contractor H made lump sum payments to irrevocably settle the benefit liability of several participants with small benefits. The annual installment to amortize these lump sum payments over fifteen years at the interest rate assumption, which is based on expected rate of return on investments and complies with 9904.412-40(b)(2) and 9904.412-50(b)(4), is $5,000. Since the plan does not meet the criteria set forth in 9904.412-50(c)(3)(ii), pension cost must be accounted for using the pay-as-you-go cost method. Pursuant to 9904.412-50(b)(3), the amount of assignable cost allocable to cost objectives of that period is $29,000, which is the sum of the amount of benefits actually paid in that period ($24,000) and the second annual installment to amortize the prior year's lump sum settlements ($5,000).

(3) Contractor I has two qualified defined-benefit pension plans that provide for fixed dollar payments to hourly employees.

(i) Under the first plan, in which the benefits are not subject to a collective bargaining agreement, the contractor's actuary believes that the contractor will be required to increase the level of benefits by specified percentages over the next several years based on an established pattern of benefit improvements. In calculating pension costs for this first plan, the contractor may not assume future benefits greater than that currently required by the plan.

(ii) With regard to the second plan, a collective bargaining agreement negotiated with the employees' labor union provides that pension benefits will increase by specified percentages over the next several years. Because the improved benefits are required to be made, the contractor can consider not only benefits increases required by the collective bargaining agreement, but may also consider subsequent benefit increases based on the average increase in benefits during the previous 6 years in computing pension costs for the current cost accounting period

in accordance with 9904.412-50(b)(5). The contractor shall limit projected benefits to the increases specified in the provisions of the existing plan, as amended by the collective bargaining agreement, in accordance with 9904.412-50(b)(5).

(4) In addition to the facts of 9904.412-60(b)(3), assume that Contractor I was required to contribute at a higher level for ERISA purposes because the plan was underfunded. To compute pension costs that are closer to the funding requirements of ERISA, Contractor I decides to "fresh start" the unfunded actuarial liability being amortized pursuant to 9904.412-50(a)(1); i.e., treat the entire amount as a newly established portion of unfunded actuarial liability, which is amortized over 10 years in accordance with 9904.412-50(a)(1)(ii). Because the contractor has changed the periods for amortizing the unfunded actuarial liability established pursuant to 9904.412-50(a)(3), the contractor has made a change in accounting practice subject to the provisions of Cost Accounting Standard 9903.302.

(c) Assignment of pension cost. (1) Contractor J maintains a qualified defined-benefit pension plan. The actuarial accrued liability for the plan is $20 million and is measured by the minimum actuarial liability in accordance with 9904.412-50(b)(7)(ii) since the criterion of 9904.412-50(b)(7)(i) has been satisfied. The actuarial value of the assets of $18 million is subtracted from the actuarial accrued liability of $20 million to determine the total unfunded actuarial liability of $2 million. Pursuant to 9904.412-50(a)(1), Contractor J has identified and is amortizing twelve separate portions of unfunded actuarial liabilities. The sum of the unamortized balances for the twelve separately maintained portions of unfunded actuarial liability equals $1.8 million. In accordance with 9904.412-50(a)(2), the contractor has separately identified, and eliminated from the computation of pension cost, $200,000 attributable to a pension cost assigned to a prior period that was not funded. The sum of the twelve amortization bases maintained pursuant to 9904.412-50(a)(1) and the amount separately identified under 9904.412-50(a)(2) equals $2 million ($1,800,000 + 200,000). Be-

CASB 9904.412-60

cause the sum of all identified portions of unfunded actuarial liability equals the total unfunded actuarial liability, the plan is in actuarial balance and Contractor J can assign pension cost to the current cost accounting period in accordance with 9904.412-40(c).

(2) Contractor K's pension cost computed for 2017, the current year, is $1.5 million. This computed cost is based on the components of pension cost described in 9904.412-40(a) and 9904.412-50(a) and is measured in accordance with 9904.412-40(b) and 9904.412-50(b). The assignable cost limitation, which is defined at 9904.412-30(a)(9), is $1.3 million. In accordance with the provisions of 9904.412-50(c)(2)(ii)(A), Contractor K's assignable pension cost for 2017 is limited to $1.3 million. In addition, all amounts that were previously being amortized pursuant to 9904.412-50(a)(1) and 9904.413-50(a) are considered fully amortized in accordance with 9904.412-50(c)(2)(ii)(B). The following year, 2018, Contractor K computes an unfunded actuarial liability of $4 million. Contractor K has not changed his actuarial assumptions nor amended the provisions of his pension plan. Contractor K has not had any pension costs disallowed or unfunded in prior periods. Contractor K must treat the entire $4 million of unfunded actuarial liability as an actuarial loss to be amortized over a ten-year period beginning in 2018 in accordance with 9904.412-50(c)(2)(ii)(C) and 9904.413-50(a)(2)(ii).

(3) Assume the same facts shown in illustration 9904.412-60(c)(2), except that in 2016, the prior year, Contractor K's assignable pension cost was $800,000, but Contractor K only funded and allocated $600,000. Pursuant to 9904.412-50(a)(2), the $200,000 of unfunded assignable pension cost was separately identified and eliminated from other portions of unfunded actuarial liability. This portion of unfunded actuarial liability was adjusted for 8% interest, which is the interest assumption for 2016 and 2017, and was brought forward to 2017 in accordance with 9904.412-50(a)(2). Therefore, $216,000 ($200,000 x 1.08) is excluded from the amount considered fully amortized in 2017. The next year, 2018, Contractor K must eliminate $233,280 ($216,000 x 1.08) from

the $4 million so that only $3,766,720 is treated as an actuarial loss in accordance with 9904.412-50(c)(2)(ii)(C).

(4) Assume, as in 9904.412-60(c)(2), the 2017 pension cost computed for Contractor K's qualified defined-benefit pension plan is $1.5 million and the assignable cost limitation is $1.7 million. The accumulated value of prepayment credits is $0. However, because of the limitation on tax-deductible contributions imposed by the Internal Revenue Code at Title 26 of the U.S.C., Contractor K cannot fund more than $1 million without incurring an excise tax, which 9904.412-50(a)(5) does not permit to be a component of pension cost. In accordance with the provisions of 9904.412-50(c)(2)(iii), Contractor K's assignable pension cost for the period is limited to $1 million. The $500,000 ($1.5 million-$1 million) of pension cost not funded is reassigned to the next ten cost accounting periods beginning in 2018 as an assignable cost deficit in accordance with 9904.412-50(a)(1)(vi).

(5) Assume the same facts for Contractor K in 9904.412-60(c)(4), except that the accumulated value of prepayment credits equals $700,000. Therefore, in addition to the $1 million tax-deductible contribution which was deposited on the first day of the plan year, Contractor K could apply up to $700,000 of the accumulated value of prepayment credits towards the pension cost computed for the period. In accordance with the provisions of 9904.412-50(c)(2)(iii), the amount of pension cost assigned to the current period shall not exceed $1,700,000, which the sum of the $1 million maximum tax-deductible amount and $700,000 accumulated value of prepayment credits. Contractor K's assignable pension cost for the period is the full $1.5 million computed for the period. A new prepayment credit of $200,000 is created by the excess funding after applying sum of the $1 million contribution and $700,000 accumulated value of prepayment credits towards the $1.5 million assigned pension cost ($700,000 + $1,000,000–$1,500,000). The $200,000 of remaining accumulated value of prepayment credits is adjusted for $14,460 of investment income allocated in accordance with

9904.412-50(a)(4) and 9904.413-50(c)(7) and the sum of $214,460 is carried forward until needed in future accounting periods in accordance with 9904.412-50(a)(4) and 9904.412-50(c)(1).

(6) Assume the same facts for Contractor K in 9904.412-60(c)(4), except that the 2017 assignable cost limitation is $1.3 million and the accumulated value of prepayment credits is $0. Pension cost of $1.5 million is computed for the cost accounting period, but the assignable cost is limited to $1.3 million in accordance with 9904.412-50(c)(2)(ii)(A). Pursuant to 9904.412-50(c)(2)(ii)(B), all existing amortization bases maintained in accordance with 9904.412-50(a)(1) are considered fully amortized. The assignable cost of $1.3 million is then compared to the maximum tax-deductible amount of $1 million. Pursuant to 9904.412-50(c)(2)(iii), Contractor K's assignable pension cost for the period is limited to $1 million. The $300,000 ($1.3 million-$1 million) excess of the assignable cost limitation over the tax-deductible maximum is assigned to future periods as an assignable cost deficit.

(7) Contractor L is currently amortizing a large decrease in unfunded actuarial liability over a period of ten years. A similarly large increase in unfunded actuarial liability is being amortized over 30 years. The absolute value of the resultant net amortization credit is greater than the normal cost so that the pension cost computed for the period is a negative $200,000. Contractor L first applies the provisions of 9904.412-50(c)(2)(i) and determines the assignable pension cost is $0. The negative pension cost of $200,000 is assigned to the next ten cost accounting periods as an assignable cost credit in accordance with 9904.412-50(a)(1)(vi). However, when Contractor L applies the provisions of 9904.412-50(c)(2)(ii), the assignable cost limitation is also $0. Because the assignable cost of $0 determined under 9904.412-50(c)(2)(i) is equal to the assignable cost limitation, the assignable cost credit of $200,000 is considered fully amortized along with all other portions of unfunded actuarial liability being amortized pursuant to 9904.412-50(a)(1). Conversely, if the assignable cost limitation had been greater

than zero, the assignable cost credit of $200,000 would have carried-forward and amortized in future periods.

(8) Contractor M has a qualified defined-benefit pension plan which is funded through a funding agency. It computes $1 million of pension cost for a cost accounting period. However, pursuant to a waiver granted under the provisions of ERISA, Contractor M is required to fund only $800,000. Under the provisions of 9904.412-50(c)(5), the remaining $200,000 shall be accounted for as an assignable cost deficit and assigned to the next five cost accounting periods in accordance with the terms of the waiver.

(9) Contractor N has a company-wide defined-benefit pension plan, wherein benefits are calculated on one consistently applied formula. That part of the formula defining benefits within ERISA limits is administered and reported as a qualified plan and funded through a funding agency. The remainder of the benefits are considered to be a supplemental or excess plan which, while it meets the criteria at 9904.412-50(c)(3)(iii) as to nonforfeitability and communication, is not funded. The costs of the qualified portion of the plan shall be comprised of those elements of costs delineated at 9904.412-40(a)(1), while the supplemental or excess portion of the plan shall be accounted for and assigned to cost accounting periods under the pay-as-you-go cost method provided at 9904.412-40(a)(3) and 9904.412-50(c)(4).

(10) Assuming the same facts as in 9904.412-60(c)(9), except that Contractor N funds its supplemental or excess plan using a so-called "Rabbi Trust" vehicle. Because the nonqualified plan is funded, the plan meets the criteria set forth at 9904.412-50(c)(3)(ii). Contractor N may account for the supplemental or excess plan in the same manner as its qualified plan, if it elects to do so pursuant to 9904.412-50(c)(3)(i).

(11) Assuming the same facts as in 9904.412-60(c)(10), except that under the nonqualified portion of the pension plan a former employee will forfeit his pension benefit if the employee goes to work for a competitor within three years of terminating

CASB 9904.412-60

employment. Since the right to a benefit cannot be affected by the unilateral action of the contractor, the right to a benefit is considered to be nonforfeitable for purposes of 9904.412-30(a)(17). The nonqualified plan still meets the criteria set forth at 9904.412-50(c)(3)(iii), and Contractor N may account for the supplemental or excess plan in the same manner as its qualified plan, if it elects to do so.

(12) Assume the same facts as in 9904.412-60(c)(11), except that Contractor N, while maintaining a "Rabbi Trust" funding vehicle elects to have the plan accounted for under the pay-as-you-go cost method so as to have greater latitude in annual funding decisions. It may so elect pursuant to 9904.412-50(c)(3)(i).

(13) The assignable pension cost for Contractor O's qualified defined-benefit plan is $600,000. For the same period Contractor O contributes $700,000 which is the minimum funding requirement under ERISA. In addition, there exists $75,000 of unfunded actuarial liability that has been separately identified pursuant to 9904.412-50(a)(2). Contractor O may use $75,000 of the contribution in excess of the assignable pension cost to fund this separately identified unfunded actuarial liability, if he so chooses. The effect of the funding is to eliminate the unassignable $75,000 portion of unfunded actuarial liability that had been separately identified and thereby eliminated from the computation of pension costs. Contractor O shall then account for the remaining $25,000 ([$700,000 - $600,000] - $75,000) of excess contribution as a prepayment credit in accordance with 9904.412-50(a)(4).

(d) Allocation of pension cost. (1) Assume the same set of facts for Contractor M in 9904.412-60(c)(8) except there was no ERISA waiver; i.e., only $800,000 was funded against $1 million of assigned pension cost for the period. Under the provisions of 9904.412-50(d)(1), only $800,000 may be allocated to Contractor M's intermediate and final cost objectives. The remaining $200,000 of assigned cost, which has not been funded, shall be separately identified and maintained in accordance with 9904.412-50(a)(2) so that

it will not be reassigned to any future accounting periods.

(2) Contractor P has a nonqualified defined-benefit pension plan which covers benefits in excess of the ERISA limits. Contractor P has elected to account for this plan in the same manner as its qualified plan and, therefore, has established a "Rabbi Trust" as the funding agency. For the current cost accounting period, the contractor computes and assigns $100,000 as pension cost. The contractor funds $65,000, which is equivalent to a funding level equal to the complement of the highest published Federal corporate income tax rate of 35. Under the provisions of 9904.412-50(d)(2), the entire $100,000 is allocable to cost objectives of the period.

(3) Assume the set of facts in 9904.412-60(d)(2), except that Contractor P's contribution to the Trust is $59,800. In that event, the provisions of 9904.412-50(d)(2)(i) would limit the amount of assigned cost allocable within the cost accounting period to the percentage of cost funded (i.e., $59,800$65,000 = 92). This results in allocable cost of $92,000 (92% of $100,000) for the cost accounting period. Under the provisions of 9904.412-40(c) and 9904.412-50(d)(2)(i), respectively, the unallocable $8,000 may not be assigned to any future cost accounting period. In addition, in accordance with 9904.412-50(a)(2), the $8,000 must be separately identified and no amount of interest on such separately identified $8,000 shall be a component of pension cost in any future cost accounting period.

(4) Again, assume the set of facts in 9904.412-60(d)(2) except that, Contractor P's contribution to the Trust is $105,000 based on an interest assumption of 8%, which is based on the expected rate of return on investments and complies with 9904.412-40(b)(2) and 9904.412-50(b)(4). Under the provisions of 9904.412-50(d)(2) the entire $100,000 is allocable to cost objectives of the period. In accordance with the provisions of 9904.412-50(c)(1) Contractor P has funded $5,000 ($105,000-$100,000) in excess of the assigned pension cost for the period. The $5,000 shall be accounted for as a prepayment credit. Pursuant

9904.412-50(a)(4), the $5,000 shall be adjusted for an allocated portion of the total investment income and expenses in accordance with 9904.412-50(a)(4) and 9904.413-50(c)(7). Allocated earnings and expenses, and the prepayment credits, shall be excluded from the actuarial value of assets used to compute the next year's pension cost. For the current period the net return on assets attributable to investment income and expenses was 6.5%. Therefore, the accumulated value of prepayment credits of $5,325 (5,000 x 1.065) may be used to fund the next year's assigned pension cost, if needed.

(5) Contractor Q maintains a nonqualified defined-benefit pension plan which satisfies the requirements of 9904.412-50(c)(3). As of the valuation date, the reported funding agency balance is $3.4 million excluding any accumulated value of prepayment credits. When the adjusted funding agency balance is added to the accumulated value of permitted unfunded accruals of $1.6 million, the market value of assets equals $5.0 million ($3.4 million + $1.6 million) in accordance with 9904.412-30(a)(13). During the plan year, retirees receive monthly benefits totalling $350,000. Pursuant to 9904.412-50(d)(2)(ii)(A), at least 32 ($1.6 million divided by $5 million) of these benefit payments shall be made from sources other than the funding agency. Contractor Q, therefore, draws $238,000 from the funding agency assets and pays the remaining $112,000 using general corporate funds.

(6) Assume the same facts as 9904.412-60(d)(5), except that by the time Contractor Q receives its actuarial valuation it has paid retirement benefits equalling $288,000 from funding agency assets. The contractor has made deposits to the funding agency equal to the tax complement of the $500,000 assignable pension cost for the period. Pursuant to 9904.412-50(d)(2)(ii)(B), the assignable $500,000 shall be reduced by the $50,000 ($288,000 – $238,000) of benefits paid from the funding agency in excess of the permitted $238,000, unless the contractor makes a deposit to replace the $50,000 inadvertently drawn from the funding agency. If this corrective action is not taken

within the time permitted by 9904.412-50(d)(4), Contractor Q shall allocate only $450,000 ($500,000 – $50,000) to final cost objectives. Furthermore, the $50,000, which was thereby attributed to benefit payments instead of funding, must be separately identified and maintained in accordance with 9904.412-50(a)(2).

(7) Contractor R has a nonqualified defined-benefit plan that meets the criteria of 9904.412-50(c)(3). For 1996, the funding agency balance was $1,250,000 and the accumulated value of permitted unfunded accruals was $600,000. During 1996 the earnings and appreciation on the assets of the funding agency equalled $125,000, benefit payments to participants totalled $300,000, and administrative expenses were $60,000. All transactions occurred on the first day of the period. In accordance with 9904.412-50(d)(2)(ii)(A), $200,000 of benefits were paid from the funding agency and $100,000 were paid directly from corporate assets. Pension cost of $400,000 was assigned to 1996. Based on the current corporate tax rate of 35%, $260,000 ($400,000 × (135%)) was deposited into the funding agency at the beginning of 1996. For 1997 the funding agency balance is $1,375,000 ($1,250,000 + $260,000 + $125,000 – $200,000 – $60,000). The actual annual earnings rate of the funding agency was 10 for 1996. Pursuant to 9904.412-50(d)(2)(iii), the accumulated value of permitted unfunded accruals is updated from 1996 to 1997 by: (i) adding $140,000 (35% × $400,000), which is the unfunded portion of the assigned cost; (ii) subtracting the $100,000 of benefits paid directly by the contractor; and (iii) increasing the value of the assets by $64,000 for imputed earnings at 10% (10% × ($600,000 + $140,000 – $100,000)). The accumulated value of permitted unfunded accruals for 1997 is $704,000 ($600,000 + $140,000 – $100,000 + $64,000).

[Final rule, 60 FR 16534, 3/30/95, effective 3/30/95; Final rule, 76 FR 81296, 12/27/2011, effective 2/27/2012]

9904.412-60.1 Illustrations—CAS Pension Harmonization Rule.

The following illustrations address the measurement, assignment and allocation of pension cost on or after the Applicability Date of the CAS Harmonization Rule. The illustrations present the measurement, assignment and allocation of pension cost for a contractor that separately computes pension costs by segment or aggregation of segments. The actuarial gain and loss recognition of changes between measurements based on the actuarial accrued liability, determined without regard to the provisions of 9904.412-50(b)7) and the minimum actuarial liability are illustrated in 9904.412-60.1(d). The structural format for 9904.412.60.1 differs from the format for 9904.412-60.

(a) *Description of the pension plan, actuarial assumptions and actuarial methods used for 9904.412-60.1 Illustrations.* (1) *Introduction:* Harmony Corporation has a defined-benefit pension plan covering employees at seven segments, of which some segments have contracts that are subject to this Standard and 9904.413, while other segments perform commercial work only. The demographic experience regarding employee terminations for employees of Segment 1 is materially different from that of the other six segments so that pursuant to 9904.413-50(c)(2)(iii) the contractor must separately compute the pension cost for Segment 1. Because the factors comprising pension cost for Segments 2 through 7 are relatively equal, the contractor computes pension cost for these six segments in the aggregate and allocates the aggregate cost to segments on a composite basis. Inactive employees are retained in the segment from which they terminated employment. The contractor has received its annual actuarial valuation for its qualified defined benefit pension plan, which bases the pension benefit on the employee's final average salary.

(2) *Actuarial Methods and Assumptions:* (i) *Salary Projections:* As permitted by 9904.412-50(b)(5), the contractor includes a projection of future salary increases and uses the projected unit credit cost method, which is an immediate gain actuarial cost method that satisfies the requirements of 9904.412-40(b)(1) and 50(b)(1), for measuring the actuarial accrued liability and normal cost. The contractor uses the accrued benefit cost method (also known as the unit

credit cost method without projection) to measure the minimum actuarial liability and minimum normal cost. The accrued benefit cost method satisfies 9904.412-50(b)(7)(ii) as well as 9904.412-40(b)(1) and 50(b)(1).

(ii) *Interest Rates:* (A) Assumed interest rate used to measure the actuarial accrued liability and normal cost: The contractor's basis for establishing the expected rate of return on investments assumption satisfies the criteria of 9904.412-40(b)(2) and 9904.412-50(b)(4). This is referred to as the "assumed interest rate" for purposes of this illustration.

(B) Corporate bond rate used to measure the minimum actuarial liability and minimum normal cost: For purposes of measuring the minimum actuarial liability and minimum normal cost the contractor has elected to use a specific set of investment grade corporate bond yield rates published by the Secretary of the Treasury for ERISA's minimum funding requirements. The basis for establishing the set of corporate bond rates meets the requirements of 9904.412-50(b)(7)(iii)(A) as permitted by 9904.412-50(b)(7)(iii)(B). This set of rates is referred to as the "corporate bond rates" for purposes of this illustration.

(iii) *Mortality:* The mortality assumption is based on a table of generational mortality rates published by the Secretary of the Treasury and reflects recent mortality improvements. This table satisfies 9904.412-40(b)(2) which requires assumptions to "represent the contractor's best estimates of anticipated experience under the plan, taking into account past experience and reasonable expectations." The specific table used for each valuation shall be identified.

(iv) *Termination of Employment:* The termination of employment (turnover) assumption is based on an experience study of Harmony Company employee terminations or causes other than retirement. Because the experience for Segment 1 was materially different from the experience for the rest of the company, the termination of employee assumption for Segment 1 was developed based on the experience of that segment only in accordance with 9904.413-50(c)(2)(iii). The termination of employment experiences for each of Segments 2 through 7 were materially similar, and therefore the termination of employee assumption for Segments 2 through 7 was developed based on the experiences of those segments in the aggregate.

(v) *Actuarial Value of Assets:* The valuation of the actuarial value of assets used for CAS 412 and 413 is based on a recognized smoothing technique that "provides equivalent recognition of appreciation and depreciation of the market value of the assets of the pension plan." The disclosed method also constrains the asset value to a corridor bounded by 80% to 120% of the market value of assets. This method for measuring the actuarial value of assets satisfies the provisions of 9904.413-50(b)(2).

(b) *Measurement of Pension Costs.* Based on the pension plan, actuarial methods and actuarial assumptions described in 9904.412-60.1(a), the Harmony Corporation determines that the pension plan, as well as Segment 1 and Segments 2 through 7, have unfunded actuarial liabilities and measures its pension cost for plan year 2017 as follows:

(1) *Asset Values:* (i) *Market Values of Assets:* The contractor accounts for the market value of assets in accordance with 9904.413-50(c)(7). The contractor has elected to separately identify the accumulated value of prepayment credits from the assets allocated to segments. The accumulated value of prepayment credits are adjusted in accordance with 9904.412-50(a)(4) and 9904.413-50(c)(7). The market value of assets as of January 1, 2017, including the accumulated value of prepayment credits, is summarized in Table 1.

Table 1—January 1, 2017, Market Value of Assets

	Total plan	Segment 1	Segments 2 through 7	Accumulated prepayments	Note
Market Value of Assets	$14,257,880	$1,693,155	$11,904,328	$660,397	1

Note 1: Information taken directly from the actuarial valuation report prepared for CAS 412 and 413 purposes and supporting documentation.

(ii) *Actuarial Value of Assets:* Based on the contractor's disclosed asset valuation method, and recognition of the asset gain or loss, which is the difference between the expected income, based on the assumed interest rate, which complies with 9904.412-40(b)(2) and 9904.412-50(b)(4), and the actual income, including realized and unrealized appreciation and depreciation for the current and four prior periods as required by 9904.413-40(b), is delayed and amortized over a five-year period. The portion of the appreciation and depreciation that is deferred until future periods is subtracted from the market value of assets to determine the actuarial value of assets for CAS 412 and 413 purposes. The actuarial value of assets cannot be less than 80%, or more than 120%, of the market value of assets. The development of the actuarial value of assets for the total plan, as well as for Segment 1 and Segments 2 through 7, as of January 1, 2017 is shown in Table 2.

Table 2—January 1, 2017, Actuarial Value of Assets

	Total plan	Segment 1	Segments 2 through 7	Accumulated prepayments	Note
Market Value at January 1, 2017	$14,257,880	$1,693,155	$11,904,328	$660,397	1
Total Deferred Appreciation ..	(37,537)	(4,398)	(31,400)	(1.739)	2

	Total plan	Segment 1	Segments 2 through 7	Accumulated prepayments	Note
Unlimited Actuarial Value of Assets	14,220,343	1,688,757	11,872,928	658,658	. . . .
CAS 413 Asset Corridor 80% of Market Value of Assets	11,406,304	1,354,524	9,523,462	528,318	. . . .
Market Value at January 1, 2017	14,257,880	1,693,155	11,904,328	660,397	1
120% of Market Value of Assets	17,109,456	2,031,786	14,285,194	792,476	. . . .
CAS Actuarial Value of Assets	14,220,343	1,688,757	11,872,928	658,658	3, 4

Note 1: See Table 1.

Note 2: Information taken directly from the actuarial valuation report prepared for CAS 412 and 413 purposes and supporting documentation.

Note 3: CAS Actuarial Value of Assets cannot be less than 80% of Market Value of Assets or more than 120% of Market Value of Assets.

Note 4: The Actuarial Value of Assets are used in determination of any Unfunded Actuarial Liability or Unfunded Actuarial Surplus regardless of whether the liability is based on the actuarial accrued liability measured without regard to 9904.412-50(b)(7) or minimum actuarial liability measured in accordance with 9904.412-50(b)(7).

(2) *Liabilities and Normal Costs:* (i) *Actuarial Accrued Liabilities and Normal Costs:* Based on the plan population data and the disclosed methods and assumptions for CAS 412 and 413 purposes, the contractor measures the actuarial accrued liability and normal cost on a going concern basis using an assumed interest rate that satisfies the requirements of 9904.412-40(b)(2) and 9904.412-50(b)(4). The actuarial accrued liability and normal cost for each segment are measured based on the termination of employment assumption unique to that segment. The actuarial accrued liability and normal cost for the total plan is the sum of the actuarial accrued liability and normal cost for the segments. The actuarial accrued liability and normal cost are shown in Table 3.

Table 3—Actuarial Accrued Liabilities and Normal Costs as of January 1, 2017

	Total plan	Segment 1	Segments 2 through 7	Notes
Actuarial Accrued Liability (AAL)	$16,325,000	$2,100,000	$14,225,000	1
Normal Cost	910,700	89,100	821,600	1
Expense Load on Normal Cost	. . . .	. . . .	. . . .	1, 2

	Total plan	Segment 1	Segments 2 through 7	Notes

Note 1: Information taken directly from the actuarial valuation report prepared for CAS 412 and 413 purposes and supporting documentation. The actuarial accrued liability and normal cost are computed using the assumed interest rate in accordance with 9904.412-40(b)(2) and 9904.412.50(b)(4).

Note 2: Expected administrative expenses are implicitly recognized as part of the assumed interest rate.

(ii) Likewise, based on the plan population data and the disclosed methods and assumptions for CAS 412 and 413 purposes, the contractor measures the minimum actuarial liability and minimum normal cost using a set of investment grade corporate bond yield rates published by the Secretary of the Treasury that satisfy the requirements of 9904.412-50(b)(7)(iii). The minimum actuarial liability and minimum normal cost for each segment are measured based on the termination of employment assumption for that segment. The minimum actuarial liability and minimum normal cost for the total plan is the sum of the actuarial accrued liability and normal cost for the segments as shown in Table 4.

Table 4—Minimum Actuarial Liabilities and Minimum Normal Costs as of January 1, 2017

	Total plan	Segment 1	Segments 2 through 7	Notes
Minimum Actuarial Liability	$16,636,000	$2,594,000	$14,042,000	1
Minimum Normal Cost	942,700	102,000	840,700	1
Expense Load on Minimum Normal Cost	82,000	8,840	73,160	1, 2

Note 1: Plan level information taken directly from the actuarial valuation report prepared for ERISA purposes and supporting documentation and equals the sum of the data for the segments. Data for the segments is taken directly from the actuarial valuation report prepared for CAS 412 and 413 purposes and supporting documentation.

Note 2: Anticipated annual administrative expenses are separately recognized as an incremental component of minimum normal cost in accordance with 9904.412-50(b)(7)(ii)(B).

(3) *CAS Pension Harmonization Test:* (i) In accordance with 9904.412-50(b)(7)(i), the contractor compares the sum of the actuarial accrued liability and normal cost plus any expense load, to the sum of the minimum actuarial liability and minimum normal cost plus any expense load. Because the contractor separately computes pension costs by segment, or aggregation of segments, the applicability of 9904.412-50(b)(7)(i) is determined separately for Segment 1 and Segments 2 through 7. See Table 5, which shows the application of the provisions of 9904.412-50(b)(7)(i), *i.e.,* the CAS pension harmonization test.

Table 5—CAS Pension Harmonization Test at January 1, 2017

	Total plan	Segment 1	Segments 2 through 7	Notes
	(Note 1)	(Note 2)	(Note 2)	
"Going Concern" Liability for Period:	. . . .	. . . .	. . . .	3
Actuarial Accrued Liability . .	. . . .	$2,100,000	$14,225,000	4
Normal Cost	. . . .	89,100	821,600	4
Expense Load on Normal Cost	. . . .	. . . .	. . . .	4, 5
Total Liability for Period	. . . .	2,189,100	15,046,600	. . . .
Minimum Liability for Period: . . .				
Minimum Actuarial Liability .	. . . .	2,594,000	14,042,000	6
Minimum Normal Cost	. . . .	102,000	840,700	6
Expense Load on Minimum Normal Cost	. . . .	8,840	73,160	6, 7
Total Minimum Liability for Period	. . . .	2,704,840	14,955,860	. . . .

Note 1: Because the contractor determines pension costs separately for Segment 1 and Segments 2 through 7, the data for the Total Plan is not needed for purposes of the 9904.412-50(b)(7)(i) determination.

Note 2: Because the contractor determines pension cost separately for Segment 1 and Segments 2 through 7, the 9904.412-50(b)(7) CAS Pension Harmonization test is applied at the segment level to determine the larger of the Total Liability for Period or the Total Minimum Liability for Period. For Segment 1, the larger Total Minimum Liability for Period determines the measurement basis for the liability and normal cost. For Segments 2 through 7, the larger Total Liability for Period determines the measurement basis for the liability and normal cost.

Note 3: The actuarial accrued liability and normal cost plus any expense load are computed using interest assumptions based on long-term expectations in accordance with 9904.412-40(b)(2) and 9904.412-50(b)(4). For purposes of Illustration 9904.412-60.1(b), the sum of these amounts are referred to as the "Going Concern" Liability for the Period.

Note 4: See Table 3.

Note 5: Because the contractor's assumed interest rate implicitly recognizes expected administrative expenses there is no explicit amount added to the normal cost.

Note 6: See Table 4.

Note 7: The contractor explicitly identifies the expected expenses as a separate component of the minimum normal cost, as required by 9904.412-50(b)(7)(ii)(B).

(ii) As shown in Table 5 for Segment 1, the total minimum liability for the period (minimum actuarial liability and minimum normal cost) of $2,704,840 exceeds the total liability for the period (actuarial accrued liability and normal cost) of $2,189,100. There- fore, the contractor must measure the pension cost for Segment 1 using the mini- mum actuarial liability and minimum normal cost as the values of the actuarial accrued liability and normal cost in accordance with 9904.412-50(b)(7)(i). In other words, the contractor substitutes the minimum actuarial liability and minimum normal cost for the actuarial accrued liability and normal cost.

(iii) Conversely, as shown in Table 5 for Segments 2 through 7, the total liability for the period of $15,046,600 exceeds the total minimum liability for the period of $14,955,860 for Segments 2 through 7. Therefore, the contractor must measure the pension cost using the actuarial accrued liability and normal cost without regard for the minimum actuarial liability and minimum normal cost.

(4) *Measurement of Current Period Pension Cost:* (i) To determine the pension cost for Segment 1, the contractor measures the unfunded actuarial liability, pension cost without regard to 9904.412-50(c)(2) limitations, and the assignable cost limitation using the actuarial accrued liability and normal cost as measured by the minimum actuarial liability

and minimum normal cost, respectively, which are based on the accrued benefit cost method. This measurement complies with the requirements of 9904.412-50(b)(7) and the definition of actuarial accrued liability, 9904.412-30(a)(2) and normal cost, 9904.412-30(a)(18).

(ii) To determine the pension cost for Segments 2 through 7, the contractor measures the unfunded actuarial liability, pension cost without regard to 9904.412-50(c)(2) limitations, and the assignable cost limitation using the actuarial accrued liability and normal cost based on the projected unit credit cost method, which is the contractor's established cost accounting method and the contractor's assumed interest rate based on long-term trends as required by 9904.412-50(b)(4).

(iii) Unfunded Actuarial Liability (Table 6):

Table 6—Unfunded Actuarial Liability as of January 1, 2017

	Total plan	Segment 1	Segments 2 through 7	Notes
	(Note 1)			
Actuarial Accrued Liability	$16,819,000	$ 2,594,000	$14,225,000	2
CAS Actuarial Value of Assets	(13,561,685)	(1,688,757)	(11,872,928)	3
Unfunded Actuarial Liability	3,257,315	905,243	2,352,072	

Note 1: Because the contractor determines pensions separately for Segment 1 and Segments 2 through 7, the values are the sum of the values for Segment 1 and Segments 2 through 7.

Note 2: For Segment 1, the actuarial accrued liability is measured by the accrued benefit cost method as required by 9904.412-50(b)(7), *i.e.,* the minimum actuarial liability as described in 9904.412-50(b)(7)(ii). See Table 4. For Segments 2 through 7, the actuarial accrued liability is measured by the projected unit credit cost method, which is the contractor's established actuarial cost method since these the 9904.412-50(b)(7)(i) criterion was not met for these segments. See Table 3.

Note 3: See Table 2. The CAS Actuarial Value of Assets is used regardless of the basis for determining the liabilities. The CAS Actuarial Value of Assets allocated to Segment 1 and Segments 2 through 7 excludes the accumulated value of prepayment credits as required by 9904.412-50(a)(4).

(iv) Measurement of the Adjusted Pension Cost (Table 7):

Table 7—Measurement of Pension Cost at January 1, 2017

	Total plan	Segment 1	Segments 2 through 7	Notes
	(Note 1)			
Normal Cost	....	$ 102,000	$821,600	2
Expense Load on Normal Cost	....	8,840	....	2, 3
Amortization Installments	....	140,900	366,097	4
Measured Pension Cost	1,439,437	251,740	1,187,697	....

Note 1: Because the contractor separately computes pension cost for Segment 1 and Segments 2 through 7, only the total pension cost is shown.

Note 2: For Segment 1, the normal cost is measured by the accrued benefit cost method as required by 9904.412-50(b)(7), *i.e.,* the minimum normal cost as described in 9904.412-50(b)(7)(ii). See Table 4. For Segments 2 through 7, the normal cost is measured by the contractor's established immediate gain cost method since these the 9904.412-50(b)(7)(i) criterion was not met for these segments. See Table 3.

Note 3: Because the criterion of 9904.412-50(b)(7)(i) was met for Segment 1, the Normal Cost is measured by the Minimum Normal Cost, which explicitly identifies the expected expenses as a separate component of the minimum normal cost in accordance with 9904.412-50(b)(7)(ii)(B). See Table 4. For Segments 2 through 7, the normal cost is measured by the contractor's established immediate gain cost method, which implicitly recognizes expenses as a decrement to expected assumed interest rate, since the 9904.412-50(b)(7)(i) criterion was not met for these segments. See Table 3.

Note 4: Net amortization installment based on the unfunded actuarial liability of $3,257,315 ($905,243 for Segment 1, and $2,352,072 for Segments 2 through 7) and the contractor's assumed interest rate in compliance with 9904.412-40(b)(2) and 9904.412-50(b)(4). See Table 6.

(c) *Assignment of Pension Cost.* In 9904.412-60.1(b), the Harmony Corporation measured the total pension cost to be $1,439,437 ($251,740 for Segment 1 and $1,187,697 for Segments 2 through 7). The contractor must now determine if any of the limitations of 9904.412-50(c)(2) apply at the segment level.

(1) *Zero Dollar Floor:* The contractor compares the measured pension cost to a zero dollar floor as required by 9904.412-50(c)(2)(i). In this case, the measured pension cost is greater than zero and no assignable cost credit is established. See Table 8.

Table 8—CAS 412-50(c)(2)(i) Zero Dollar Floor as of January 1, 2017

	Total plan	Segment 1	Segments 2 through 7	Notes
	(Note 1)			
Measured Pension Cost ≥ $0	....	$251,740	$1,187,697	2

CASB 9904.412-60.1

	Total plan	Segment 1	Segments 2 through 7	Notes
Assignable Cost Credit	. . . .	. . . .	. . . .	3

Note 1: Because the provisions of CAS 412-50(c)(2)(i) are applied at the segment level, no values are shown for the Total Plan.

Note 2: See Table 7. The Assignable Pension Cost in accordance with 9904.412-50(c)(2)(i) is the greater of zero or the Harmonized Pension Cost.

Note 3: There is no Assignable Cost Credit since the Measured Pension Cost is greater than zero.

(2) *Assignable Cost Limitation:* (i) As required by 9904.412-50(c)(2)(ii), the contractor measures the assignable cost limitation amount. The pension cost assigned to the period cannot exceed the assignable cost limitation amount. Because the measured pension cost for Segment 1 met the harmonization criterion of 9904.412-50(b)(7)(i), the assignable cost limitation is based on the sum of the actuarial accrued liability and normal cost plus expense load, using the accrued benefit cost method in accordance with 9904.412-50(b)(7)(ii). Therefore, the actuarial accrued liability and normal cost plus expense load are measured by the minimum actuarial liability and minimum normal cost plus expense load. See Table 9.

Table 9—CAS 412-50(c)(2)(ii) Assignable Cost Limitation as of January 1, 2017

	Total plan	Segment 1	Segments 2 through 7	Notes
	(Note 1)			
Actuarial Accrued Liability	. . . .	$2,594,000	$14,225,000	2
Normal Cost	. . . .	102,000	821,600	3
Expense Load on Normal Cost	. . . .	8,840	. . . .	4
Total Liability for Period	. . . .	$2,704,840	$15,046,600	. . . .
CAS Actuarial Value of Plan Assets	. . . .	(1,688,757)	(11,872,928)	5
(A) Assignable Cost Limitation Amount . . .	. . . .	$1,016,083	$3,173,672	6
(B) 412-50(c)(2)(i) Assigned Cost	. . . .	$251,740	$1,187,697	7
(C) 412-50(c)(2)(ii) Assigned Cost	$1,439,437	$251,740	$1,187,697	8

Note 1: Because the assignable cost limitation is applied at the segment level when pension costs are separately calculated by segment or aggregation of segments, no values are shown for the Total Plan other than the Assigned Cost after consideration of the Assignable Cost Limit.

	Total plan	Segment 1	Segments 2 through 7	Notes

Note 2: For Segment 1, the actuarial accrued liability is measured by the accrued benefit cost method as required by 9904.412-50(b)(7), *i.e.,* the minimum actuarial liability as described in 9904.412-50(b)(7)(ii)(A). See Table 4. For Segments 2 through 7, the actuarial accrued liability is measured by the contractor's established immediate gain cost method since these the 9904.412-50(b)(7)(i) criterion was not met for these segments. See Table 3.

Note 3: For Segment 1, the normal cost is measured by the accrued benefit cost method as required by 9904.412-50(b)(7), *i.e.,* the minimum normal cost as described in 9904.412-50(b)(7)(ii)(B). See Table 4. For Segments 2 through 7, the normal cost is measured by the contractor's established immediate gain cost method since these the 9904.412-50(b)(7)(i) criterion was not met for these segments. See Table 3.

Note 4: For Segment 1, the normal cost is measured by the accrued benefit cost method as required by 9904.412-50(b)(7), *i.e.,* the minimum normal cost as described in 9904.412-50(b)(7)(ii)(B), which explicitly identifies the expected expenses as a separate component of the minimum normal cost. See Table 4. For Segments 2 through 7, the normal cost is measured by the contractor's established immediate gain cost method, which implicitly recognizes expenses as a decrement to the assumed interest rate since these the 9904.412-50(b)(7)(i) criterion was not met for these segments. See Table 3.

Note 5: See Table 2. The CAS Actuarial Value of Assets is used regardless of the basis for determining the liabilities. The CAS Actuarial Value of Assets allocated to Segment 1 and Segments 2 through 7 excludes the accumulated value of prepayment credits as required by 9904.412-50(a)(4).

Note 6: The Assignable Cost Limitation cannot be less than $0.

Note 7: See Illustration 9904.412-60.1(c)(1), Table 8.

Note 8: Lesser of lines (A) or (B).

(ii) As shown in Table 9, the contractor determines that the measured pension costs for Segment 1 and Segments 2 through 7 do not exceed the assignable cost limitation and are not limited.

(3) *Measurement of Tax-Deductible Limitation on Assignable Pension Cost:* (i) Finally, after limiting the measured pension cost in accordance with 9904.412-50(c)(2)(i) and (ii), the contractor checks to ensure that the total assigned pension cost will not exceed $15,674,697, which is the sum of the maximum tax-deductible contribution ($15,014,300), which is developed in the actuarial valuation prepared for ERISA, and the accumulated value of prepayment credits ($660,397) shown in Table 1. Since the tax-deductible contribution and accumulated value of prepayment credits are maintained for the plan as a whole, these values are allocated to segments based on the assignable pension cost after adjustment, if any, for the assignable cost limitation in accordance with 9904.413-50(c)(1)(ii). See Table 10.

Table 10—CAS 412-50(c)(2)(iii) Tax-Deductible Limitation as of January 1, 2017

	Total plan	Segment 1	Segments 2 through 7	Notes
Maximum Tax-deductible Amount . . .	$15,014,300	$2,625,818	$12,388,482	1, 2
Accumulated Prepayment Credits . .	660,397	115,495	544,902	3, 4

	Total plan	Segment 1	Segments 2 through 7	Notes
(A) 412-50(c)(2)(iii) Limitation	$15,674,697	$2,741,313	$12,933,384	....
(B) 412-50(c)(2)(ii) Assigned Cost	$1,439,437	$251,740	$1,187,697	5
Assigned Pension Cost	$1,439,437	$251,740	$1,187,697	6

Note 1: The Maximum Deductible Amount for the Total Plan is obtained from the valuation report prepared for ERISA purposes.

Note 2: The Maximum Tax-deductible Amount for the Total Plan is allocated to segments based on the assigned cost after application of 9904.412-50(c)(2)(ii) in accordance with 9904.413-50(c)(1)(i) for purposes of this assignment limitation test.

Note 3: The Accumulated Prepayment Credits for the Total Plan are allocated to segments based on the assigned cost after application of 9904.412-50(c)(2)(ii) in accordance with 9904.413-50(c)(1)(i) for purposes of this assignment limitation test.

Note 4: See Table 1.

Note 5: See Table 9.

Note 6: Lesser of lines (A) or (B).

(ii) For Segment 1, the assignable pension cost of $251,740, measured after considering the assignable cost limitation, does not exceed the 9904.412-50(c)(2)(iii) limit of $2,741,313. For Segments 2 through 7, the assignable pension cost of $1,187,697, measured after considering the assignable cost limitation, does not exceed the 9904.412-50(c)(2)(iii) limit of $12,933,384.

(d) *Actuarial Gain and Loss—Change in Liability Basis.* (1) Assume the same facts shown in 9904.412-60.1(b) for Segment 1 of the Harmony Corporation for 2017. Table 11 shows the actuarial liabilities and normal costs plus any expense loads for Segment 1 for 2016 through 2018.

Table 11—Summary of Liabilities for Segment 1 as of January 1

	2016	2017	2018	Notes
"Going Concern" Liabilities for the Period:				
Actuarial Accrued Liability	$1,915,000	$2,100,000	$2,305,000	1
Normal Cost	89,600	89,100	99,500	1
Expense Load on Normal Cost	....	....	....	1, 2
Total Liability for Period	$2,004,600	$2,189,100	$2,404,500	....
Minimum Liabilities for the Period:				
Minimum Actuarial Liability	$1,901,000	$2,594,000	$2,212,000	3
Minimum Normal Cost .	83,800	102,000	96,500	3

CASB 9904.412-60.1

	2016	2017	2018	Notes
Expense Load on Minimum Normal Cost .	8,300	8,840	9,300	3, 4
Total Minimum Liability for Period	$1,993,100	$2,704,840	$2,317,800	....
Interest Basis as Determined by Segment's Liabilities for Period	9904.412-50 (b)(4)	9904.412-50 (b)(7)(iii)	9904.412-50 (b)(4)	5

Note 1: See Table 3 for 2017 values. For 2016 and 2018, the data for Segment 1 is taken directly from the actuarial valuation report prepared for CAS 412 and 413 purposes and supporting documentation, including subtotals of the data by segment.

Note 2: Because the contractor's interest assumption, which satisfies the requirements of 9904.412-40(b)(2) and 9904.412-50(b)(4), implicitly recognizes expected administrative expenses there is no explicit amount shown for the normal cost.

Note 3: See Table 4 for 2017 values. For 2016 and 2018, the data for Segment 1 is taken directly from the actuarial valuation report prepared for ERISA purposes and supporting documentation, including subtotals of the data by segment. The values for 2016 are based on the transitional minimum actuarial liability and transitional minimum normal cost measured in accordance with 9904.412-64.1(a) and (b).

Note 4: For purposes of determining minimum normal cost, the contractor explicitly identifies the expected administrative expense as a separate component as required by 9904.412-50(b)(7)(ii)(B).

Note 5: For determining the pension cost for the period, the measurements are based on the actuarial accrued liability and normal cost unless the total minimum liability for the period exceeds the "Going Concern" total liability for the period. The measurement basis was separately determined for each segment in accordance with 9904.412-50(b)(7)(i).

(2) For 2016, the sum of the minimum actuarial liability and minimum normal cost does not exceed the sum of the actuarial accrued liability and normal cost. Therefore the criterion of 9904.412-50(b)(7)(i) is not met, and the actuarial accrued liability and normal cost are used to compute the pension cost for 2016. For 2017, the sum of the minimum actuarial liability and minimum normal cost exceeds the sum of the actuarial accrued liability and normal cost, and therefore the pension cost is computed using minimum actuarial liability and minimum normal cost as required by 9904.412-50(b)(7)(i). For 2018, the sum of the minimum actuarial liability and minimum normal cost does not exceed the sum of the actuarial accrued liability and normal cost, and the actuarial accrued liability and normal cost are used to compute the pension cost for 2018 because the criterion of 9904.412-50(b)(7)(i) is not met. Table 12 shows the measurement of the unfunded actuarial liability for 2016 through 2018.

Table 12—Unfunded Actuarial Liability for Segment 1 as of January 1

	2016	2017	2018	Notes
Current Year Actuarial Liability Basis	9904.412-50 (b)(4)	9904.412-50(b) (7)(iii)	9904.412-50 (b)(4)	1
Actuarial Accrued Liability	$1,915,000	$2,594,000	$2,305,000	1

CASB 9904.412-60.1

	2016	2017	2018	Notes
CAS Actuarial Value of Assets	(1,500,000)	(1,688,757)	(1,894,486)	2
Unfunded Actuarial Liability (Actual) ...	$415,000	$905,243	$410,514	....

Note 1: See Table 11.

Note 2: The 2017 CAS Actuarial Value of Assets is developed in Table 2. For 2016 and 2018, the Actuarial Value of Assets for Segment 1 is taken directly from the actuarial valuation report prepared for CAS 412 and 413 purposes and supporting documentation.

(3) Except for changes in the value of the assumed interest rate used to measure the minimum actuarial liability and minimum normal cost, there were no changes to the pension plan's actuarial assumptions or actuarial cost methods during the period of 2016 through 2018. The contractor's actuary measured the expected unfunded actuarial liability and determined the actuarial gain or loss for 2017 and 2018 as shown in Table 13.

Table 13—Measurement of Actuarial Gain or Loss for Segment 1 as of January 1

	2016	2017	2018	Notes
Actual Unfunded Actuarial Liability	(Note 1)	$905,243	$410,514	2
Expected Unfunded Actuarial Liability	....	(381,455)	(848,210)	3
Actuarial Loss (Gain) .	....	$523,788	$(437,696)	....

Note 1: The determination of the actuarial gain or loss that occurred during 2015 and measured on 2016 is outside the scope of this Illustration.

Note 2: See Table 12.

Note 3: Information taken directly from the actuarial valuation report prepared for CAS 412 and 413 purposes and supporting documentation. The expected unfunded actuarial liability is based on the prior unfunded actuarial liability updated based on the assumed interest rate in compliance with 9904.412-40(b)(2) and 9904.412-50(b)(4). Note that in accordance with 9904.412-50(b)(7)(iii)(D), the corporate bond yield rate is only used to determine the minimum actuarial liability but not to adjust the liability for the passage of time.

(4) According to the actuarial valuation report, the 2017 actuarial loss of $523,788 includes a $494,000 actuarial loss due to a change in measurement basis from using an actuarial accrued liability of $2,100,000 to using a minimum actuarial liability of $2,594,000, including the effect of any change in the interest rate basis. (See Table 11 for the actuarial accrued liability and the minimum actuarial liability.) The $494,000 loss ($2,594,000-$2,100,000) due to the change in the liability basis is amortized as part of the total actuarial loss of $523,788 over a ten-year period in accordance with 9904.412-50(a)(1)(v) and 9904.413-50(a)(2)(ii). Similarly, the next year's valuation report shows a 2018 actuarial gain of $437,696, which includes a $93,000 actuarial gain ($2,305,000-$2,212,000) due to a change from a minimum actuarial liability back to an actuarial accrued liability basis, which includes the effect of any change in interest rate basis. The $93,000 gain due the change in the liability basis will be amortized as part of the total $437,696 actuarial gain over a ten-year period in accordance with 9904.412-50(a)(1) and 9904.413-50(a)(2)(ii).

CASB 9904.412-60.1

[Final rule, 76 FR 81296, 12/27/2011, effective 2/27/2012; Technical correcting amendment, 77 FR 43542, 7/25/2012, effective 8/24/2012]

9904.412-61 [Reserved]

9904.412-62 Exemption.

None for this Standard.

9904.412-63 Effective date.

(a) This Standard is effective as of February 27, 2012, hereafter known as the "Effective Date," and is applicable for cost accounting periods after June 30, 2012, hereafter known as the "Implementation Date."

(b) Following the award of a contract or subcontract subject to this Standard on or after the Effective Date, contractors shall follow this Standard, as amended, beginning with its next cost accounting period beginning after the later of the Implementation Date or the award date of a contract or subcontract to which this Standard is applicable. The first day of the cost accounting period that this Standard, as amended, is first applicable to a contractor or subcontractor is the "Applicability Date of the CAS Pension Harmonization Rule" for purposes of this Standard. Prior to the Applicability Date of the CAS Pension Harmonization Rule, contractors or subcontractors shall follow the Standard in 9904.412 in effect prior to the Effective Date.

(1) Following the award of a contract or subcontract subject to this Standard received on or after the Effective Date, contractors with contracts or subcontracts subject to this Standard that were received prior to the Effective Date shall continue to follow the Standard in 9904.412 in effect prior to the Effective Date. Beginning with the Applicability Date of the CAS Pension Harmonization Rule, such contractors shall follow this Standard, as amended, for all contracts or subcontracts subject to this Standard.

(2) Following the award of a contract or subcontract subject to this Standard received during the period beginning on or after the date published in the **Federal Register** and ending before the Effective Date, contractors shall follow the Standard in

9904.412 in effect prior to the Effective Date. If another contract or subcontract, subject to this Standard, is received on or after the Effective Date, the provisions of 9904.412-63(b)(1) shall apply.

[Final rule, 60 FR 16534, 3/30/95, effective 3/30/95; Final rule, 76 FR 81296, 12/27/2011, effective 2/27/2012; Technical correcting amendment, 77 FR 43542, 7/25/2012, effective 8/24/2012]

9904.412-64 Transition method.

To be acceptable, any method of transition from compliance with Standard 9904.412 in effect prior to March 30, 1995, to compliance with the Standard effective March 30, 1995, must follow the equitable principle that costs, which have been previously provided for, shall not be redundantly provided for under revised methods. Conversely, costs that have not previously been provided for must be provided for under the revised method. This transition subsection is not intended to qualify for purposes of assignment or allocation, pension costs which have previously been disallowed for reasons other than ERISA tax-deductibility limitations. The sum of all portions of unfunded actuarial liability identified pursuant to Standard 9904.412, effective March 30, 1995, including such portions of unfunded actuarial liability determined for transition purposes, is subject to the provisions of 9904.412-40(c) on requirements for assignment. The method, or methods, employed to achieve an equitable transition shall be consistent with the provisions of Standard 9904.412, effective March 30, 1995, and shall be approved by the contracting officer. Examples and illustrations of such transition methods include, but are not limited to, the following:

(a) Reassignment of certain prior unfunded accruals.

(1) Any portion of pension cost for a qualified defined-benefit pension plan, assigned to a cost accounting period prior to March 30, 1995, which was not funded because such cost exceeded the maximum tax-deductible amount, determined in accordance with ERISA, shall be assigned to subsequent accounting periods, including an adjustment for interest, as an assignable cost deficit.

However, such costs shall be assigned to periods on or after March 30, 1995, only to the extent that such costs have not previously been allocated as cost or price to contracts subject to this Standard.

(2) Alternatively, the transition method described in paragraph (d) of this subsection may be applied separately to costs subject to paragraph (a)(1) of this subsection.

(b) Reassignment of certain prior unallocated credits.

(1) Any portion of pension cost for a defined-benefit pension plan, assigned to a cost accounting period prior to March 30, 1995, which was not allocated as a cost or price credit to contracts subject to this Standard because such cost was less than zero, shall be assigned to subsequent accounting periods, including an adjustment for interest, as an assignable cost credit.

(2) Alternatively, the transition method described in paragraph (d) of this subsection may be applied separately to costs subject to paragraph (b)(1) of this subsection.

(c) Accounting for certain prior allocated unfunded accruals. Any portion of unfunded pension cost for a nonqualified defined-benefit pension plan, assigned to a cost accounting period prior to March 30, 1995, that was allocated as cost or price to contracts subject to this Standard, shall be recognized in subsequent accounting periods, including adjustments for imputed interest and benefit payments, as an accumulated value of permitted unfunded accruals.

(d) "Fresh start" alternative transition method. The transition methods of paragraphs (a)(1), (b)(1), and (c) of this subsection may be implemented using the so-called "fresh start" method whereby a portion of the unfunded actuarial liability of a defined-benefit pension plan, which occurs in the first cost accounting period after March 30, 1995, shall be treated in the same manner as an actuarial gain or loss. Such portion of unfunded actuarial liability shall exclude any portion of unfunded actuarial liability that must continue to be separately identified and maintained in accordance with 9904.412-50(a)(2), including interest adjustments. If the contracting officer already has approved a different amortization period for the fresh start amortization, then such amortization period shall continue.

(e) Change to pay-as-you-go method. A change in accounting method subject to 9903.302 will have occurred whenever costs of a nonqualified defined-benefit pension plan have been accounted for on an accrual basis prior to March 30, 1995, and the contractor must change to the pay-as-you-go cost method because the plan does not meet the requirement of 9904.412-50(c)(3), either by election or otherwise. In such case, any portion of unfunded pension cost, assigned to a cost accounting period prior to March 30, 1995 that was allocated as cost or price to contracts subject to this Standard, shall be assigned to future accounting periods, including adjustments for imputed interest and benefit payments, as an accumulated value of permitted unfunded accruals. Costs computed under the pay-as-you-go cost method shall be charged against such accumulated value of permitted unfunded accruals before such costs may be allocated to contracts.

(f) Actuarial assumptions. The actuarial assumptions used to calculate assignable cost deficits, assignable cost credits, or accumulated values of permitted unfunded accruals for transition purposes shall be consistent with the long term assumptions used for valuation purposes for such prior periods unless the contracting officer has previously approved the use of other reasonable assumptions.

(g) Transition illustrations. Unless otherwise noted, paragraphs (g)(1) through (9) of this subsection address pension costs and transition amounts determined for the first cost accounting period beginning on or after the date this revised Standard becomes applicable to a contractor. For purposes of these illustrations an interest assumption of 7% is presumed to be in effect for all periods.

(1) For the cost accounting period immediately preceding the date this revised Standard was applicable to a contractor, Contractor S computed and assigned pension cost of $1 million for a qualified defined-benefit pension plan. The contractor made a contribution equal to the maximum tax-deductible amount of $800,000 for the period

CASB 9904.412-64

leaving $200,000 of assigned cost unfunded for the period. Except for this $200,000, no other assigned pension costs have ever been unfunded or otherwise disallowed. Using the transition method of paragraph (a)(1) of this subsection, the contractor shall establish an assignable cost deficit equal to $214,000 ($200,000 × 1.07), which is the prior unfunded assigned cost plus interest. If this assignable cost deficit amount, plus all other portions of unfunded actuarial liability identified in accordance with 9904.412-50(a)(1) and (2), equal the total unfunded actuarial liability, pension cost may be assigned to the current period.

(2) Assume that Contractor S in 9904.412-64(g)(1) priced the entire $1 million into firm fixed-price contracts. In this case, no assignable cost deficit amount may be established. In addition, the $214,000 ($200,000 × 1.07) shall be separately identified and maintained in accordance with 9904.412-50(a)(2). If all portions of unfunded actuarial liability identified in accordance with 9904.412-50(a)(1) and (2), equal the total unfunded actuarial liability, pension cost may be assigned to the period.

(3) Assume the same facts as in 9904.412-64(g)(1), except Contractor S only funded and allocated $500,000. The $300,000 of assigned cost that was not funded, but could have been funded without exceeding the tax-deductible maximum, may not be recognized as an assignable cost deficit. Instead, the $300,000 must be separately identified and maintained in accordance with 9904.412-50(a)(2). If the $321,000 ($300,000 × 1.07) plus the $214,000 already identified as an assignable cost deficit plus all other portions of unfunded actuarial liability identified in accordance with 9904.412-50(a)(1) and (2), equal the total unfunded actuarial liability, pension cost may be assigned to the period.

(4) Assume that, for Contractor S in 9904.412-64(g)(3), the only portion of unfunded actuarial liability that must be identified under 9904.412-50(a)(2) is the $321,000. If Contractor S chooses to use the "fresh start" transition method, the $321,000 of unfunded assigned cost must be subtracted from the total unfunded actuarial liability in

accordance with 9904.412-63(d). The net amount of unfunded actuarial liability shall then be amortized over a period of fifteen years as an actuarial loss in accordance with 9904.412-50(a)(1)(v) and Cost Accounting Standard 9904.413.

(5) For the cost accounting period immediately preceding the date this revised Standard becomes applicable to a contractor, Contractor T computed and assigned pension cost of negative $400,000 for a qualified defined-benefit plan. Because the contractor could not withdraw assets from the trust fund, the contracting officer agreed that instead of allocating a current period credit to contracts, the negative costs would be carried forward, with interest, and offset against future pension costs allocated to the contract. Using the transition method of paragraph (b)(1) of this subsection, the contractor shall establish an assignable cost credit equal to $428,000 ($400,000 × 1.07). If this assignable cost credit amount, plus all other portions of unfunded actuarial liability identified in accordance with 9904.412-50(a)(1) and (2), equals the total unfunded actuarial liability, pension cost may be assigned to the period.

(6) Assume that in 9904.412-64(g)(5), following guidance issued by the contracting agency the contracting officer had deemed the cost for the prior period to be $0. In order to satisfy the requirements of 9904.412-40(c) and assign pension cost to the current period, Contractor S must account for the prior period negative accruals that have not been specifically identified. Following the transition method of paragraph (b)(1) of this subsection, the contractor shall identify $428,000 as an assignable cost credit.

(7) Assume the facts of 9904.412-64(g)(5), except Contractor S uses the "fresh start" transition method. In addition, for the current period the plan is overfunded since the actuarial value of the assets is greater than the actuarial accrued liability. In this case, an actuarial gain equal to the negative unfunded actuarial liability; i.e., actuarial surplus, is recognized since there are no portions of unfunded actuarial liability that must be identified under 9904.412-50(a)(2).

CASB 9904.412-64

(8) Since March 28, 1989, Contractor U has computed, assigned, and allocated pension costs for a nonqualified defined-benefit plan on an accrual basis. The value of these past accruals, increased for imputed interest at 7 and decreased for benefits paid by the contractor, is equal to $2 million as of the beginning of the current period. Contractor U elects to establish a "Rabbi trust" and the plan meets the other criteria at 9904.412-50(c)(3). Using the transition method of paragraph (c) of this subsection, Contractor U shall recognize the $2 million as the accumulated value of permitted unfunded accruals, which will then be included in the market value and actuarial value of the assets. Because the accumulated value of permitted unfunded accruals is exactly equal to the current period market value of the assets, 100 of benefits for the current period must be paid from sources other than the funding agency in accordance with 9904.412-50(d)(2)(ii).

(9) Assume that Contractor U in 9904.412-64(g)(8) establishes a funding agency, but elects to use the pay-as-you-go method for current and future pension costs. Furthermore, plan participants receive $500,000 in benefits on the last day of the current period. Using the transition method of paragraph (e) of this subsection to ensure prior costs are not redundantly provided for, the contractor shall establish assets; i.e., an accumulated value of permitted unfunded accruals, of $2 million. Since these assets are sufficient to provide for the current benefit payments, no pension costs can be allocated in this period. Furthermore, previously priced contracts subject to this Standard shall be adjusted in accordance with 9903.302. The accumulated value of permitted unfunded accruals shall be carried forward to the next period by adding $140,000 (7% × $2 million) of imputed interest, and subtracting the $500,000 of benefit payments made by the contractor. The accumulated value of permitted unfunded accruals for the next period equals $1,640,000 ($2 million + $140,000$500,000).

[Final rule, 60 FR 16534, 3/30/95, effective 3/30/95; Corrected, 60 FR 20248, 4/25/95]

9904.412-64.1 Transition Method for the CAS Pension Harmonization Rule.

Contractors or subcontractors that become subject to the Standard, as amended, during the Pension Harmonization Transition Period shall recognize the change in cost accounting method in accordance with paragraphs (a) and (b).

(a) The Pension Harmonization Rule Transition Period is the five cost accounting periods beginning with a contractor's first cost accounting period beginning after June 30, 2012, and is independent of the receipt date of a contract or subcontract subject to this Standard. The Pension Harmonization Rule Transition Period begins on the first day of a contractor's first cost accounting period that begins after June 30, 2012.

(b) Phase in of the Minimum Actuarial Liability and Minimum Normal Cost. During each successive accounting period of Pension Harmonization Rule Transition Period, the contractor shall recognize on a scheduled basis the amount by which the minimum actuarial liability differs from the actuarial accrued liability; and the amount by which the sum of the minimum normal cost plus any expense load differs from the sum of the normal cost plus any expense load.

(1) For purposes of determining the amount of the difference, the minimum actuarial liability and minimum normal cost shall be measured in accordance with 9904.412-50(b)(7)(ii).

(2) During each successive accounting period of the Pension Harmonization Rule Transition Period, the transitional minimum actuarial liability shall be set equal to the actuarial accrued liability adjusted by an amount equal to the difference between the minimum actuarial liability and actuarial accrued liability, multiplied by the scheduled applicable percentage for that period. The sum of the transitional minimum normal cost plus any expense load shall be set equal to the sum of normal cost plus any expense load, adjusted by an amount equal to the difference between the minimum normal cost and the normal cost, plus expense loads, multiplied by the scheduled applicable percentage for that period.

CASB 9904.412-64.1

(3) The scheduled applicable percentages for each successive accounting period of the Pension Harmonization Rule Transition Period are as follows: 0% for the First Cost Accounting Period, 25% for the Second Cost Accounting Period, 50% for the Third Cost Accounting Period, 75% for the Fourth Cost Accounting Period, and 100% for the Fifth Cost Accounting Period.

(4) The transitional minimum actuarial liability and transitional minimum normal cost measured in accordance with this provision shall be used for purposes of the 9904.412-50(b)(7) minimum actuarial liability and minimum normal cost.

(5) The actuarial gain or loss attributable to experience since the prior valuation, measured as of the First Cost Accounting Period of the Pension Harmonization Rule Transition Period, shall be amortized over a ten-year period in accordance with 9904.413-50(a)(2)(ii).

(c) Transition Illustration. Assume the same facts for the Harmony Corporation in Illustration 9904.412-60.1(a) and (b), except that this is the Fourth Cost Accounting Period of the Pension Harmonization Rule Transition Period. As in Illustration 9904.412-60.1(a) and (b), the contractor separately computes pension costs for Segment 1, and computes pension costs for Segments 2 through 7 in the aggregate. The contractor has two actuarial valuations prepared: one measures the actuarial accrued liability and normal cost using the contractor's expected rate of return on investments assumption, in accordance with 9904.412-40(b)(2) and

9904.412-50(b)(4), and the other valuation measures the minimum actuarial liability and minimum normal cost based on the assumed current yields on investment quality corporate bonds in accordance with 9904.412-50(b)(7)(iii)(A). The actuarial valuations present the values subtotaled for each segment and in total for the plan as a whole.

(1) The contractor applies 9904.412-64.1(b) as follows:

(i) (A) For Segment 1, the $494,000 ($2,594,000—$2,100,000) difference between the minimum actuarial liability and the actuarial accrued liability is multiplied by 75%. Therefore for Segment 1, the minimum actuarial liability for purposes of 9904.412-50(b)(7) is adjusted to a transitional minimum actuarial liability of $2,470,500 ($2,100,000 + [75% × $494,000]).

(B) For Segments 2 through 7, the ($183,000) difference ($14,042,000-$14,225,000) between the minimum actuarial liability and the actuarial accrued liability is multiplied by 75%. For Segment 2 through 7, the minimum actuarial liability for purposes of 9904.412-50(b)(7) is adjusted to a transitional minimum actuarial liability of $14,087,750 ($14,225,000 + [75% × ($183,000)]).

(C) The computation of the transitional minimum actuarial liability that incrementally recognizes the difference between the minimum actuarial liability and the actuarial accrued liability for Segment 1, and for Segments 2 through 7, is shown in Table 1 below:

Table 1—Development of Transitional Minimum Actuarial Liability for Fourth Transition Period

	Total plan	Segment 1	Segments 2 through 7	Notes
	(Note 1)	. . . .	. . . .	. . . .
Minimum Actuarial Liability	. . . .	$2,594,000 (2,100,000)	$14,042,000 (14,225,000)	2 3
Actuarial Accrued Liability	. . . .	(2,100,000)	(14,225,000)	2 3
Actuarial Accrued Liability Difference	. . . .	$494,000	$(183,000)	4

	Total plan	Segment 1	Segments 2 through 7	Notes
Phase In Percentage (Period 4)		75%	75%	5
Phase In Liability Difference		$370,500	$(137,250)	6
Actuarial Accrued Liability		2,100,000	14,225,000	6
Transitional Minimum:				
Actuarial Liability		$2,470,500	$14,087,750	....

Note 1: The values for the Total Plan are not shown because the 9904.412-50(b)(7)(i) threshold criterion is applied separately for each segment.

Note 2: See Illustration 9904.412-60.1(b)(2)(ii), Table 4.

Note 3: See Illustration 9904.412-60.1(b)(2)(i), Table 3.

Note 4: The phase in percentage will be applied to positive or negative differences in the actuarial liabilities, since the purpose of the phase in is to incrementally move the measurement away from the actuarial accrued liability to the minimum actuarial liability, regardless of the direction of the movement.

Note 5: Appropriate transition percentage for the Fourth Cost Accounting Period of the Pension Harmonization Rule Transition Period as stipulated in 9904.412-64.1(b)(3).

Note 6: The actuarial accrued liability is adjusted by the phase in difference between liabilities, either positive or negative, in accordance with 9904.412-64.1(b)(2).

(ii) (A) For Segment 1, the $21,740 ($110,840-$89,100) difference between the minimum normal cost and the normal cost, plus expense loads, is multiplied by 75%. Therefore for Segment 1, the minimum normal cost plus expense load, for purposes of 9904.412-50(b)(7), is adjusted to a transitional minimum normal cost plus expense load of $105,405 ($89,100 + [75% × $21,740]).

(B) For Segments 2 through 7, the 92,260 ($913,860-$821,600) difference between the minimum normal cost and the normal cost,

plus expense loads, is multiplied by 75%. Therefore, for Segments 2 through 7, the minimum normal cost for purposes of 9904.412-50(b)(7) is adjusted to a transitional minimum normal cost plus expense load of $890,795 ($821,600 + [75% × $92,260]).

(C) The computation of the transitional minimum normal cost plus expense load for Segment 1, and for Segments 2 through 7, is shown in Table 2 below:

Table 2—Development of Transitional Minimum Normal Cost for Fourth Transition Period

	Total plan	Segment 1	Segments 2 through 7	Notes
	(Note 1)	....	....	....
Minimum Normal Cost		$102,000	$840,700	2
Expense Load on Normal Cost		8,840	73,160	2, 3
Minimum Normal Cost Plus Expense Load		$110,840	$913,860	2
Normal Cost Plus Expense Load		(89,100)	(821,600)	4

CASB 9904.412-64.1

	Total plan	Segment 1	Segments 2 through 7	Notes
Difference		$21,740	$92,260	5
Phase In Percentage (Period 4)		75%	75%	6
Phase In Normal Cost Difference		$16,305	$69,195	7
Normal Cost Plus Expense Load		89,100	821,600	7
Transitional Minimum: Normal Cost Plus Expense Load		$105,405	$890,795	....

Note 1: The values for the Total Plan are not shown because the 9904.412-50(b)(7)(i) threshold criterion is applied separately for each segment.

Note 2: See Illustration 9904.412-60.1(b)(2)(ii), Table 4.

Note 3: For minimum normal cost valuation purposes, the contractor explicitly identifies the expected administrative expenses as a separate component of minimum normal cost.

Note 4: See Illustration 9904.412-60.1(b)(2)(i), Table 3. Expected expenses are implicitly recognized as part of the contractor's expected rate of return on investments assumption.

Note 5: The phase in percentage will be applied to positive and negative differences in the normal costs plus expense loads, since the purpose of the phase in is to incrementally move the measurement from the normal cost plus expense load, to the minimum normal cost plus expense load, regardless of the direction of the movement.

Note 6: Appropriate transition percentage for the Fourth Cost Accounting Period of the Pension Harmonization Rule Transition Period stipulated in 9904.412-64.1(b)(3).

Note 7: The sum of the normal cost plus expense load is adjusted by the phase in difference between normal costs, either positive or negative, in accordance with 9904.412-64.1(b)(2).

(2) The contractor applies the provisions of with 9904.412-50(b)(7)(i) using the transitional minimum actuarial liability and transitional minimum normal cost plus expense load, in accordance with 9904.412-64.1(b)(4).

(i) The comparison of the sum of the actuarial accrued liability and normal cost plus expense load, and the sum of the transitional minimum actuarial liability and minimum normal cost plus expense load, for Segment 1, and for Segments 2 through 7, is summarized in Table 3 below:

Table 3—Summary of Liability and Normal Cost Values for Fourth Transition Period

	Total plan	Segment 1	Segments 2 through 7	Notes
	(Note 1)	....	....	....
"Going Concern" Liabilities for Period:				
Actuarial Accrued Liability		$2,100,000	$14,225,000	2
Normal Cost Plus Expense Load		89,100	821,600	3

	Total plan	Segment 1	Segments 2 through 7	Notes
Total Liability for Period	. . . .	2,189,100	15,046,600	. . . .
Transitional Minimum Liabilities for the Period:				
Transitional Minimum Actuarial Liability	. . . .	2,470,500	14,087,750	1
Transitional Minimum Normal Cost Plus Expense Load	. . . .	105,405	890,795	3
Total Transitional Minimum Liability for Period	. . . .	2,575,905	14,978,545	4

Note 1: The values for the Total Plan are not shown because the 9904.412-50(b)(7)(i) threshold criterion is applied separately for each segment.

Note 2: See Table 1.

Note 3: See Table 2.

Note 4: If the threshold criterion is met, then the pension cost for the period is measured based on the Transitional Minimum Actuarial Liability and Transition Normal Cost Plus Expense Load.

(ii) For Segment 1, the Total Transitional Minimum Liability for the Period of $2,575,905 exceeds the total liability for the period of $2,189,100. (See Table 3.) Therefore, in accordance with 9904.412-50(b)(7)(i), the pension cost for Segment 1 is measured using the actuarial accrued liability and normal cost as measured by the transitional minimum actuarial liability and transitional minimum normal cost, which are based on the accrued benefit cost method. This measurement complies with the requirements of 9904.412-50(b)(7) and with the definition of actuarial accrued liability, 9904.412-30(a)(2), and normal cost, 9904.412-30(a)(18).

(iii) For Segments 2 through 7, the total liability for the period of $15,046,600 exceeds the Total Transitional Minimum Liability for the Period of $14,978,545. (See Table 3.) Therefore, in accordance with 9904.412-50(b)(7)(i), the pension cost for Segment 2 through 7 is measured using actuarial accrued liability and normal cost, which are based on the projected benefit cost method.

(3) The contractor computes the pension cost for the period in accordance with the provisions of 9904.412-50(b)(7)(i), which considers the transitional minimum actuarial liability and transitional minimum normal cost plus expense load, in accordance with 9904.412-64.1(b).

(i) The contractor computes the unfunded actuarial liability as shown in Table 4 below:

Table 4—Unfunded Actuarial Liability for Fourth Transition Period

	Total Plan	Segment 1	Segments 2 through 7	Notes
	(Note 1)			
Actuarial Accrued Liability	. . . .	$2,470,500	$14,225,000	2
CAS Actuarial Value of Assets	. . . .	(1,688,757)	(11,872,928)	3

	Total Plan	Segment 1	Segments 2 through 7	Notes
Unfunded Actuarial Liability	....	781,743	2,352,072	....

Note 1: The values for the Total Plan are not shown because the 9904.412-50(b)(7)(i) threshold criterion is applied separately for each segment.

Note 2: Because the Pension Harmonization criterion of 9904.412-50(b)(7)(i) has been met for Segment 1, the actuarial accrued liability is measured by the transitional minimum actuarial liability as required by 9904.412-64.1(b)(4). See Table 3. Because the Pension Harmonization criterion of 9904.412-50(b)(7)(i) was not satisfied for Segments 2 through 7, the actuarial accrued liability is based on the actuarial assumptions that reflect long-term trends in accordance with 9904.412-50(b)(4), *i.e.,* the transitional minimum actuarial liability does not apply.

Note 3: See Illustration 9904.412-60.1(b)(1)(ii), Table 2.

(ii) Measurement of the Pension Cost for the current period (Table 5):

Table 5—Pension Cost for Fourth Transition Period

	Total plan	Segment 1	Segments 2 through 7	Notes
	(Note 1)			
Normal Cost Plus Expense Load	....	$105,405	$821,600	2
Amortization Installments	....	101,990	314,437	3, 4
Pension Cost Computed for the Period	1,343,432	207,395	1,136,037	

Note 1: Except for the Total Pension Cost Computed for the Period, the values for the Total Plan are not shown because the 9904.412-50(b)(7)(i) threshold criterion is applied separately for each segment.

Note 2: See Table 3. Because the Pension Harmonization criterion of 9904.412-50(b)(7)(i) has been met for Segment 1, the sum of the normal cost plus the expense load is measured by the sum of the transitional minimum normal cost plus the expense load, as required by 9904.412-64.1(a). Because the Pension Harmonization criterion of 9904.412-50(b)(7)(i) was not satisfied for Segments 2 through 7, the sum of the normal cost plus any applicable expense load is based on the contractor's actuarial assumptions reflecting long-term trends in accordance with 9904.412-40(b)(2) and 9904.412-50(b)(4), *i.e.,* the transitional minimum normal cost plus the expense load does not apply.

Note 3: Net amortization installment based on the unfunded actuarial liability of $781,743 for Segment 1, and $2,352,072 for Segments 2 through 7, including an interest equivalent on the unamortized portion of such liability. See Table 4. The interest adjustment is based on the contractor's interest rate assumption in compliance with 9904.412-40(b)(2) and 9904.412-50(b)(4).

Note 4: See 9904.64-1(c)(4) for details concerning the recognition of the unfunded actuarial liability during the first Pension Harmonization Rule Transition Period.

CASB 9904.412-64.1

(4) The Silvertone Corporation separately computes pension costs for Segment 1, and computes pension costs for Segments 2 through 7 in the aggregate.

(i) For the First Cost Accounting Period of the Pension Harmonization Rule Transition Period, the difference between the actuarial accrued liability and the minimum actuarial liability, and the difference between the normal cost and the minimum normal cost, are multiplied by 0%. Therefore the transitional minimum actuarial liability and transitional minimum normal are equal to the actuarial accrued liability and normal cost. The total transitional minimum liability for the period does not exceed the total liability for the period in conformity with the criterion of 9904.412-50(b)(7)(i). Therefore, the pension cost for the First Cost Accounting Period of the Pension Harmonization Rule Transition Period is computed using the actuarial accrued liability and normal cost.

(ii) The actuarial gain attributable to experience during the prior period that is measured for the cost accounting period is amortized over a ten-year period in accordance with 9904.412-50(a)(1)(v) and 9904.413-50(a)(2)(ii).

(iii) The contractor computes the pension cost for First Cost Accounting Period of the Pension Harmonization Rule Transition Period as shown in Table 6 below.

Table 6—Computation of the Pension for the First Transition Period

	Total plan	Segment 1	Segments 2 through 7	Notes
	(Note 1)			
Amortization of Unfunded Liability Net Amortization Installment from Prior Periods	....	$81,019	$523,801	2
January 1, 2013, Actuarial Loss (Gain) Amortization Installment	....	(9,369)	(68,740)	3
Net Amortization Installment	....	71,650	455,061	....
Normal Cost plus expense load ..	....	78,400	715,000	4
Pension Cost Computed for the Period	....	150,050	1,170,061	

Note 1: The values for the Total Plan are not shown because the 9904.412-50(b)(7)(i) threshold criterion is applied separately for each segment.

Note 2: Amortization installments of actuarial gains and losses, and other portions of the unfunded actuarial liability identified prior to January 1, 2013, in accordance with 9904.412-50(a)(1)(v) and 9904.413-50(b)(2)(ii), including an interest adjustment based on the contractor's long-term interest assumption in compliance with 9904.412-40(b)(2) and 9904.412-50(b)(4).

	Total plan	Segment 1	Segments 2 through 7	Notes

Note 3: The actuarial gains for both Segment 1, and Segments 2 through 7, as measured as of January 1, 2013, are amortized over a ten-year period in accordance with 9904.413-50(a)(2)(ii) and 9904.412-64-1(b)(4). Note that although the source of the actuarial gains was the deviation between assumed and actual changes during the prior period, the gain is measured on January 1, 2013, and so the ten-year amortization period applies in the current period, including an interest adjustment based on the contractor's long-term interest assumption in compliance with 9904.412-40(b)(2) and 9904.412-50(b)(4).

Note 4: For the first period of the Pension Harmonization Rule transition period, the adjustment to the sum of the actuarial accrued liability and normal cost is adjusted by $0. Therefore the sum of the transitional minimum actuarial liability and transitional minimum normal cost plus expense load is equal to the sum of the actuarial accrued liability and normal cost plus expense load, and the criterion of 9904.412-50(b)(7)(i) was not met for either Segment 1, or Segments 2 through 7. The sum of the normal cost plus expense load is based on the sum of the going concern normal cost plus expense load.

[Final rule, 76 FR 81296, 12/27/2011, effective 2/27/2012; Technical correcting amendment, 77 FR 43542, 7/25/2012, effective 8/24/2012]

9904.413 Adjustment and allocation of pension cost. (No Text)

9904.413-10 [Reserved]

9904.413-20 Purpose.

A purpose of this Standard is to provide guidance for adjusting pension cost by measuring actuarial gains and losses and assigning such gains and losses to cost accounting periods. The Standard also provides the bases on which pension cost shall be allocated to segments of an organization. The provisions of this Cost Accounting Standard should enhance uniformity and consistency in accounting for pension costs.

9904.413-30 Definitions.

(a) The following are definitions of terms which are prominent in this Standard. Other terms defined elsewhere in this chapter 99 shall have the meaning ascribed to them in those definitions unless paragraph (b) of this subsection requires otherwise.

(1) *Accrued benefit cost method* means an actuarial cost method under which units of benefits are assigned to each cost accounting period and are valued as they accrue; that is, based on the services performed by each employee in the period involved. The measure of normal cost under this method for each cost accounting period is the present value of the units of benefit deemed to be credited to employees for service in that period. The measure of the actuarial accrued liability at a plan's measurement date is the present value of the units of benefit credited to employees for service prior to that date. (This method is also known as the Unit Credit cost method without salary projection.)

(2) *Actuarial accrued liability* means pension cost attributable, under the actuarial cost method in use, to years prior to the current period considered by a particular actuarial valuation. As of such date, the actuarial accrued liability represents the excess of the present value of future benefits and administrative expenses over the present value of future normal costs for all plan participants and beneficiaries. The excess of the actuarial accrued liability over the actuarial value of the assets of a pension plan is the Unfunded Actuarial Liability. The excess of the actuarial value of the assets of a pension plan over the actuarial accrued liability is an actuarial surplus and is treated as a negative unfunded actuarial liability.

(3) *Actuarial assumption* means an estimate of future conditions affecting pension cost; for example, mortality rate, employee turnover, compensation levels, earnings on pension plan assets, changes in values of pension plan assets.

CASB 9904.413

(4) *Actuarial cost method* means a technique which uses actuarial assumptions to measure the present value of future pension benefits and pension plan administrative expenses, and which assigns the cost of such benefits and expenses to cost accounting periods. The actuarial cost method includes the asset valuation method used to determine the actuarial value of the assets of a pension plan.

(5) *Actuarial gain and loss* means the effect on pension cost resulting from differences between actuarial assumptions and actual experience.

(6) *Actuarial valuation* means the determination, as of a specified date, of the normal cost, actuarial accrued liability, actuarial value of the assets of a pension plan, and other relevant values for the pension plan.

(7) *Curtailment of benefits* means an event; e.g., a plan amendment, in which the pension plan is frozen and no further material benefits accrue. Future service may be the basis for vesting of nonvested benefits existing at the time of the curtailment. The plan may hold assets, pay benefits already accrued, and receive additional contributions for unfunded benefits. Employees may or may not continue working for the contractor.

(8) *Funding agency* means an organization or individual which provides facilities to receive and accumulate assets to be used either for the payment of benefits under a pension plan, or for the purchase of such benefits, provided such accumulated assets form a part of a pension plan established for the exclusive benefit of the plan participants and their beneficiaries. The fair market value of the assets held by the funding agency as of a specified date is the Funding Agency Balance as of that date.

(9) *Immediate-gain actuarial cost method* means any of the several cost methods under which actuarial gains and losses are included as part of the unfunded actuarial liability of the pension plan, rather than as part of the normal cost of the plan.

(10) *Market value of the assets* means the sum of the funding agency balance plus the accumulated value of any permitted unfunded accruals belonging to a pension plan.

The Actuarial Value of the Assets means the value of cash, investments, permitted unfunded accruals, and other property belonging to a pension plan, as used by the actuary for the purpose of an actuarial valuation.

(11) *Normal cost* means the annual cost attributable, under the actuarial cost method in use, to current and future years as of a particular valuation date, excluding any payment in respect of an unfunded actuarial liability.

(12) *Pension plan* means a deferred compensation plan established and maintained by one or more employers to provide systematically for the payment of benefits to plan participants after their retirement, provided that the benefits are paid for life or are payable for life at the option of the employees. Additional benefits such as permanent and total disability and death payments, and survivorship payments to beneficiaries of deceased employees may be an integral part of a pension plan.

(13) *Pension plan participant* means any employee or former employee of an employer, or any member or former member of an employee organization, who is or may become eligible to receive a benefit from a pension plan which covers employees of such employer or members of such organization who have satisfied the plan's participation requirements, or whose beneficiaries are receiving or may be eligible to receive any such benefit. A participant whose employment status with the employer has not been terminated is an active participant of the employer's pension plan.

(14) *Pension plan termination* means an event; i.e., plan amendment, in which either the pension plan ceases to exist and all benefits are settled by purchase of annuities or other means, or the trusteeship of the plan is assumed by the Pension Benefit Guarantee Corporation or other conservator. The plan may or may not be replaced by another plan.

(15) *Permitted unfunded accruals* means the amount of pension cost for nonqualified defined-benefit pension plans that is not required to be funded under 9904.412-50(d)(2). The Accumulated Value of Permitted Unfunded Accruals means the value, as of the measurement date, of the

CASB 9904.413-30

permitted unfunded accruals adjusted for imputed earnings and for benefits paid by the contractor.

(16) *Prepayment credit* means the amount funded in excess of the pension cost assigned to a cost accounting period that is carried forward for future recognition. The Accumulated Value of Prepayment Credits means the value, as of the measurement date, of the prepayment credits adjusted for income and expenses in accordance with 9904.413-50(c)(7) and decreased for amounts used to fund pension costs or liabilities, whether assignable or not.

(17) *Projected benefit cost method* means either (i) any of the several actuarial cost methods which distribute the estimated total cost of all of the employees' prospective benefits over a period of years, usually their working careers, or (ii) a modification of the accrued benefit cost method that considers projected compensation levels.

(18) *Qualified pension plan* means a pension plan comprising a definite written program communicated to and for the exclusive benefit of employees which meets the criteria deemed essential by the Internal Revenue Service as set forth in the Internal Revenue Code for preferential tax treatment regarding contributions, investments, and distributions. Any other plan is a nonqualified pension plan.

(19) *Segment* means one of two or more divisions, product departments, plants, or other subdivisions of an organization reporting directly to a home office, usually identified with responsibility for profit and/or producing a product or service. The term includes Government-owned contractor-operated (GOCO) facilities, and joint ventures and subsidiaries (domestic and foreign) in which the organization has a majority ownership. The term also includes those joint ventures and subsidiaries (domestic and foreign) in which the organization has less than a majority ownership, but over which it exercises control.

(20) *Segment closing* means that a segment has (i) been sold or ownership has been otherwise transferred, (ii) discontinued operations, or (iii) discontinued doing or ac-

tively seeking Government business under contracts subject to this Standard.

(21) *Termination of employment gain or loss* means an actuarial gain or loss resulting from the difference between the assumed and actual rates at which plan participants separate from employment for reasons other than retirement, disability, or death.

(b) The following modifications of terms defined elsewhere in this Chapter 99 are applicable to this Standard: None.

[Final rule, 60 FR 16534, 3/30/95, effective 3/30/95; Final rule, 76 FR 81296, 12/27/2011, effective 2/27/2012]

9904.413-40 Fundamental requirement.

(a) *Assignment of actuarial gains and losses.* Actuarial gains and losses shall be calculated annually and shall be assigned to the cost accounting period for which the actuarial valuation is made and subsequent periods.

(b) *Valuation of the assets of a pension plan.* The actuarial value of the assets of a pension plan shall be determined under an asset valuation method which takes into account unrealized appreciation and depreciation of the market value of the assets of the pension plan, including the accumulated value of permitted unfunded accruals, and shall be used in measuring the components of pension costs.

(c) *Allocation of pension cost to segments.* Contractors shall allocate pension costs to each segment having participants in a pension plan.

(1) A separate calculation of pension costs for a segment is required when the conditions set forth in 9904.413-50(c)(2) or (3) are present. When these conditions are not present, allocations may be made by calculating a composite pension cost for two or more segments and allocating this cost to these segments by means of an allocation base.

(2) When pension costs are separately computed for a segment or segments, the provisions of Cost Accounting Standard 9904.412 regarding the assignable cost limitation shall be based on the actuarial value of assets, actuarial accrued liability and normal

cost for the segment or segments for purposes of such computations. In addition, for purposes of 9904.412-50(c)(2)(iii), the amount of pension cost assignable to a segment or segments shall not exceed the sum of:

(i) The maximum tax-deductible amount computed for the plan as a whole, and

(ii) The accumulated value of prepayment credits not already allocated to segments apportioned among the segment(s).

[Final rule, 60 FR 16534, 3/30/95, effective 3/30/95; Final rule, 76 FR 81296, 12/27/2011, effective 2/27/2012]

9904.413-50 Techniques for application.

(a) Assignment of actuarial gains and losses. (1) In accordance with the provisions of Cost Accounting Standard 9904.412, actuarial gains and losses shall be identified separately from other unfunded actuarial liabilities.

(2) Actuarial gains and losses shall be amortized as required by 9904.412-50(a)(1)(v).

(i) For periods beginning prior to the "Applicability Date of the CAS Pension Harmonization Rule," actuarial gains and losses determined under a pension plan whose costs are measured by an immediate-gain actuarial cost method shall be amortized over a fifteen-year period in equal annual installments, beginning with the date as of which the actuarial valuation is made.

(ii) For periods beginning on or after the "Applicability Date of the CAS Pension Harmonization Rule," such actuarial gains and losses shall be amortized over a ten-year period in equal annual installments, beginning with the date as of which the actuarial valuation is made.

(iii) The installment for a cost accounting period shall consist of an element for amortization of the gain or loss, and an element for interest on the unamortized balance at the beginning of the period. If the actuarial gain or loss determined for a cost accounting period is not material, the entire gain or loss may be included as a component of the current or ensuing year's pension cost.

(3) Pension plan terminations and curtailments of benefits shall be subject to adjustment in accordance with 9904.413-50(c)(12).

(b) Valuation of the assets of a pension plan. (1) The actuarial value of the assets of a pension plan shall be used:

(i) In measuring actuarial gains and losses, and

(ii) For purposes of measuring other components of pension cost.

(2) The actuarial value of the assets of a pension plan may be determined by the use of any recognized asset valuation method which provides equivalent recognition of appreciation and depreciation of the market value of the assets of the pension plan. However, the actuarial value of the assets produced by the method used shall fall within a corridor from 80 to 120 percent of the market value of the assets, determined as of the valuation date. If the method produces a value that falls outside the corridor, the actuarial value of the assets shall be adjusted to equal the nearest boundary of the corridor.

(3) The method selected for valuing pension plan assets shall be consistently applied from year to year within each plan.

(4) The provisions of paragraphs (b) (1) through (3) of this subsection are not applicable to plans that are treated as defined-contribution plans in accordance with 9904.412-50(a)(6).

(5) The market and actuarial values of the assets of a pension plan shall not be adjusted for any fee, reserve charge, or other investment charge for withdrawals from or termination of an investment contract, trust agreement, or other funding arrangement, unless such fee is determined in an arm's length transaction, and actually incurred and paid.

(6) The market value of the assets of a pension plan shall include the present value of contributions received after the date the market value of plan assets is measured.

(i) The assumed rate of interest, established in accordance with 9904.412-40(b)(2) and 9904.412-50(b)(4), shall be used to determine the present value of such receivable contributions as of the valuation date.

CASB 9904.413-50

(ii) The market value of plan assets measured in accordance with paragraphs (b)(6)(i) of this section shall be the basis for measuring the actuarial value of plan assets in accordance with this Standard.

(c) Allocation of pension cost to segments. (1) For contractors who compute a composite pension cost covering plan participants in two or more segments, the base to be used for allocating such costs shall be representative of the factors on which the pension benefits are based. For example, a base consisting of salaries and wages shall be used for pension costs that are calculated as a percentage of salaries and wages; a base consisting of the number of participants shall be used for pension costs that are calculated as an amount per participant. If pension costs are separately calculated for one or more segments, the contractor shall make a distribution among the segments for the maximum tax-deductible amount and the contribution to the funding agency as follows:

(i) When apportioning to the segments the sum of (A) the maximum tax-deductible amount, which is determined for a qualified defined-benefit pension plan as a whole pursuant to the Internal Revenue Code at Title 26 of the U.S. C., as amended, and (B) the accumulated value of the prepayment credits not already allocated to segments, the contractor shall use a base that considers the otherwise assignable pension costs or the funding levels of the individual segments.

(ii) When apportioning amounts deposited to a funding agency to segments, contractors shall use a base that is representative of the assignable pension costs, determined in accordance with 9904.412-50(c) for the individual segments. However, for qualified defined-benefit pension plans, the contractor may first apportion amounts funded to the segment or segments subject to this Standard.

(2) Separate pension cost for a segment shall be calculated whenever any of the following conditions exist for that segment, provided that such condition(s) materially affect the amount of pension cost allocated to the segment:

(i) There is a material termination of employment gain or loss attributable to the segment,

(ii) The level of benefits, eligibility for benefits, or age distribution is materially different for the segment than for the average of all segments, or

(iii) The appropriate actuarial assumptions are, in the aggregate, materially different for the segment than for the average of all segments. Calculations of termination of employment gains and losses shall give consideration to factors such as unexpected early retirements, benefits becoming fully vested, and reinstatements or transfers without loss of benefits. An amount may be estimated for future reemployments.

(3) Pension cost shall also be separately calculated for a segment under circumstances where—

(i) The pension plan for that segment becomes merged with that of another segment, or the pension plan is divided into two or more pension plans, and in either case,

(ii) The ratios of market value of the assets to actuarial accrued liabilities for each of the merged or separated plans are materially different from one another after applying the benefits in effect after the pension plan merger or pension plan division.

(4) For a segment whose pension costs are required to be calculated separately pursuant to paragraphs (c) (2) or (3) of this subsection, such calculations shall be prospective only; pension costs need not be redetermined for prior years.

(5) For a segment whose pension costs are either required to be calculated separately pursuant to paragraph (c)(2) or (c)(3) of this subsection or calculated separately at the election of the contractor, there shall be an initial allocation of a share in the undivided market value of the assets of the pension plan to that segment, as follows:

(i) If the necessary data are readily determinable, the funding agency balance to be allocated to the segment shall be the amount contributed by, or on behalf of, the segment, increased by income received on such assets, and decreased by benefits and expenses paid from such assets. Likewise, the

CASB 9904.413-50

accumulated value of permitted unfunded accruals to be allocated to the segment shall be the amount of permitted unfunded accruals assigned to the segment, increased by interest imputed to such assets, and decreased by benefits paid from sources other than the funding agency; or

(ii) If the data specified in paragraph (c)(5)(i) of this subsection are not readily determinable for certain prior periods, the market value of the assets of the pension plan shall be allocated to the segment as of the earliest date such data are available. Such allocation shall be based on the ratio of the actuarial accrued liability of the segment to the plan as a whole, determined in a manner consistent with the immediate gain actuarial cost method or methods used to compute pension cost. Such assets shall be brought forward as described in paragraph (c)(7) of this subsection.

(iii) The actuarial value of the assets of the pension plan shall be allocated to the segment in the same proportion as the market value of the assets.

(6) If, prior to the time a contractor is required to use this Standard, it has been calculating pension cost separately for individual segments, the amount of assets previously allocated to those segments need not be changed.

(7) After the initial allocation of assets, the contractor shall maintain a record of the portion of subsequent contributions, permitted unfunded accruals, income, benefit payments, and expenses attributable to the segment, and paid from the assets of the pension plan. Income shall include a portion of any investment gains and losses attributable to the assets of the pension plan. Income and expenses of the pension plan assets shall be allocated to the segment in the same proportion that the average value of assets allocated to the segment bears to the average value of total pension plan assets, including the accumulated value of prepayment credits, for the period for which income and expenses are being allocated.

(8) If plan participants transfer among segments, contractors need not transfer assets or actuarial accrued liabilities, unless a transfer is sufficiently large to distort the segment's ratio of pension plan assets to actuarial accrued liabilities determined using the accrued benefit cost method. If assets and liabilities are transferred, the amount of assets transferred shall be equal to the actuarial accrued liabilities transferred, determined using the accrued benefit cost method and long-term assumptions in accordance with 9904.412-40(b)(2) and 9904.412-50(b)(4).

(9) Contractors who separately calculate the pension cost of one or more segments may calculate such cost either for all pension plan participants assignable to the segment(s) or for only the active participants of the segment(s). If costs are calculated only for active participants, a separate segment shall be created for all of the inactive participants of the pension plan and the cost thereof shall be calculated. When a contractor makes such an election, assets shall be allocated to the segment for inactive participants in accordance with paragraphs (c)(5), (6), and (7) of this subsection. When an employee of a segment becomes inactive, assets shall be transferred from that segment to the segment established to accumulate the assets and actuarial liabilities for the inactive plan participants. The amount of assets transferred shall be equal to the actuarial accrued liabilities, determined under the accrued benefit cost method and long-term assumptions in accordance with 9904.412-40(b)(2) and 9904.412-50(b)(4), for these inactive plan participants. If inactive participants become active, assets and liabilities shall similarly be transferred to the segments to which the participants are assigned. Such transfers need be made only as of the last day of a cost accounting period. The total annual pension cost for a segment having active employees shall be the amount calculated for the segment and an allocated portion of the pension cost calculated for the inactive participants. Such an allocation shall be on the same basis as that set forth in paragraph (c)(1) of this subsection.

(10) Where pension cost is separately calculated for one or more segments, the actuarial cost method used for a plan shall be the same for all segments. Unless a separate calculation of pension cost for a segment is

CASB 9904.413-50

made because of a condition set forth in paragraph (c)(2)(iii) of this subsection, the same actuarial assumptions may be used for all segments covered by a plan.

(11) If a pension plan has participants in the home office of a company, the home office shall be treated as a segment for purposes of allocating the cost of the pension plan. Pension cost allocated to a home office shall be a part of the costs to be allocated in accordance with the appropriate requirements of Cost Accounting Standard 9904.403.

(12) If a segment is closed, if there is a pension plan termination, or if there is a curtailment of benefits, the contractor shall determine the difference between the actuarial accrued liability for the segment and the market value of the assets allocated to the segment, irrespective of whether or not the pension plan is terminated. The difference between the market value of the assets and the actuarial accrued liability for the segment represents an adjustment of previously-determined pension costs.

(i) The determination of the actuarial accrued liability shall be made using the accrued benefit cost method. The actuarial assumptions employed shall be consistent with the current and prior long term assumptions used in the measurement of pension costs. If there is a pension plan termination, the actuarial accrued liability shall be measured as the amount paid to irrevocably settle all benefit obligations or paid to the Pension Benefit Guarantee Corporation.

(ii) In computing the market value of assets for the segment, if the contractor has not already allocated assets to the segment, such an allocation shall be made in accordance with the requirements of paragraphs (c)(5)(i) and (ii) of this subsection. The market value of the assets shall be reduced by the accumulated value of prepayment credits, if any. Conversely, the market value of the assets shall be increased by the current value of any unfunded actuarial liability separately identified and maintained in accordance with 9904.412-50(a)(2).

(iii) The calculation of the difference between the market value of the assets and the

actuarial accrued liability shall be made as of the date of the event (e.g., contract termination, plan amendment, plant closure) that caused the closing of the segment, pension plan termination, or curtailment of benefits. If such a date is not readily determinable, or if its use can result in an inequitable calculation, the contracting parties shall agree on an appropriate date.

(iv) Pension plan improvements adopted within 60 months of the date of the event which increase the actuarial accrued liability shall be recognized on a pro rata basis using the number of months the date of adoption preceded the event date. Plan improvements mandated by law or collective bargaining agreement are not subject to this phase-in.

(v) If a segment is closed due to a sale or other transfer of ownership to a successor in interest in the contracts of the segment and all of the pension plan assets and actuarial accrued liabilities pertaining to the closed segment are transferred to the successor segment, then no adjustment amount pursuant to this paragraph (c)(12) is required. If only some of the pension plan assets and actuarial accrued liabilities of the closed segment are transferred, then the adjustment amount required under this paragraph (c)(12) shall be determined based on the pension plan assets and actuarial accrued liabilities remaining with the contractor. In either case, the effect of the transferred assets and liabilities is carried forward and recognized in the accounting for pension cost at the successor contractor.

(vi) The Government's share of the adjustment amount determined for a segment shall be the product of the adjustment amount and a fraction. The adjustment amount shall be reduced for any excise tax imposed upon assets withdrawn from the funding agency of a qualified pension plan. The numerator of such fraction shall be the sum of the pension plan costs allocated to all contracts and subcontracts (including Foreign Military Sales) subject to this Standard during a period of years representative of the Government's participation in the pension plan. The denominator of such fraction shall be the total pension costs assigned to cost accounting periods during those same years. This amount shall represent an adjustment of contract prices or cost allowance as appropriate. The adjustment may be recognized by modifying a single contract, several but not all contracts, or all contracts, or by use of any other suitable technique.

(vii) The full amount of the Government's share of an adjustment is allocable, without limit, as a credit or charge during the cost accounting period in which the event occurred and contract prices/costs will be adjusted accordingly. However, if the contractor continues to perform Government contracts, the contracting parties may negotiate an amortization schedule, including interest adjustments. Any amortization agreement shall consider the magnitude of the adjustment credit or charge, and the size and nature of the continuing contracts.

(viii) If a benefit curtailment is caused by a cessation of benefit accruals mandated by the Employee Retirement Income Security Act of 1974 (ERISA), 29 U.S.C. 1001 *et seq.*, as amended based on the plan's funding level, then no adjustment for the curtailment of benefit pursuant to this paragraph (c)(12) is required. Instead, the curtailment of benefits shall be recognized as follows:

(A) If the written plan document provides that benefit accruals are nonforfeitable once employment service has been rendered, and shall be retroactively restored if, and when, the benefit accrual limitation ceases, then the contractor may elect to recognize the expected benefit accruals in the actuarial accrued liability and normal cost during the period of cessation for the determination of pension cost in accordance with the provisions of 9904-412 and 413.

(B) Otherwise, the curtailment of benefits shall be recognized as an actuarial gain or loss for the period. The subsequent restoration of missed benefit accruals shall be recognized as an actuarial gain or loss in the period in which the restoration occurs.

[Final rule, 60 FR 16534, 3/30/95, effective 3/30/95; Final rule, 76 FR 81296, 12/27/2011, effective 2/27/2012]

9904.413-60 Illustrations.

(a) *Assignment of actuarial gains and losses.* Contractor A has a defined-benefit pension plan whose costs are measured under an immediate-gain actuarial cost method. The contractor makes actuarial valuations every other year. In the past, at each valuation date, the contractor has calculated the actuarial gains and losses that have occurred since the previous valuation date, and has merged such gains and losses with the unfunded actuarial liabilities that are being amortized. Pursuant to 9904.413-40(a), the contractor must make an actuarial valuation annually, and any actuarial gains or losses measured must be separately amortized over a specific period of years beginning with the period for which the actuarial valuation is made in accordance with 9904.413-50(a)(1) and (2). If the actuarial gain or loss is measured for a period beginning prior to the "Applicability Date for the CAS Pension Harmonization Rule," the gain or loss shall be amortized over a fifteen-year period. For gains and losses measured for periods beginning on or after the "Applicability Date for the CAS Pension Harmonization Rule," the gain or loss shall be amortized over a ten-year period.

(b)(1) Valuation of the assets of a pension plan. Contractor B has a qualified defined-benefit pension plan, the assets of which are invested in equity securities, debt securities, and real property. The contractor, whose cost accounting period is the calendar year, has an annual actuarial valuation of the pension plan assets in June of each year; the effective date of the valuation is the beginning of that year. The contractor's method for valuing the assets of the pension plan is as follows: debt securities expected to be held to maturity are valued on an amortized basis running from initial cost at purchase to par value at maturity; land and buildings are valued at cost less depreciation taken to date; all equity securities and debt securities not expected to be held to maturity are valued on the basis of a five-year moving average of market values. In making an actuarial valuation, the contractor must compare the values reached under the asset valuation method used with the market value of all the assets as required by 9904.413-40(b). In this case, the assets are valued as of January 1 of that year. The contractor established the following values as of the valuation date.

	Asset valuation method	Market
Cash	$100,000	100,000
Equity securities	6,000,000	7,800,000
Debt securities, expected to be held to maturity	550,000	600,000
Other debt securities	600,000	750,000
Land and Buildings, net of depreciation	400,000	750,000
Total	7,650,000	10,000,000

(2) Section 9904.413-50(b)(2) requires that the actuarial value of the assets of the pension plan fall within a corridor from 80 to 120 percent of market. The corridor for the plan's assets as of January 1 is from $12 million to $8 million. Because the asset value reached by the contractor, $7,650,000, falls outside that corridor, the value reached must be adjusted to equal the nearest boundary of the corridor: $8 million. In subsequent years the contractor must continue to use the same method for valuing assets in accordance with 9904.413-50(b)(3). If the value produced falls inside the corridor, such value shall be used in measuring pension costs.

(3) Assume that besides the market value of assets of $10 million that Contractor B has on the valuation date of January 1, 2017, the contractor makes a contribution of $100,000 on July 1, 2017, to cover its prior year's pension cost. Based on the contractor's assumed interest rate of 8% which complies with 9904.412-40(b)(2) and 9904.412.-50(b)(5), the contribution is discounted for the six-month period from January 1, 2017 to July 1, 2017. For contract cost accounting purposes, the contractor measures $96,225 as the present value (PV) of the $100,000 contribution on January 1, 2017 (discounted at 8% per annum for one half year using compound interest, i.e., Net PV = $100,000/$1.08^{0.5}$), and therefore recognizes $10,096,225 as the market value of assets as required by 9904.413-50(b)(6)(ii). The actuarial value of assets on January 1, 2017, must also reflect $96,225 as the present value of the July 1, 2017, contribution of $100,000.

(c) Allocation of pension costs to segments. (1) Contractor C has a defined-benefit pension plan covering employees at five segments. Pension cost is computed by use of an immediate-gain actuarial cost method. One segment (X) is devoted primarily to performing work for the Government. During the current cost accounting period, Segment X had a large and unforeseeable reduction of employees because of a contract termination at the convenience of the Government and because the contractor did not receive an anticipated follow-on contract to one that was completed during the period. The segment does continue to perform work under several other Government contracts. As a consequence of this termination of employment gain, a separate calculation of the pension cost for Segment X would result in materially different allocation of costs to the segment than would a composite calculation and allocation by means of a base. Accordingly, pursuant to 9904.413-50(c)(2), the contractor must calculate a separate pension cost for Segment X. In doing so, the entire termination of employment gain must be assigned to Segment X and amortized over fifteen years. If the actuarial assumptions for Segment X continue to be substantially the same as for the other segments, the termination of employment gain may be separately amortized and allocated only to Segment X; all other Segment X computations may be included as part of the composite calculation. After the termination of employment gain is amortized, the contractor is no longer required to separately calculate the costs for

CASB 9904.413-60

Segment X unless subsequent events require each separate calculation.

(2) Contractor D has a defined-benefit pension plan covering employees at ten segments, all of which have some contracts subject to this Standard. The contractor's calculation of normal cost is based on a percentage of payroll for all employees covered by the plan. One of the segments (Segment Y) is entirely devoted to Government work. The contractor's policy is to place junior employees in this segment. The salary scale assumption for employees of the segment is so different from that of the other segments that the pension cost for Segment Y would be materially different if computed separately. Pursuant to 9904.413-50(c)(2)(iii), the contractor must compute the pension cost for Segment Y as if it were a separate pension plan. Therefore, the contractor must allocate a portion of the market value of pension plan's assets to Segment Y in accordance with 9904.413-50(c)(5). Memorandum records may be used in making the allocation. However, because the necessary records only exist for the last five years, 9904.413-50(c)(5)(ii) permits an initial allocation to be made as of the earliest date such records are available. The initial allocation must be made on the basis of the immediate gain actuarial cost method or methods used to calculate prior years' pension cost for the plan. Once the assets have been allocated, they shall be brought forward to the current period as described in 9904.413-50(c)(7). A portion of the undivided actuarial value of assets shall then be allocated to the segment based on the segment's proportion of the market value of assets in accordance with 9904.413-50(c)(5)(iii). In future cost accounting periods, the contractor shall make separate pension cost calculations for Segment Y based on the appropriate salary scale assumption. Because the factors comprising pension cost for the other nine segments are relatively equal, the contractor may compute pension cost for these nine segments by using composite factors. As required by 9904.413-50(c)(1), the base to be used for allocating such costs shall be representative of the factors on which the pension benefits are based.

(3) Contractor E has a defined-benefit pension plan which covers employees at twelve segments. The contractor uses composite actuarial assumptions to develop a pension cost for all segments. Three of these segments primarily perform Government work; the work at the other nine segments is primarily commercial. Employee turnover at the segments performing commercial work is relatively stable. However, employment experience at the Government segments has been very volatile; there have been large fluctuations in employment levels and the contractor assumes that this pattern of employment will continue to occur. It is evident that separate termination of employment assumptions for the Government segments and the commercial segments will result in materially different pension costs for the Government segments. Therefore, the cost for these segments must be separately calculated, using the appropriate termination of employment assumptions for these segments in accordance with 9904.413-50(c)(2)(iii).

(4) Contractor F has a defined-benefit pension plan covering employees at 25 segments. Twelve of these segments primarily perform Government work; the remaining segments perform primarily commercial work. The contractor's records show that the termination of employment experience and projections for the twelve segments are so different from that of the average of all of the segments that separate pension cost calculations are required for these segments pursuant to 9904.413-50(c)(2). However, because the termination of employment experience and projections are about the same for all twelve segments, Contractor F may calculate a composite pension cost for the twelve segments and allocate the cost to these segments by use of an appropriate allocation base in accordance with 9904.413-50(c)(1).

(5) After this Standard becomes applicable to Contractor G, it acquires Contractor H and makes it Segment H. Prior to the merger, each contractor had its own defined-benefit pension plan. Under the terms of the merger, Contractor H's pension plan and plan assets were merged with those of Contractor G. The actuarial assumptions, current

salary scale, and other plan characteristics are about the same for Segment H and Contractor G's other segments. However, based on the same benefits at the time of the merger, the plan of Contractor H had a disproportionately larger unfunded actuarial liability than did Contractor G's plan. Any combining of the assets and actuarial liabilities of both plans would result in materially different pension cost allocation to Contractor G's segments than if pension cost were computed for Segment H on the basis that it had a separate pension plan. Accordingly, pursuant to 9904.413-50(c)(3), Contractor G must allocate to Segment H a portion of the assets of the combined plan. The amount to be allocated shall be the market value of Segment H's pension plan assets at the date of the merger determined in accordance with 9904.413-50(c)(5), and shall be adjusted for subsequent receipts and expenditures applicable to the segment in accordance with 9904.413-50(c)(7). Pursuant to 9904.413-40(b)(1) and 9904.413-50(c)(5)(iii), Contractor G must use these amounts of assets as the basis for determining the actuarial value of assets used for calculating the annual pension cost applicable to Segment H.

(6) Contractor I has a defined-benefit pension plan covering employees at seven segments. The contractor has been making a composite pension cost calculation for all of the segments. However, the contractor determines that, pursuant to this Standard, separate pension costs must be calculated for one of the segments. In accordance with 9904.413-50(c)(9), the contractor elects to allocate pension plan assets only for the active participants of that segment. The contractor must then create a segment to accumulate the assets and actuarial accrued liabilities for the plan's inactive participants. When active participants of a segment become inactive, the contractor must transfer assets to the segment for inactive participants equal to the actuarial accrued liabilities for the participants that become inactive.

(7) Contractor J has a defined-benefit pension plan covering employees at ten segments. The contractor makes a composite pension cost calculation for all segments.

The contractor's records show that the termination of employment experience for one segment, which is performing primarily Government work, has been significantly different from the average termination of employment experience of the other segments. Moreover, the contractor assumes that such different experience will continue. Because of this fact, and because the application of a different termination of employment assumption would result in significantly different costs being charged the Government, the contractor must develop separate pension cost for that segment. In accordance with 9904.413-50(c)(2)(iii), the amount of pension cost must be based on an acceptable termination of employment assumption for that segment; however, as provided in 9904.413-50(c)(10), all other assumptions for that segment may be the same as those for the remaining segments.

(8) Contractor K has a five-year contract to operate a Government-owned facility. The employees of that facility are covered by the contractor's overall qualified defined-benefit pension plan which covers salaried and hourly employees at other locations. At the conclusion of the five-year period, the Government decides not to renew the contract. Although some employees are hired by the successor contractor, because Contractor K no longer operates the facility, it meets the 9904.413-30(a)(20)(iii) definition of a segment closing. Contractor K must compute the actuarial accrued liability for the pension plan for that facility using the accrued benefit cost method as of the date the contract expired in accordance with 9904.413-50(c)(12)(i). Because many of Contractor K's employees are terminated from the pension plan, the Internal Revenue Service considers it to be a partial plan termination, and thus requires that the terminated employees become fully vested in their accrued benefits to the extent such benefits are funded. Taking this mandated benefit improvement into consideration in accordance with 9904.413-50(c)(12)(iv), the actuary calculates the actuarial accrued liability to be $12.5 million. The contractor must then determine the market value of the pension plan assets allocable to the facility, in accordance with 9904.413-50(c)(5), as of the

date agreed to by the contracting parties pursuant to 9904.413-50(c)(12)(iii), the date the contract expired. In making this determination, the contractor is able to do a full historical reconstruction of the market value of the assets allocated to the segment. In this case, the market value of the segment's assets amounted to $13.8 million. Thus, for this facility the value of pension plan assets exceeded the actuarial accrued liability by $1.3 million. Pursuant to 9904.413-50(c)(12)(vi), this amount indicates the extent to which the Government over-contributed to the pension plan for the segment and, accordingly, is the amount of the adjustment due to the Government.

(9) Contractor L operated a segment over the last five years during which 80 of its work was performed under Government CAS-covered contracts. The Government work was equally divided each year between fixed-price and cost-type contracts. The employees of the facility are covered by a funded nonqualified defined-benefit pension plan accounted for in accordance with 9904.412-50(c)(3). For each of the last five years the highest Federal corporate income tax rate has been 30. Pension costs of $1 million per year were computed using a projected benefit cost method. Contractor L funded at the complement of the tax rate ($700,000 per year). The pension plan assets held by the funding agency earned 8 each year. At the end of the five-year period, the funding agency balance; i.e., the market value of invested assets, was $4.4 million. As of that date, the accumulated value of permitted unfunded accruals; i.e., the current value of the $300,000 not funded each year, is $1.9 million. As defined by 9904.413-30(a)(20)(i), a segment closing occurs when Contractor L sells the segment at the end of the fifth year. Thus, for this segment, the market value of the assets of the pension plan determined in accordance with 9904.413-30(a)(10) is $6.3 million, which is, the sum of the funding account balance ($4.4 million) and the accumulated value of permitted unfunded accruals ($1.9 million). Pursuant to 9904.413-50(c)(12)(i), the contractor uses the accrued benefit cost method to calculate an actuarial accrued liability of $5 million as of that date. There is no transfer of plan

assets or liabilities to the buyer. The difference between the market value of the assets and the actuarial accrued liability for the segment is $1.3 million ($6.3 million—$5 million). Pursuant to 9904.413-50(c)(12)(vi), the adjustment due the Government for its 80 share of previously-determined pension costs for CAS-covered contracts is $1.04 million (80 times $1.3 million). Because contractor L has no other Government contracts the $1.04 million is a credit due to the Government.

(10) Assume the same facts as in 9904.413-60(c)(9), except that Contractor L continues to perform substantial Government contract work through other segments. After considering the amount of the adjustment and the current level of contracts, the contracting officer and the contractor establish an amortization schedule so that the $1.04 million is recognized as credits against ongoing contracts in five level annual installments, including an interest adjustment based on the interest assumption used to compute pension costs for the continuing contracts. This amortization schedule satisfies the requirements of 9904.413-50(c)(12))(vii).

(11) Assume the same facts as in 9904.413-60(c)(9). As part of the transfer of ownership, Contractor L also transfers all pension liabilities and assets of the segment to the buyer. Pursuant to 9904.413-50(c)(12)(v), the segment closing adjustment amount for the current period is transferred to the buyer and is subsumed in the future pension cost accounting of the buyer. If the transferred liabilities and assets of the segment are merged into the buyer's pension plan which has a different ratio of market value of pension plan assets to actuarial accrued liabilities, then pension costs must be separately computed in accordance with 9904.413-50(c)(3).

(12) Contractor M sells its only Government segment. Through a contract novation, the buyer assumes responsibility for performance of the segment's Government contracts. Just prior to the sale, the actuarial accrued liability under the actuarial cost method in use is $18 million, and the market value of assets allocated to the segment of

$22 million. In accordance with the sales agreement, Contractor M is required to transfer $20 million of plan assets to the new plan sponsored by the buyer. In determining the segment closing adjustment under 9904.413-50(c)(12), the actuarial accrued liability and the market value of assets are reduced by the amounts transferred to the buyer's new plan in accordance with the terms of the sales agreement. The adjustment amount, which is the difference between the remaining assets ($2 million) and the remaining actuarial liability ($0), is $2 million.

(13) Contractor N has three segments that perform primarily government work and has been separately calculating pension costs for each segment. As part of a corporate reorganization, the contractor closes the production facility for Segment A and transfers all of that segment's contracts and employees to Segments B and C, the two remaining government segments. The pension assets from Segment A are allocated to the remaining segments based on the actuarial accrued liability of the transferred employees. Because Segment A has discontinued operations, a segment closing has occurred pursuant to 9904.413-30(a)(20)(ii). However, because all pension assets and liabilities have been transferred to other segments or to successors in interest of the contracts of Segment A, an immediate period adjustment is not required pursuant to 9904.413-50(c)(12)(v).

(14) Contractor O does not renew its government contract and decides to not seek additional government contracts for the affected segment. The contractor reduces the work force of the segment that had been dedicated to the government contract and converts the segment's operations to purely commercial work. In accordance with 9904.413-30(a)(20)(iii), the segment has closed. Immediately prior to the end of the contract the market value of the segment's assets was $20 million and the actuarial accrued liability determined under the actuarial cost method in use was $22 million. An actuarial accrued liability of $16 million is determined using the accrued benefit cost method as required by

9904.413-50(c)(12)(i). The segment closing adjustment is $4 million ($20 million—$16 million).

(15) Contractor P terminated its underfunded defined-benefit pension plan for hourly employees. The market value of the assets for the pension plan is $100 million. Although the actuarial accrued liability exceeds the $100 million of assets, the termination liability for benefits guaranteed by the Pension Benefit Guarantee Corporation (PBGC) is only $85 million. Therefore, the $15 million of assets in excess of the liability for guaranteed benefits are allocated to plan participants in accordance with PBGC regulations. The PBGC does not impose an assessment for unfunded guaranteed benefits against the contractor. The adjustment amount determined under 9904.413-50(c)(12) is zero.

(16) Assume the same facts as 9904.413-60(c)(15), except that the termination liability for benefits guaranteed by the Pension Benefit Guarantee Corporation (PBGC) is $120 million. The PBGC imposes a $20 million ($120 million—$100 Million) assessment against Contractor P for the unfunded guaranteed benefits. The contractor then determines the Government's share of the pension plan termination adjustment charge of $20 million in accordance with 9904.413-50(c)(12)(vi). In accordance with 9904.413-50(c)(12)(vii), the cognizant Federal official may negotiate an amortization schedule based on the contractor's schedule of payments to the PBGC.

(17) Assume the same facts as in 9904.413-60(c)(16), except that pursuant to 9904.412-50(a)(2) Contractor P has an unassignable portion of unfunded actuarial liability for prior unfunded pension costs which equals $8 million. The $8 million represents the value of assets that would have been available had all assignable costs been funded and, therefore, must be added to the assets used to determine the pension plan termination adjustment in accordance with 9904.413-50(c)(12)(ii). In this case, the adjustment charge is determined to be $12 million ($20 million-$8 million).

(18) Contractor Q terminates its qualified defined-benefit pension plan without estab-

lishing a replacement plan. At termination, the market value of assets is $85 million. All obligations for benefits are irrevocably transferred to an insurance company by the purchase of annuity contracts at a cost of $55 million, which thereby determines the actuarial liability in accordance with 9904.413-50(c)(12)(i). The contractor receives a reversion of $30 million ($85 million - $55 million). The adjustment is equal to the reversion amount, which is the excess of the market value of assets over the actuarial liability. However, the Internal Revenue Code imposes a 50% excise tax of $15 million (50% of $30 million) on the reversion amount. In accordance with 9904.413-50(c)(12)(vi), the $30 million adjustment amount is reduced by the $15 million excise tax. Pursuant to 9904.413-50(c)(12)(vi), a share of the $15 million net adjustment ($30 million - $15 million) shall be allocated, without limitation, as a credit to CAS-covered contracts.

(19) Assume that, in addition to the facts of 9904.413-60(c)(18), Contractor Q has an accumulated value of prepayment credits of $10 million. Contractor Q has $3 million of unfunded actuarial liability separately identified and maintained pursuant to 9904.412-50(a)(2). The assets used to determine the adjustment amount equal $78 million. This amount is determined as the market value of assets ($85 million) minus the accumulated value of prepayment credits ($10 million) plus the portion of unfunded actuarial liability maintained pursuant to 9904.412-50(a)(2) ($3 million). Therefore, the difference between the assets and the actuarial liability is $23 million ($78 million—$55 million). In accordance with 9904.413-50(c)(12)(vi), the $23 million adjustment is reduced by the $15 million excise tax to equal $8 million. The contracting officer determines that the pension cost data of the most recent eight years reasonably reflects the government's participation in the pension plan. The sum of costs allocated to fixed-price and cost-type contracts subject to this Standard over the eight-year period is $21 million. The sum of costs assigned to cost accounting periods during the last eight years equals $42 million. Therefore, the government's share of the net adjustment is 50

($21 million divided by $42 million) of the $8 million and equals $4 million.

(20) Contractor R maintains a qualified defined-benefit pension plan. Contractor R amends the pension plan to eliminate the earning of any future benefits; however the participants do continue to earn vesting service. Pursuant to 9904.413-30(a)(7), a curtailment of benefits has occurred. An actuarial accrued liability of $78 million is determined under the accrued benefit cost method using the interest assumption used for the last four actuarial valuations. The market value of assets, determined in accordance with 9904.413-50(c)(12)(ii), is $90 million. Contractor R shall determine the Government's share of the adjustment in accordance with 9904.413-50(c)(12)(vi). The contractor then shall allocate that share of the $12 million adjustment ($90 million—$78 million) determined under 9904.413-50(c)(12) to CAS-covered contracts. The full amount of adjustment shall be made without limitation in the current cost accounting period unless arrangements to amortize the adjustment are permitted and negotiated pursuant to 9904.413-50(c)(12)(vii).

(21) Contractor S amends its qualified defined-benefit pension plan to "freeze" all accrued benefits at their current level. Although not required by law, the amendment also provides that all accrued benefits are fully vested. Contractor S must determine the adjustment for the curtailment of benefits. Fifteen months prior to the date of the plan amendment freezing benefits, Contractor S voluntarily amended the plan to increase benefits. This voluntary amendment resulted in an overall increase of over 10. All actuarial accrued liabilities are computed using the accrued benefit cost method. The actuarial accrued liability for all accrued benefits is $1.8 million. The actuarial accrued liability for vested benefits immediately prior to the current plan amendment is $1.6 million. The actuarial accrued liability determined for vested benefits based on the plan provisions before the voluntary amendment is $1.4 million. The $1.4 million actuarial liability is based on benefit provisions that have been in effect for six years and is fully recognized. However, the

$200,000 increase in liability due to the voluntary benefit improvement adopted 15 months ago must be phased in on a pro rata basis over 60 months. Therefore, only 25% (15 months divided by 60 months) of the $200,000 increase, or $50,000, can be included in the curtailment liability. The current amendment voluntarily increasing vesting was just adopted and, therefore, none of the associated increase in actuarial accrued liability can be included. Accordingly, in accordance with 9904.413-50(c)(12)(iv), Contractor S determines the adjustment for the curtailment of benefits using an actuarial accrued liability of $1.45 million ($1.4 million plus $50,000).

(22) Contractor T has maintained separate qualified defined-benefit plans for Segments A and B and has separately computed pension costs for each segment. Both segments perform work under contracts subject to this Standard. On the first day of the current cost accounting period, Contractor T merges the two pension plans so that segments A and B are now covered by a single pension plan. Because the ratio of assets to liabilities for each plan is materially different from that of the merged plan, the contractor continues the separate computation of pension costs for each segment pursuant to 9904.413-50(c)(3). After considering the assignable cost limitations for each segment, Contractor T determines the potentially assignable pension cost is $12,000 for Segment A and $24,000 for Segment B. The maximum tax-deductible amount for the merged plan is $30,000, which is $6,000 less than the sum of the otherwise assignable costs for the segments ($36,000). To determine the portion of the total maximum tax-deductible amount applicable to each segment on a reasonable basis, the contractor prorates the $30,000 by the pension cost determined for each segment after considering the assignable cost limitations for each segment. Therefore, in accordance with 9904.413-50(c)(1)(i), the assignable pension cost is $10,000 for Segment A ($30,000 times $12,000 divided by $36,000) and $20,000 for Segment B ($30,000 times $24,000 divided by $36,000). Contractor T funds the full $30,000 and allocates the assignable pension cost for each segment to final cost objectives.

(23) Assume the same facts as in 9904.413-60(c)(22), except that the tax-deductible maximum is $40,000 and the ERISA minimum funding requirement is $18,000. Since funding of the accrued pension cost is not constrained by tax-deductibility, Contractor T determines the assignable pension cost to be $12,000 for Segment A and $24,000 for Segment B. If the contractor funds $36,000, the full assigned pension cost of each segment can be allocated to final cost objectives. However, because the contractor funds only the ERISA minimum of $18,000, the contractor must apportion the $18,000 contribution to each segment on a basis that reflects the assignable pension cost of each segment in accordance with 9904.413-50(c)(1)(ii). To measure the funding level of each segment, Contractor T uses an ERISA minimum funding requirement separately determined for each segment, as if the segment were a separate plan. On this basis, the allocable pension cost is determined to be $8,000 for Segment A and $10,000 for Segment B. In accordance with 9904.412-50(a)(2), Contractor T must separately identify, and eliminate from future cost computations, $4,000 ($12,000-$8,000) for Segment A and $14,000 ($24,000-$10,000) for Segment B.

(24) Assume the same facts as in 9904.413-60(c)(23), except that Segment B performs only commercial work. As permitted by 9904.413-50(c)(1)(ii), the contractor first applies $12,000 of the contribution amount to Segment A, which is performing work under Government contracts, for purposes of 9904.412-50(d)(1). The remaining $6,000 is applied to Segment B. The full assigned pension cost of $12,000 for Segment A is funded and such amount is allocable to CAS-covered contracts. Pursuant to 9904.412-50(a)(2), the contractor separately identifies, and eliminates from future pension costs, the $18,000 ($24,000-$6,000) of unfunded assigned cost for Segment B.

(25) Contractor U has a qualified defined-benefit pension plan covering employees at two segments that perform work on contracts subject to this Standard. The ratio of the actuarial value of assets to actuarial accrued liabilities is significantly different between the two segments. Therefore,

Contractor U is required to compute pension cost separately for each segment. The actuarial value of assets allocated to Segment A exceeds the actuarial accrued liability by $50,000. Segment B has an unfunded actuarial liability of $20,000. Thus, the pension plan as a whole has an actuarial surplus of $30,000. Pension cost of $5,000 is computed for Segment B and is less than Segment B's assignable cost limitation of $9,000. The tax-deductible maximum is $0 for the plan as whole and, therefore, $0 for each segment. Contractor U will deem all existing amortization bases maintained for Segment A to be fully amortized in accordance with 9904.412-50(c)(2)(ii). For Segment B, the amortization of existing portions of unfunded actuarial liability continues unabated. Furthermore, pursuant to 9904.412-50(c)(2)(iii), the contractor establishes an additional amortization base for Segment B for the assignable cost deficit of $5,000.

(26) Assume the same facts as Illustration 9904.413-60(c)(20), except that ERISA required Contractor R to cease benefit accruals. In this case, the segment closing adjustment is exempted by 9904.413-50(c)(12)(viii). If the written plan document provides that benefit accruals will automatically be retroactively reinstated when permitted by ERISA, then the pension cost measured pursuant to CAS 412 and this Standard for contract costing purposes may continue to recognize the benefit accruals, if the contractor has so elected. If there is evidence that the contractor might revoke the plan provision to restore the missed benefit accruals, then the contractor shall not make such election. Otherwise, the pension cost measured pursuant to CAS 412 and this Standard shall not recognize any benefit accruals until, and unless, the plan is subsequently amended to reinstate the accruals. Furthermore, when the plan is amended, the change in the actuarial accrued liability shall be measured as an actuarial gain or loss, and amortized in accordance with 9904.412-50(a)(1)(v) and 9904.413-50(a)(2)(ii).

[Final rule, 60 FR 16534, 3/30/95, effective 3/30/95; corrected, 60 FR 20248,

4/25/95, corrected 61 FR 58011, 11/12/96; Final rule, 76 FR 81296, 12/27/2011, effective 2/27/2012; Technical correcting amendment, 77 FR 43542, 7/25/2012, effective 8/24/2012]

9904.413-61 [Reserved]

9904.413-62 Exemption.
None for this Standard.

9904.413-63 Effective date.
(a) This Standard is effective as February 27, 2012, hereafter known as the "Effective Date," and is applicable for cost accounting periods after June 30, 2012, hereafter known as the "Implementation Date."

(b) Following the award of a contract or subcontract subject to this Standard on or after the Effective Date, contractors shall follow this Standard, as amended, beginning with its next cost accounting period beginning after the later of the Implementation Date or the award date of a contract or subcontract to which this Standard is applicable. The first day of the cost accounting period that this Standard, as amended, is first applicable to a contractor or subcontractor is the "Applicability Date of the CAS Pension Harmonization Rule" for purposes of this Standard. Prior to the Applicability Date of the CAS Pension Harmonization Rule, contractors or subcontractors shall follow the Standard in 9904.413 in effect prior to the Effective Date.

(1) Following the award of a contract or subcontract subject to this Standard received on or after the Effective Date, contractors with contracts or subcontracts subject to this Standard that were received prior to the Effective Date shall continue to follow the Standard in 9904.413 in effect prior to the Effective Date. Beginning with the Applicability Date of the CAS Pension Harmonization Rule, such contractors shall follow this Standard, as amended, for all contracts or subcontracts subject to this Standard.

(2) Following the award of a contract or subcontract subject to this Standard received during the period beginning on or after the date published in the **Federal Register** and ending before the Effective Date,

contractors shall follow the Standard in 9904.413 in effect prior to the Effective Date. If another contract or subcontract, subject to this Standard, is received on or after the Effective Date, the provisions of 9904.413-63(b)(1) shall apply.

[Final rule, 60 FR 16534, 3/30/95, effective 3/30/95; Final rule, 76 FR 81296, 12/27/2011, effective 2/27/2012; Technical correcting amendment, 77 FR 43542, 7/25/2012, effective 8/24/2012]

9904.413-64 Transition method.

(a) To be acceptable, any method of transition from compliance with Standard 9904.413 in effect prior to March 30, 1995, to compliance with Standard 9904.413 in effect as of March 30, 1995, must follow the equitable principle that costs, which have been previously provided for, shall not be redundantly provided for under revised methods. Conversely, costs that have not previously been provided for must be provided for under the revised method. This transition subsection is not intended to qualify for purposes of assignment or allocation, pension costs which have previously been disallowed for reasons other than ERISA funding limitations.

(b) The sum of all portions of unfunded actuarial liability identified pursuant to Standard 9904.413, effective March 30, 1995, including such portions of unfunded actuarial liability determined for transition purposes, is subject to the requirements for assignment of 9904.412-40(c).

(c) Furthermore, this Standard, effective March 30, 1995, clarifies, but is not intended to create, rights of the contracting parties, and specifies techniques for determining adjustments pursuant to 9904.413-50(c)(12). These rights and techniques should be used to resolve outstanding issues that will affect pension costs of contracts subject to this Standard.

(d) The method, or methods, employed to achieve an equitable transition shall be consistent with the provisions of this Standard and shall be approved by the contracting officer.

(e) All adjustments shall be prospective only. However, costs/prices of prior and existing contracts not subject to price adjustment may be considered in determining the appropriate transition method or adjustment amount for the computation of costs/prices of contracts subject to this Standard.

[Final rule, 60 FR 16534, 3/30/95, effective 3/30/95]

9904.413-64.1 Transition Method for the CAS Pension Harmonization Rule.

The transition method for the CAS Pension Harmonization Rule under this Standard shall be in accordance with 9904.412.64.1 Transition Method for CAS Pension Harmonization Rule.

[Final rule, 76 FR 81296, 12/27/2011, effective 2/27/2012]

9904.414 Cost accounting standard—cost of money as an element of the cost of facilities capital. (No Text)

9904.414-10 [Reserved]

9904.414-20 Purpose.

The purpose of this Cost Accounting Standard is to establish criteria for the measurement and allocation of the cost of capital committed to facilities as an element of contract cost. Consistent application of these criteria will improve cost measurement by providing for allocation of cost of contractor investment in facilities capital to negotiated contracts.

9904.414-30 Definitions.

(a) The following are definitions of terms which are prominent in this Standard. Other terms defined elsewhere in this Part 99 shall have the meanings ascribed to them in those definitions unless paragraph (b) of this subsection, requires otherwise.

(1) *Business Unit* means any segment of an organization, or an entire business organization, which is not divided into segments.

(2) *Cost of capital committed to facilities* means an imputed cost determined by applying a cost of money rate to facilities capital.

(3) *Facilities capital* means the net book value of tangible capital assets and of those

intangible capital assets that are subject to amortization.

(4) *Intangible capital asset* means an asset that has no physical substance, has more than minimal value, and is expected to be held by an enterprise for continued use or possession beyond the current accounting period for the benefits it yields.

(5) *Tangible capital asset* means an asset that has physical substance, more than minimal value, and is expected to be held by an enterprise for continued use or possession beyond the current accounting period for the services it yields.

(b) The following modifications of terms defined elsewhere in this chapter 99 are applicable to this Standard: None.

9904.414-40 Fundamental requirement.

(a) A contractor's facilities capital shall be measured and allocated in accordance with the criteria set forth in this Standard. The allocated amount shall be used as a base to which a cost of money rate is applied.

(b) The cost of money rate shall be based on rates determined by the Secretary of the Treasury, pursuant to Public Law 92-41 (85 stat. 97).

(c) The cost of capital committed to facilities shall be separately computed for each contract using facilities capital cost of money factors computed for each cost accounting period.

9904.414-50 Techniques for application.

(a) The investment base used in computing the cost of money for facilities capital shall be computed from accounting data used for contract cost purposes. The form and instructions stipulated in this Standard shall be used to make the computation.

(b) The cost of money rate for any cost accounting period shall be the arithmetic mean of the interest rates specified by the Secretary of the Treasury pursuant to Public Law 92-41 (85 stat. 97). Where the cost of money must be determined on a prospective basis, the cost of money rate shall be based on the most recent available rate published by the secretary of the Treasury.

(c) (1) A facilities capital cost of money factor shall be determined for each indirect cost pool to which a significant amount of facilities capital has been allocated and which is used to allocate indirect costs to final cost objectives.

(2) The facilities capital cost of money factor for an indirect cost pool shall be determined in accordance with Form CASB CMF, and its instructions which are set forth in appendix A to 9904.414. One form will serve for all the indirect cost pools of a business unit.

(3) For each CAS-covered contract, the applicable cost of capital committed to facilities for a given cost accounting period is the sum of the products obtained by multiplying the amount of allocation base units (such as direct labor hours, or dollars of total cost input) identified with the contract for the cost accounting period by the facilities capital cost of money factor for the corresponding indirect cost pool. In the case of process cost accounting systems, the contracting parties may agree to substitute an appropriate statistical measure for the allocation base units identified with the contract.

9904.414-60 Illustrations.

The use of Form CASB CMF and other computations anticipated for this Cost Accounting Standard are illustrated in appendix B to 9904.414.

9904.414-61 [Reserved]

9904.414-62 Exemption.

(a) For contractors who are not subject to full CAS-coverage as of the date of publication of this part 99 as a final rule, this Standard shall apply only to those fully-covered contracts with subsequent dates of award and pricing certification.

(b) This Standard shall not apply where compensation for the use of tangible capital assets is based on use rates or allowances provided for by other appropriate Federal procurement regulations such as those governing:

(1) Educational institutions,

(2) State, local, and Federally recognized Indian tribal governments, or

CASB 9904.414-62

(3) Construction equipment rates (see 48 CFR 31.105(d)).

9904.414-63 Effective date.

This Standard is effective as of April 17, 1992.

APPENDIX A TO 9904.414—
INSTRUCTIONS FOR FORM CASB CMF:

Form CASB-CMF

FORM APPROVED OMB NUMBER 0348-0051

APPENDIX A
FACILITIES CAPITAL
COST OF MONEY FACTORS COMPUTATION

CONTRACTOR:

BUSINESS UNIT:

ADDRESS:

COST ACCOUNTING PERIOD:	1. APPLICABLE COST OF MONEY RATE ____%	2. ACCUMULATION & DIRECT DISTRIBUTION OF N.B.V.	3. ALLOCATION OF UNDISTRIBUTED BASIS OF ALLOCATION	4. TOTAL NET BOOK VALUE COLUMNS 2 + 3	5. COST OF MONEY FOR THE COST ACCOUNTING PERIOD COLUMNS 1 × 4	6. ALLOCATION BASE FOR THE PERIOD IN UNIT(S) OF MEASURE	7. FACILITIES CAPITAL COST OF MONEY FACTORS COLUMNS 5/6
BUSINESS UNIT FACILITIES CAPITAL RECORDED							
LEASED PROPERTY							
CORPORATE OR GROUP							
TOTAL							
UNDISTRIBUTED							
DISTRIBUTED							
OVERHEAD POOLS							
G & A EXPENSE POOLS							
TOTAL							

BILLING CODE 3110-01-C

CASB App. A 9904.414

Purpose

The purpose of this form is to (a) accumulate total facilities capital net book values allocated to each business unit for the contractor cost accounting period, and (b) convert those values to facilities capital cost of money factors applicable to each overhead or G&A expense allocation base employed within a business unit.

Basis

All data pertain to the cost accounting period for which the contractor prepares overhead and C&A expense allocations. The cost of money computations should be compatible with those allocation procedures. More specifically, facilities capital values used should be the same values that are used to generate depreciation or amortization that is allowed for Federal Government contract costing purposes; land which is integral to the regular operation of the business unit shall be included.

Applicable Cost of Money Rate (Col. 1)

Enter here the rate as computed in accordance with 9904.414-50(b).

Accumulation and Direct Distribution of Net Book Value (Col. 2)

Recorded, Leased Property, Corporate.

The net book value of facilities capital items in this column shall represent the average balances outstanding during the cost accounting period. This applies both to items that are subject to periodic depreciation or amortization and also to such items as land that are not subject to periodic write-offs. Unless there is a major fluctuation, it will be adequate to ascertain the net book value of these assets at the beginning and end of each cost accounting period, and to compute an average of those two sets of figures. "Recorded" facilities are the facilities capital items owned by the contractor, carried on the books of the business unit, and used in its regular business activity. "Leased property" is the capitalized value of leases for which constructive costs of ownership are allowed in lieu of rental costs under Government procurement regulations. Corporate or group facilities are the business unit's allocable share of corporate-owned and leased facilities. The net book value of items of facilities capital which are held or controlled by the home office shall be allocated to the business unit on a basis consistent with the home office expense allocation.

Distributed and Undistributed.

All facilities capital items that are identified in the contractor's records as solely applicable to an organizational unit corresponding to a specific overhead, G&A or other indirect cost pool which is used to allocate indirect costs to final cost objectives. are listed against the applicable pools and are classified as "distributed." "Undistributed" is the remainder of the business unit's facilities capital. The sum of "distributed" and "undistributed" must also correspond to the amount shown on the "total" line.

Allocation of Distributed.

List in the narrative column all the overhead and G&A expense pools to which "distributed" facilities capital items have been allocated. Enter the corresponding amounts in (Col. 2). The sum of all the amounts shown against specific overhead and G&A expense pools must correspond to the amount shown in the "distributed" line.

Allocation of Undistributed (Col. 3)

Business unit "undistributed" facilities are allocated to overhead and the G&A expense pools on any reasonable basis that approximates the actual absorption of depreciation or amortization of such facilities. For instance, the basis of allocation of undistributed assets in each business unit between, e.g., engineering overhead pool and the manufacturing overhead pool, should be related to the manner in which the expenses generated by these assets are allocated between the two overhead pools. Detailed analysis of this allocation is not required where essentially the same results can be obtained by other means. Where the cost accounting system for purposes of Government contract costing uses more than one "charging rate" for allocating indirect costs accumulated in a single cost pool, one representative base may be substituted for the multiplicity of bases used in the allocation process. The net book value of service center facilities capital items appropriately allocated should be included in this column. The sum of the entries in Column 3 is equal to the entry in the undistributed line, Column 2.

A supporting work sheet of this allocation should be prepared if there is more than one service center or other similar "intermediate" cost objective involved in the reallocation process.

Alternative Allocation Process—As an alternative to the above allocation process all the undistributed assets for one or more service centers or similar intermediate cost objectives may be allocated to the G&A expense pool. Consequently, the

CASB App. A 9904.414

cost of money for these undistributed assets will be distributed to the final cost objectives on the same basis that is used to allocate G&A expense. This procedure may be adopted for any cost accounting period only when the contracting parties agree (a) that the depreciation or amortization generated by these undistributed assets is immaterial, or (b) that the results of this alternative procedure are not likely to differ materially from those which would be obtained under the "regular" allocation process described previously.

Total Net Book Value (Col. 4)

The sum of Columns 2 and 3. The total of this column should agree with the business unit's total shown in Column 2.

Cost of Money for the Cost Accounting Period (Col. 5)

Multiply the amounts in Column 4 by the percentage rate in Column 1.

Allocation Base for the Period (Col. 6)

Show here the total units of measure used to allocate overhead and G&A expense pools (e.g., direct labor dollars, machine hours, total cost input, etc.). Include service centers that make charges to final cost objectives. Each base unit-of-measure must be compatible with the bases used for applying overhead in the Federal Government contract cost computation. The total base unit of measure used for allocation in this column refers to all work done in an organizational unit associated with the indirect cost pool and not to Government work alone.

Facilities Capital Cost of Money Factors (Col. 7)

The quotients of cost of money for the cost accounting period (Col. 5) separately divided by the corresponding overhead or G&A expense allocation bases (Col. 6). Carry each computation to five decimal places. This factor represents the cost of money applicable to facilities capital allocated to each unit of measure of the overhead or G&A expense allocation base.

[Corrected, 57 FR 43776, 9/22/92]

APPENDIX B TO 9904.414— EXAMPLE—ABC CORPORATION

ABC Corporation has a home office that controls three operating divisions (Business Units A, B & C). The home office includes an administrative computer center whose costs are allocated separately to the business units. The separate allocation conforms to the requirements specified in the Cost Accounting Standard No. 403. Tables I through VI deal with home office expense allocations to business units.

The A Division is a business unit as defined by the CASB, and it uses one engineering and one manufacturing overhead pool to accumulate costs for charging overhead to final cost objectives. In addition, the indirect cost allocation process also uses two "service centers" with their own indirect cost pools: Occupancy and technical computer center.

The costs accumulated in the occupancy pool are allocated among manufacturing overhead, engineering overhead, and the technical computer center on the basis of floor space occupied. The costs accumulated in the technical computer center cost pool are allocated to users on the basis of a CPU hourly rate. Some of these allocations are made to engineering or manufacturing overhead while others are allocated direct to final cost objectives.

At the business unit level, all the indirect expense incurred is regarded either as an engineering or manufacturing expense. Thus the sole item that enters into the business unit G&A expense pool is the allocation received by the A Division from the home office.

Operating results for the A Division are given in Table VII. Facilities capital items for the division are given in Table IX.

The example is based on a single set of illustrative contract cost data given in Table VIII. Since two methods, the "regular" and the "alternative" method, are potentially available for computing cost of money on facilities capital items two sets of different results can be considered.

In addition, total cost input is used in the example as the allocation base for the G&A expense. Two variations of this example have been prepared to illustrate the impact of excluding or including cost of money from total cost input. Variation I, summarized in Table XIII, excludes cost of money from the cost input allocation base. Variation II, summarized in Tables XVII and XVIII, includes cost of money in the cost input allocation base.

Throughout the example, where appropriate, cross references have been made to the text of the relevant parts of the Standard.

	Dec. 31, 1974	Dec. 31, 1975
Administrative computer center facilities capital	$550,000	$450,000
Other home office facilities capital	420,000	380,000
Total	970,000	830,000

The assets in the above table generate allowable depreciation or amortization, as explained in Instructions for Form CASB CMF (Basis). Thus, they should be included in the asset base for cost of money computation.

TABLE II.—HOME OFFICE FACILITIES CAPITAL ANNUAL AVERAGE BALANCES

Administrative computer center facilities capital	$500,000
Other home office facilities capital	400,000
Total	900,000

The above averages are based on data in Table I computed in accordance with the criteria in Instructions for Form CASB CMF (Recorded, Leased Property, Corporate).

$970,000 + $830,000 = $1,800,000 [1] 2 = $900,000

TABLE III.—HOME OFFICE DEPRECIATION AND AMORTIZATION FOR 1975

Administrative computer center facilities capital	$100,000
Other home office facilities capital	40,000
Total	140,000

	Total expense	Allocation of business units		
		A	B	C
Administrative computer center	$1,800,000	$900,000	$900,000	...
Other home office	4,800,000	2,400,000	1,200,000	$1,200,000
Total	6,600,000	3,300,000	2,100,000	1,200,000

The above allocation is carried out in accordance with CAS 403. The expense allocated to individual business units above includes depreciation and amortization as reflected in Table V.

CASB App. B 9904.414

	Total depreciation and amortization expense	Allocation of business units		
		A	B	C
Administrative computer center	$100,000	$50,000	$50,000	...
Other home office	40,000	20,000	10,000	$10,000
Total.............................	140,000	70,000	60,000	10,000

(a) Depreciation and amortization allocation in Table V converted to percentages.

	Total depreciation and amortization expense (in percent)	Allocation of business units (in percent)		
		A	B	C
Administrative computer center	100	50	50	...
Other home office	100	50	25	25

(b) Application of percentages in (a) to average net book values in Table II, in accordance with criteria in Instructions for Form CASB CMF (Recorded, Leased Property, Corporate).

	Total net book value	Allocation of business units		
		A	B	C
Administrative computer center facilities capital................................	$500,000	$250,000	$250,000	...
Other home office facilities capital	400,000	200,000	100,000	$100,000
Total	900,000	450,000	350,000	100,000

	Total cost input and other work G. & A.	Fixed price CAS-covered contracts	Cost reimbursement CAS-covered contracts	Commercial and other work
Direct material:				
Purchased parts	$2,000,000	$100,000	$100,000	$1,800,000
Subcontract items...................	21,530,000	11,750,000	7,205,000	2,575,000
Total	23,530,000	11,850,000	7,305,000	4,375,000
Direct labor and overhead:				
Engineering labor	2,000,000	1,500,000	500,000	. . .
Engineering overhead (80 pct of direct engineering labor)................	1,600,000	1,200,000	400,000	. . .
Manufacturing labor	3,000,000	1,200,000	200,000	1,600,000
Manufacturing overhead (200 pct of direct management labor)................	6,000,000	2,400,000	400,000	3,200,000
Other direct charges:				
Technical computer center direct charge 2,280 h at $250/h	570,000	200,000	370,000	. . .
Total cost input (excluding cost of money) ..	36,700,000	18,350,000	9,175,000	9,175,000
G. & A. (8.99 pct of cost input)	3,300,000	1,650,000	825,000	825,000
Total	40,000,000	20,000,000	10,000,000	10,000,000

TABLE VIII.—COST DATA FOR THE CONTRACT

Purchased parts..	$85,000
Subcontract items	990,000
Technical computer time 280 h at $250/h...	70,000
Engineering labor	330,000
Engineering overhead at 80 pct	264,000
Manufacturing labor	1,210,000
Manufacturing overhead at 200 pct	2,420,000
Total cost input (excluding cost of money).....................................	5,369,000
G. & A. at 8.99 pct	483,000
Total cost input and G.& A. (excluding cost of money)	5,852,000

TABLE IX.—DIVISION A FACILITIES CAPITAL

Average net book values are computed in accordance with Instructions to Form CASB CMF. Average figures only are given, the underlying beginning and ending balances for 1975 have not been reproduced.

Name of indirect cost pool the asset is associated with	Average net book value	Annual depreciation
Engineering overhead	$320,000	$40,000
Manufacturing overhead	4,500,000	900,000
Technical computer center	450,000	90,000
Occupancy	3,000,000	200,000
Facilities capital recorded by division A (see Form CASB CMF instructions for description of recorded)............................	8,270,000	1,230,000
Allocated from home office, table VI	450,000	. . .
Total division A...	8,720,000	. . .

CASB App. B 9904.414

TABLE X.—ALLOCATION OF UNDISTRIBUTED FACILITIES CAPITAL

(a) *Occupancy Pool Assets.* Total occupancy pool expenses are assumed to be $1,000,000 of which $200,000 is depreciation per Table IX. Allocation of the $3,000,000 net book value of assets per Table IX is performed on the basis of floor space utilization.

Indirect cost pool	Occupancy expenses and depreciation allocation	Percent of total floor space utilized	Asset allocation
Engineering	$ 200,000	20	$ 600,000
Manufacturing	750,000	75	2,250,000
Technical computer	50,000	5	150,000
Total	1,000,000	100	3,000,000

(b) *Technical Computer Center Assets.* Total technical computer center expenses for the year are assumed to be $770,000 including $90,000 depreciation per Table IX and $50,000 charge from the occupancy pool per paragraph (a) of this table. A charging rate of $250 per hour is computed assuming a total of 3,080 chargeable CPU hours per annum. The net book value of assets amounting to $600,000 ($450,000 per Table IX plus the $150,000 allocated per (a) above) is allocated on the basis of CPU hours utilized.

Overhead pool or cost objective	Hours charged	Amount charged	Percent	Asset allocation
Fixed price contracts, table VII	800	$200,000	26	$156,000
Cost reimbursement contracts, table VII	1,480	370,000	48	288,000
Engineering overhead pool	800	200,000	26	156,000
Total	3,080	770,000	100	600,000

(c) Summary of Undistributed Facilities Capital Allocation. Undistributed (per Table IX).

Technical computer center	$ 450,000
Occupancy	3,000,000
Total	3,450,000

(c) Summary of Undistributed Facilities Capital Allocation. Undistributed (per Table IX).

Overhead pool	(a)	(b)	Total
Engineering	$ 600,000	$ 156,000	$ 756,000
Manufacturing	2,250,000	. . .	2,250,000
Technical computer center (direct charge to contracts)	. . .	444,000	444,000
Total	2,850,000	600,000	3,450,000

Form CASB-CMF

TABLE XI
FACILITIES CAPITAL
COST OF MONEY FACTORS COMPUTATION
("Regular" Method—Cost of Money Excluded from Total Cost Input)

CONTRACTOR: ABC Corp.

BUSINESS UNIT: A Division

ADDRESS:

COST ACCOUNTING PERIOD: Y.E. 12/31/75

	1. APPLICABLE COST OF MONEY RATE 8%	2. ACCUMULATION & DIRECT DISTRIBUTION OF N.B.V.	3. ALLOCATION OF UNDISTRIBUTED — BASIS OF ALLOCATION	4. TOTAL NET BOOK VALUE — COLUMNS 2 + 3	5. COST OF MONEY FOR THE COST ACCOUNTING PERIOD — COLUMNS 1 × 4	6. ALLOCATION BASE FOR THE PERIOD — IN UNIT(S) OF MEASURE	7. FACILITIES CAPITAL COST OF MONEY FACTORS — COLUMNS 5/6
BUSINESS UNIT FACILITIES CAPITAL							
RECORDED	Table IX	8,270,000					
LEASED PROPERTY		450,000					
CORPORATE OR GROUP	Table VI						
TOTAL		8,720,000					
UNDISTRIBUTED		3,450,000	Worksheet / Table X			Table VII	
DISTRIBUTED		5,270,000					
OVERHEAD POOLS							
Engineering	Table IX	320,000	756,000	1,076,000	86,080	$ 2,000,000	.04304
Manufacturing	Table IX	4,500,000	2,250,000	6,750,000	540,000	$ 3,000,000	.18
Technical Computer			444,000	444,000	35,520	2,280 hr	15.57895
G & A EXPENSE POOLS							
G&A Expense	Table VI	450,000		450,000	36,000	$36,700,600	.00098
TOTAL		5,270,000	3,450,000	8,720,000	697,600	/////////////	/////////////

CASB App. B 9904.414

Form CASB-CMF

TABLE XII
FACILITIES CAPITAL
COST OF MONEY FACTORS COMPUTATION
("Alternative" Method—Cost of Money Excluded from Total Cost Input)

CONTRACTOR: ABC Corp.   ADDRESS:

BUSINESS UNIT: A Division

COST ACCOUNTING PERIOD: Y.E. 12/31/75	1. APPLICABLE COST OF MONEY RATE 8 %	2. ACCUMULATION & DIRECT DISTRIBUTION OF N.B.V.	3. ALLOCATION OF UNDISTRIBUTED — BASIS OF ALLOCATION	4. TOTAL NET BOOK VALUE — COLUMNS 2 + 3	5. COST OF MONEY FOR THE COST ACCOUNTING PERIOD — COLUMNS 1 × 4	6. ALLOCATION BASE FOR THE PERIOD — IN UNIT(S) OF MEASURE	7. FACILITIES CAPITAL COST OF MONEY FACTORS — COLUMNS 5/6
BUSINESS UNIT FACILITIES CAPITAL							
RECORDED	Table IX	8,270,000					
LEASED PROPERTY							
CORPORATE OR GROUP	Table VI	450,000					
TOTAL		8,720,000					
UNDISTRIBUTED		3,450,000	All to G&A Expense Pool				
DISTRIBUTED		5,270,000					
OVERHEAD POOLS							
Engineering	Table IX	320,000		320,000	25,600	$ 2,000,000	.0128
Manufacturing	Table IX	4,500,000		4,500,000	360,000	$ 3,000,000	.12
						Table VII	
G & A EXPENSE POOLS							
G&A Expense	Table VI	450,000	3,450,000	3,900,000	312,000	$36,700,600	.00850
TOTAL		5,270,000	3,450,000	8,720,000	697,600	////////////	////////////

TABLE XIII.—SUMMARY OF COST OF MONEY COMPUTATION ON FACILITIES CAPITAL

[Cost of money excluded from total cost input]

Allocation base	Allocated to contract, table VIII	Computation using regular facilities, capital cost of money factor, table XI	Amount	Computation using alternative facilities capital, cost of money factor, table XI	Amount
Engineering labor	$330,000	0.04304	$14,203	0.0128	$4,244
Manufacturing labor	1,210,000	.18	217,800	.12	145,200
Technical computer time	[1] 280	15.57895	4,362	....	....
Cost input	$5,369,000	.00098	5,261	.00850	45,636
Total cost of money on facilities capital	....	....	241,626	....	195,060

[1] Hours.

VARIATION II—TOTAL COST INPUT ALLOCATION BASE INCLUDES COST OF MONEY

TABLE XIV.—RECOMPUTATION OF "A" DIVISION TOTAL COST INPUT TO REFLECT INCLUSION OF COST OF MONEY

(a) Regular method:	
Total cost input per table VII	$36,700,000
Cost of money applicable to facilities capital identified with overhead pools per subtotal in column 5, table XV	661,600
Total cost input including cost of money	37,361,600
(b) Alternative method:	
Total cost input per table VII	36,700,000
Cost of money applicable to facilities capital identified with overhead pools per subtotal in column 5, table XVI	385,600
Total cost input including cost of money	37,085,900

CASB App. B 9904.414

Form CASB-CMF

TABLE XV
FACILITIES CAPITAL
COST OF MONEY FACTORS COMPUTATION
("Regular" Method—Cost of Money Included in Total Cost Input)

CONTRACTOR: ABC Corp.

BUSINESS UNIT: A Division

ADDRESS:

COST ACCOUNTING PERIOD: Y.E. 12/31/75

		1. APPLICABLE COST OF MONEY RATE 8 %	2. ACCUMULATION & DIRECT DISTRIBUTION OF N.B.V.	3. ALLOCATION OF UNDISTRIBUTED — BASIS OF ALLOCATION	4. TOTAL NET BOOK VALUE — COLUMNS 2 + 3	5. COST OF MONEY FOR THE COST ACCOUNTING PERIOD — COLUMNS 1 × 4	6. ALLOCATION BASE FOR THE PERIOD — IN UNIT(S) OF MEASURE	7. FACILITIES CAPITAL COST OF MONEY FACTORS — COLUMNS 5/6
BUSINESS UNIT FACILITIES CAPITAL	RECORDED	Table IX	8,270,000					
	LEASED PROPERTY		450,000					
	CORPORATE OR GROUP	Table VI						
	TOTAL		8,720,000					
	UNDISTRIBUTED		3,450,000	Worksheet				
	DISTRIBUTED		5,270,000	Table X				
OVERHEAD POOLS	Engineering	Table IX	320,000	756,000	1,076,000	86,080	$ 2,000,000	.04304
	Manufacturing	Table IX	4,500,000	2,250,000	6,750,000	540,000	$ 3,000,000	.18
	Technical Computer			444,000	444,000	35,520	2,280 hr	15.57895
	Subtotal: Cost of Money to be included in Total Cost Input					661,600	Table VII & Table XIV	
G & A EXPENSE POOLS	G&A Expense	Table VI	450,000		450,000	36,000	$37,361,600	.00096
TOTAL			5,270,000	3,450,000	8,720,000	697,600	/////////////	/////////////

Form CASB-CMF

TABLE XVI
FACILITIES CAPITAL
COST OF MONEY FACTORS COMPUTATION
("Alternative" Method—Cost of Money Included in Total Cost Input)

CONTRACTOR: ABC Corp. ADDRESS:

BUSINESS UNIT: A Division

COST ACCOUNTING PERIOD: Y.E. 12/31/75

		1. APPLICABLE COST OF MONEY RATE 8 %	2. ACCUMULATION & DIRECT DISTRIBUTION OF N.B.V.	3. ALLOCATION OF UNDISTRIBUTED — BASIS OF ALLOCATION	4. TOTAL NET BOOK VALUE COLUMNS 2 + 3	5. COST OF MONEY FOR THE COST ACCOUNTING PERIOD COLUMNS 1 × 4	6. ALLOCATION BASE FOR THE PERIOD IN UNIT(S) OF MEASURE	7. FACILITIES CAPITAL COST OF MONEY FACTORS COLUMNS 5/6
BUSINESS UNIT FACILITIES CAPITAL	RECORDED	Table IX	8,270,000					
	LEASED PROPERTY							
	CORPORATE OR GROUP	Table VI	450,000	All to G&A Expense Pool			Table VII & Table XIV	
	TOTAL		8,720,000					
	UNDISTRIBUTED		3,450,000					
	DISTRIBUTED		5,270,000					
OVERHEAD POOLS	Engineering	Table IX	320,000	Expense Pool	320,000	25,600	$ 2,000,000	.0128
	Manufacturing	Table IX	4,500,000		4,500,000	360,000	$ 3,000,000	.12
	Subtotal: Cost of Money to be included in Total Cost Input					385,600		
G & A EXPENSE POOLS	G&A Expense	Table VI	450,000	3,450,000	3,900,000	312,000	$37,085,600	.00841
TOTAL			5,270,000	3,450,000	8,720,000	697,600	/////////////	/////////////

TABLE XVII.—SUMMARY OF COST OF MONEY COMPUTATION ON FACILITIES CAPITAL

[Cost of money included in total cost input—regular method]

Allocation base	Allocated to contract, table VIII	Computation using regular facilities, capital cost of money factor, table XV	Amount
Engineering labor	$ 330,000	0.04304	$ 14,203
Manufacturing labor	1,210,000	.18	217,800
Technical computer time	[1] 280	15.57895	4,362
Cost of money related to overheads	....	....	236,365
Cost of money above to be included in cost input	236,365	....	....
Cost input, table VIII	5,369,000	....	....
Cost input including cost of money	5,605,365	.00096	5,381
Total cost of money on facilities capital	....	....	241,674

[1] Hours.

TABLE XVIII.—SUMMARY OF COST OF MONEY COMPUTATION ON FACILITIES CAPITAL

[Cost of money included in total cost input—alternative method]

Allocation base	Allocated to contract, table VIII	Computation using alternative facilities, capital cost of money factor, table XVI	Amount
Engineering labor	$ 330,000	0.0128	$ 4,224
Manufacturing labor	1,210,000	.12	145,200
Cost of money related to overheads	....	....	149,424
Cost of money above to be included in cost input	149,424	....	....
Cost input, table VIII	5,369,000	....	....
Cost input including cost of money	5,518,424	.00841	46,410
Total cost of money on facilities capital	5,518,424	....	195,834

[Corrected, 57 FR 34081 and 57 FR 34167, 8/3/92]

9904.415 Accounting for the cost of deferred compensation. (No Text)

9904.415-10 [Reserved]

9904.415-20 Purpose.

(a) The purpose of this Standard 9904.415 is to provide criteria for the measurement of the cost of deferred compensation and the assignment of such cost to cost accounting periods. The application of these criteria should increase the probability that the cost of deferred compensation is allocated to cost objectives in a uniform and consistent manner.

(b) This Standard is applicable to the cost of all deferred compensation except the following which are covered in other Cost Accounting Standards:

(1) The cost for compensated personal absence, and

(2) The cost for pension plans that do not meet the definition of an Employee Stock Ownership Plan (ESOP).

[Final rule, 73 FR 23961, 5/1/2008, effective 6/2/2008]

9904.415-30 Definitions.

(a) The following are definitions of terms which are prominent in this Standard 9904.415. Other terms defined elsewhere in this Chapter 99 shall have the meanings ascribed to them in those definitions unless paragraph (b) of this section requires otherwise.

(1) *Deferred compensation* means an award made by an employer to compensate an employee in a future cost accounting period or periods for services rendered in one or more cost accounting periods prior to the date of the receipt of compensation by the employee. This definition shall not include the amount of year end accruals for salaries, wages, or bonuses that are to be paid within a reasonable period of time after the end of a cost accounting period.

(2) *Employee Stock Ownership Plan (ESOP)* means:

(i) An employee benefit plan that is described by the Employee Retirement Income Security Act of 1974 (ERISA) and the Internal Revenue Code (IRC) of 1986 as a stock bonus plan, or combination stock bonus and money purchase pension plan, designed to invest primarily in employer stock, and

(ii) Any other deferred compensation plan designed to invest primarily in the stock of the contractor's corporation including, but not limited to, plans covered by ERISA.

(3) Fair value means the amount that a seller would reasonably expect to receive in a current arm's length transaction between a willing buyer and a willing seller, other than a forced or liquidation sale.

(b) The following modifications of terms defined elsewhere in this Chapter 99 are applicable to this Standard:

(1) *Market value* means the current or prevailing price of a stock or other property as indicated by market quotations.

(2) [Reserved]

[Final rule, 73 FR 23961, 5/1/2008, effective 6/2/2008]

9904.415-40 Fundamental requirement.

(a) The cost of deferred compensation shall be assigned to the cost accounting period in which the contractor incurs an obligation to compensate the employee. In the event no obligation is incurred prior to payment, the cost of deferred compensation shall be the amount paid and shall be assigned to the cost accounting period in which the payment is made.

(b) Measurement of deferred compensation costs.

(1) For deferred compensation other than ESOPs, the deferred compensation cost shall be the present value of the future benefits to be paid by the contractor.

(2) For an ESOP, the deferred compensation cost shall be the amount contributed to the ESOP by the contractor.

(c) The cost of each award of deferred compensation shall be considered separately for purposes of measurement and assignment of such costs to cost accounting periods. However, if the cost of deferred compensation for the employees covered by a deferred compensation plan can be measured and assigned with reasonable accuracy on a group basis, separate computations for each employee are not required.

[Final rule, 73 FR 23961, 5/1/2008, effective 6/2/2008]

9904.415-50 Techniques for application.

(a) The contractor shall be deemed to have incurred an obligation for the cost of deferred compensation when all of the following conditions have been met. However, for awards which require that the employee perform future service in order to receive the benefits, the obligation is deemed to have been incurred as the future service is performed for that part of the award attributable to such future service:

(1) There is a requirement to make the future payment(s) which the contractor cannot unilaterally avoid.

(2) The deferred compensation award is to be satisfied by a future payment of money, other assets, or shares of stock of the contractor.

(3) The amount of the future payment can be measured with reasonable accuracy.

(4) The recipient of the award is known.

(5) If the terms of the award require that certain events must occur before an employee is entitled to receive the benefits, there is a reasonable probability that such events will occur.

(6) For stock options, there must be a reasonable probability that the options ultimately will be exercised.

(b) If any of the conditions in 9904.415-50(a) is not met, the cost of deferred compensation shall be assignable only to the cost accounting period or periods in which the compensation is paid to the employee.

(c) If the cost of deferred compensation can be estimated with reasonable accuracy on a group basis, including consideration of probable forfeitures, such estimate may be used as the basis for measuring and assigning the present value of future benefits.

(d) The following provisions are applicable for plans, other than ESOPs, that meet the conditions of 9904.415-50(a) and the compensation is to be paid in money.

(1) If the deferred compensation award provides that the amount to be paid shall include the principal of the award plus interest at a rate fixed at the date of award, such interest shall be included in the computation of the amount of the future benefit. If no interest is included in the award, the amount of the future benefit is the amount of the award.

(2) If the deferred compensation award provides for payment of principal plus interest at a rate not fixed at the time of award but based on a specified index which is determinable in each applicable cost accounting period; e.g., a published corporate bond rate, such interest shall be included in the computation of the amount of future benefit. The interest rate to be used shall be the rate in effect at the close of the period in which the cost of deferred compensation is assignable. Since that interest rate is likely to vary from the actual rates in future periods, adjustments shall be made in any such future period in which the variation in rates materially affects the cost of deferred compensation.

(3) If the deferred compensation award provides for payment of principal plus interest at a rate not based on a specified index, or not determinable in each applicable year, the—

(i) Cost of deferred compensation for the principal of the award shall be measured by the present value of the future benefits of the principal, and shall be assigned to the cost accounting period in which the employer incurs an obligation to compensate the employee; and

(ii) Interest on such awards shall be assigned to the cost accounting period(s) in which the payment of the deferred compensation is made.

(4) If the terms of the award require that the employee perform future service in order to receive benefits, the cost of the deferred compensation shall be appropriately assigned to the periods of current and future service based on the facts and circumstances of the award. The cost of deferred compen-

CASB 9904.415-50

sation for each cost accounting period shall be the present value of the future benefits of the deferred compensation calculated as of the end of each such period to which such cost is assigned.

(5) In computing the present value of the future benefits, the discount rate shall be equal to the interest rate as determined by the Secretary of the Treasury pursuant to Public Law 92-41, 85 stat. 97 at the time the cost is assignable.

(6) If the award is made under a plan which requires irrevocable funding for payment to the employee in a future cost accounting period together with all interest earned thereon, the amount assignable to the period of award shall be the amount irrevocably funded.

(7) In computing the assignable cost for a cost accounting period, any forfeitures which reduce the employer's obligation for payment of deferred compensation shall be a reduction of contract costs in the period in which the forfeiture occurred. The amount of the reduction for a forfeiture shall be the amount of the award that was assigned to a prior period, plus interest compounded annually, using the same Treasury rate that was used as the discount rate at the time the cost was assigned. For irrevocably funded plans, pursuant to 9904.415-50(d)(6), the amount of the reduction for a forfeiture shall be the amount initially funded plus or minus a pro-rata share of the gains and losses of the fund.

(8) If the cost of deferred compensation for group plans measured in accordance with 9904.415-50(c) is determined to be greater than the amounts initially assigned because the forfeiture was overestimated, the additional cost shall be assignable to the cost accounting period in which such cost is ascertainable.

(e) The following provisions are applicable for plans, other than ESOPs, that meet the conditions of 9904.415-50(a) and the compensation is received by the employee in other than money. The measurements set forth in this paragraph constitute the present value of future benefits for awards made in other than money and, therefore, shall be deemed to be a reasonable measure of the amount of the future payment:

(1) If the award is made in the stock of the contractor, the cost of deferred compensation for such awards shall be based on the market value of the stock on the measurement date; i.e., the first date the number of shares awarded is known. Market value is the current or prevailing price of the security as indicated by market quotations. If such values are unavailable or not appropriate (thin market, volatile price movements, etc.) an acceptable alternative is the fair value of the stock.

(2) If an award is made in the form of options to employees to purchase stock of the contractor, the cost of deferred compensation of such award shall be the amount by which the market value of the stock exceeds the option price multiplied by the number of shares awarded on the measurement date; i.e., the first date on which both the option price and the number of shares is known. If the option price on the measurement date is equal to or greater than the market value of the stock, no cost shall be deemed to have been incurred for contract costing purposes.

(3) If the terms of an award of stock or stock option require that the employee perform future service in order to receive the stock or to exercise the option, the cost of the deferred compensation shall be appropriately assigned to the periods of current and future service based on the facts and circumstances of the award. The cost to be assigned shall be the value of the stock or stock option at the measurement date as prescribed in 9904.415-50(e)(1) or (e)(2).

(4) If an award is made in the form of an asset other than cash, the cost of deferred compensation for such award shall be based on the market value of the asset at the time the award is made. If a market value is not available, the fair value of the asset shall be used.

(5) If the terms of an award, made in the form of an asset other than cash, require that the employee perform future service in order to receive the asset, the cost of the deferred compensation shall be appropriately assigned to the periods of current and future service based on the facts and circum-

CASB 9904.415-50

stances of the award. The cost to be assigned shall be the value of the asset at the time of award as prescribed in 9904.415-50(e)(4).

(6) In computing the assignable cost for a cost accounting period, any forfeitures which reduce the employer's obligation for payment of deferred compensation shall be a reduction of contract costs in the period in which the forfeiture occurred. The amount of the reduction shall be equal to the amount of the award that was assigned to a prior period, plus interest compounded annually, using the Treasury rate (see 9904.415-50(d)(5)) that was in effect at the time the cost was assigned. If the recipient of the award of stock options voluntarily fails to exercise such options, such failure shall not constitute a forfeiture under provisions of this Standard.

(7) Stock option awards or any other form of stock purchase plans containing all of the following characteristics shall be considered noncompensatory and not covered by this Standard:

(i) Substantially all full-time employees meeting limited employment qualifications may participate.

(ii) Stock is offered equally to eligible employees or based on a uniform percentage of salary or wages.

(iii) An option or a purchase right must be exercisable within a reasonable period.

(iv) The discount from the market price of the stock is no greater than would be reasonable in an offer of stock to stockholders or others.

(f)(1) For an ESOP, the contractor's cost shall be measured by the contractor's contribution, including interest and dividends if applicable, to the ESOP. The measurement of contributions made in the form of stock of the corporation or property, shall be based on the market value of the stock or property at the time the contributions are made. If the market value is not available, then fair value of the stock or property shall be used.

(2) A contractor's contribution to an ESOP shall be assignable to a cost accounting period only to the extent that the stock, cash, or any combination thereof resulting from

the contribution is awarded to employees and allocated to individual employee accounts by the tax filing date for that period, including any permissible extensions thereof. All stock or cash that is allocated to the individual employee accounts between the end of the cost accounting period and the tax filing date for that period must be assigned to the cost accounting period in which the employee is awarded the stock or cash. Any portion of the stock or cash resulting from a contractor's contribution that is not awarded to employees or allocated to individual employee accounts by the tax filing date for that period, including any permissible extensions thereof, shall be assigned to a future cost accounting period or periods when the remaining portion of stock or cash has been awarded to employees and allocated to individual employee accounts. This stock shall retain the value established when it was originally purchased by or otherwise made available to the ESOP.

[Final rule, 73 FR 23961, 5/1/2008, effective 6/2/2008]

9904.415-60 Illustrations.

(a) Contractor A has a deferred compensation plan in which all cash awards are increased each year by an interest factor equivalent to the long-term borrowing rate of the contractor prevailing during each such year. The interest factor based on a variable long-term borrowing rate meets the criteria of 9904.415-50(d)(2). Consequently, the cost of deferred compensation for Contractor A shall be measured by the present value of the future benefits and shall be assigned to the cost accounting period in which the contractor initially incurs an obligation to compensate the employee. If the long-term borrowing rate for Contractor A was 9 percent at the close of the period to which the cost of deferred compensation was assignable, then that rate should be used to calculate the future benefit. Any adjustment in the cost of deferred compensation which results from a material change in the 9 percent rate in future applicable periods shall be made in each such future period or periods (see 9904.415-50(d)(2)).

(b) Contractor B made a deferred compensation award of $10,000 to an employee on December 31, 1976, for services performed in 1976 to be paid in equal annual payments of $2,000 starting at December 31, 1981. The terms of the award do not provide for an interest factor to be included in the payment; consequently, according to provisions of 9904.415-50(d)(1), interest may not be included in the computation of the future benefits. The assignable cost for 1976 is computed as follows, assuming that the interest rate determined by the Secretary of the Treasury (pursuant to Public Law 92-41, 85 Stat. 97) at the time of the award is 8 percent and the conditions set forth in 9904.415-50(a) are met.

Year	Amount of future payment × discount rate 8-percent present value factor = present value
1981	$2,000 × 0.6805 = $1,361
1982	2,000 × .6301 = 1,260
1983	2,000 × .5834 = 1,167
1984	2,000 × .5402 = 1,080
1985	2,000 × .5002 = 1,000
Assignable cost for 1976.	5,868

(c) Contractor C awarded stock options for 1,000 shares of the contractor to key employees on December 31, 1976, under a deferred compensation plan requiring 2 years of additional service before the awards can be exercised. The facts and circumstances of the awards indicate that the deferred compensation applies only to the periods of future service. The market price of the stock was $26 per share, the option price was $22, and the interest rate established by the Secretary of the Treasury in effect at the time of award was 8 percent.

(1) In accordance with 9904.415-50(e)(2), the cost of the stock options is the amount by which the current value of the stock exceeds the option price multiplied by the number of shares awarded on the measurement date. Thus, the total cost of the stock options is 1,000 shares multiplied by the difference of the option price and the market price ($26-22) or $4,000.

(2) Under provisions of 9904.415-50(e)(3), the cost for stock options is assigned to each future cost accounting period in which employee service is required and is computed as follows:

Year of required service:

	Assignable Cost[1]
1977	$2,000
1978	2,000

Year of required service:

	Assignable Cost[1]
Total amount of award	4,000

[1] Note that this illustration assumes that the facts and circumstances of the award indicate that the award relates equally to each period of future service. Thus, the assignable cost was allocated on a pro-rata basis.

(d)(1) Contractor D has a deferred compensation plan that specifies that an employee receiving a cash award must remain with the company for 3 calendar years after the award in order to qualify and receive the award and the facts and circumstances indicate that the deferred compensation applies only to the periods of future service. In accordance with 9904.415-50(d)(4), the cost of deferred compensation is assignable to the periods of future service. Thus, the amount of cost of deferred compensation to be assigned by Contractor D for each of the 3 years shall be the present value of the future benefits of the deferred compensation award calculated as of the end of each such period to which such cost is assigned.

(2) Under this plan, Contractor D made an award to an employee of $3,000 to be paid at the end of the third year. The assignable

CASB 9904.415-60

cost for each of the 3 years is computed as follows:

Year[1]	Amount of future payment	Present value factor[2] treasury rate[3]		Assignable cost for each year
1	$1,000	0.8573 (8 pct for 2 yr)	=	$ 857.30
2	1,000	0.9302 (7.5 pct for 1 yr)	=	930.20
3	1,000	1.000 (8 pct for 0 yr)	=	1,000.00

[1] Note that in accordance with the facts and circumstances of the award no deferred compensation is assignable to the period in which the award is made and that the award relates equally to each period of future service.

[2] Note that since the costs are measured at the end of each year of required service, the present value factors are based on the number of years from the year of assignment to the date of payment.

[3] Note that the prevailing Treasury rate changed from year 1 to year 2.

(e)(1) Contractor E has a deferred compensation plan that specifies that an employee receiving a cash award must remain with the company for 2 calendar years after the award in order to qualify and receive the award. Contractor E made an award of $6,000 at the end of 1976 to an employee to be paid at the end of 1978. However, the employee voluntarily terminated his employment before the end of 1977. The facts and circumstances of the award indicate that $2,000 of the award represents compensation for services rendered in the period of award (1976). The remaining portion of the award represents compensation for services to be rendered in future periods. The assignable cost for 1976, which was the only period to which costs were assigned before termination, was the present value of $2,000, the amount of the award attributable to the services of that period. Thus, the cost assigned for 1976 was:

Amount of future payment × Discount rate present value factor for 2 yr at 8 pct = Assignable cost

$2,000 × 0.8573 = $1,714.60

(2) According to provisions of 9904.415-50(d)(7), the amount of the forfeiture shall be the amount of the cost that was assigned to a prior period, plus interest compounded annually, from the year the cost was assigned to the year of forfeiture, using the same Treasury rate (see 9904.415-50(d)(5)) that was used as the discount rate at the time the cost was assigned. The IRS rate in effect at the date of award was 8 percent.

(3) The amount of the forfeiture is computed as follows:

Assignable cost × Discount rate future value for 1 yr at 8 pct = Forfeiture

$1,714.60 × 1.08 = $1,851.77

(f) Contractor F has a non-leveraged ESOP. Under the contractor's plan, employees are awarded 5,000 shares of stock for the year ended December 31, 2007. On February 5, 2008, when the shares have a market value of $10.00 each, the 5,000 shares are contributed to the ESOP and allocated to the individual employee accounts. The total measured and assigned deferred compensation cost for FY 2007 is $50,000 (5,000 $10 = $50,000). The market value of the contractor's stock when awarded to the employees, whether higher or lower than the $10.00 per share market value when the contractor's contribution was made to the ESOP, is irrelevant to the measurement of the contractor's ESOP costs.

CASB 9904.415-60

(g) Contractor G has a leveraged ESOP. Under the contractor's plan, employees are awarded 10,000 shares of stock for the year ended December 31, 2007. On February 15, 2008, the contractor contributes $780,000 in cash to the ESOP trust (ESOT) to satisfy the principal and interest payment on the ESOT loan for FY 2007, resulting in the bank releasing 9,000 shares of stock, and 1,000 shares of stock valued at $60,000 to the ESOT, representing the balance of the 10,000 shares. On February 22, 2008, the ESOP allocates 10,000 shares to the individual employee accounts. The total measured and assigned deferred compensation cost for FY 2007 is $840,000—the contractor's total contribution required to satisfy the deferred compensation obligation totaling 10,000 shares.

(h) (1) Contractor H has a leveraged ESOP. Under the contractor's plan, employees are awarded 8,000 shares of stock for the year ended December 31, 2007. On January 31, 2008, the contractor contributes $500,000 in cash to the ESOT to satisfy the principal and interest payment on the ESOT loan for 2007, resulting in the bank releasing 10,000 shares of stock. On February 10, 2008, 8,000 shares are allocated to individual employee accounts, satisfying the deferred compensation obligation for 2007. The total measured deferred compensation cost for 2007 is $500,000—the contractor's contribution for the cost accounting period. However, the total assignable deferred compensation cost for 2007 is $400,000—the portion of the contribution that satisfies the 2007 deferred compensation obligation of 8,000 shares [(8,000 shares / 10,000 shares) × $500,000 = $400,000]. The remaining $100,000 of the contribution made in 2007 is assignable to future periods in which the remaining 2,000 shares of stock are awarded to employees and allocated to individual employee accounts.

(2) At December 31, 2008, the employees are awarded 12,000 shares of stock. On January 31, 2009, Contractor H contributes $500,000 in cash to the ESOT to satisfy the principal and interest payment on the ESOT loan for 2008, resulting in the bank releasing 10,000 shares of stock. On February 10,

2009, 12,000 shares are allocated to individual employee accounts satisfying the deferred compensation obligation for 2008. The total deferred compensation assignable to 2008 is $600,000, the cost of the 12,000 shares awarded to employees and allocated to individual employee accounts for 2008. The cost of the award is comprised of the contractor's contribution for the current cost accounting period (10,000 shares at $500,000) and the 2007 contribution carryover (2,000 shares at $100,000).

(i) Contractor I has a leveraged ESOP. Under the contractor's plan, employees are awarded 10,000 shares for FY 2007, which ended December 31, 2007. On February 10, 2008, Contractor I contributes $700,000 in cash to satisfy the principal and interest payment for the ESOP loan for FY 2007. This contribution results in the bank releasing 10,000 shares of stock. On March 1, 2008, the ESOP allocates the 10,000 shares to individual employee accounts satisfying the 2007 obligation. The 10,000 shares of stock must be assigned to FY 2007 (these shares cannot be assigned to 2008).

[Final rule, 73 FR 23961, 5/1/2008, effective 6/2/2008]

9904.415-61 [Reserved]

9904.415-62 Exemption.

None for this Standard.

9904.415-63 Effective date.

(a) This Standard 9904.415 is effective as of June 2, 2008.

(b) This Standard shall be followed by each contractor on or after the start of its next cost accounting period beginning after the receipt of a contract or subcontract to which this Standard is applicable.

(c) Contractors with prior CAS-covered contracts with full coverage shall continue to follow Standard 9904.415 in effect prior to June 2, 2008 until this Standard, effective June 2, 2008, becomes applicable following receipt of a contract or subcontract to which this revised Standard applies.

(d) For contractors and subcontractors that have established advance agreements prior to June 2, 2008 regarding the recognition of the costs of existing ESOPs, the awarding agency and contractor shall comply with the provisions of such advance agreement(s) for these existing ESOPs, regardless of whether the ESOP was previously subject to CAS 412 or 415. These advance agreements may be modified, by mutual agreement, to incorporate the requirements effective on June 2, 2008.

[Final rule, 73 FR 23961, 5/1/2008, effective 6/2/2008]

9904.416 Accounting for insurance costs. (No Text)

9904.416-10 [Reserved].

9904.416-20 Purpose.

The purpose of this standard is to provide criteria for the measurement of insurance costs, the assignment of such costs to cost accounting periods, and their allocation to cost objectives. The application of these criteria should increase the probability that insurance costs are allocated to cost objectives in a uniform and consistent manner.

9904.416-30 Definitions.

(a) The following are definitions of terms which are prominent in this Standard. Other terms defined elsewhere in this Part 99 shall have the meanings ascribed to them in those definitions unless paragraph (b) of this subsection, requires otherwise.

(1) *Actual cash value* means the cost of replacing damaged property with other property of like kind and quality in the physical condition of the property immediately prior to the damage.

(2) *Insurance administration expenses* means the contractor's costs of administering an insurance program, e.g., the costs of operating an insurance or risk-management department, processing claims, actuarial fees, and service fee paid to insurance companies, trustees, or technical consultants.

(3) *Projected average loss* means the estimated long-term average loss per period for periods of comparable exposure to risk of loss.

(4) *Self-insurance* means the assumption or retention of the risk or loss by the con-

tractor, whether voluntarily or involuntarily. Self-insurance includes the deductible portion of purchased insurance.

(5) *Self-insurance charge* means a cost which represents the projected average loss under a self-insurance plan.

(b) The following modifications of terms defined elsewhere in this Chapter 99 are applicable to this Standard: None.

9904.416-40 Fundamental requirement.

(a) The amount of insurance cost to be assigned to a cost accounting period is the projected average loss for that period plus insurance administration expenses in that period.

(b) The allocation of insurance costs to cost objectives shall be based on the beneficial or causal relationship between the insurance costs and the benefiting or causing cost objectives.

9904.416-50 Techniques for application.

(a) Measurement of projected average loss.

(1) For exposure to risk of loss which is covered by the purchase of insurance or by payments to a trusteed fund, the premium or payment, adjusted in accordance with the following criteria, shall represent the projected average loss:

(i) The premium cost applicable to a given policy term shall be assigned pro rata among the cost accounting periods covered by the policy term, except as provided in subdivisions (a)(1)(ii) through (vi) of this subsection. A refund, dividend or additional assessment shall become an adjustment to the pro rata premium costs for the earliest cost accounting period in which the refund or dividend is actually or constructively received or in which the additional assessment is payable.

(ii) Where insurance is purchased specifically for, and directly allocated to, a single final cost objective, the premium need not be prorated among cost accounting periods.

(iii) Any part of a premium or payment to an insurer or trustee, or any part of a dividend or premium refund retained by an insurer or trustee which would be includable as a deposit in published financial statements prepared in accordance with generally accepted accounting principles shall be accounted for as a deposit for the purpose of determining insurance costs.

(iv) Any part of a premium or payment to an insurer or to a trustee, or any part of a dividend or premium refund retained by an insurer, for inclusion in a reserve or fund established and maintained on behalf of the insured or the policyholder or trustor, shall be accounted for as a deposit unless the following conditions are met:

(A) The objectives of the reserve or fund are clearly stated in writing.

(B) Measurement of the amount required for the reserve or fund is actuarially determined and is consistent with the objectives of the reserve or fund.

(C) Payments and additions to the reserve or fund are made in a systematic and consistent manner.

(D) If payments to accomplish the stated objectives of the reserve or fund are made from a source other than the reserve or fund, the payments into the reserve or fund are reduced accordingly.

(v) If an objective of an insurance program is to prefund insurance coverage on retired persons, then, in addition to the requirements imposed by subdivision (a)(1)(iv) of this subsection, the:

(A) Payments must be made to an insurer or trustee to establish and maintain a fund or reserve for that purpose;

(B) Policyholder or trustor must have no right of recapture of the reserve or fund so long as any active or retired participant in the program remains alive, unless the interests of such remaining participants are satisfied through adequate reinsurance or otherwise; and

(C) Amount added to the reserve or fund in any cost accounting period must not be greater than an amount which would be required to apportion the cost of the insurance coverage fairly over the working lives of the active employees in the plan. If a contractor

establishes a terminal-funded plan for retired persons or converts from a pay-as-you-go plan to a terminal-funded plan, the actuarial present value of benefits applicable to employees already retired shall be amortized over a period of 15 years.

(vi) The contractor may adopt and consistently follow a practice of determining insurance costs based on the estimated premium and assessments net of estimated refunds and dividends. If this practice is adopted, then any difference between an estimated and actual refund, dividend, or assessment shall become an adjustment to the pro rata net premium costs for the earliest cost accounting period in which the refund or dividend is actually or constructively received or in which the additional assessment is payable.

(2) For exposure to risk of loss which is not covered by the purchase of insurance or by payments to a trusteed fund, the contractor shall follow a program of self-insurance accounting according to the following criteria:

(i) Except as provided in subdivisions (a)(2)(ii) and (iii) of this subsection, actual losses shall not become a part of insurance costs. Instead, the contractor shall make a self-insurance charge for each period for each type of self-insured risk which shall represent the projected average loss for that period. If insurance could be purchased against the self-insured risk, the cost of such insurance may be used as an estimate of the projected average loss; if this method is used, the self-insurance charge plus insurance administration expenses may be equal to, but shall not exceed, the cost of comparable purchased insurance plus the associated insurance administration expenses. However, the contractor's actual loss experience shall be evaluated regularly, and self-insurance charges for subsequent periods shall reflect such experience in the same manner as would purchased insurance. If insurance could not be purchased against the self-insured risk, the amount of the self-insurance charge for each period shall be based on the contractor's experience, relevant industry experience, and anticipated conditions in accordance with accepted actuarial principles.

(ii) Where it is probable that the actual amount of losses which will occur in a cost accounting period will not differ significantly from the projected average loss for that period, the actual amount of losses in that period may be considered to represent the projected average loss for that period in lieu of a self-insurance charge.

(iii) Under self-insurance programs for retired persons, only actual losses shall be considered to represent the projected average loss unless a reserve or fund is established in accordance with 9904.416-50(a)(1)(v).

(iv) The self-insurance charge shall be determined in a manner which will give appropriate recognition to any indemnification agreement which exists between the contracting parties.

(3) In measuring actual losses under subparagraph (a)(2) of this subsection:

(i) The amount of a loss shall be measured by:

(A) the actual cash value of property destroyed,

(B) amounts paid or accrued to repair damage,

(C) amounts paid or accrued to estates and beneficiaries, and

(D) amounts paid or accrued to compensate claimants, including subrogation.

Where the amount of a loss which is represented by a liability to a third party is uncertain, the estimate of the loss shall be the amount which would be includable as an accrued liability in financial statements prepared in accordance with generally accepted accounting principles.

(ii) If a loss has been incurred and the amount of the liability to a claimant is fixed or reasonably certain, but actual payment of the liability will not take place for more than 1 year after the loss is incurred, the amount of the loss to be recognized currently shall be the present value of the future payments, determined by using a discount rate equal to the interest rate as determined by the Secretary of the Treasury pursuant to Public Law 92-41, 85 stat. 97 in effect at the time the loss is recognized. Alternatively, where settle-

ment will consist of a series of payments over an indefinite time period, as in workmen's compensation, the contractor may follow a consistent policy of recognizing only the actual amounts paid in the period of payment.

(4) The contractor may elect to recognize immaterial amounts of self-insured losses or insurance administration expenses as part of other expense categories rather than as "insurance costs."

(b) Allocation of insurance costs. (1) Where actual losses are recognized as an estimate of the projected average loss, in accordance with 9904.416-50(a)(2), or where actual loss experience is determined for the purpose of developing self-insurance charges by segment, a loss which is incurred in a given segment shall be identified with that segment. However, if the contractor's home office is, in effect, a reinsurer of its segments against catastrophic losses, a portion of such catastrophic losses shall be allocated to, or identified with, the home office.

(2) Insurance costs shall be allocated on the basis of the factors used to determine the premium, assessment, refund, dividend, or self-insurance charge, except that insurance costs incurred by a segment or allocated to a segment from a home office may be combined with costs of other indirect cost pools if the resultant allocation to each final cost objective is substantially the same as it would have been if separately allocated under this provision.

(3) Insurance administration expenses which are material in relation to total insurance costs shall be allocated on the same basis as the related premium costs or self-insurance charge.

(c) Records. The contractor shall maintain such records as may be necessary to substantiate the amounts of premiums, refunds, dividends, losses, and self-insurance charges, paid or accrued, and the measurement and allocation of insurance costs. Memorandum records may be used to reflect any material differences between insurance costs as determined in accordance with this standard and as includable in financial

CASB 9904.416-50

statements prepared in accordance with generally accepted accounting principles.

[Corrected, 57 FR 34168, 8/3/92; Corrected, 57 FR 43776, 9/22/92]

9904.416-60 Illustrations.

(a) Contractor A pays a company-wide property and casualty insurance premium for the policy term July 1, 1980, to July 1, 1983, and includes the entire amount as cost in its cost accounting period which ended December 31, 1980. This is a violation of 9904.416-50(a)(1)(i) in that only one-sixth of the policy term fell within the cost accounting period which ended December 31, 1980, and therefore only one-sixth of the premium should have been included in cost in that cost accounting period.

(b) Contractor B has a retrospectively rated worker's compensation insurance program. The policy term corresponds with the contractor's cost accounting period. Premium refunds are normally received and applied in the following cost accounting period. The contractor's practice is to include the entire gross premium in insurance cost in the cost accounting period in which it is paid and to credit the refund against insurance cost in the cost accounting period in which it is received. This practice conforms with 9904.416-50(a)(1)(i). The contractor could also, under the provisions of 9904.416-50(a)(1)(vi), have followed a consistent practice of estimating such refunds in advance and including the estimated net premium in insurance cost.

(c) Contractor C establishes a self-insured program of life insurance for active and retired persons. The contractor pays death benefits directly to the beneficiaries of deceased employees and includes such payments in insurance costs at the time of payment. This practice complies with 9904.416-50(a)(2)(iii) which requires that only the actual losses be recognized unless a trusteed reserve or fund is established in accordance with 9904.416-50(a)(1)(v).

(d) Instead of paying death benefits directly, contractor D purchases annual group term life insurance on active and retired persons and charges the premiums to insurance costs (with proper recognition for refunds and dividends). Contractor D's retired persons wish to be protected against possible discontinuance of the program. Contractor D, therefore, establishes a trusteed fund. As each employee retires, contractor D deposits in the fund an amount which is equal to the premium on a paid-up policy for that employee, and he advises the trustee that the fund is to be used to continue to pay premiums on retired persons in the event the program is discontinued. The contractor also continues to purchase group term insurance on both active employees and retired persons and charges both the premiums and the deposits to insurance costs. This practice does not comply with 9904.416-50(a)(1)(iv)(D) which requires that if payments to accomplish the stated objectives of the reserve or funds are made from a source other than the reserve or fund, the payments into the fund shall be reduced accordingly.

Note: In this instance the contractor could comply with the standard by paying from the fund that portion of the group term premium which represented the retired persons or by reducing the deposits to the fund by an equivalent amount in accordance with 9904.416-50(a)(1)(iv)(D). This practice would also comply with the requirement of 9904.416-50(a)(1)(v)(C) that the amount added to the fund not be greater than an amount which would be required to fairly allocate the cost over the working lives of the active employees in the plan.

(e) Contractor E wishes to provide assurance of his life insurance program continuance to both active and retired employees. He establishes a trusteed fund in accordance with 9904.416-50(a)(1)(iv) and (v) and thereafter pays into the fund each year for each active employee an actuarially determined amount which will accumulate to the equivalent of the premium on a paid-up life insurance policy at retirement. He charges the annual payments to insurance costs. Benefits are paid directly from the fund (or the fund is used to pay the annual premiums on group term life insurance for all employees). This practice also complies with the requirement of 9904.416-50(a)(1)(v)(C) that the amount added to the fund not be greater than an amount which would be required to fairly allocate the cost over the working lives of the active employees in the plan.

(f) Contractor F has a fire insurance policy which provides that the first $50,000 of any fire loss will be borne by the contractor. Because the risk of loss is dispersed among many physical units of property and the average potential loss per unit is relatively low, the actual losses in any period may be expected not to differ significantly from the projected average loss. Therefore, the contractor intends to let the actual losses represent the projected average loss for this exposure to risk. Property with an actual cash value of $80,000 is destroyed in a fire. The contractor charges the $50,000 of the loss not covered by the policy to insurance costs for contract costing purposes. The practice complies with the requirement of 9904.416-50(a)(2). However, had the contractor's plan been to make a self-insurance charge for such losses, then any difference between the self-insurance charge and actual losses in that cost accounting period would not have been allocable as an insurance cost.

(g) Contractor G is preparing to enter into a Government contract to produce explosive devices. The contractor is unable to purchase adequate insurance protection and must act as a self-insurer. There is a significant possibility of a major loss, against which the Government will not undertake to indemnify the contractor. The contractor, therefore, intends to make a self-insurance charge for this exposure to risk. The contractor may, in accordance with 9904.416-50(a)(2)(i), use data obtained from other contractors or any other reasonable method of estimating the projected average loss in order to determine the self-insurance charge.

(h) Contractor H purchases liability insurance for all of its motor vehicles in a single, company-wide policy which contains a $50,000 deductible provision. However, the company's management policy provides that when a loss is incurred in a segment, only the first $5,000 of the loss will be charged to the segment; the balance of the loss will be absorbed at the home-office level and reallocated among all segments. Because the risk

of loss is dispersed among many physical units and the maximum potential loss per occurrence is limited, the actual losses in any cost accounting period may be expected not to differ significantly from the projected average loss. Therefore, the contractor intends to let the actual losses represent the projected average loss for this exposure to risk. An analysis of the loss experience shows that many past losses exceeded $5,000. Contractor H's practice of allocating the loss in excess of $5,000 to the home office is a violation of 9904.416-50(b)(1). The limit of $5,000 cannot realistically be considered a measure of a "catastrophic" loss when losses frequently exceed this amount, and the use of a limit this low would obscure segment loss experience.

9904.416-61 [Reserved]

9904.416-62 Exemption.

None for this Standard.

9904.416-63 Effective date.

This Standard is effective as of April 17, 1992. Contractors with prior CAS-covered contracts with full coverage shall continue this Standard's applicability upon receipt of a contract to which this Standard is applicable. For contractors with no previous contracts subject to this Standard, this Standard shall be applied beginning with the contractor's next full fiscal year beginning after the receipt of a contract to which this Standard is applicable.

9904.417 Cost of money as an element of the cost of capital assets under construction. (No Text)

9904.417-10 [Reserved]

9904.417-20 Purpose.

The purpose of this Cost Accounting Standard is to establish criteria for the measurement of the cost of money attributable to capital assets under construction, fabrication, or development as an element of the cost of those assets. Consistent application of these criteria will improve cost measurement by providing for recognition of cost of contractor investment in assets under construction, and will provide greater uniformity in accounting for asset acquisition costs.

9904.417-30 Definitions.

(a) The following are definitions of terms which are prominent in this Standard. Other terms defined elsewhere in this Part 99 shall have the meanings ascribed to them in those definitions unless paragraph (b) of this subsection, requires otherwise.

(1) *Intangible capital asset* means an asset that has no physical substance, has more than minimal value, and is expected to be held by an enterprise for continued use or possession beyond the current accounting period for the benefits it yields.

(2) *Tangible capital asset* means an asset that has physical substance, more than minimal value, and is expected to be held by an enterprise for continued use or possession beyond the current accounting period for the services it yields.

(b) The following modifications of terms defined elsewhere in this chapter 99 are applicable to this Standard: None.

9904.417-40 Fundamental requirement.

The cost of money applicable to the investment in tangible and intangible capital assets being constructed, fabricated, or developed for a contractor's own use shall be included in the capitalized acquisition cost of such assets.

9904.417-50 Techniques for application.

(a) The cost of money for an asset shall be calculated as follows:

(1) The cost of money rate used shall be based on interest rates determined by the Secretary of the Treasury pursuant to Public Law 92-41 (85 stat. 97).

(2) A representative investment amount shall be determined each cost accounting period for each capital asset being constructed, fabricated, or developed giving appropriate consideration to the rate at which costs of construction are incurred.

(3) Other methods for calculating the cost of money to be capitalized, such as the method used for financial accounting and

reporting, may be used, provided the resulting amount does not differ materially from the amount calculated by use of paragraphs (a)(1) and (2) of this subsection.

(b) If substantially all the activities necessary to get the asset ready for its intended use are discontinued, cost of money shall not be capitalized for the period of discontinuance. However, if such discontinuance arises out of causes beyond the control and without the fault or negligence of the contractor, cessation of cost of money capitalization is not required.

9904.417-60 Illustrations.

(a) A contractor decided to build a major addition to his plant using both his own labor and outside subcontractors. It took 13 months to complete the building. The first 10 months of the construction period were in one cost accounting period. At the end of the cost accounting period the total charges, including cost of money computed in accordance with 9904.414, accumulated in the construction-in-progress account for this project amounted to $750,000. However, most of these construction costs were incurred towards the end of the cost accounting period. In developing a method for determining a representative investment amount, appropriate consideration must be given to the rate at which costs have been incurred in accordance with 9904.417-50(a)(2). Therefore, the contractor averaged the 10 month-end balances and determined that the average investment in the project was $245,000. Two cost of money rates were in effect during the 10-month period; their time-weighted average was determined to be 8.6 percent. Application of the 8.6 percent rate for ten-twelfths of a year to the representative balance of $245,000 resulted in the determination that $17,558 should be added to the construction-in-progress account in recognition of the cost of money related to this project in its first cost accounting period. The project was completed with the addition of $750,000 of additional costs during the first 3 months of the subsequent cost accounting period. The contractor considered the 3 month-end balances (which included the $17,558 capitalized cost of money described in the preceding paragraph) and determined that the representative balance was $1,234,000. The cost of money rate in effect during this 3-month period was 7.75 percent. Applying the rate of 7.75 percent for one-fourth of a year to the balance of $1,234,000 resulted in a determination that $23,909 should be added to the construction-in-progress account in recognition of the cost of money while under construction in the second cost accounting period. The capitalized project was put into service at the recognized cost of acquisition of $1,541,467 which consists of the "regular" costs of $1,500,000 plus $17,558 and $23,909 cost of money. This practice is in accordance with 9904.417-50(a) and other applicable provisions of the Standard.

Note: An alternative technique would be to make separate calculations, using an appropriate investment amount and cost of money rate, for each month. The sum of the monthly cost of money amounts could be entered in the construction-in-progress account once each cost accounting period.

(b) A contractor built a major addition with identical basic data to those described in 9904.417-60(a) except that the costs were incurred at a fairly uniform rate throughout the period. Because of the pattern of cost incurrence, the contractor used beginning and ending balances of the cost accounting period to find the representative amounts. For the first cost accounting period the representative investment amount was the average of the beginning and ending balances (zero and $750,000), or $375,000. Application of the average interest rate of 8.6 percent for ten-twelfths of a year resulted in the determination that $26,875 should be added to the construction-in-progress account in recognition of the cost of money related to this project in its first cost accounting period. During the subsequent 3 months the contractor used the representative balance of $1,151,875, derived by averaging the beginning balance of $776,875 ($750,000 "regular" cost plus the $26,875 imputed cost from the prior period) and the balance at the end, $1,526,875. Applying the 7.75 percent cost of money rate to this balance for a 3-month period resulted in a determination that $22,317 should be added to the construction-

in-progress account in recognition of the cost of money while under construction in the second cost accounting period. The capitalized project was put into service at the recognized cost of acquisition of $1,549,192 which consists of the "regular" costs of $1,500,000 plus $26,875 and $22,317 imputed cost of money. This practice is in accordance with 9904.417-50(a) and other applicable provisions of the Standard.

Note: If this contractor, acting in accordance with established Standards for financial accounting, allocated a portion of its paid interest expense to this construction project and the resultant acquisition cost for financial reporting purposes was not materially different from $1,549,192, the contractor could, in accordance with 9904.417-50(a)(iii), use the same acquisition cost for contract costing purposes.

[Corrected, 57 FR 34081, 8/3/92]

9904.417-61 [Reserved]

9904.417-62 Exemption.

None for this Standard.

9904.417-63 Effective date.

This Standard is effective as of April 17, 1992. Contractors with prior CAS-covered contracts with full coverage shall continue this Standard's applicability upon receipt of a contract to which this Standard is applicable. For contractors with no previous contracts subject to this Standard, this Standard shall be applied beginning with the contractor's next full fiscal year beginning after the receipt of a contract to which this Standard is applicable.

9904.418 Allocation of direct and indirect costs. (No Text)

9904.418-10 [Reserved]

9904.418-20 Purpose.

The purpose of this Cost Accounting Standard is to provide for consistent determination of direct and indirect costs; to provide criteria for the accumulation of indirect costs, including service center and overhead costs, in indirect cost pools; and, to provide guidance relating to the selection of allocation measures based on the beneficial or causal relationship between an indirect cost pool and cost objectives. Consistent application of these criteria and guidance will improve classification of costs as direct and indirect and the allocation of indirect costs.

9904.418-30 Definitions.

(a) The following are definitions of terms which are prominent in this Standard. Other terms defined elsewhere in this chapter 99 shall have the meanings ascribed to them in those definitions unless paragraph (b) of this subsection, requires otherwise.

(1) *Allocate* means to assign an item of cost, or a group of items of cost, to one or more cost objectives. This term includes both direct assignment of cost and the reassignment of a share from an indirect cost pool.

(2) *Direct cost* means any cost which is identified specifically with a particular final cost objective. Direct costs are not limited to items which are incorporated in the end product as material or labor. Costs identified specifically with a contract are direct costs of that contract. All costs identified specifically with other final cost objectives of the contractor are direct costs of those cost objectives.

(3) *Indirect cost* means any cost not directly identified with a single final cost objective, but identified with two or more final cost objectives or with at least one intermediate cost objective.

(4) *Indirect cost pool* means a grouping of incurred costs identified with two or more cost objectives but not identified specifically with any final cost objective.

(b) The following modifications of terms defined elsewhere in this chapter 99 are applicable to this Standard: None.

9904.418-40 Fundamental requirements.

(a) A business unit shall have a written statement of accounting policies and practices for classifying costs as direct or indirect which shall be consistently applied.

(b) Indirect costs shall be accumulated in indirect cost pools which are homogeneous.

(c) Pooled costs shall be allocated to cost objectives in reasonable proportion to the beneficial or causal relationship of the pooled costs to cost objectives as follows:

(1) If a material amount of the costs included in a cost pool are costs of management or supervision of activities involving direct labor or direct material costs, resource consumption cannot be specifically identified with cost objectives. In that circumstance, a base shall be used which is representative of the activity being managed or supervised.

(2) If the cost pool does not contain a material amount of the costs of management or supervision of activities involving direct labor or direct material costs, resource consumption can be specifically identified with cost objectives. The pooled cost shall be allocated based on the specific identifiability of resource consumption with cost objectives by means of one of the following allocation bases:

(i) A resource consumption measure,

(ii) An output measure, or

(iii) A surrogate that is representative of resources consumed.

The base shall be selected in accordance with the criteria set out in 9904.418-50(e).

(d) To the extent that any cost allocations are required by the provisions of other Cost Accounting Standards, such allocations are not subject to the provisions of this Standard.

(e) This Standard does not cover accounting for the costs of special facilities where such costs are accounted for in separate indirect cost pools.

9904.418-50 Techniques for application.

(a) Determination of direct cost and indirect cost. (1) The business unit's written policy classifying costs as direct or indirect shall be in conformity with the requirements of this Standard.

(2) In accounting for direct costs a business unit shall use actual costs, except that

(i) Standard costs for material and labor may be used as provided in 9904.407; or

(ii) An average cost or pre-established rate for labor may be used provided that

(A) The functions performed are not materially disparate and employees involved are interchangeable with respect to the functions performed, or

(B) The functions performed are materially disparate but the employees involved either all work in a single production unit yielding homogeneous outputs, or perform their respective functions as an integral team. Whenever average cost or preestablished rates for labor are used, the variances, if material, shall be disposed of at least annually by allocation to cost objectives in proportion to the costs previously allocated to these cost objectives.

(3) Labor or material costs identified specifically with one of the particular cost objectives listed in paragraph (d)(3) of this subsection shall be accounted for as direct labor or direct material costs.

(b) Homogeneous indirect cost pools. (1) An indirect cost pool is homogeneous if each significant activity whose costs are included therein has the same or a similar beneficial or causal relationship to cost objectives as the other activities whose costs are included in the cost pool. It is also homogeneous if the allocation of the costs of the activities included in the cost pool result in an allocation to cost objectives which is not materially different from the allocation that would result if the costs of the activities were allocated separately.

(2) An indirect cost pool is not homogeneous if the costs of all significant activities in the cost pool do not have the same or a similar beneficial or causal relationship to cost objectives and, if the costs were allocated separately, the resulting allocation would be materially different. The determination of materiality shall be made using the criteria provided in 9903.305.

(3) A homogeneous indirect cost pool shall include all indirect costs identified with the activity to which the pool relates.

(c) Change in Allocation Base. No change in an existing indirect cost pool allocation base is required if the allocation resulting from the existing base does not differ materially from the allocation that results from the use of the base determined to be most appropriate in accordance with the criteria set forth in paragraphs (d) and (e) of this subsection. The determination of materiality shall be made using the criteria provided in Subpart 9903.305.

(d) Allocation measures for an indirect cost pool which includes a material amount of the costs of management or supervision of activities involving direct labor or direct material costs. (1) The costs of the management or supervision of activities involving direct labor or direct material costs do not have a direct and definitive relationship to the benefiting cost objectives and cannot be allocated on measures of a specific beneficial or causal relationship. In that circumstance, the base selected to measure the allocation of the pooled costs to cost objectives shall be a base representative of the activity being managed or supervised.

(2) The base used to represent the activity being managed or supervised shall be determined by the application of the criteria below. All significant elements of the selected base shall be included.

(i) A direct labor hour base or direct labor cost base shall be used, whichever in the aggregate is more likely to vary in proportion to the costs included in the cost pool being allocated, except that:

(ii) A machine-hour base is appropriate if the costs in the cost pool are comprised predominantly of facility related costs, such as depreciation, maintenance, and utilities; or

(iii) A units-of-production base is appropriate if there is common production of comparable units; or

(iv) A material cost base is appropriate if the activity being managed or supervised is a material related activity.

(3) Indirect cost pools which include material amounts of the costs of management or supervision of activities involving direct labor or direct material costs shall be allocated to:

(i) Final cost objectives;

(ii) Goods produced for stock or product inventory;

(iii) Independent research and development and bid and proposal projects;

(iv) Cost centers used to accumulate costs identified with a process cost system (i.e., process cost centers);

(v) Goods or services produced or acquired for other segments of the contractor and for other cost objectives of a business unit; and

(vi) Self-construction, fabrication, betterment, improvement, or installation of tangible capital assets.

(e) Allocation measures for indirect cost pools that do not include material amounts of the costs of management or supervision of activities involving direct labor or direct material costs. Homogeneous indirect cost pools of this type have a direct and definitive relationship between the activities in the pool and benefiting cost objectives. The pooled costs shall be allocated using an appropriate measure of resource consumption. This determination shall be made in accordance with the following criteria taking into consideration the individual circumstances:

(1) The best representation of the beneficial or causal relationship between an indirect cost pool and the benefiting cost objectives is a measure of resource consumption of the activities of the indirect cost pool.

(2) (i) If consumption measures are unavailable or impractical to ascertain, the next best representation of the beneficial or causal relationship for allocation is a measure of the output of the activities of the indirect cost pool. Thus, the output is substituted for a direct measure of the consumption of resources.

(ii) The use of the basic unit of output will not reflect the proportional consumption of resources in circumstances in which the level of resource consumption varies among the units of output produced. Where a material difference will result, either the output measure shall be modified or more than one output measure shall be used to reflect the resources consumed to perform the activity.

(3) If neither resources consumed nor output of the activities can be measured practically, a surrogate that varies in proportion to the services received shall be used to measure the resources consumed. Generally, such surrogates measure the activity of the cost objectives receiving the service.

(4) Allocation of indirect cost pools which benefit one another may be accomplished by use of:

(i) The cross-allocation (reciprocal) method,

(ii) The sequential method, or

(iii) Another method the results of which approximate those achieved by either of the methods in subdivisions (e) (4) (i) or (e) (4) (ii) of this subsection.

(5) Where the activities represented by an indirect cost pool provide services to two or more cost objectives simultaneously, the cost of such services shall be prorated between or among the cost objectives in reasonable proportion to the beneficial or causal relationship between the services and the cost objectives.

(f) Special allocation. Where a particular cost objective in relation to other cost objectives receives significantly more or less benefit from an indirect cost pool than would be reflected by the allocation of such costs using a base determined pursuant to paragraphs (d) and (e) of this subsection, the Government and contractor may agree to a special allocation from that indirect cost pool to the particular cost objective commensurate with the benefits received. The amount of a special allocation to any such cost objective made pursuant to such an agreement shall be excluded from the indirect cost pool and the particular cost objective's allocation base data shall be excluded from the base used to allocate the pool.

(g) Use of preestablished rates for indirect costs. (1) Preestablished rates, based on either forecasted actual or standard cost, may be used in allocating an indirect cost pool.

(2) Preestablished rates shall reflect the costs and activities anticipated for the cost accounting period except as provided in paragraph (g) (3) of this subsection. Such preestablished rates shall be reviewed at

least annually, and revised as necessary to reflect the anticipated conditions.

(3) The contracting parties may agree on preestablished rates which are not based on costs and activities anticipated for a cost accounting period. The contractor shall have and consistently apply written policies for the establishment of these rates.

(4) Under paragraphs (g)(2) and (3) of this subsection where variances of a cost accounting period are material, these variances shall be disposed of by allocating them to cost objectives in proportion to the costs previously allocated to these cost objectives by use of the preestablished rates.

(5) If preestablished rates are revised during a cost accounting period and if the variances accumulated to the time of the revision are significant, the costs allocated to that time shall be adjusted to the amounts which would have been allocated using the revised preestablished rates.

9904.418-60 Illustrations.

(a) Business Unit A has various classifications of engineers whose time is spent in working directly on the production of the goods or services called for by contracts and other final cost objectives. In keeping with its written policy, detailed time records are kept of the hours worked by these engineers, showing the job/account numbers representing various cost objectives. On the basis of these detailed time records, Unit A allocates the labor costs of these engineers as direct labor costs of final cost objectives. This practice is in accordance with the requirements of 9904.418-50(a)(1).

(b) Business Unit B has a fabrication department, employees of which perform various functions on units of the work-in-process of multiple final cost objectives. These employees are grouped by labor skills and are interchangeable within the skill grouping. The average wage rate for each group is multiplied by the hours worked on each cost objective by employees in that group. The contractor classifies these costs as direct labor costs of each final cost objective. This cost accounting treatment is in accordance with the provisions of 9904.418-50(a)(2)(ii)(B).

(c) Business Unit C accumulates the costs relating to building ownership, maintenance, and utility into one indirect cost pool designated "Occupancy Costs" for allocation to cost objectives. Each of these activities has the same or a similar beneficial or causal relationship to the cost objectives occupying a space. Unit C's practice is in conformance with the provisions of 9904.418-50(b)(1).

(d) Business Unit D includes the indirect costs of machining and assembling activities in a single manufacturing overhead pool. The machining activity does not have the same or similar beneficial or causal relationship to cost objectives as the assembling activity. Also, the allocation of the cost of the machining activity to cost objectives would be significantly different if allocated separately from the cost of the assembling activity. Unit D's single manufacturing overhead pool is not homogeneous in accordance with the provisions of 9904.418-50(b), and separate pools must be established in accordance with 9904.418-40(b).

(e) In accordance with 9904.418-50(b)(3), Business Unit E includes all the cost of occupancy in an indirect cost pool. In selecting an allocation measure for this indirect cost pool, the contractor establishes that it is impractical to ascertain a measurement of the consumption of resources in relation to the use of facilities by individual cost objectives. An output base, the number of square feet of space provided to users, can be measured practically; however, the cost to provide facilities is significantly different for various types of facilities such as warehouse, factory, and office and each type of facility requires a different level of resource consumption to provide the same number of square feet of usable space. Allocation on a basic unit measure of square feet of space occupied will not adequately reflect the proportional consumption of resources. Unit E establishes a weighted square foot measure for allocating occupancy costs, which reflects the different levels of resource consumption required to provide the different types of facilities. This practice is in conformance with provisions of 9904.418-50(e)(2)(ii).

(f) Business Unit F has an indirect cost pool containing a significant amount of material-related costs. The contractor allocates these costs between his machining overhead cost pool and his assembly overhead cost pool. The business unit finds it impractical to use an allocation measure based on either consumption or output. The business unit selects a dollars of material-issued base which varies in proportion to the services rendered. The dollars of material-issued base is a surrogate base which conforms to the provisions of 9904.418-50(e)(3).

(g) Business Unit G has a machining activity for which it develops a separate overhead rate. using direct labor cost as the allocation base. The machining activity occasionally does significant amounts of work for other activities of the business unit. The labor used in doing the work for other activities is of the same nature as that used for contract work. However, the machining labor for other activities is not included in the base used to allocate the overhead costs of the machining activity. This practice is not in conformance with 9904.418-50(d)(2). Unit G must include the cost of labor doing work for the other activities in the allocation base for the machining activity indirect cost pool.

(h) Business Unit H accounts for the costs of company aircraft in a separate homogeneous indirect cost pool and allocates the cost to benefiting cost objectives using flight hours. Unit H prorates the cost of a single flight between benefiting cost objectives whenever simultaneous services have been rendered. Manager of Contract 2 learns of the trip and goes along with Manager of Contract 1. Unit H prorates the cost of the trip between Contract 1 and Contract 2. This practice is in conformance with the provision of 9904.418-50(e)(5).

(i) During a cost accounting period, Business Unit I allocates the cost of its flight services indirect cost pool to other indirect cost pools and final cost objectives using a preestablished rate. The preestablished rate is based on an estimate of the actual costs and activity for the cost accounting period. For the cost accounting period, Unit I establishes a rate of $200 per hour for use of the flight services activity. In March, the contractor's operating environment changes significantly; the contractor now expects a

significant increase in the cost of this activity during the remainder of the year. Unit I estimates the rate for the entire cost accounting period to be $240 an hour. Pursuant to the provisions of 9904.418-50(g)(4), the Business Unit may revise its rate to the expected $240 an hour. If the accumulated variances are significant, the business unit must also adjust the costs previously allocated to reflect the revised rates.

9904.418-61 [Reserved]

9904.418-62 Exemptions.

This Standard shall not apply to contracts and grants with state, local, and Federally recognized Indian tribal governments.

9904.418-63 Effective date.

This Standard is effective as of April 17, 1992. Contractors with prior CAS-covered contracts with full coverage shall continue this Standard's applicability upon receipt of a contract to which this Standard is applicable. For contractors with no previous contracts subject to this Standard, this Standard shall be applied beginning with the contractor's second full fiscal year beginning after the receipt of a contract to which this Standard is applicable.

9904.420 Accounting for independent research and development costs and bid and proposal costs. (No Text)

9904.420-10 [Reserved]

9904.420-20 Purpose.

The purpose of this Cost Accounting Standard is to provide criteria for the accumulation of independent research and development costs and bid and proposal costs and for the allocation of such costs to cost objectives based on the beneficial or causal relationship between such costs and cost objectives. Consistent application of these criteria will improve cost allocation.

9904.420-30 Definitions.

(a) The following are definitions of terms which are prominent in this Standard. Other terms defined elsewhere in this Chapter 99 shall have the meanings ascribed to them in

CASB 9904.420-30

those definitions unless paragraph (b) of this subsection, requires otherwise.

(1) *Allocate* means to assign an item of cost, or a group of items of cost, to one or more cost objectives. This term includes both direct assignment of cost and the reassignment of a share from an indirect cost pool.

(2) *Bid and proposal (B&P) cost* means the cost incurred in preparing, submitting, or supporting any bid or proposal which effort is neither sponsored by a grant, nor required in the performance of a contract.

(3) *Business unit* means any segment of an organization, or an entire business organization which is not divided into segments.

(4) *General and administrative (G&A) expense* means any management, financial, and other expenses which is incurred by or allocated to a business unit and which is for the general management and administration of the business unit as a whole. G&A expense does not include those management expenses whose beneficial or causal relationship to cost objectives can be more directly measured by a base other than a cost input base representing the total activity of a business unit during a cost accounting period.

(5) *Home office* means an office responsible for directing or managing two or more, but not necessarily all, segments of an organization. It typically establishes policy for, and provides guidance to the segments in their operations. It usually performs management, supervisory, or administrative functions, and may also perform service functions in support of the operations of the various segments. An organization which has intermediate levels, such as groups, may have several home offices which report to a common home office. An intermediate organization may be both a segment and a home office.

(6) *Independent research and development* means the cost of effort which is neither sponsored by a grant, nor required in the performance of a contract, and which falls within any of the following three areas:

(i) Basic and applied research,

(ii) Development, and

(iii) Systems and other concept formulation studies.

(7) *Indirect cost* means any cost not directly identified with a single final cost objective, but identified with two or more final cost objectives or with at least one intermediate cost objective.

(8) *Segment* means one of two or more divisions, product departments, plants, or other subdivisions of an organization reporting directly to a home office, usually identified with responsibility for profit and/or producing a product or service. The term includes Government-owned contractor-operated (GOCO) facilities, and joint ventures and subsidiaries (domestic and foreign) in which the organization has a majority ownership. The term also includes those joint ventures and subsidiaries (domestic and foreign) in which the organization has less than a majority of ownership, but over which it exercises control.

(b) The following modifications of terms defined elsewhere in this Chapter 99 are applicable to this Standard: None.

9904.420-40 Fundamental requirement.

(a) The basic unit for the identification and accumulation of Independent Research and Development (IR&D) and Bid and Proposal (B&P) costs shall be the individual IR&D or B&P project.

(b) The IR&D and B&P project costs shall consist of all allocable costs, except business unit general and administrative expenses.

(c) The IR&D and B&P cost pools consist of all IR&D and B&P project costs and other allocable costs, except business unit general and administrative expenses.

(d) The IR&D and B&P cost pools of a home office shall be allocated to segments on the basis of the beneficial or causal relationship between the IR&D and B&P costs and the segments reporting to that home office.

(e) The IR&D and B&P cost pools of a business unit shall be allocated to the final cost objectives of that business unit on the basis of the beneficial or causal relationship between the IR&D and B&P costs and the final cost objectives.

(f)(1) The B&P costs incurred in a cost accounting period shall not be assigned to any other cost accounting period.

(2) The IR&D costs incurred in a cost accounting period shall not be assigned to any other cost accounting period, except as may be permitted pursuant to provisions of existing laws, regulations, and other controlling factors.

9904.420-50 Techniques for application.

(a) The IR&D and B&P project costs shall include (1) costs, which if incurred in like circumstances for a final cost objective, would be treated as direct costs of that final cost objective, and (2) the overhead costs of productive activities and other indirect costs related to the project based on the contractor's cost accounting practice or applicable Cost Accounting Standards for allocation of indirect costs.

(b) The IR&D and B&P cost pools for a segment consist of the project costs plus allocable home office IR&D and B&P costs.

(c) When the costs of individual IR&D or B&P efforts are not material in amount, these costs may be accumulated in one or more project(s) within each of these two types of effort.

(d) The costs of any work performed by one segment for another segment shall not be treated as IR&D costs or B&P costs of the performing segment unless the work is a part of an IR&D or B&P project of the performing segment. If such work is part of a performing segment's IR&D or B&P project, the project will be transferred to the home office to be allocated in accordance with paragraph (e) of this subsection.

(e) The costs of IR&D and B&P projects accumulated at a home office shall be allocated to its segments as follows:

(1) Projects which can be identified with a specific segment(s) shall have their costs allocated to such segment(s).

(2) The costs of all other IR&D and B&P projects shall be allocated among all segments by means of the same base used by

the company to allocate its residual expenses in accordance with 9904.403; provided, however, where a particular segment receives significantly more or less benefit from the IR&D or B&P costs than would be reflected by the allocation of such costs to the segment by the base, the Government and the contractor may agree to a special allocation of the IR&D or B&P costs to such segment commensurate with the benefits received. The amount of a special allocation to any segment made pursuant to such an agreement shall be excluded from the IR&D and B&P cost pools to be allocated to other segments and the base data of any such segment shall be excluded from the base used to allocate these pools.

(f) The costs of IR&D and B&P projects accumulated at a business unit shall be allocated to cost objectives as follows:

(1) Where costs of any IR&D or B&P project benefit more than one segment of the organization, the amounts to be allocated to each segment shall be determined in accordance with paragraph (e) of this subsection.

(2) The IR&D and B&P cost pools which are not allocated under subparagraph (f)(1) of this subsection, shall be allocated to all final cost objectives of the business unit by means of the same base used by the business unit to allocate its general and administrative expenses in accordance with 9904.410-50; provided, however, where a particular final cost objective receives significantly more or less benefit from IR&D or B&P cost than would be reflected by the allocation of such costs the Government and the contractor may agree to a special allocation of the IR&D or B&P costs to such final cost objective commensurate with the benefits received. The amount of special allocation to any such final cost objective made pursuant to such an agreement shall be excluded from the IR&D and B&P cost pools to be allocated to other final cost objectives and the particular final cost objective's base data shall be excluded from the base used to allocate these pools.

(g) Notwithstanding the provisions of paragraph (d), (e) or (f) of this subsection, the costs of IR&D and B&P projects allocable to a home office pursuant to 9904.420-50(d) may be allocated directly to the receiving segments, provided that such allocation not be substantially different from the allocation that would be made if they were first passed through home office accounts.

9904.420-60 Illustrations.

(a) Business Unit A's engineering department in accordance with its established accounting practice, charges administrative effort including typing to its overhead cost pool. In submitting a proposal, the engineering department assigns several typists to the proposal project on a full time basis and charges the typists' time directly to the proposal project, rather than to its overhead pool. Because the engineering department under its established accounting practice does not charge the cost of typing directly to final cost objectives, the direct charge does not meet with the requirements of 9904.420-50(a).

(b) Company B has five segments. The company undertakes an IR&D project which is part of IR&D plans of segments X, Y, and Z, and will be of general benefit to all five segments. The company designates Segment Z as the project leader in performing the project. In accumulating the costs, each segment allocates overhead to its part of the project but does not allocate segment G&A. The IR&D costs are then allocated to the home office by each segment. The costs are combined with other IR&D costs that benefit the company as a whole. The costs are allocated to all five segments by means of the same base by which the company allocates its residual home office expense costs of all segments. This practice meets the requirements of 9904.420-40(b), 9904.420-50(e)(2), and 9904.420-50(f)(1).

(c) Business Unit C normally accounts for its B&P effort by individual project. It accumulates directly allocated costs and departmental overhead costs by project. The business unit also submits large numbers of bids and proposals whose individual costs of preparation are not material in amount. The business unit collects the cost of these efforts under a single project. Since the cost of preparing each individual bid and proposal is not material, the practice of accumulating

these costs in a single project meets the requirements of 9904.420-50(c).

(d) Segment D requests that Segment Y provide support for a Segment D IR&D project. The work being performed by Segment Y is similar in nature to Segment Y's normal product and is not part of its annual IR&D plan. Segment Y allocates to the project all costs it allocates to other final cost objectives, including G&A expense. Segment Y then directly transfers the cost of the project to Segment D in accordance with its normal intersegment transfer procedure. The accounting treatment meets the requirements of 9904.420-50(d) and 9904.410.

(e)(1) Contractor E has six operating segments and a research segment. The research segment performs work under

(i) Research and development contracts,

(ii) Projects which are not part of its own IR&D plan but are specifically in support of other segments' IR&D projects, and

(iii) IR&D projects for the benefit of the company as a whole.

(2) The research segment directly allocates the cost of the projects in support of another segment's IR&D projects, including an allocation of its general and administrative expenses, to the receiving segment. This practice meets the requirements of 9904.420-50(d).

(3) The costs of the IR&D projects which benefit the company as a whole exclude any allocation of the research segment's general and administrative expenses and are transferred to the home office. The home office allocates these costs on the same base it uses to allocate its residual expenses to all seven segments. This practice meets the requirements of 9904.420-50(e)(2) and (f)(1).

(f) Company F accumulates at the home office the costs of IR&D and B&P projects which generally benefit all segments of the company except Segment X. The company and the contracting officer agree that the nature of the business activity of Segment X is such that the home office IR&D and B&P effort is neither caused by nor provides any benefit to that segment. For the purpose of allocating its home office residual expenses, the company uses a base as provided in

9904.403. For the purpose of allocating the home office IR&D and B&P costs, the company removes the data of Segment X from the base used for the allocation of its residual expenses. This practice meets the requirements of 9904.420-50(e)(2).

(g) Company G has 10 segments. Segment X performs IR&D projects, the results of which benefit it and two other segments but none of the other seven segments. The cost of those projects performed by Segment X are transferred to the home office and allocated to the three segments on the basis of the benefits received by the three segments. This practice meets the requirements of 9904.420-50(e)(1) and 9904.420-50(f)(1).

9904.420-61 [Reserved]

9904.420-62 Exemptions.

This Standard shall not apply to contracts and grants with state, local, and Federally recognized Indian tribal governments.

9904.420-63 Effective date.

This Standard is effective as of April 17, 1992. Contractors with prior CAS-covered contracts with full coverage shall continue this Standard's applicability upon receipt of a contract to which this Standard is applicable. For contractors with no previous contracts subject to this Standard, this Standard shall be applied beginning with the contractor's second full fiscal year beginning after the receipt of a contract to which this Standard is applicable.

PART 9905—COST ACCOUNTING STANDARDS FOR EDUCATIONAL INSTITUTIONS
Table of Contents

PART 9905—COST ACCOUNTING STANDARDS FOR EDUCATIONAL INSTITUTIONS

9905.501 Cost accounting standard—consistency in estimating, accumulating and reporting costs by educational institutions. (No Text)

9905.501-10 [Reserved]

[Final rule, 59 FR 55746, 11/8/94, effective 1/9/95]

9905.501-20 Purpose.

The purpose of this Cost Accounting Standard is to ensure that each educational institution's practices used in estimating costs for a proposal are consistent with cost accounting practices used by the institution in accumulating and reporting costs. Consistency in the application of cost accounting practices is necessary to enhance the likelihood that comparable transactions are treated alike. With respect to individual contracts, the consistent application of cost accounting practices will facilitate the preparation of reliable cost estimates used in pricing a proposal and their comparison with the costs of performance of the resulting contract. Such comparisons provide one important basis for financial control over costs during contract performance and aid in establishing accountability for costs in the manner agreed to by both parties at the time of contracting. The comparisons also provide an improved basis for evaluating estimating capabilities.

[Final rule, 59 FR 55746, 11/8/94, effective 1/9/95]

9905.501-30 Definitions.

(a) The following are definitions of terms which are prominent in this Standard. Other terms defined elsewhere in this Chapter 99 shall have the meanings ascribed to them in those definitions unless paragraph (b) of this subsection requires otherwise.

(1) *Accumulating costs* means the collecting of cost data in an organized manner, such as through a system of accounts.

(2) *Actual cost* means an amount determined on the basis of cost incurred (as distinguished from forecasted cost), including standard cost properly adjusted for applicable variance.

(3) *Estimating costs* means the process of forecasting a future result in terms of cost, based upon information available at the time.

(4) *Indirect cost pool* means a grouping of incurred costs identified with two or more objectives but not identified specifically with any final cost objective.

(5) *Pricing* means the process of establishing the amount or amounts to be paid in return for goods or services.

(6) *Proposal* means any offer or other submission used as a basis for pricing a contract, contract modification or termination settlement or for securing payments thereunder.

(7) *Reporting costs* means the providing of cost information to others.

(b) The following modifications of terms defined elsewhere in this Chapter 99 are applicable to this Standard: None.

[Final rule, 59 FR 55746, 11/8/94, effective 1/9/95]

9905.501-40 Fundamental requirement.

(a) An educational institution's practices used in estimating costs in pricing a proposal shall be consistent with the institution's cost accounting practices used in accumulating and reporting costs.

(b) An educational institution's cost accounting practices used in accumulating and reporting actual costs for a contract shall be consistent with the institution's practices used in estimating costs in pricing the related proposal.

(c) The grouping of homogeneous costs in estimates prepared for proposal purposes shall not per se be deemed an inconsistent application of cost accounting practices under paragraphs (a) and (b) of this subsection when such costs are accumulated and reported in greater detail on an actual cost basis during contract performance.

[Final rule, 59 FR 55746, 11/8/94, effective 1/9/95]

CASB 9905.501-40

9905.501-50 Techniques for application.

(a) The standard allows grouping of homogeneous costs in order to cover those cases where it is not practicable to estimate contract costs by individual cost element. However, costs estimated for proposal purposes shall be presented in such a manner and in such detail that any significant cost can be compared with the actual cost accumulated and reported therefor. In any event, the cost accounting practices used in estimating costs in pricing a proposal and in accumulating and reporting costs on the resulting contract shall be consistent with respect to:

(1) The classification of elements of cost as direct or indirect;

(2) The indirect cost pools to which each element of cost is charged or proposed to be charged; and

(3) The methods of allocating indirect costs to the contract.

(b) Adherence to the requirement of 9905.501-40(a) of this standard shall be determined as of the date of award of the contract, unless the contractor has submitted cost or pricing data pursuant to 10 U.S.C. 2306(a) or 41 U.S.C. 254(d) (Pub. L. 87-653), in which case adherence to the requirement of 9905.501-40(a) shall be determined as of the date of final agreement on price, as shown on the signed certificate of current cost or pricing data. Notwithstanding 9905.501-40(b), changes in established cost accounting practices during contract performance may be made in accordance with Part 9903 (48 CFR part 9903).

(c) The standard does not prescribe the amount of detail required in accumulating and reporting costs. The basic requirement which must be met, however, is that for any significant amount of estimated cost, the contractor must be able to accumulate and report actual cost at a level which permits sufficient and meaningful comparison with its estimates. The amount of detail required may vary considerably depending on how the proposed costs were estimated, the data presented in justification or lack thereof, and the significance of each situation. Accord-

ingly, it is neither appropriate nor practical to prescribe a single set of accounting practices which would be consistent in all situations with the practices of estimating costs. Therefore, the amount of accounting and statistical detail to be required and maintained in accounting for estimated costs has been and continues to be a matter to be decided by Government procurement authorities on the basis of the individual facts and circumstances.

[Final rule, 59 FR 55746, 11/8/94, effective 1/9/95]

9905.501-60 [Reserved]

[Final rule, 59 FR 55746, 11/8/94, effective 1/9/95]

9905.501-61 [Reserved]

[Final rule, 59 FR 55746, 11/8/94, effective 1/9/95]

9905.501-62 Exemption.

None for this Standard.

[Final rule, 59 FR 55746, 11/8/94, effective 1/9/95]

9905.501-63 Effective date.

This Standard is effective as of January 9, 1995. [Final rule, 59 FR 55746, 11/8/94, effective 1/9/95]

9905.502 Cost accounting standard—consistency in allocating costs incurred for the same purpose by educational institutions. (No Text)

9905.502-10 [Reserved]

[Final rule, 59 FR 55746, 11/8/94, effective 1/9/95]

9905.502-20 Purpose.

The purpose of this Standard is to require that each type of cost is allocated only once and on only one basis to any contract or other cost objective. The criteria for determining the allocation of costs to a contract or other cost objective should be the same for all similar objectives. Adherence to these cost accounting concepts is necessary to guard against the overcharging of some cost objectives and to prevent double counting. Double counting occurs most commonly when cost items are allocated directly to a cost objective without eliminating like cost items from indirect cost pools which are allocated to that cost objective.

[Final rule, 59 FR 55746, 11/8/94, effective 1/9/95]

9905.502-30 Definitions.

(a) The following are definitions of terms which are prominent in this Standard. Other terms defined elsewhere in this Chapter 99 shall have the meanings ascribed to them in those definitions unless paragraph (b) of this subsection requires otherwise.

(1) *Allocate* means to assign an item of cost, or a group of items of cost, to one or more cost objectives. This term includes both direct assignment of cost and the reassignment of a share from an indirect cost pool.

(2) *Cost objective* means a function, organizational subdivision, contract, or other work unit for which cost data are desired and for which provision is made to accumulate and measure the cost of processes, products, jobs, capitalized projects, etc.

(3) *Direct cost* means any cost which is identified specifically with a particular final cost objective. Direct costs are not limited to items which are incorporated in the end product as material or labor. Costs identified specifically with a contract are direct costs of that contract. All costs identified specifically with other final cost objectives of the educational institution are direct costs of those cost objectives.

(4) *Final cost objective* means a cost objective which has allocated to it both direct and indirect costs, and in the educational institution's accumulation system, is one of the final accumulation points.

(5) *Indirect cost* means any cost not directly identified with a single final cost objective, but identified with two or more final cost objectives or with at least one intermediate cost objective.

(6) *Indirect cost pool* means a grouping of incurred costs identified with two or more cost objectives but not identified with any final cost objective.

(7) *Intermediate cost objective* means a cost objective that is used to accumulate indirect costs or service center costs that are subsequently allocated to one or more indirect cost pools and/or final cost objectives.

(b) The following modifications of terms defined elsewhere in this Chapter 99 are applicable to this Standard: None.

[Final rule, 59 FR 55746, 11/8/94, effective 1/9/95]

9905.502-40 Fundamental requirement.

All costs incurred for the same purpose, in like circumstances, are either direct costs only or indirect costs only with respect to final cost objectives. No final cost objective shall have allocated to it as an indirect cost any cost, if other costs incurred for the same purpose, in like circumstances, have been included as a direct cost of that or any other final cost objective. Further, no final cost objective shall have allocated to it as a direct cost any cost, if other costs incurred for the same purpose, in like circumstances, have been included in any indirect cost pool to be allocated to that or any other final cost objective.

[Final rule, 59 FR 55746, 11/8/94, effective 1/9/95]

9905.502-50 Techniques for application.

(a) The Fundamental Requirement is stated in terms of cost incurred and is equally applicable to estimates of costs to be incurred as used in contract proposals.

(b) The Disclosure Statement to be submitted by the educational institution will require that the institution set forth its cost accounting practices with regard to the distinction between direct and indirect costs. In addition, for those types of cost which are sometimes accounted for as direct and sometimes accounted for as indirect, the educational institution will set forth in its Disclosure Statement the specific criteria and circumstances for making such distinctions. In essence, the Disclosure Statement submitted by the educational institution, by distinguishing between direct and indirect costs, and by describing the criteria and cir-

CASB 9905.502-50

cumstances for allocating those items which are sometimes direct and sometimes indirect, will be determinative as to whether or not costs are incurred for the same purpose. Disclosure Statement as used herein refers to the statement required to be submitted by educational institutions as a condition of contracting as set forth in Subpart 9903.2.

(c) In the event that an educational institution has not submitted a Disclosure Statement, the determination of whether specific costs are directly allocable to contracts shall be based upon the educational institution's cost accounting practices used at the time of contract proposal.

(d) Whenever costs which serve the same purpose cannot equitably be indirectly allocated to one or more final cost objectives in accordance with the educational institution's disclosed accounting practices, the educational institution may either use a method for reassigning all such costs which would provide an equitable distribution to all final cost objectives, or directly assign all such costs to final cost objectives with which they are specifically identified. In the event the educational institution decides to make a change for either purpose, the Disclosure Statement shall be amended to reflect the revised accounting practices involved.

(e) Any direct cost of minor dollar amount may be treated as an indirect cost for reasons of practicality where the accounting treatment for such cost is consistently applied to all final cost objectives, provided that such treatment produces results which are substantially the same as the results which would have been obtained if such cost had been treated as a direct cost.

[Final rule, 59 FR 55746, 11/8/94, effective 1/9/95]

9905.502-60 Illustrations.

(a) Illustrations of costs which are incurred for the same purpose:

(1) An educational institution normally allocates all travel as an indirect cost and previously disclosed this accounting practice to the Government. For purposes of a new proposal, the educational institution intends to allocate the travel costs of personnel whose time is accounted for as direct labor directly to the contract. Since travel costs of personnel whose time is accounted for as direct labor working on other contracts are costs which are incurred for the same purpose, these costs may no longer be included within indirect cost pools for purposes of allocation to any covered Government contract. The educational institution's Disclosure Statement must be amended for the proposed changes in accounting practices.

(2) An educational institution normally allocates purchasing activity costs indirectly and allocates this cost to instruction and research on the basis of modified total costs. A proposal for a new contract requires a disproportionate amount of subcontract administration to be performed by the purchasing activity. The educational institution prefers to continue to allocate purchasing activity costs indirectly. In order to equitably allocate the total purchasing activity costs, the educational institution may use a method for allocating all such costs which would provide an equitable distribution to all applicable indirect cost pools. For example, the institution may use the number of transactions processed rather than its former allocation base of modified total costs. The educational institution's Disclosure Statement must be amended for the proposed changes in accounting practices.

(b) Illustrations of costs which are not incurred for the same purpose:

(1) An educational institution normally allocates special test equipment costs directly to contracts. The costs of general purpose test equipment are normally included in the indirect cost pool which is allocated to contracts. Both of these accounting practices were previously disclosed to the Government. Since both types of costs involved were not incurred for the same purpose in accordance with the criteria set forth in the educational institution's Disclosure Statement, the allocation of general purpose test equipment costs from the indirect cost pool to the contract, in addition to the directly allocated special test equipment costs, is not considered a violation of the Standard.

(2) An educational institution proposes to perform a contract which will require three firemen on 24-hour duty at a fixed-post to

provide protection against damage to highly inflammable materials used on the contract. The educational institution presently has a firefighting force of 10 employees for general protection of its facilities. The educational institution's costs for these latter firemen are treated as indirect costs and allocated to all contracts; however, it wants to allocate the three fixed-post firemen directly to the particular contract requiring them and also allocate a portion of the cost of the general firefighting force to the same contract. The institution may do so but only on condition that its disclosed practices indicate that the costs of the separate classes of firemen serve different purposes and that it is the institution's practice to allocate the general firefighting force indirectly and to allocate fixed-post firemen directly.

[Final rule, 59 FR 55746, 11/8/94, effective 1/9/95]

9905.502-61 Interpretation.

(a) 9905.502, Cost Accounting Standard—Consistency in Allocating Costs Incurred for the Same Purpose by Educational Institutions, provides, in 9905.502-40, that "*** no final cost objective shall have allocated to it as a direct cost any cost, if other costs incurred for the same purpose, in like circumstances, have been included in any indirect cost pool to be allocated to that or any other final cost objective."

(b) This interpretation deals with the way 9905.502 applies to the treatment of costs incurred in preparing, submitting, and supporting proposals. In essence, it is addressed to whether or not, under the Standard, all such costs are incurred for the same purpose, in like circumstances.

(c) Under 9905.502, costs incurred in preparing, submitting, and supporting proposals pursuant to a specific requirement of an existing contract are considered to have been incurred in different circumstances from the circumstances under which costs are incurred in preparing proposals which do not result from such a specific requirement. The circumstances are different because the costs of preparing proposals specifically required by the provisions of an existing contract relate only to that contract while other proposal costs relate to all work of the educational institution.

(d) This interpretation does not preclude the allocation, as indirect costs, of costs incurred in preparing all proposals. The cost accounting practices used by the educational institution, however, must be followed consistently and the method used to reallocate such costs, of course, must provide an equitable distribution to all final cost objectives.

[Final rule, 59 FR 55746, 11/8/94, effective 1/9/95]

9905.502-62 Exemption.

None for this Standard.

[Final rule, 59 FR 55746, 11/8/94, effective 1/9/95]

9905.502-63 Effective date.

This Standard is effective as of January 9, 1995.

[Final rule, 59 FR 55746, 11/8/94, effective 1/9/95]

9905.505 Accounting for unallowable costs—Educational institutions. (No Text)

9905.505-10 [Reserved]

[Final rule, 59 FR 55746, 11/8/94, effective 1/9/95]

9905.505-20 Purpose.

(a)(1) The purpose of this Cost Accounting Standard is to facilitate the negotiation, audit, administration and settlement of contracts by establishing guidelines covering:

(i) Identification of costs specifically described as unallowable, at the time such costs first become defined or authoritatively designated as unallowable, and

(ii) The cost accounting treatment to be accorded such identified unallowable costs in order to promote the consistent application of sound cost accounting principles covering all incurred costs.

(2) The Standard is predicated on the proposition that costs incurred in carrying on the activities of an educational institution—regardless of the allowability of such costs under Government contracts—are allocable to the cost objectives with which they are

CASB 9905.505-20

identified on the basis of their beneficial or causal relationships.

(b) This Standard does not govern the allowability of costs. This is a function of the appropriate procurement or reviewing authority.

[Final rule, 59 FR 55746, 11/8/94, effective 1/9/95]

9905.505-30 Definitions.

(a) The following are definitions of terms which are prominent in this Standard. Other terms defined elsewhere in this Chapter 99 shall have the meanings ascribed to them in those definitions unless paragraph (b) of this subsection requires otherwise.

(1) *Directly associated cost* means any cost which is generated solely as a result of the incurrence of another cost, and which would not have been incurred had the other cost not been incurred.

(2) *Expressly unallowable cost* means a particular item or type of cost which, under the express provisions of an applicable law, regulation, or contract, is specifically named and stated to be unallowable.

(3) *Indirect cost* means any cost not directly identified with a single final cost objective, but identified with two or more final cost objectives or with at least one intermediate cost objective.

(4) *Unallowable cost* means any cost which, under the provisions of any pertinent law, regulation, or contract, cannot be included in prices, cost reimbursements, or settlements under a Government contract to which it is allocable.

(b) The following modifications of terms defined elsewhere in this Chapter 99 are applicable to this Standard: None.

[Final rule, 59 FR 55746, 11/8/94, effective 1/9/95]

9905.505-40 Fundamental requirement.

(a) Costs expressly unallowable or mutually agreed to be unallowable, including costs mutually agreed to be unallowable directly associated costs, shall be identified and excluded from any billing, claim, or proposal applicable to a Government contract.

(b) Costs which specifically become designated as unallowable as a result of a written decision furnished by a contracting officer pursuant to contract disputes procedures shall be identified if included in or used in the computation of any billing, claim, or proposal applicable to a Government contract. This identification requirement applies also to any costs incurred for the same purpose under like circumstances as the costs specifically identified as unallowable under either this paragraph or paragraph (a) of this subsection.

(c) Costs which, in a contracting officer's written decision furnished pursuant to contract disputes procedures, are designated as unallowable directly associated costs of unallowable costs covered by either paragraph (a) or (b) of this subsection shall be accorded the identification required by paragraph (b) of this subsection.

(d) The costs of any work project not contractually authorized, whether or not related to performance of a proposed or existing contract, shall be accounted for, to the extent appropriate, in a manner which permits ready separation from the costs of authorized work projects.

(e) All unallowable costs covered by paragraphs (a) through (d) of this subsection shall be subject to the same cost accounting principles governing cost allocability as allowable costs. In circumstances where these unallowable costs normally would be part of a regular indirect cost allocation base or bases, they shall remain in such base or bases. Where a directly associated cost is part of a category of costs normally included in an indirect-cost pool that will be allocated over a base containing the unallowable cost with which it is associated, such a directly associated cost shall be retained in the indirect-cost pool and be allocated through the regular allocation process.

(f) Where the total of the allocable and otherwise allowable costs exceeds a limitation-of-cost or ceiling-price provision in a contract, full direct and indirect cost allocation shall be made to the contract cost objective, in accordance with established cost accounting practices and Standards which regularly govern a given entity's allocations to Government contract cost objectives. In any determination of unallowable cost overrun, the amount thereof shall be identified in terms of the excess of allowable costs over the ceiling amount, rather than through specific identification of particular cost items or cost elements.

[Final rule, 59 FR 55746, 11/8/94, effective 1/9/95]

9905.505-50 Techniques for application.

(a) The detail and depth of records required as backup support for proposals, billings, or claims shall be that which is adequate to establish and maintain visibility of identified unallowable costs (including directly associated costs), their accounting status in terms of their allocability to contract cost objectives, and the cost accounting treatment which has been accorded such costs. Adherence to this cost accounting principle does not require that allocation of unallowable costs to final cost objectives be made in the detailed cost accounting records. It does require that unallowable costs be given appropriate consideration in any cost accounting determinations governing the content of allocation bases used for distributing indirect costs to cost objectives. Unallowable costs involved in the determination of rates used for standard costs, or for indirect-cost bidding or billing, need be identified only at the time rates are proposed, established, revised or adjusted.

(b)(1) The visibility requirement of paragraph (a) of this subsection, may be satisfied by any form of cost identification which is adequate for purposes of contract cost determination and verification. The Standard does not require such cost identification for purposes which are not relevant to the determination of Government contract cost. Thus, to provide visibility for incurred costs, acceptable alternative practices would include:

(i) The segregation of unallowable costs in separate accounts maintained for this purpose in the regular books of account,

(ii) The development and maintenance of separate accounting records or workpapers, or

(iii) The use of any less formal cost accounting techniques which establishes and maintains adequate cost identification to permit audit verification of the accounting recognition given unallowable costs.

(2) Educational institutions may satisfy the visibility requirements for estimated costs either:

(i) By designation and description (in backup data, workpapers, etc.) of the amounts and types of any unallowable costs which have specifically been identified and recognized in making the estimates, or

(ii) By description of any other estimating technique employed to provide appropriate recognition of any unallowable costs pertinent to the estimates.

(c) Specific identification of unallowable costs is not required in circumstances where, based upon considerations of materiality, the Government and the educational institution reach agreement on an alternate method that satisfies the purpose of the Standard.

[Final rule, 59 FR 55746, 11/8/94, effective 1/9/95]

9905.505-60 Illustrations.

(a) An auditor recommends disallowance of certain direct labor and direct material costs, for which a billing has been submitted under a contract, on the basis that these particular costs were not required for performance and were not authorized by the contract. The contracting officer issues a written decision which supports the auditor's position that the questioned costs are unallowable. Following receipt of the contracting officer's decision, the educational institution must clearly identify the disallowed direct labor and direct material costs in the institution's accounting records and reports covering any subsequent submission which includes such costs. Also, if the educational institution's base for allocation of any indirect cost pool relevant to the subject contract consists of direct labor, direct material, total prime cost, total cost input, etc., the institution must include the disallowed direct labor and material costs in its allocation base for such pool. Had the contracting officer's decision been against the auditor, the educational institution would not, of course, have been required to account separately for the costs questioned by the auditor.

(b) An educational institution incurs, and separately identifies, as a part of a service center or expense pool, certain costs which are expressly unallowable under the existing and currently effective regulations. If the costs of the service center or indirect expense pool are regularly a part of the educational institution's base for allocation of other indirect expenses, the educational institution must allocate the other indirect expenses to contracts and other final cost objectives by means of a base which includes the identified unallowable indirect costs.

(c) An auditor recommends disallowance of certain indirect costs. The educational institution claims that the costs in question are allowable under the provisions of Office Of Management and Budget Circular A-21, Cost Principles For Educational Institutions; the auditor disagrees. The issue is referred to the contracting officer for resolution pursuant to the contract disputes clause. The contracting officer issues a written decision supporting the auditor's position that the total costs questioned are unallowable under the Circular. Following receipt of the contracting officer's decision, the educational institution must identify the disallowed costs and specific other costs incurred for the same purpose in like circumstances in any subsequent estimating, cost accumulation or reporting for Government contracts, in which such costs are included. If the contracting officer's decision had supported the educational institution's contention, the costs questioned by the auditor would have been allowable and the educational institution would not have been required to provide special identification.

(d) An educational institution incurred certain unallowable costs that were charged indirectly as general administration and general expenses (GA&GE). In the educational institution's proposals for final indirect cost rates to be applied in determining allowable contract costs, the educational institution identified and excluded the expressly unallowable GA&GE costs form the applicable

indirect cost pools. In addition, during the course of negotiation of indirect cost rates to be used for bidding and billing purposes, the educational institution agreed to classify as unallowable cost, various directly associated costs of the identifiable unallowable costs. On the basis of negotiations and agreements between the educational institution and the contracting officer's authorized representatives, indirect cost rates were established, based on the net balance of allowable GA&GE. Application of the rates negotiated to proposals, and to billings, for covered contracts constitutes compliance with the Standard.

(e) An employee, whose salary, travel, and subsistence expenses are charged regularly to the general administration and general expenses (GA&GE), an indirect cost category, takes several business associates on what is clearly a business entertainment trip. The entertainment costs of such trips is expressly unallowable because it constitutes entertainment expense prohibited by OMB Circular A-21, and is separately identified by the educational institution. In these circumstances, the employee's travel and subsistence expenses would be directly associated costs for identification with the unallowable entertainment expense. However, unless this type of activity constituted a significant part of the employee's regular duties and responsibilities on which his salary was based, no part of the employee's salary would be required to be identified as a directly associated cost of the unallowable entertainment expense.

[Final rule, 59 FR 55746, 11/8/94, effective 1/9/95]

9905.505-61 [Reserved]

[Final rule, 59 FR 55746, 11/8/94, effective 1/9/95]

9905.505-62 Exemption.

None for this Standard.

[Final rule, 59 FR 55746, 11/8/94, effective 1/9/95]

9905.505-63 Effective date.

This Standard is effective as of January 9, 1995.

[Final rule, 59 FR 55746, 11/8/94, effective 1/9/95]

9905.506 Cost accounting period— Educational institutions. (No Text)

9905.506-10 [Reserved]

[Final rule, 59 FR 55746, 11/8/94, effective 1/9/95]

9905.506-20 Purpose.

The purpose of this Cost Accounting Standard is to provide criteria for the selection of the time periods to be used as cost accounting periods for contract cost estimating, accumulating, and reporting. This Standard will reduce the effects of variations in the flow of costs within each cost accounting period. It will also enhance objectivity, consistency, and verifiability, and promote uniformity and comparability in contract cost measurements.

[Final rule, 59 FR 55746, 11/8/94, effective 1/9/95]

9905.506-30 Definitions.

(a) The following are definitions of terms which are prominent in this Standard. Other terms defined elsewhere in this Part 99 shall have the meanings ascribed to them in those definitions unless paragraph (b) of this subsection requires otherwise.

(1) *Allocate* means to assign an item of cost, or a group of items of cost, to one or more cost objectives. This term includes both direct assignment of cost and the reassignment of a share from an indirect cost pool.

(2) *Cost objective* means a function, organizational subdivision, contract, or other work unit for which cost data are desired and for which provision is made to accumulate and measure the cost of processes, products, jobs, capitalized projects, etc.

(3) *Fiscal year* means the accounting period for which annual financial statements are regularly prepared, generally a period of 12 months, 52 weeks, or 53 weeks.

(4) *Indirect cost pool* means a grouping of incurred costs identified with two or more cost objectives but not identified specifically with any final cost objective.

(b) The following modifications of terms defined elsewhere in this Chapter 99 are applicable to this Standard: None.

[Final rule, 59 FR 55746, 11/8/94, effective 1/9/95]

9905.506-40 Fundamental requirement.

(a) Educational institutions shall use their fiscal year as their cost accounting period, except that:

(1) Costs of an indirect function which exists for only a part of a cost accounting period may be allocated to cost objectives of that same part of the period as provided in 9905.506-50(a).

(2) An annual period other than the fiscal year may, as provided in 9905.506-50(d), be used as the cost accounting period if its use is an established practice of the institution.

(3) A transitional cost accounting period other than a year shall be used whenever a change of fiscal year occurs.

(b) An institution shall follow consistent practices in the selection of the cost accounting period or periods in which any types of expense and any types of adjustment to expense (including prior period adjustments) are accumulated and allocated.

(c) The same cost accounting period shall be used for accumulating costs in an indirect cost pool as for establishing its allocation base, except that the contracting parties may agree to use a different period for establishing an allocation base as provided in 9905.506-50(e).

[Final rule, 59 FR 55746, 11/8/94, effective 1/9/95]

9905.506-50 Techniques for application.

(a) The cost of an indirect function which exists for only a part of a cost accounting period may be allocated on the basis of data for that part of the cost accounting period if the cost is:

(1) Material in amount,

(2) Accumulated in a separate indirect cost pool or expense pool, and

CASB 9905.506-50

(3) Allocated on the basis of an appropriate direct measure of the activity or output of the function during that part of the period.

(b) The practices required by 9905.506-40(b) of this Standard shall include appropriate practices for deferrals, accruals, and other adjustments to be used in identifying the cost accounting periods among which any types of expense and any types of adjustment to expense are distributed. If an expense, such as insurance or employee leave, is identified with a fixed, recurring, annual period which is different from the institution's cost accounting period, the Standard permits continued use of that different period. Such expenses shall be distributed to cost accounting periods in accordance with the institution's established practices for accruals, deferrals, and other adjustments.

(c) Indirect cost allocation rates, based on estimates, which are used for the purpose of expediting the closing of contracts which are terminated or completed prior to the end of a cost accounting period need not be those finally determined or negotiated for that cost accounting period. They shall, however, be developed to represent a full cost accounting period, except as provided in paragraph (a) of this subsection.

(d) An institution may, upon mutual agreement with the Government, use as its cost accounting period a fixed annual period other than its fiscal year, if the use of such a period is an established practice of the institution and is consistently used for managing and controlling revenues and disbursements, and appropriate accruals, deferrals or other adjustments are made with respect to such annual periods.

(e) The contracting parties may agree to use an annual period which does not coincide precisely with the cost accounting period for developing the data used in establishing an allocation base: Provided,

(1) The practice is necessary to obtain significant administrative convenience,

(2) The practice is consistently followed by the institution,

(3) The annual period used is representative of the activity of the cost accounting period for which the indirect costs to be allocated are accumulated, and

(4) The practice can reasonably be estimated to provide a distribution to cost objectives of the cost accounting period not materially different from that which otherwise would be obtained.

(f)(1) When a transitional cost accounting period is required under the provisions of 9905.506-40(a)(3), the institution may select any one of the following:

(i) The period, less than a year in length, extending from the end of its previous cost accounting period to the beginning of its next regular cost accounting period,

(ii) A period in excess of a year, but not longer than 15 months, obtained by combining the period described in paragraph (f)(1) of this subsection with the previous cost accounting period, or

(iii) A period in excess of a year, but not longer than 15 months, obtained by combining the period described in subparagraph (f)(1) of this subsection with the next regular cost accounting period.

(2) A change in the institution's cost accounting period is a change in accounting practices for which an adjustment in the contract price may be required in accordance with subdivision (a)(4)(ii) or (iii) of the contract clause set out at 9903.201-4(e).

[Final rule, 59 FR 55746, 11/8/94, effective 1/9/95]

9905.506-60 Illustrations.

(a) An institution allocates indirect expenses for Organized Research on the basis of a modified total direct cost base. In a proposal for a covered contract, it estimates the allocable expenses based solely on the estimated amount of indirect costs allocated to Organized Research and the amount of the modified total direct cost base estimated to be incurred during the 8 months in which performance is scheduled to be commenced and completed. Such a proposal would be in violation of the requirements of this Standard that the calculation of the amounts of both the indirect cost pools and the allocation bases be based on the contractor's cost accounting period.

(b) An institution whose cost accounting period is the calendar year, installs a computer service center to begin operations on May 1. The operating expense related to the new service center is expected to be material in amount, will be accumulated in an intermediate cost objective, and will be allocated to the benefiting cost objectives on the basis of measured usage. The total operating expenses of the computer service center for the 8-month part of the cost accounting period may be allocated to the benefiting cost objectives of that same 8-month period.

(c) An institution changes its fiscal year from a calendar year to the 12-month period ending May 31. For financial reporting purposes, it has a 5-month transitional "fiscal year." The same 5-month period must be used as the transitional cost accounting period; it may not be combined as provided in 9905.506-50(f), because the transitional period would be longer than 15 months. The new fiscal year must be adopted thereafter as its regular cost accounting period. The change in its cost accounting period is a change in accounting practices; adjustments of the contract prices may thereafter be required in accordance with subdivision (a)(4) (ii) or (iii) of the contract clause at 9903.2014(e).

(d) Financial reports are prepared on a calendar year basis on a university-wide basis. However, the contracting segment does all internal financial planning, budgeting, and internal reporting on the basis of a twelve month period ended June 30. The contracting parties agree to use the period ended June 30 and they agree to overhead rates on the June 30 basis. They also agree on a technique for prorating fiscal year as-

signment of the university's central system office expenses between such June 30 periods. This practice is permitted by the Standard.

(e) Most financial accounts and contract cost records are maintained on the basis of a fiscal year which ends November 30 each year. However, employee vacation allowances are regularly managed on the basis of a "vacation year" which ends September 30 each year. Vacation expenses are estimated uniformly during each "vacation year." Adjustments are made each October to adjust the accrued liability to actual, and the estimating rates are modified to the extent deemed appropriate. This use of a separate annual period for determining the amounts of vacation expense is permitted under 9905.506-50(b).

[Final rule, 59 FR 55746, 11/8/94, effective 1/9/95]

9905.506-61 [Reserved]

[Final rule, 59 FR 55746, 11/8/94, effective 1/9/95]

9905.506-62 Exemption.

None for this Standard.

[Final rule, 59 FR 55746, 11/8/94, effective 1/9/95]

9905.506-63 Effective date.

This Standard is effective as of January 9, 1995. For institutions with no previous CAS-covered contracts, this Standard shall be applied as of the start of its next fiscal year beginning after receipt of a contract to which this Standard is applicable.

[Final rule, 59 FR 55746, 11/8/94, effective 1/9/95]

Cost Accounting Standards Board Regulations

Topical Index
References are to section (§) numbers

274   Cost Accounting Standards Board Regulations
Topical Index
References are to section (§) numbers

Consistency in allocating costs incurred for the same purpose, CAS 402—continued

Consistency in estimating, accumulating and reporting costs, CAS 401

Consistency in estimating costs—see also Educational institutions, consistency in estimating, accumulating and reporting costs, CAS 501

Contract coverage

Cost accounting period, CAS 406

Cost accounting period—educational institutions, CAS 506

Cost accounting standards

Cost accounting standards—continued

Cost Accounting Standards Board Regulations

Cost accounting standards for educational institutions

Cost accounting standards for educational institutions—continued
. cost accounting standard
. . consistency in estimating, accumulating and reporting costs by educational institutions . . . 9905.501
. definitions . . . 9905.501.30
. effective date . . . 9905.501.63
. exemption . . . 9905.501.62
. fundamental requirement . . . 9905.501.40
. purpose . . . 9905.501.20

Cost of money as an element of the cost of capital assets under construction, CAS 417
. definitions . . . 9904.417.30
. effective date . . . 9904.417.63
. exemption . . . 9904.417.62
. fundamental requirement . . . 9904.417.40
. illustrations . . . 9904.417.60
. purpose . . . 9904.417.20
. techniques for application . . . 9904.417.50

Cost of money as an element of the cost of facilities capital, CAS 414
. Appendix B . . . 9904.414
. definitions . . . 9904.414.30
. effective date . . . 9904.414.63
. exemption . . . 9904.414.62
. fundamental requirement . . . 9904.414.40
. illustrations . . . 9904.414.60
. purpose . . . 9904.414.20
. techniques for application . . . 9904.414.50

D

Deferred compensation, CAS 415
. definitions . . . 9904.415.30
. effective date . . . 9904.415.63
. exemption . . . 9904.415.62
. fundamental requirement . . . 9904.415.40
. illustrations . . . 9904.415.60
. purpose . . . 9904.415.20
. techniques for application . . . 9904.415.50

Definitions
. accrued benefit cost method . . . 9903.301; 9904.412.30; 9904.413.30
. accumulating costs . . . 9903.301; 9904.401.30; 9905.501.30
. actual cash value . . . 9903.301; 9904.416.30
. actual cost . . . 9903.301; 9904.401.30; 9905.501.30
. actuarial accrued liability . . . 9904.412.30; 9904.413.30
. actuarial assumption . . . 9903.301; 9904.412.30; 9904.413.30
. actuarial cost method . . . 9903.301; 9904.412.30; 9904.413.30
. actuarial gain and loss . . . 9903.301; 9904.412.30; 9904.413.30
. actuarial liability . . . 9903.301
. actuarial valuation . . . 9903.301; 9904.412.30; 9904.413.30

Definitions—continued
. allocate . . . 9903.301; 9904.402.30; 9904.403.30; 9904.406.30; 9904.410.30; 9904.411.30; 9904.418.30; 9904.420.30; 9905.502.30; 9905.506.30
. allocation of cost to cost objectives . . . 9903.302.1
. asset accountability unit . . . 9903.301; 9904.404.30
. assignable cost credit . . . 9904.412.30
. assignable cost deficit . . . 9904.412.30
. assignable cost limitation . . . 9904.412.30
. assignment of cost to cost accounting periods . . . 9903.301; 9903.302.1
. bid and proposal (B&P) cost . . . 9904.420.30; 9903.301
. business unit . . . 9903.201.2; 9903.301; 9904.410.30; 9904.411.30; 9904.414.30; 9904.420.30
. CAS-covered contract . . . 9903.301
. category of material . . . 9903.301; 9904.411.30
. change to a cost accounting practice . . . 9903.301; 9903.302.2
. compensated personal absence . . . 9903.301; 9904.408.30
. cost accounting practice . . . 9903.301; 9903.302.1
. cost input . . . 9903.301; 9904.410.30
. cost objective . . . 9903.301; 9904.402.30; 9904.406.30; 9904.410.30; 9904.411.30; 9905.502.30; 9905.506.30
. cost of capital committed to facilities . . . 9903.301; 9904.414.30
. currently performing . . . 9903.301
. curtailment of benefits . . . 9904.413.30
. deferred compensation . . . 9903.301; 9904.415.30
. defined-benefit pension plan . . . 9903.301; 9904.412.30
. defined-contribution pension plan . . . 9904.412.30; 9903.301
. direct cost . . . 9903.301; 9904.402.30; 9904.418.30; 9905.502.30
. directly associated cost . . . 9903.301; 9904.405.30; 9905.505.30
. disclosure statement . . . 9903.301
. educational institution . . . 9903.201.2; 9903.301
. entitlement . . . 9903.301; 9904.408.30
. estimating costs . . . 9903.301; 9904.401.30; 9905.501.30
. expressly unallowable cost . . . 9903.301; 9905.505.30; 9904.405.30
. facilities capital . . . 9903.301; 9904.414.30
. final cost objective . . . 9903.301; 9904.402.30; 9904.410.30; 9905.502.30
. fiscal year . . . 9903.301; 9904.406.30; 9905.506.30
. funded pension cost . . . 9903.301; 9904.412.30
. funding agency . . . 9903.301; 9904.412.30; 9904.413.30
. general and administrative (G&A) expense . . . 9903.301; 9904.410.30; 9904.420.30
. home office . . . 9903.301; 9904.403.30; 9904.420.30
. immediate-gain actuarial cost method . . . 9903.301; 9904.412.30; 9904.413.30

276   Cost Accounting Standards Board Regulations
Topical Index
References are to section (§) numbers